Women at War

ALSO BY ROSEMARIE SKAINE

Power and Gender:
Issues in Sexual Dominance and Harassment
(McFarland, 1996)

WOMEN AT WAR

Gender Issues of
Americans in Combat

by

ROSEMARIE SKAINE

McFarland & Company, Inc., Publishers
Jefferson, North Carolina, and London

Cover: U.S. Marine Corps servicewoman.

British Library Cataloguing-in-Publication data are available

Library of Congress Cataloguing-in-Publication Data

Skaine, Rosemarie.
    Women at war : gender issues of Americans in combat / by
Rosemarie Skaine.
        p.   cm.
    Includes bibliographical references and index.
    ISBN 0-7864-0570-8 (sewn softcover : 50# alkaline paper) ∞
    1. Women in combat—United States.   2. United States—
Armed Forces—Women.   3. Sex discrimination in employment—
United States.
    I. Title.   98-35231
    UB418.W65K56   1999   CIP
    355'.0082'0973—dc21

Manufactured in the United States of America

McFarland & Company, Inc., Publishers
    Box 611, Jefferson, North Carolina 28640

In memory of
my brother
William H. Keller,
who would have served in the armed forces
if his health had permitted

Acknowledgments

With the help of the following people, this book became a reality. I am deeply grateful for their patience, mentoring, encouragement, perseverance, and in the case of the military women, undaunting courage. Without them, I would not have gone beyond the horizon.

James C. Skaine, communication studies, University of Northern Iowa, provided assistance and support.

CAPT Rosemary Mariner, U.S. Navy (USN), offered me strategic initial introduction and direction. MAJ Lillian Pfluke, U.S. Army (Ret.), provided generous but rigorous mentoring and focus. Col. Kelly Hamilton, U.S. Air Force (Ret.), was a source of inspiration.

To RADM D.M. "Mac" Williams, Jr., U.S. Navy (Ret.), former Naval Investigative Service (NIS) Commander, offered expert guidance on military law, and kindness in a multitude of helpful ways. Linda Oliver, Officer of General Counsel, U.S. Navy (USN), presently detailed to White House Office of Counsel, provided support and sense of direction.

Several members of the first class of women at West Point unselfishly shared their perspectives with me, in particular, Danna Maller, former U.S. Army (USA) captain; MAJ Jane McKeon, USA (Ret.); and Mary Whitley, former USA captain.

Assistance also came from MAJ Mary Finch, USA, Deputy TRADOC System Manager for Unmanned Aerial Vehicles, a former member of the U.S. Presidential Commission on the Assignment of Women in the Armed Forces; COL Barbara Lee, Assistant, Office of Assistant Secretary of Army, The Pentagon, and MAJ Angela M. Manos, Executive Officer and Deputy Division Provost Marshal, 10th Military Policy Battalion, 10th Mountain Division, Ft. Drum, New York, USA, and former advisor to Army Chief of Staff, GEN Gordon R. Sullivan.

Linda Grant De Pauw, professor of history at George Washington University and president of The MINERVA Center, Pasadena, Maryland, assisted me through her dedication to the edification of military women. Holly K.

Hemphill, chair, Defense Advisory Committee on Women in the Services (DACOWITS), provided insights and help. CAPT Georgia C. Sadler, USN (Ret.), Women's Research and Education Institute, offered assistance. BGen. Wilma Vaught, U.S. Air Force (USAF) (Ret.), president, Women in Military Service for America Memorial Foundation, Inc. (WIMSA), provided inspiring words I shall always remember. Kathryn Sheldon, curator, WIMSA, reached out to assist me in my research.

ADM Stanley R. Arthur, USN (Ret.) former Vice Chief of Naval Operations, former Commander, U.S. Seventh Fleet, and Commander, U.S. Naval Forces Central command for Operations Desert Shield and Desert Storm, provided advice, patience, and ongoing willingness to help. RADM Paul T. Gillcrist, aviator, USN (Ret.), offered assistance, inspiration, and encouragement.

Senator Charles Grassley (R-Iowa) provided help in attaining Freedom of Information Act (FOIA) requests and worked to involve a constituent in the government process. Senator Grassley's regional director, Fred Schuster, is to be commended for his ongoing and tireless dedication to the quality of life and realization of democracy for American citizens.

Barbara Sweatt, former specialist in the 1980s, USA, and editor, *Athena Women's Veterans Journal*, offered support. CPT Sharon Grant Wildwind, U.S. Army Nurse Corps (Ret.), and CAPT Doris M. Sterner, USN (Ret.), helped me understand more fully the force of medical corps in and around the services.

Officers at the Cedar Falls, Iowa, Recruiting Station: SFC Richard D. Stroup, Station Commander, USA; William Plotner, Electronics Technician Chief (Aviation Warfare Qualified) (ETC[AW]), USN; Sgt Bill Kohl, U.S. Marine Corps (USMC); and SSgt Christopher Sweet, USAF.

The academicians who assisted with our college youth survey presented in Chapter 6 include Terry Besser, Iowa State University; Clinton Jesser, Department of Sociology, Northern Illinois University-DeKalb; Dean Knudsen, chair, Department of Sociology, Purdue University; Debra Clements Lemke, chair, Department of Sociology, Western Maryland College; Andrew J. Potts, Economics and Management, University of Southern Maine; LTC Timothy A. Rippe, USA professor of Military Science–ROTC (Ret.), University of Northern Iowa; Ronald Roberts, Department of Sociology, and Surendar Yadava, statistician, Department of Sociology, University of Northern Iowa.

My thanks also go to a multitude of other military personnel and civilians who helped enlighten and educate: Lt Col Greg Morin, USMC Department Director, Military Police Division; Kris Warner, Family Advocacy Program, USMC; Seaman Apprentice (SA) Vanessa L. Encarnacion, Ceremonial Guard, USN; MAJ Susan Kellett-Forsyth, USA, Operation Joint Endeavor; Sgt Maj Charlene K. Wiese, USMC, Headquarters, Barstow; CDR John Calande, U.S. Naval Academy, 1963; Sgt. Beth Adams, former police officer, Los Angeles Police Department; Martha Rudd, USA Public Affairs; Gy Sgt Sylvia

Gethicker, Camp LeJeune, Public Affairs, USMC; LT Brenda Malone, USN, Public Affairs; and Rebecca Hancock Cameron, Ph.D., Air Force historian. Other individuals at the University of Northern Iowa I wish to thank include, in particular, Cpl Timothy S. Sexton, U.S. Marine Corps Reserve (USMCR); Professor Tom Lindsay, Department of Political Science; Professors Virgil C. Noack and Kristin Mack, Department of Sociology, Anthropology, and Criminology (DSAC), The Family; Professor Eric Henderson, J.D., anthropologist, DSAC; and Richard Webb, graduate student, DSAC, who provided inspiration, acceptance, and poetry.

I thank Judy Arnold, David Hackbart, Leslie Pfiffner, Thomas R. Sherman, Kathryn Sherman, Christopher I. Thornell, Lance E. Vanderloo, and Lois Breis for their wordless songs of support.

I thank Warren V. Keller, my father, for his love and inspiration.

My appreciation also goes to my good friend, Mary Nelson, who always has time to do a good deed, and to my friend of yesteryear, Cass Paley—invincible summers can become invincible seasons.

Contents

Preface

Writing women into history, particularly into military history and specifically into combat history, is no easy feat. First of all, women in general were written fully into history only within the last 45 years. Second, military history chronicles only some of the culturally accepted roles. Linda Grant De Pauw, a professor of history at George Washington University, and founder and president of The MINERVA Center in Pasadena, Maryland, says that women are underrepresented in war because the "mythology of warfare" recognizes only the roles of "warriors, victims and whores."[1] The first role is reserved for men and the latter two generally for women. This explains the lack of attention women have received and the fact that women joined military forces secretly or under assumed male names.[2]

The Persian Gulf War, however, provided impetus for recognition and change. During the Gulf War, "the whole face of what we considered combat changed. Scud missiles were launched country to country; there is no longer a defining boundary," according to Col. Kelly Hamilton, U.S. Air Force (Ret.), senior woman pilot in the Air Force and former Assistant Director of Operations for Strategic Planning, Air Mobility Command.[3] Nowhere was this more true than in combat aviation, which Hamilton says involved more standoff tactics and aerial engagement and more air to ground strategy.

Along with the changing nature of combat itself, the Gulf War presented us with the changing nature of the role of the Americans in combat. As Col. Hamilton explains, "The key turning point of the war was the way the press handled it. It had a big impact on us and the public. When asked how they felt about women being put in harm's way, or having a woman go to war and leave her family, the American public responded, 'Yeah, my neighbor, daughter, mom is there.' This conflict was an awakening for the people in the U.S. They suddenly realized there were a lot of women in the military. These women weren't wonder women; they were all-around gals. I can tell you military men and women are professionals who take their job seriously."[4] Mady Wechsler Segal and Amanda Faith Hansen support Hamilton's position, say-

1

ing, "The Persian Gulf War brought women's military roles into extensive public scrutiny. The mass media brought home the reality of women's participation in the armed forces."[5]

The combatant role is elusive and difficult to define in spite of recent legal progress and growing public awareness. Even in direct combat, however, women had already been serving, and some of the men who served with them looked the other way, allowing them to take on an unofficial combatant role. Today these men remember the women combatants with honor and respect. In some cases, women could legally serve in combat through temporary assignment. Military women tell me, "We've been doing it." Military women expected to lead their troops in battle when the rear became a front.[6] In past centuries, women served in combat dressed as men. It was believed that men would follow a woman into battle only if she was dressed as a man.

From 1948 to 1991, only one major frontier remained unchanged: the law. The reason, some say, is that the group called the "American public" was as difficult to define as combat itself. "The American public didn't want it," argued some. Now, even as the law has changed, some policy, particularly Army and Marine Corps, prohibits the assignment of women into certain combat units that are in direct collocation with the enemy. Policy is not only slower to keep pace but sometimes unclear in its definition of what units actually collocate.

Another factor that makes it difficult to chronicle women's combat history comes from women themselves. The first women to officially serve in combat in the new legal frontier may be afraid of getting tagged as women rather than soldiers, sailors, or marines; therefore we do not hear a great deal about their service. Concerns about "feminization" of the military and acceptance of women in the military suggest possible research implication. Jeanne M. Lieberman says that women don't have a war story tradition and that "an analysis of women's 'war stories' might shed light on the issue."[7] The Women in the Military Service for America Memorial Foundation (WIMSA) has compiled histories of military women from which such an analysis may be undertaken. The WIMSA Memorial, at Arlington National Cemetery, was dedicated in 1997.

Organizations such as the Defense Advisory Committee on Women in the Services (DACOWITS) visit military installations to see that women are actually serving in slots created for them. In November 1951, Secretary of Defense GEN George C. Marshall founded DACOWITS. The Secretary invited 50 civilian women to meet with him. Anna Rosenberg, Assistant Secretary of Defense for Manpower, Personnel, and Reserve, served as chairman-hostess for this group, whose mission was to "advise the Secretary on how to obtain more women for the Armed Forces, increase their retention rate, and better use their capabilities."[8] DACOWITS now focuses on women being successful in the open assignments. Holly K. Hemphill, the chair of DACOWITS, says that when an assignment is not open, they ask, "What is it about this job that makes it restricted?"[9] They make efforts to learn more about closed positions, such as missile systems. They ask questions such as, "The Multiple Launch Rocket System (MLRS) collocates, but it stays and operates independently so is that a job that should be closed even under the current definition?"[10] All in all, Hemphill believes positive movement is here for women in the military. Men and women alike are now more amenable to change, and the clock is not likely to be turned back.

Views on whether women should serve in combat vary greatly both in and out of the military community. One woman told me that nobody wants to serve in combat but cold-blooded killers. But the United States has never been occupied. What would happen to our untrained women then? If the American public can't handle the image of a toddler clinging to a woman who must leave for military service,[11] how would an untrained woman protect that child in a situation of occupation? Men are taught to protect women, but what if, in the final analysis, some men would save only themselves? A sensible answer is, of course, that when men and women are taught to kill, they must also be taught when to stop killing. That is the responsibility of all those who train soldiers.

In an age of peacekeeping and tactical weapons, it is more likely that some will find women in combat more acceptable. It is also more probable, say some, that women will be killed. In congressional hearings and in history it is revealed that women have been killed during military conflicts. If the enemy destroys an Army supply line, it affects the direct combat unit. In the Navy fleet, the noncombatant vessel may take the hit before the combatant vessel. Military women in all services told me over and over again, "We've been doing it [combat] anyway." They also say that when the need arises—for instance, if male soldiers are too scarce—women will be used, so why not train all people? The U.S. Marine Corps has begun such a training program in the "Crucible."[12]

If we want to assure the continuance of our nation, women have to know how to defend themselves and their country. If all people were trained, we would have a better chance as a society to survive or be peaceful.

Peace is not gained without strength. In military terms this means readiness. Women, when trained, stand ready to preserve our nation and peace, and by increasing their own ability to survive, they increase their children's chances for survival.

Tables

Abbreviations

Official ranks and branches as used in this book.

ADM	Admiral, U.S. Navy
Amn	Airman, U.S. Air Force
ANC	U.S. Army Nurse Corps
B Gen	Brigadier General, U.S. Marine Corps
BG	Brigadier General, U.S. Army
BGen.	Brigadier General, U.S. Air Force
CAPT	Captain, U.S. Navy
Capt	Captain, U.S. Marine Corps
Capt.	Captain, U.S. Air Force
CDR	Commander, U.S. Navy
CNO	Chief of Naval Operations
COL	Colonel, U.S. Army
Col	Colonel, U.S. Marine Corps
Col.	Colonel, U.S. Air Force
Cpl	Corporal, U.S. Marine Corps
CPT	Captain, U.S. Army
1st Lt.	First Lieutenant, U.S. Air Force
1LT	First Lieutenant, U.S. Army
GEN	General, U.S. Army
Gen	General, U.S. Marine Corps
Gen.	General, U.S. Air Force
Gy Sgt	Gunnery Sergeant, U.S. Marine Corps
JAG	Judge Advocate General
JAGC	Judge Advocate General Corps
LCDR	Lieutenant Commander, U.S. Navy
LCpl	Lance Corporal, U.S. Marine Corps
LT	Lieutenant, U.S. Navy
Lt Col	Lieutenant Colonel, U.S. Marine Corps
Lt. Col.	Lieutenant Colonel, U.S. Air Force

LTC	Lieutenant Colonel, U.S. Army
LGen.	Lieutenant General, U.S. Air Force
Lt Gen	Lieutenant General, U.S. Marine Corps
LTG	Lieutenant General, U.S. Army
MAJ	Major, U.S. Army
Maj.	Major, U.S. Air Force
Maj Gen	Major General, U.S. Marine Corps
MG	Major General, U.S. Army
MGen.	Major General, U.S. Air Force
NROTC	Naval Reserve Officer Training Corps
OJAG	Office of the Judge Advocate General
Pvt	Private, U.S. Marine Corps
RADM	Rear Admiral, U.S. Navy
Ret.	retired
RMC	Chief Radioman, U.S. Navy
SECDEF	Secretary of Defense
SECNAV	Secretary of the Navy
SECNAVINST	Secretary of the Navy Instruction
2nd Lt.	Second Lieutenant, U.S. Air Force
SFC	Sergeant First Class, U.S. Army
SGM	Sergeant Major, U.S. Army
SGMA	Sergeant Major of the Army, U.S. Army
SGT	Sergeant, U.S. Army
Sgt	Sergeant, U.S. Marine Corps
Sgt Maj	Sergeant Major, U.S. Marine Corps
SSgt	Staff Sergeant, U.S. Air Force
SOF	Special Operations Forces
SPAR	Coast Guard Women's Reserve (from Coast Guard motto "*Semper Paratus*—Always Ready")
SPC	Specialist, U.S. Army
TSgt	Technical Sergeant, U.S. Air Force
USA	U.S. Army
USAF	U.S. Air Force
USAR	U.S. Army Reserve
USMC	U.S. Marine Corps
USMCR	U.S. Marine Corps Reserve
USN	U.S. Navy
USNR	U.S. Navy Reserve
VADM	Vice Admiral, U.S. Navy
WAC	Women's Army Corps
WAFS	Women in the Air Force
WASP	Women Air Force Service Pilots
WAVES	Women Accepted for Voluntary Emergency Service

Introduction

A soldier is a soldier.
—CAPT Rosemary Mariner, U.S. Navy[1]

PROFILE OF A SOLDIER

I am a physically fit and mentally tough leader of soldiers. I am the current national military triathlon champion, two-time national military cycling champion, two-time European interservice ski champion. I earned a varsity letter in ski jumping on the men's ski team at West Point and captained the women's lacrosse team. I play rugby. I have achieved a maximum score on every PT test taken in 12 years of service. I am physical, aggressive, and very competitive. I am a leader who can inspire people to their own personal bests by providing a powerful example and through my genuine and infectious enthusiasm for adventure and challenge. Men will follow me, will bond with me, will respect me, and we will fight as a team. They have done so in all the infantry training I have been exposed to, including the jungle operations training course in Panama, Airborne training at Fort Benning, as an instructor during Recondo training at West Point, and throughout my troop leading experience in the field at Ft. Bragg, Germany, and Ft. Lewis.

But I still have not addressed a fundamental question: do I have what it takes to ram my bayonet through my enemy's chest? First of all, very few deaths in modern combat are the result of bayonet wounds. Secondly, no man can answer that question with certainty until faced with that situation. Most importantly, though, that is a question I have had to think about already. [Women soldiers] are issued bayonets and we are trained to use them.

The real question, then, is am I comfortable with a vocation whose primary purpose is to close with and destroy the enemy? Once one comes to terms with using force to impose our nation's will on others by killing people and by risking one's own life (which every soldier, sailor, airman, and Marine must come to terms with), the only question

9

that remains is how one wants to contribute to that mission. Is it by flying airplanes or steaming ships or fixing trucks or flipping hamburgers?
My choice is to engage in the direct physical confrontation of the
infantry, to close with and kill or capture the enemy, to hold the high
ground. In my view, the essence of conflict.
   I can do it. I want to do it. I should be given the chance to do it.[2]

   Why, you ask, is this highly qualified soldier having to ask for an opportunity to serve? The soldier's qualifications are unusually high. This soldier,
MAJ Lillian Pfluke, U.S. Army (Ret.), is familiar with asking her country to
let her serve in the infantry and being turned down. In 1979, as her senior class-
mates at West Point were choosing their branches of service, Pfluke wrote a
letter to the Secretary of the Army requesting an exception to the combat
exclusion policy to allow her to serve in the infantry. Her reasons were that
infantry training had always given her the most personal satisfaction of all the
training and she believed the infantry was where she could best contribute and
where her personal strengths and attributes could be best utilized by our nation.
Nevertheless, the Secretary of the Army refused her request.
   Thirteen years later, in 1992, she testified before the U.S. Presidential
Commission on the Assignment of Women in the Armed Forces that her attitudes, matured and refined by experience, and her desire to serve in the infantry
were stronger than ever, as was her conviction that such service would make
best use of her talents. Why did she want to be in the infantry? Pfluke testified:

   Why does anyone want to be in the infantry? Like most infantry men
   I know, I want to dedicate my life to the ultimate challenge faced by
   the infantry, well-styled: the Queen of Battle. While I know the life
   can be harsh, with intense physical demands and few amenities, I do
   want to measure myself against what the infantry does. I enjoy the
   outdoors, braving the elements, carrying everything I need on my
   back and finding my way in the woods. I enjoy cross-country skiing
   and sport parachuting. I especially enjoy pushing myself to my personal physical limits. I enjoy risk, challenge, and adventure.[3]

   Major Pfluke would be a qualified ground-combat soldier. She has the
physical qualifications and the desire. Opponents of women in combat say
physical qualifications alone do not make a person able to serve in combat. A
combat soldier, they say, must have a desire and a certain frame of mind.
Opponents also wonder whether women can do what is necessary with the
enemy. Leadership should ask that same question of men considered for serving in combat. Undoubtedly, a male soldier asks it of himself.
   Major Pfluke addresses other issues in her testimony. Service in any aspect
of the military is valuable. No one type of service to our country is better than
another. All people who serve and have served our country I personally thank
and respect. Many women as well as men would have preferred not to fight,

but many women who wanted to serve in a combat role were not allowed to do so. They had no choice but to serve in the ways permitted. Some women served in combat either in temporary positions or because a crisis was the mother of invention. In an emergency, soldiers do what they have to do.

Military leaders I have interviewed value all soldiers. RADM Paul T. Gillcrist, U.S. Navy (Ret.), says, "A good manager and leader should never tell a part of his organization that they are not really a part of the team. At least, not if the leader ever expects to need them in times of emergency."[4] Gillcrist was addressing the issue of teamwork in a fighter squadron in an air wing during deployment in the Vietnam War. He believes this philosophy is applicable to service women.[5] Gillcrist notes that all service women, whatever their assignment, are important to a mission.

Major Pfluke's story draws a sympathetic response. She has tremendous qualifications, but she believes there was no way she would have been allowed to reach her potential in the United States Army. When asked, "Is the reason [you did not reach your potential] because you were not allowed into ground combat?" Pfluke quickly responded, "Yes, absolutely." Major Pfluke feels the Army wasted her talent. "Ground combat is what is important to the Army. It picks its senior leaders from ground combat branches."[6] No one joins the Army to be a general, she added, but in an exit interview, GEN Gordon R. Sullivan, then Army Chief of Staff, said to her, "Lil, you could have been a general." In a follow-up note Pfluke replied, "No, I didn't want to be a general in a support branch, I only want to be a lieutenant colonel in the infantry."

CAPT Rosemary Mariner, U.S. Navy (USN), shares Pfluke's philosophy that the services should match people with jobs.[7] "A soldier is a soldier," Mariner emphatically states.[8] She explains that "it is the common identity of being a soldier first that transcends the differences of gender and unites highly competitive people to serve under a common purpose. Participation based upon individual ability also insures the strongest possible national defense.... The support of all the people is fundamental to victory."[9]

Mariner adds: "The military is about what you command. It is impossible for any member of the military who is restricted by class to have full advantage of opportunity. The uppermost positions are the unified combatant commands which are the ultimate war fighter positions. The positions I and other women held were legally defined as operations support positions. We were not even in the race for a combatant command position. There is a distinction between promotions and commands."[10] Mariner believes that no senior woman officer today is really in the running for a combatant command because women don't have the necessary experience. Until recently, the highest ranking women were two-star admirals, and they were largely restricted to operations support. "The younger women, just like the men, have the possibility of acquiring the necessary experience to put them in competition in the future," she added.

"The combatant command equality women will rise not just to a rank, but to a command. This distinction is not without a difference."[11]

In 1993, Mariner wrote, "Commanders must give women equal access to a level playing field on which each competitor either succeeds or fails based on individual merit." Mariner believes that as a result of changes in the law and in policy, women will fight as well as die in our next war. "While a gender-neutral meritocracy may be difficult to achieve, an initial step is to promote a shared common identity and purpose: man or woman, a soldier is a soldier *first*."[12] Some men who have served with women in the military are quick to agree that previously women could not reach their full potential. ADM Stanley R. Arthur, USN (Ret.), said that he had served with a woman who as a cadet in a Naval Reserve Officer Training Corps (NROTC) program was the very best midshipman. "There was no career path for her," he explained. "She went to college at the NROTC and related to a typical role. She went into intelligence. That wasn't her strongest suit. She was a leader. She didn't have line officer opportunities."[13]

In response to some who opposed having women fly in combat squadrons, Gillcrist asked, "When was the last time you flew in tactical formation with a female?"[14] "Never," was the opponents' response.

Gillcrist said, "Well, I have," pointing to a woman in the group with whom he had flown. "I would take her into combat tomorrow. I know what I am talking about." Gillcrist's experience is not unusual. Congressional hearings have heavily documented Gillcrist's position. In 1993, RADM Philip M. Quast, Assistant Chief of Naval Operations (CNO), Surface Warfare; VADM Ronald J. Zlatoper, Deputy CNO, Manpower, Personnel and Training, and Chief of Naval Personnel; and CAPT James F. Amerault, former Commanding Officer, USS *Samuel Gompers*, testified that their experiences with women were positive.[15]

It is difficult for women to realize their full potential in the Army and Marine Corps (see Chapter 5). In 1994, Congressman Ike Skelton (D-Mo.), chair, Military Forces and Personnel Subcommittee, said some people had expressed concern that the assignment policy which went into effect on October 1 would result in women being assigned to Army and Marine Corps units with a direct ground combat mission and that the so-called tripwire in the 1994 bill had been violated without the required notification.[16] (The military is not entirely free from civilian monitoring because of what is referred to as the tripwire bill; see Chapter 2.) Congressman Jon Kyl (R-Ariz.), ranking minority member, said that the decision had been especially controversial in the army. Kyl believed that the arguments reflected "the service's struggle to find the right balance between career opportunity for women and readiness of units." Areas of concern outlined in the Authorization Report of 1994 include "the impact of changes in assignment policy for women on the constitutionality of an all-male military selective service and the need to establish gender-neutral physical performance standards for military positions being opened up for both men and women."[17]

Congressman Stephen E. Buyer (R-Ind.) asked whether the American public is ready "to see one of its daughters [as a female soldier] half-naked dragged by a rope through the streets of a foreign capital after she is shot down delivering combat troops to a fire fight?... That happened in Somalia."[18] These and other issues are addressed throughout this book.

Women I interviewed who were denied a career path are quick to point out that young women today do not face the same problems. We must honor the earlier women, the forerunners, because they helped make change occur. Mariner characterizes the struggle to assign women to combat units as coming about because of a watershed, Desert Storm, and she further sees the repeal of the law that restricted women as the coming down of the military's "Berlin Wall." "It looked like it would never come down," Mariner recalls. "It took 20 years—all types of people [to bring down the barrier against allowing women in combat]."

In Desert Storm, male and female noncombatants were performing many of the same tasks that some combatant men had performed in earlier conflicts as well. According to Mariner, Desert Storm demonstrated that "codifying is absurd."

Letters of praise for women who served in the marines during Desert Storm and Shield make it clear that they "worked and lived side by side with their male counterparts, held key billets, and shared in the harsh living conditions."[19] Most of these women were performing under the classification the law allowed, but like their predecessors, they were, realistically speaking, in combat. The compelling stories of MAJ Marie T. Rossi, who was killed; MAJ Rhonda Cornum, who was captured;[20] and other women such as Col. Kelly Hamilton, U.S. Air Force (Ret.), who served in combat in the Gulf War and lived to tell about it, will be featured in this book. Knowing firsthand that she was in fact in combat in the Gulf War, Hamilton, like other women, became active in advocating the repeal of the combat exclusion laws after she came home.[21]

Many interviewees, regardless of their position on the issue, said it is critical to remember that the soldier we are discussing is a very young person. Some thought age added to the difficulty in training, whether that training addressed mixed gender units or actual combat. "How," one person said to me, "can you expect someone trained to be a cold-blooded killer to discontinue that behavior once conflict subsides?"

"That," according to one military officer, "is the commander's challenge."

It is little wonder that the real controversy surrounds allowing women in ground combat. Most agree that ground combat is gruesome, but that should not be the basis for barring women from combat. This book examines the reasons given for their exclusion. To explore this exclusion, I have interviewed

high-ranking combat commanders as well as other military and civilian people. Some reasons for the exclusion of women from combat are very real concerns; others are smoke screen issues. Education is sorely needed on the abilities
of both genders. Nonetheless, some in our culture have a problem with the possibility of women serving in ground combat regardless of what studies report.
For these people, a cultural dissonance sets in when women are allowed in combat.[22] To change society takes a long time, and institutions within society must
also change. Leaders of the military institution may not admit some of their
true objections, such as not wanting to share coveted high ranks, economic
gain, or realization of individual potential. These objections may manifest
themselves in inappropriate behavior toward women.[23]

The strain on family ties is well known to anyone who has served in the
military, whether in war or in the endless preparation for the possibility of war,
as Gillcrist notes:

> I'm going to miss you, sweetheart.... Nancy hated these good-byes
> more than I did. It was not so much the lonely nights. It was the des-
> olate feeling of struggling through a busy day, doing the chores, being
> both father and mother to four young children, and then, when it was
> over, having no one to discuss the problems with.[24]

Now that women can serve in some parts of combat, the issue of a woman's
family role, especially in parenting, has become a subject for debate.

This book will examine not only the history of women in combat, but the
contemporary women in combat. It begins with important definitions. Chapter 1 addresses the prime question of what war is. The answer is not as simple
as it may seem on the surface. Chapter 2 engages the question of what combat is. The definition of combat has enabled women to be placed in certain
positions, and excluded them from others.

Chapters 3 and 4 examine the evolution of women's involvement in war
and combat. Chapter 3 provides historical perspective on the role of women
in war and combat, while Chapter 4 examines the contemporary scene.

Chapter 5 analyzes the role of law and policy in the position of women
in the military and combat. Recent law and policy have opened more positions
for women, but policy still acts as a bar to combat positions for women in the
army.

Chapter 6, which is coauthored with James C. Skaine, assesses the American public and its role in the controversy surrounding women in the military
and combat. Some societal attitudes support the position that women should
not be in combat, but polls of the American public support women being in
the military and being assigned to combat.

Chapter 7 places the controversy within the context of sociological theory. Theories include: Goffman's total institution, conflict, role and feminist.
Sociobiology and ethics are also included in this chapter.

Issues involved in the controversy include readiness (Chapter 8), cohesion (Chapter 9), ability (Chapter 10), sexual issues (Chapter 11), equal opportunity (Chapter 12), and family (Chapter 13). These issues are being argued and investigated at the same time that law and policy are changing to include women in more combat positions, but many issues remain to be resolved.

In Chapter 14, "Toward Strength and Equality," attention focuses on the brutal consequence of war and even peacekeeping: the death of the soldier. The final frontier is and always has been that women and men fly, fight, and die alongside one another.

Chapter 1

What Is War?

War is an odd beast which kills when least expected.
—Col. Kelly Hamilton, U.S. Air Force (Ret.)[1]

"What is war?" may seem to be a question too obvious to need an answer. We talk about war and use the word war frequently. A search of a database for the word *war* produced nearly four million appearances.[2] That we use the word frequently does not mean, however, that we agree on its definition or its consequences. Nowadays we must add the words "peacekeeping" and "armed conflict" to our war vocabulary. These actions, my military friends tell me, pose no less threat to those who serve.

In 1985 the *Chicago Tribune* had an article which examined the state of war in the world.[3] Jonathan Broder, Ray Mosely, and Ron Yates begin in this way:

> "War is hell," said Gen. George S. Patton, who fought his way through the biggest of them all. He echoed the sentiment of the Roman philosopher Seneca, whose summation of the folly of war was equally pithy: "Men practice war; beasts do not." There is almost universal agreement about the iniquity of war, but it remains mankind's worst habit, one seemingly impossible to shake off. In this respect, new generations do not learn from the mistakes of the past. As civilization progresses in a technical sense, the resort to war becomes ever more frequent.[4]

Broder, Mosely, and Yates point out that there have been between 150 and 300 wars around the globe since World War II "depending on how you define war" and that each month 41,000 people around the world die in armed conflict.[5] The toll of 41,000 is the average toll since World War II ended, which adds up to almost 20 million lives, three out of every five of them civilians.[6]

Richard Rhodes has studied the casualties of war and says that wars have

17

claimed more than 100 million lives worldwide since 1700. He defines war as "an armed conflict including one or more governments and causing the death of 1,000 or more people per year."[7] Rhodes has found that the ratio of civilians to combatants in the death toll has also increased steadily. "Historically, about 50 percent of war-related deaths were civilian—but by the 1970s, civilians accounted for 73 percent of war deaths, and in the 1980s so far, the figure has risen to 85 percent."[8] According to Linda Grant De Pauw, professor of history at George Washington University and president of The MINERVA Center of Pasadena, Maryland, civilian women and children are killed in vastly greater numbers than are soldiers in war.[9] In 1995 a United Nations report stated: "Civilian victims, mostly women and children, often outnumber casualties among combatants. In addition, women often become caregivers for injured combatants and find themselves, as a result of conflict, unexpectedly cast as sole manager of household, sole parent, and caretaker of elderly relatives."[10] The casualties of war are only partially measured by the number of deaths. The injuries and damage to individuals and to the parties engaged in war are incalculable. Casualties, however, only partially define what war is.

The Brutality of Conflict

No one denies the brutality of conflict. People who have served in combat in past conflicts testify to that. On the eve of the major involvement of the United States in Bosnia, RADM Paul T. Gillcrist wrote:

> Two quotes by Hal Moore and Joe Galloway (*We Were Soldiers Once ... and Young*) ought to be required reading for all who aspire to be politicians, statesmen, public servants or journalists. And, it is especially appropriate on the eve of our major involvement in Bosnia. [Moore and Galloway wrote] about our soldiers in Vietnam:[11]
>
>> We were the children of the 1950s and John F. Kennedy's stalwarts of the early 1960s. He told the world that Americans would "pay any price, bear any burden, meet any hardship" in the defense of freedom. We were the down payment on that costly contract, but the man who signed it was not there when we fulfilled his promise. John F. Kennedy waited for us on a hill in Arlington National Cemetery, and in time we came by the thousands to fill those slopes with our white marble markers and to ask on the murmur of the wind if that was truly the future he had envisioned for us.[12]

De Pauw notes that combat in twentieth-century warfare has resulted in "killing a larger number of noncombatants, most of them women and children. This is called 'collateral damage' and is considered an unavoidable byproduct of combat."[13] De Pauw (whose book *Battle Cries and Lullabies: A Brief History of Women in War* covers the globe for the period 650 B.C. to the present) says, "My research shows that women have always and everywhere been involved in war."[14] Women have always been part of those for whom the bell tolls in war.

War Crimes and Atrocities

The United States has never had a policy of condoning rape in war. Sometimes a nation that goes to war maintains that whatever methods were used were necessary. According to Pfluke, the United States complies with the Geneva Convention's rules of war. Atrocities discussed in this section are violations of "codified behavior that we take very seriously," says Pfluke. "There are one-and-a-half-million males in the armed services. Not all men commit atrocities. Generalizations should not be made."[15]

Rape has been documented throughout history.[16] In some instances men are raped.[17] One particularly terrible version of rape is genocidal rape, which, as described in Article II of the 1948 UN Convention, is a crime of genocide.[18] Beverly Allen believes that the commissions of experts appointed in October 1992 by UN Secretary General Boutros Boutros-Ghali to examine the breaches of the Geneva Conventions and other international humanitarian law is a step in the right direction.[19]

The Geneva Convention of 1949 relative to the protection of civilians during a war and the additional protocols of 1977 provide that women shall especially be protected against any attack on their honor, in particular the humiliating and degrading acts of rape, enforced prostitution, or indecent assault. Likewise, the Vienna Declaration and Programme of Action adopted by the World Conference on Human Rights states: "Violations of the human rights of women in situations of armed conflict are violations of the fundamental principles of international human rights and humanitarian law."[20] Among the violations cited are murder, rape, including systematic rape, sexual slavery, and forced pregnancy.

It is encouraging that in 1995 the United Nation's Fourth World Conference on Women in Beijing urged governments to make commitments to improve women's status. The "Armed Conflict" commitment states: "Governments are to convert military resources to peaceful purposes to reduce the impact of armed conflict on women."[21]

International law prohibits attacks on civilians. This law is sometimes systematically ignored, however, and human rights, especially of women, children, the elderly, and the disabled are often violated. The Beijing Report discusses violations of the human rights of women, especially rape and systematic rape of women in war situations. The report urges condemnation, cessation, and punishment of such acts. Some human rights violations begin during the conquest of a country and are perpetuated through state and military repression.

The Beijing Report urges implementation of equal access for women as well as participation of women in power structures and their full involvement in all efforts for conflict prevention and resolution as important ways to move toward a more peaceful world peace. The Beijing report states:

> Although women have begun to play an important role in conflict resolution, peace-keeping and defense and foreign affairs mechanisms, they are underrepresented in decision-making positions. If women are to play an equal part in securing and maintaining peace, they must be empowered politically and economically and represented adequately at all levels of decision-making."[22]

First Lady Hillary Rodham Clinton emphasized human rights in a speech at the UN Fourth World Conference on Women. The Bosnia conflict hung unspoken in the air as she lamented that "thousands of women are subjected to rape as a tactic or prize of war."[23]

"DADDY, WHAT IS WAR?"[24]

On his last night before he went to the war in Vietnam, LTG Harold G. Moore tried his best to explain war to his six-year-old daughter, Cecile. Her look of bewilderment only grew, writes Moore. The most common description of war or peacekeeping missions offered to me is, "War is brutal." One only has to read Moore and Galloway's *We Were Soldiers Once ... and Young* to come to a very quick agreement that war is brutal.

> The small bloody hole in the ground was crowded with men. One man, 25 years of age, lay crumpled in the red dirt, dead from an AK-47 round through his throat; another, crouched low, bleeding from a shrapnel wound; and still another, slumped, with a bullet hole in his left shoulder and armpit. All men lay watching bullets kick the dirt at the edge of the hole.[25]

War's effects on the family are often harsh. In the Persian Gulf War, MGen. Jeanne Holm writes, it was often the wife and mother leaving the husband and father at home.[26] When TSgt Deborah Knight's unit was called up to deploy to Saudi Arabia, she had to leave behind her four-year-old son. *Courage Under Fire*, a contemporary movie, demonstrates many of the issues for women in combat. The heroine dies in battle, leaving behind a small daughter.

Holm dedicated her recent book on women in the military to MAJ Marie Rossi, who died in the Persian Gulf War.[27] According to Philip Bigler, thirty-two-year-old Rossi "volunteered to fly a mission despite the onset of bad weather. Rossi had gained distinction during the war for her bravery and for having flown into combat. In many ways, she had become a symbol of the ever-expanding role of women in the United States military."[28] Rossi's Chinook helicopter crashed, killing both her and her crew. Her proud family eulogized her bravery, leadership, and example to others. Rossi's headstone reads, "First Female Combat Commander to Fly in Battle." Bigler notes the appropriateness of the bronze plaque of a helicopter and the inscribed sentiment: "May our men and women stand strong and equal."

Many people believe that both mother and father should parent, but that in the youngest years of childhood, it is the mother who can best give the type of nurturing needed. The dual-military career family and single military parent carry an ominous responsibility; particularly when both parents in a dual military family deploy at the same time. The possibility of producing orphaned children is a serious one. John Whyte, a neighbor of my father, stated a position widely-held in society: "We know women can do combat, the question is, do we want them to?"

Deployment of soldiers to a war zone affects not only their children but their parents and other family members. Col. Kelly Hamilton, U.S. Air Force (Ret.), was the senior woman pilot in the Air Force in the Gulf War and was Assistant Director of Operations for Strategic Planning for the Air Mobility Command. In a letter home to her father dated 3 A.M., Jan. 15, 1991, on what she calls "Showdown Day during the Gulf War," Col. Hamilton wrote:

> It's early in the morning here and I've been working on changes to one of our big missions. Three of us have been working since about nine last night. With all that is going on in the world "today" the atmosphere is tense. I'm sure that you and the rest of the family are awaiting this noon deadline [for Saddam Hussein] with mixed thoughts as well.... The prospect [of war] does not frighten me as this is what I have trained for all my life.... The deadline weighs heavily on all involved but the conversations here are ones of serious dedication. I think we have all taken this opportunity to reflect on our decision to serve.... I do not for a moment regret my decision to serve.... The decision to join the military is the decision to fight and die for our great country."[29]

Col. Hamilton wrote that many young men and women were working 12–14 hours a day, far from home, but were satisfied to know the payback for their efforts was continued freedom.

TRAINING FOR WAR OR CONFLICT

Training for the possibility of war or conflict also takes its toll; military service personnel occasionally die in training. In some cases, a paragraph concerning a fatal accident may appear in a newspaper or a sentence will be spoken on a newscast. In others, no wide media coverage is given. Since women are now allowed in most combat situations, the watchful world scrutinizes the outcomes of training mishaps of women.

LT Kara Hultgreen, a female Navy F-14 fighter pilot, died in a training exercise crash off the California coast on October 25, 1994. The controversy surrounding her aircraft mishap is examined in Chapter 2. That chapter explores Hultgreen's personal battle to succeed in the field of carrier aviation, where women had not previously had an opportunity to succeed. An interview with RADM Paul Gillcrist, a former naval aviator, helps us understand the F-14A's problems.[30] He reminds us that history illustrates that male aviators have been on the edge of the sword, lived, and died as did Hultgreen and, as she did, have performed their missions.

Military academies where the future combat leaders of military service are trained are not immune from the one irrevocable result of combatant life. Training, testing, and serving is not in vain. Said former Secretary of the Navy James Webb, Jr.: "I went to a funeral the other day.... It was Saturday, I guess. It was my best friend. It was sad. His wife was crying. But you know, I thought, watching him go under like that, I thought, he isn't really gone. He's alive as long as this place [academy] is alive."[31] The academies are facing much change, but it is in these institutions that hope remains.

ILLNESSES RESULTING FROM COMBAT

Mere mention of the use of nuclear bombs in World War II and the use of nerve gases in both world wars drive home rather quickly the brutality and often finality of illness resulting from war. Moore and Galloway tell of soldiers who contracted malaria while serving in Vietnam.[32] Wars almost inevitably bring with them possible disease in the short-term or long-term. Press reports indicate some veterans of the Gulf War suffer from "the Gulf War Syndrome."[33]

EFFECTS OF WAR AND CONFLICT

Whatever the fate of a soldier, he or she is not the only one affected by war or conflict. The soldier's family members are affected, and on a higher level, society and the global society are also affected. How the individual, institutions, systems and subsystems are affected depends on their position in the war or conflict.

Congress decides, reflecting the views or wishes of the American people, whether the military includes draftees as well as volunteers. The military goes to war at the instruction of the president as commander in chief and with congressional authorization. Congress does not have to declare war for conflict to occur. Sometimes the issue may be simply debated by Congress, and sometimes the military forces respond to contingencies that don't involve the political system. The location and type of battle fought is usually, however, a political decision. The military then actually fights the war. Gerald Linderman notes: "Every war begins as one war and becomes two, that watched by civilians and that fought by the soldiers. Separation may begin soon after a society declares itself at war."[34] Combat changes the soldiers more than it does even the most ardent civilian. Linderman maintains the difference in outlooks brings tension and struggle, and it is important for political leaders to keep the "two wars" proximate. Leaders should help civilians to understand the realities of war better. Otherwise, the morale and cohesiveness of the nation's forces may be endangered, putting the nation itself at risk.

Chapter 2

What Is Combat?

First Female Combat Commander to Fly in Battle
May our men and women stand strong and equal
—Inscriptions on MAJ Marie Rossi's Headstone[1]

Issues

What is combat? What does the law mean when it says women are not allowed to serve in combat? What is U.S. policy regarding whether women can serve in combat and how is this policy made? If people agreed upon a definition of combat, the law and policy would have to be broadly interpreted (see Chapter 5). Many military women think they have "been doin' it." Linda Bird Francke writes, "the book I intended to write about women in the military had less to do with women than with men in the military," and that "the combat issue was never about women but about men."[2] When some military men are asked what they think about women in combat, they say, "Women have been doing it anyway" and they just "looked the other way." Women have served legally in temporary combat positions; on May 12, 1993, the Navy had 158 women on temporary duty on 20 combatants.[3] In the Gulf War, some women were employed in positions which exposed them to direct combat. But these women did not get the promotions or pay commensurate with what they did. To a certain extent it can be argued that these women got the same pay as men in comparable positions and that they had the opportunity for promotion within a noncombatant unit. These women could not realize their potential, however, because in the long run, they were not allowed to enter another "career" track—combat positions. The men who serve in a noncombatant unit are allowed, if qualified, to enter the combatant units. Women in noncombatant units may get the same pay, but not the same opportunity. Two arguments in favor of allowing women to serve in a combat role are that the old front line no longer exists because present day conflicts are peacekeeping tasks and that modern weaponry is more technologically operated than in the past. During

World War II, the bombing included the infrastructure: units that made ammunition for the front line in addition to military targets. Today, targets most often are military personnel, supply depots, transportation, and communication centers. To examine combat in the context of the fifteenth century, we can consider Town A, a walled town that is being besieged by King B and his knights. King B is not as concerned about killing people as he is with capturing Town A. The people in the fields taking care of the water supply are the ones King B targets. Modern warfare may achieve its goals by knocking out gas trucks and not concentrating solely on "combat" units because, after interdicting the supplies, you slow down the troops in direct combat. Mary Whitley, a former captain in the Army Transportation Corps, agrees that women are and have been in combat and notes there are "hokey" rules that change all the time.[5] Whitley states: "When I say the rules change, I am referring to rules like gender requirements for certain jobs in the Field Artillery [FA] and Air Defense Artillery [ADA] which have changed several times in the past fifteen years. This causes women to lose opportunities to serve in positions which may later be required to progress in their career, e.g., they may not be able to hold a command position in FA or ADA if they did not serve as an ADA platoon leader or company commander."[6]

Barbara Sweatt, former specialist in the Army, spent four years in combat support during the 1980s. "We were always ready to go," Sweatt says, "but we never had to go." When asked if she thinks she would have been fit for combat, Sweatt responded with an eyeopener:

> Let me answer this by telling you about the unit I was in near Frankfurt, Germany. Supported units pulled forward to the Fulda Gap where the Russians could get into West Germany—it was the only place you got tanks through. We were told that our life expectancy was 45 minutes. We understood that the Russian battle plan was to hit support units first. DACOWITS started about this time. I remember I got sent to hear a panel of DACOWITS women. Another female soldier asked the panel, "What happens if [combat occurs]?" There was a Colonel, the only man in the room, who said, "I think I can answer that. I was told if women were in my battalion, the women have to come with me." Most women did not realize they would go into combat. I did realize that I would go, but I thought I would be further from the action [than I was]. I was 23.[7]

Something was wrong. The definition of combat was wrong. CAPT Georgia Sadler, U.S. Navy (Ret.) and director of the Women in the Military Project of the Women's Research and Education Institute (WREI), says, "If the laws and policies were intended to keep women out of harm's way, they failed completely in the Persian Gulf War."[8] Col. Kelly Hamilton, U.S. Air Force (Ret.), who was flying combat support missions in the Gulf War from the beginning of the "outbreak of hostilities," writes: "As you may know only Fighters and

Bombers and Attack Aircraft may log 'actual combat' time. Once again we will prove the definition of combat to mean the ability to shoot at, or inflict damage on, the enemy. It has nothing to do with being at risk. Hopefully, the American public will see the high tech aspect of war and recognize that brain and agility are the key elements to 'combat' aircraft, not brawn."[9] Hamilton adds that more aircraft and crews are sent to expanded forward locations. How does the military know for sure when it is in a combat zone? Does being in the forward zone in the air and on the ground and not "shooting" make combat a grey area in the Air Force, Army, Navy, or Marine Corps? Does warfare from the sea make combat a grey area in the Navy?

In 1991, President George Bush appointed the U.S. Presidential Commission on the Assignment of Women in the Armed Forces. In 1992 the Commission said the definition of combat was the key to understanding women in combat.[10] Today the definition is a combination of law and policy. Women have been allowed in more combat positions as a result of the Gulf War, the Presidential Commission, the repeal of the combat exclusion laws, a series of congressional hearings from 1990 to 1994, the election of President Clinton, and the efforts of countless individuals. Are all positions promised really opened? No, but many are. Definition is basic to understanding combat assignments, particularly, direct combat.

Direct Combat at the Time of the Persian Gulf War

No statute has restricted the Army from assigning women to combat positions. Title 10 U.S. Code § 3013 authorizes the Secretary of the Army to determine policy. The Secretary developed policies that "exclude women from 'routine engagement in direct combat.'"[11] The Army justified its policy on the basis of congressional intent manifested in the Navy and Air Force exclusionary statutes.

In 1988 the Secretary of Defense drafted the Risk Rule, which attempted to standardize positions closed to women across the services. "Non-combat units can be closed to women on grounds of risks or exposure to direct combat, hostile fire, or capture provided the type, degree, and duration of such risks are *equal to or greater than* that experienced by combat units in the same theater of operations".[12] The Presidential Commission held that because "the line between direct combat and support units is sometimes blurred, the [1988] Risk Rule provides the best mechanism available for maintaining consistency in assignment policies and integrity of the relationship between support and direct land combat units."[13]

Definition of Direct Ground Combat

Army and Marine Corps directives announced on July 29, 1994, are based on the new "rule" and "definition" of combat announced by Defense Secretary Les Aspin on January 13, 1994.

A. Rule. Service members are eligible to be assigned to all positions for which they are qualified, except that women shall be excluded from assignment to units below the brigade level whose primary mission is to engage in direct combat on the ground as defined below:

B. Definition. Direct ground combat is engaging an enemy on the ground with individual or crew served weapons, while being exposed to hostile fire and to a high probability of direct physical contact with the hostile force's personnel. Direct ground combat takes place well forward on the battle field while locating and closing with the enemy to defeat them by fire, maneuver, or shock effect.[14]

The new rule replaced the Defense Department's long-standing Risk Rule, which was designed to limit the exposure of women in noncombat units to front-line combat on land, sea, and in the air. Both provisions represent a significant departure from previous policy.[15] MAJ Lillian Pfluke, U.S. Army (Ret.), however, says there was not a "significant departure from previous policy. The policy is the same as the previous policy, but in different words. It was the Risk Rule which was rescinded."[16] In 1994, Edwin Dorn, Under Secretary of Defense, Personnel and Readiness, said that rescinding the Risk Rule policy allows the assignment of women, who serve in career fields that are otherwise open, to all ground units *except* for units below the brigade level whose primary mission is to engage in direct ground combat.[17]

Background

In February 1978, Deputy Secretary of Defense Charles Duncan testified before Congress that combat meant being engaged by an enemy in armed combat in a geographic area designated as a combat zone. A combat mission occurred when a military unit sought out, reconnoitered, or engaged an enemy. Duncan affirmed that women have served in combat and received commensurate pay and awards for combat duty in World War II, Korea, and Vietnam. Nurses, though considered noncombatants, served in combat. Therefore he concluded, "the Department of Defense (DOD) does not believe that the term provides a useful basis for expanding the opportunities for women in the service."[18]

In 1991, according to the Committee on Military Affairs and Justice of the Association of the Bar of the City of New York, the five terms relevant to the definition of combat are "combat mission," "close combat," "direct combat," "combat support," and "combat service support." Many of the definitions were inconsistent from one service to the other and did not always comply with DOD policy. "Combat mission" was the only term used to establish combat exclusion in 10 U.S. Code § 6015, applicable to the Navy and Marine Corps, and § 8549, applicable to the Air Force, but the term was not defined statutorily.[19]

The term "close combat" was defined by the DOD in 1978 as "engaging an enemy with individual or crew-served weapons while being exposed to direct enemy fire, a high probability of direct physical contact with the enemy's personnel, and a substantial risk of capture."[20] In 1985 the word *and* was replaced by the word *or*. No women serve in "close combat" positions in any of the armed forces.

"Direct combat," an Army term defined in 1982, expanded the DOD's close combat definition by adding, "engaging any enemy with individual or crew-served weapons while being exposed to direct enemy fire, a high probability of direct physical contact with the enemy's personnel, and a substantial risk of capture. Direct combat takes place while closing with the enemy by fire, maneuver, or shock effect in order to destroy or capture him, or while repelling his assault by fire, close combat or counterattack."[21] No women serve in direct combat positions.

The Marine Corps defines "direct combat operations" as "seeking out, reconnoitering, or engaging in <u>offensive</u> action". Women therefore could be assigned to combat support and combat service support units in a designated hostile fire area that might involve a "<u>defensive</u>" combat action.[22]

"Combat support" was defined as providing operational assistance to combat troops. "Combat service support" was defined as a position that provided logistical, technical, and administrative services to the combat arm. Women in all the services serve in these positions.

The DOD Task Force Report studied the "risk" interpretation of the law and the risk in the restricting of women in noncombat positions. The Risk Rule stated in part, "risk of exposure to direct combat, hostile fire, or capture ... equal to or greater than that experienced by associated combat units with which they are normally associated in a given theater of operations." In 1991, thinking the Risk Rule would change the services' interpretations, the Committee on Military Affairs and Justice of the Association of the Bar of the City of New York concluded that to believe the Risk Rule a valid method, one must assume the risk itself can be predicted, measured, quantified, and compared, and require that the thresholds of the services be the same.

NAVY BACKGROUND

In 1987, in response to the Navy Women's Study Group (NWSG), the Secretary of the Navy changed the combat definition from "'seek out, reconnoiter, <u>or</u> engage the enemy (emphasis added),'" to "'seek out, reconnoiter, <u>and</u> engage the enemy (emphasis added),'" in order to narrow the definition of combat mission."[23] As a result, additional positions aboard combat services support ships were opened to women. The NWSG recommended, however, expanding the combat definition to add the collective task group concept. This had the effect under the Risk Rule of excluding women from assignment to support ships that operated as an integrated part of a collective task group. In 1990 the study group again reexamined the definition of combat, and as a result the Secretary of the Navy removed the collective task group concept. The Navy's definition included the language: "A *primary* mission of an individual unit, ship or aircraft to seek out, reconnoiter, and engage an enemy, (emphasis added)." This change allowed review of an individual vessel to be followed by application of the Risk Rule to that vessel in order to determine whether women could be permanently assigned to that vessel.

The study group also recommended Navy units and platforms be reviewed in light of the changed combat definition to ensure that women were not precluded from permanent assignment to units, vessels, and aircraft. Force reduction required retirement of vessels that mandated a change in employment of some vessels. If certain platforms are not open to women, decommissioning ships to achieve the force reduction would result in decreased opportunities for women to serve at sea. The Navy therefore reassessed the mission of a number of ships and determined that individually they did not have a "*primary*" combat mission. The ships thus became noncombatant, and no change was required. Because these vessels had a secondary combat mission or were routinely assigned to a task group, women had been previously precluded from permanent assignment to them, but under the changed definition of "combat mission" they were not. The Navy determined that the risk of direct combat, exposure to hostile fire, or capture for the support ships was less than for the combat vessel with which they normally appeared.[24]

SIMILAR RISKS

The testimony of VADM Ronald J. Zlatoper, Deputy Chief of Naval Operations, Manpower, Personnel and Training, Chief of Naval Personnel (CNP), in the 1993 hearings indicates that the risks may not in fact be less for the noncombatant vessel than for the combatant vessel. In Desert Storm, the USS *Shasta*, one of eight ships assigned to Zlatoper's battle group, had 44 women on board. Zlatoper was aboard the USS *Ranger*, which was 150 miles further away from the mines in the Persian Gulf. Any Iraqi aircraft that came out to shoot an Exocet missile would have had an opportunity to shoot at the *Shasta*, the noncombatant ship with its 44 women, before the aircraft got to the *Ranger*. What does Zlatoper's testimony tell us about attitudes toward women in combat?[25] Does it tell us that women can die but cannot fight?

Congresswoman Patricia Schroeder (D-Colo.), chair of the House Military Installations and Facilities Subcommittee, noted three years earlier in 1990 that an Army recruiting commercial illustrated just that point. The commercial portrayed a female soldier operating a "noncombat" communications van during field maneuvers. Schroeder responded:

I think all of us know that if you were in real battle, the first person you usually try to hit is the person running the communications van. So it appears that women can be the first killed, but they are not allowed at the front line and supposedly in battle. I think that really shows you how tenuous so many of these classifications really are. Looking at those commercials, I think, brings it all home.[26]

In 1993, RADM Philip M. Quast, Assistant Chief of Naval Operations (CNO), Surface Warfare, evaluated combat in the Navy in a way that recalled Schroeder's 1990 opinion about the Army combat lines. Naval warfare is no longer taking place on the sea, but from the sea, thus making combat a grey area. "It is difficult in this area to determine when you are in combat and when you are not."[27] The invisible lines of combat zones are artificialities.

In 1997, Sadler wrote:

[The Gulf War] clearly illustrated the difficulty of differentiating between support and combat. Air Force women were not permitted to fly fighter planes, but they flew the tankers that refueled the fighters over Iraq. Female Army pilots, excluded from piloting heavily-armed attack helicopters, flew soldiers and supplies in the first assault wave 50 miles into Iraq aboard more vulnerable, lightly-armed helicopters. Navy women pilots could not be in the cockpits of fighter aircraft, but were flying helicopters from ships that were in waters filled with mines.[28]

As noted earlier, prior to 1993 the Department of the Navy implemented the 1979–91 statutes by defining combat missions as involving an "individual ship/aircraft that individually or collectively as a naval task organization has a primary objective to seek out, reconnoiter, and engage the enemy." The Risk Rule was used as a proper criterion for closing noncombat positions or units to women when there was a risk of direct combat, exposure to hostile fire, or capture equal to or greater than that of the combat units with which they were normally associated. Once women were assigned to a particular class of ship, however, those units were expected to perform their intended mission and assignments were not reassessed under the Risk Rule during a national emergency.[29]

In December 1991, Congress repealed 10 U.S. Code § 8549 which had prohibited the assignment of women to Air Force aircraft engaged in combat missions. The legislation that removed the restrictions passed without too much difficulty. The Presidential Commission on the Assignment of Women in the Armed Forces voted 8 to 7 in 1992, however, to recommend that Congress reenact the combat aviation exclusion.[30] After President Clinton was elected, he and Congress disregarded the Commission's vote by moving toward repeal of the restrictive laws and assignment policies.[31]

The war in the Persian Gulf demonstrated that women could work in dangerous environments. This was the catalyst for Congress to repeal the laws prohibiting women from being assigned to combat aircraft. Women were also allowed to fly high performance aircraft. "The modern battlefield where mobility and long-range standoff weapons made even rear echelon lethal, the argument that women should not be exposed to danger no longer has any meaning," stated Congresswoman Beverly B. Byron (D–Md.).[32] The Navy was directed to open many additional positions aboard ships and develop a proposal to repeal the remaining restrictions preventing women from serving aboard combatant ships.

In 1993, according to Secretary of Defense Les Aspin, both the number and role of women in the military had evolved, with the number increasing substantially since the 1980s. In 1993, women comprised 11.5 percent of the active force and 13 percent of the selected reserve. The total military strength was at its lowest since the Korean War, and Aspin predicted that by the end of 1994 the active force would be over 25 percent smaller than it was in 1987. As the number of women increased, opportunities for women also expanded. Prior to the historic decision to open some combat positions on ships, 87 percent of all skill categories representing over one million jobs were already open to women.[33]

Many factors contributed to this repeal of the air combat prohibition. In addition to the ambiguity in the use of the term *combat*, there were changes in society and the military. The Anita Hill–Clarence Thomas Senate hearings wherein Hill alleged that Clarence Thomas, nominee to the U.S. Supreme Court, had sexually harassed her and the publicity arising from charges made by LT Paula Coughlin, U.S. Navy (USN), that sexual harassment had occurred in 1991 at Tailhook contributed to the change in women's role in the military and society.

ARMY BACKGROUND

The Army's struggle has been and is the most difficult (see Chapter 5). There is no statute limiting the assignment of Army women. Restrictions are imposed as a matter of policy consistent with the statutory restrictions on the other services that existed prior to 1994. In the aftermath of the 1989 invasion of Panama in Operation Just Cause, Congresswoman Schroeder introduced legislation in 1990 to allow women in combat in the Army. She stated that women had served in combat roles in the Revolutionary Army, World War II, and Vietnam and that the outdated exclusion laws did not reflect the opinion of the American public. According to Schroeder, we were not maintaining a more combat-effective force by this exclusion, and we were in fact denying the military the skilled and qualified personnel that it needed.[34]

Congressman G. V. (Sonny) Montgomery (D-Miss.) said he did not see the necessity of legislation because if the Army wanted to change, they could change their regulation, and put women in combat.[35] In the 1990 hearings,

Schroeder argued that because there was no statutory combat exclusion in the case of the Army, testing the effectiveness of women in these roles would reveal whether it would be worthwhile to remove the exclusion in the Air Force and the Navy.[36] We will see in Chapter 5 that the evolution Schroeder proposed did not seem logical to those making Army policy. The Army and Marine Corps still have not completely removed their combat restriction policies. No statutory limitation on women serving in combat exists any longer, but military policy does restrict women.

ARMY POLICY AND DEFINITIONS

According to LTC Timothy A. Rippe, U.S. Army (USA), University of Northern Iowa professor of Military Science–ROTC (Ret.), "Proximity to the front line and the risk factors associated with it in terms of combat used to be the criteria by which certain positions were open to women."[37] Rippe agrees that the Gulf War helped to change the earlier Army policy. "In any position you are assigned in the military, you have the potential for being exposed to combat. No longer is there a front line per se, so the old cold war criteria doesn't stand. Now there are certain restrictions for females, for example, in the infantry, armor and some special positions in the artillery and engineers. Positions that are in close proximity to combat."[38]

Rippe verifies that there has been change: "The new definition, opened ... positions for helicopter flying for females. The University of Northern Iowa commissioned a female who went to flight school and is now training to fly the Apache aircraft, a helicopter for combat."[39] According to Rippe:

> The past policy was problematic. It drew a zone on the ground women couldn't be in. Policy was created in the cold war days. Combat could have included the entire German area of operations, for example, with units with women in them exposed to combat in the rear areas, as well as, areas in close proximity to the front lines. It was an unrealistic policy. Implementing a policy which excludes women from the most violent roles is more realistic policy. Although it is not a perfect policy yet.[40]

Military policy is not immune to civilian political guidance. This is particularly true in the matter of ground combat. A congressional hearing was held in 1994 precisely to exercise congressional oversight and monitor military policy in the assignment of Army and Marine Corps women under the new definition of ground combat. Although Congressman Ike Skelton (D-Mo.), chair of the Military Forces and Personnel Subcommittee of the House Committee on Armed Services, believed that the letter of the law had been met, there was some concern that women might be assigned into combat as a matter of policy.

The most common question I have heard from civilians as I researched this book was: How can women not be admitted into ground combat if no law prohibits it? When the answer is given that policy prohibits women serving in ground combat, many military and civilian proponents of assigning women to combat roles do not understand. The military is not entirely free from civilian monitoring because of what Skelton calls the tripwire bill. Skelton points out, however, that the subcommittee and Congress as a whole have consistently maintained the position that women should not serve in direct ground combat. In addition to the repeal exclusions, they left in the tripwire bill a notification requirement that Skelton describes thusly:

> The position [that women cannot serve in combat] is why the 1994 *Defense Authorization Act* contained a 90-day notification requirement for any proposed assignment policy that would require women serving in units with direct ground combat mission. Specifically, the statute states that notification is required if the Secretary of Defense proposes to make any change in the ground combat exclusion policy. That policy being that female members of the armed forces are restricted from assignments to units and positions whose missions require routine engagement in direct combat on the ground.[41]

It should be noted that the legislation does not say anything about the military prerogative to assign women to combat positions should necessity dictate. Yet it must be acknowledged and can best be demonstrated from the conflicts since the beginning of time, but more recently the conflicts of Vietnam, Grenada, Panama, and Desert Storm, that if necessity arises, female military personnel go where the military tells them.

Current Army Policy

In 1993 Army policy incorporated guidance on the Department of Defense Risk Rule:

> Army policy was that Army women served in all units except those whose mission was to engage in direct combat or those units whose routine mission required physical collocation with direct combat units. The Army defined direct combat as engaging an enemy with individual or crew served weapons while being exposed to direct enemy fire, a high probability of direct physical contact with the enemy's personnel and a substantial risk of capture.[42]

LTG Theodore G. Stroup, Jr., Deputy Chief of Staff for Personnel, USA, testified that the 1994 definition for direct combat eliminated the phrase "substantial risk of capture," but the Army assignment policy remained the same.

The 1994 rescission of the DOD Risk Rule allowed the Army to reevaluate all positions closed by application of the Risk Rule while continuing to exclude women from assignments to units below the brigade level whose primary mission is direct ground combat. The Risk Rule only applied to noncombat positions; consequently, Stroup testified, the Army's combat exclusion policy was not materially changed and the Army did not change the basic exclusion of women from direct ground combat.[43]

Under Secretary of Defense Edwin Dorn testified that prior to the January 13, 1994, policy memorandum, neither the armed services nor the Department of Defense had a specific Ground Combat Exclusion Policy.[44] Each service had incorporated applicable laws and the Risk Rule into an ersatz combat exclusion policy. With the repeal of combat exclusion laws, the Risk Rule was no longer appropriate. To ensure consistency across the services with these changes, DOD officials believed that the actual establishment of a DOD definition of direct ground combat and an associated assignment rule was essential. Under the new policy, Dorn stated, the same fields that had been closed to women (i.e., armor, infantry, field artillery, and ground combat Special Operations Forces such as Army Special Forces, Rangers, Navy Special Forces [SEALS], and Air Force Combat Controllers units and career fields) remained closed.

Stroup testified that the Army first looked at whether the unit's primary mission was to engage in direct ground combat. After that determination was made, the Army looked at whether a unit should be closed based on its collocation with a direct ground combat unit. "Collocation occurs on the battlefield when units operate in such a close proximity to the other direct ground combat units that they are almost indistinguishable from direct ground combat units—in terms of the physical demands on the soldier, source of support, possible physical contact with the enemy force. These aspects affected the units differently and subsequently each unit was considered on an individual basis."[45]

Lt Gen George R. Christmas, Deputy Chief of Staff for Manpower and Reserve Affairs, U.S. Marine Corps (USMC), states that the major increases that come from career opportunities for women in the Marines are in aviation. The direct combat units, those that locate, close with, and destroy the enemy by fire, maneuver, and shock effect remain closed.[46]

Christmas testified that women will not serve in the infantry regiments and below, artillery battalions and below, all armored units (tanks, amphibious assault vehicles, and light armored reconnaissance vehicles), combat engineer battalions, reconnaissance units, riverine assault craft units, and low-altitude air defense units.

Christmas says that the Marine Corps had worked closely with the Army and had made the same changes the Army did, except that the Combat Engineer Battalion Headquarters Company would remain closed. Marine doctrine calls for the Combat Engineer Battalion Headquarters to provide decentralized support for front-line units. The Army has significantly more combat engineer capability, which allows for differing concepts of command and control. The only difference in training technique is that women will not receive instruction in ambush techniques like the men.[47]

Since there is no law prohibiting women from serving in ground combat, the definition of combat for policy issues is arrived at through a written military policy and a philosophy of Congress that attempts to reflect the greater society. Both Congress and the military realize that the latter may have to interpret philosophy and policy and place women in combat in times of necessity and crisis to defend our country.

The definition of combat goes hand in hand with units being open or closed to military women. Whether military women are in selected units reflects interpretation of policy and the execution of policy. In 1991 the Marines reported that three career fields were closed to women: infantry, combat arms, and combat support (artillery). The Army prohibited women from 10 percent of its fields, the Navy restricted 13 out of 99 and the Air Force opened all but 4 areas. The percentages of total positions open in 1991 compared with 1996 appear in Table 2.1.

Further interpretation of philosophy and policy is necessary in the actual opening up of military units for the assignment of women. Congress and organizations like DACOWITS exercise even more oversight responsibility as they seek to find out whether women are not only in the units that are open, but are indeed serving in the positions and the roles new policy allows. Many proponents of women in combat question the acculturation positions that allow women to serve in combat in aviation and at sea, but not on the ground. Is it the way a woman is at risk that we are limiting? To answer this question, we return to the policy criteria that form the basis for the restriction and ask what is the validity of the criteria, keeping in mind that policy is open to interpretation by the appropriate military and civilian personnel. Two other important questions for which some advocates are seeking to find answers are: Should some units be opened that now are not, such as the Multiple Launch Rocket System (MLRS) unit? And if women are not in such units, why aren't they? These and other questions are examined in this book.

Illustrations of Combat in a Support Assignment

The successful portrayal of women soldiers by the media during the Gulf War was a primary reason for the repeal of the statutory restrictions of 10 U.S. Code § 6015. The following illustrations of military women in combat give shape and reality to an otherwise intellectual concept for those of us who have never been in a combat zone.

In the Gulf War, many women's assignments were support assignments, but they were performed in a combat environment. Many women who served

Table 2.1
**Percentages of Total Positions Open to Women in All Services
1991 and 1996**

Service	*1991*	*1996*
Air Force	97%	99%
Army	52%	91%
Coast Guard	100%	100%
Navy	59%	97%
Marine Corps	33%	62%

Source: Carolyn Becraft in Committee on Military Affairs and Justice of the Association of the Bar of the City of New York, "The Combat Exclusion Laws: An Idea Whose Time Has Gone," May 17, 1991, 21–22, note 82, for 1991, and testimony at congressional hearings for 1996.

in support assignments in previous wars also found this to be true. The concept that female and male noncombatants cannot legally shoot back because of their unit assignment does not make sense to these noncombatants.

Army Reservist Becky Creighton's Persian Gulf War experience is an excellent illustration that the military, in times of necessity, does what it has to do. Creighton was trained as an artillery repair technician, but the Army needed drivers. Creighton was "pressed into emergency service as a fuel truck driver."[48] The Army transferred her from her first assignment with the 26th Support Battalion of the 1st Armored Division since the noncommissioned officers of Bravo Company didn't want her because she was a woman. When she moved to Alpha Company, a sergeant gave her a 30-minute driving lesson, but left the lesson saying that he would teach her to reverse on the next day. The Iraqi invasion did not start on February 25, 1991, as everyone, including the sergeant, expected. The invasion started a day early. Creighton, who had not learned how to drive in reverse, had to keep her 34-ton fuel truck with its 5,000 gallons of helicopter fuel going forward across an exploding Iraqi minefield.

Col. Kelly Hamilton was called upon to do what she always did, but her duties held a new significance. Stationed in Bunker Hill, Indiana, at Grissom Air Force Base, Hamilton was Director of Aircrew Scheduling and Training. As part of her duties, she oversaw who flew what flights based upon training requirements and experience levels. "My boss, the Director of Operations, and I met with the squadron commanders to determine the line up. During this meeting, I was called away. Upon my return, I was informed by a senior enlisted woman that, in my absence, my boss had directed that all women be removed from the crews, stating that women would not deploy."[49] Hamilton was stunned.

"At the time of the Gulf War, we still had combat exclusion laws that were lingering in some minds," says Hamilton, "I checked this out with my Director. He said he had gotten no directives but this is the way he viewed this law." Hamilton advised him that she didn't agree because since 1978 women had been certified for the Single Integrated Operational Plan (SIOP). Women stood by a week at a time along with their male counterparts as part of an integral crew ready to respond in a matter of minutes to get their aircraft off the ground, should the "balloon go up." "We had earned, and proudly wore, the Combat Crew ribbon. I found it difficult to accept the view that it was never the Air Force's intention to send us to war should the occasion arise," says Hamilton. She asked her director to reconsider his interpretation, which she believed wasn't correct because "the crews had trained and flown as integral crews." The next morning the director rescinded his direction and Hamilton's crews deployed with women the following week. As the senior female pilot, Hamilton did have an impact. She had influenced policy in a positive manner. "Very few people are aware that these kinds of conversations are going on," adds Hamilton. "Combat relationship is being in a high threat area and being able to provide air refueling for fighters, bombers, and reconnaissance aircraft which sometimes includes going into high threat areas." Because of her experience in Desert Storm, Hamilton was heavily involved in the effort to change the combat exclusion law when she returned home. The face of combat had changed. Not only were the actual lines blurred, says Hamilton, but the Gulf War was very different from any other conflict. "It was the beginning of true recognition that what scenarios we had looked at over the years that what the next war would be like, was indeed happening: stand off (less face to face encounters and more distant targeting based on reconnaissance and intelligence information), aerial engagement (less focus on air to air battle), and more air to ground (more emphasis on destruction of communications, command and control and infrastructure—use of smart bombs and missiles)." Hamilton and her crew were, indeed, combat aviators.

Desert Shield and Desert Storm were definitely progress. Women were recognized within the military and within society at large as excellent soldiers.[50] Women who served in the Marine Headquarters Battalion numbered 10 officers, 66 enlisted women, and 4 Navy corpsmen. Several women served in critical billets, were deployed with forward and rear elements, and served in a field environment for 90 continuous days.

Specific women honored include Lt Col M. K. Lowery, Assistant Chief of Staff, who successfully accomplished her assigned tasks in rigorous winter desert warfare in a combat zone. First Lt N. E. McCarthy helped transport enemy prisoners of war and assisted in locating enemy equipment, command bunkers, caches, maps and overlays for further exploitation.[51]

Gen Charles C. Krulak, present Commandant of the Marine Corps and previously Commanding General, 2d Force Service Support Group, wrote of two "most noteworthy" women, Lt Col Ruthann Poole and Maj Ginger Jacocks, who operated the vehicles that transported Marines to the holding area. "During and since the war, these drivers have passed through the breaches in the minefields on hundreds of occasions."[52]

TESTING AND TRAINING AS PREPARATION FOR COMBAT

The shouted words "eject, eject," sounding the combination of alarm and hope for aircraft recovery, may have been the last words LT Kara Hultgreen, a Navy F-14A Tomcat fighter pilot, heard in her young life of 29 years. On October 24, 1994, at 15:01, off the coast of San Diego, California, her aircraft hit the water during her aborted carrier landing approach and was destroyed. The mission was a carrier qualification refresher. Destination: USS *Abraham Lincoln*. Damage and costs: aircraft, destroyed; two drop tanks, $111,900. Personal information, injuries, and costs: "Souls on board, two."[53] Reality check. Although the male pilot survived, the factual statement "Souls on board, two" is a solemn reminder of death amidst the otherwise austere report.

RADM Jay P. Yakeley, Commander, Carrier Group THREE, spelled out Hultgreen's narrow margin:

> There were four seconds critical to the outcome of this mishap:
> *15:01:12* Aircraft rolls out of an overshooting start with a left engine stall.
> *15:01:16* Starboard engine is in afterburner, left wing down, excessive left yaw rate, angle of attack above 20 units.[54]

According to Yakeley, the window of opportunity for a successful recovery was missed. The tasks that would have had to be accomplished to prevent the mishap had to happen within those four short seconds. VADM R. J. Spane, Commander of the Naval Air Force, U.S. Pacific Fleet, wrote, "All too often we forget how narrow the margin of safety is in naval carrier aviation. This pilot did her best to keep this aircraft flying under conditions that were all but impossible."[55]

Military personnel often describe issues or events in terms of a heartbeat. It isn't long until you get a very clear understanding of what a heartbeat means to military personnel. In the case of Hultgreen's mishap, any required tasks had to be accomplished in a very few seconds. As Yakeley speculated, if Hultgreen had ejected just 0.4 of a second earlier, she might have survived. In all likelihood, Hultgreen was a heartbeat away from life.

In 1995, journalist Michael Kilian reported that the F-14 engines were old and unreliable and were supposed to have been replaced ten years earlier.[56] Congress approved the program, but the Defense Department killed the refitting project to save money. Hultgreen's squadron never got new engines, and ten of its pilots died. Hultgreen, Kilian says, was not among those ten, because she was a woman.

RADM Paul Gillcrist, veteran aviator, tried to get the F-14 engines replaced. He says that the immediate steps some say Hultgreen should have taken to save the aircraft are hard to do. "She may have had an incipient problem we don't know about. So I don't second guess her at all."[57] In 1992, Gillcrist, former Director of Navy Aviation Plans and Programs, criticized the Navy for pursuing the wrong path in developing the next generation's combat aircraft.[58] Gillcrist stated: "The adamant position of the Defense Department in canceling the F-14D program has forced the U.S. Navy to accept a less capable maritime air superiority airplane (FA-18 E/F) and to continue pursuing the AX [Attack Advanced] program. The decision … may well prove to be a fatal judgment for aircraft carriers." Gillcrist argued that the Navy's rationale behind the AX program is "a combination of economics and flawed logic." In his 1994 book, *Tomcat! The Grumman F-14 Story*, Gillcrist writes, "I do not believe that anyone who has ever flown the F-14A Tomcat would argue with the statement that the airplane's greatest single weakness is the engine."[59]

Gillcrist adds: "The F-14A was not the Navy's newest aircraft. The F-14D has corrected the problems of the F-14A. Hultgreen was in the F-14A, the oldest aircraft and she had all the problems."[60] Gillcrist says it took 19 years to complete the transition to an all F-14 fighter force. In *Tomcat!* he gives a moving description of the danger navy pilots face:

> Naval warfare is an evolving art. But, it is not a pretty art form. It is raw, bloody, painful, shocking, demanding of the highest of human heroics and always conducted "in harm's way." Capitulation is not simply a waving of the white flag. The raging sea is the ultimate winner of all naval engagements. The losers have, historically, succumbed to the crushing depths of the ocean and the voracious denizens which abound in them. At sea, defeat is not a pretty picture, because the sea is the ultimate enemy![61]

Hultgreen fell into harm's way and lost her life, but historically, she gives us a positive legacy in that she was a pioneering female carrier aviator.

Military women in general have not had an easy path. Some roles have been more difficult than others even though the law has changed. Male naval aviators have been particularly resistant.[62] It is believed that disgruntled aviators placed online the mishap investigation report (MIR) after Kara Hultgreen was killed in October 1994. Anonymous faxes circulated that questioned her qualifications.[63] In 1994, MGen. Jeanne M. Holm dismissed the criticism as unfounded and asserted that it was inconceivable that Hultgreen was not qualified. The "slams" are there, she said, because the combat pilot community resists the entrance of women into the field.[64] Former Navy public-affairs officer and women's issue activist Bobbie Carleton's words are revealing, "[It is] unheard of to attack the flight record of a dead pilot."[65] Attorney Susan Barnes, who represents some of the Navy's female combat aviators, is aware that in 1992 there may have been at least two petitions from the West Coast F-14 and FA-18 communities presented to the President's Commission in opposition to the opening of combat aviation to women.[66]

CAPT Rosemary Mariner knew Hultgreen very well because Hultgreen was in her sister squadron. "Kara was an exceptional person," Mariner said. "She [could] maintain her sense of humor and not have her spirit broken. [She was a] natural-born fighter pilot." Mariner finds the treatment of Hultgreen's death appalling. She had never seen a pilot maligned by peers after a fatal accident and considers those who maligned Hultgreen to be a vocal minority of loud mouths. "The issue," says Mariner, "is not pilot error, but how her death was exploited by people who had a different agenda. I find this unconscionable."[67]

Captain Mariner believes it is important not to characterize Hultgreen as a victim "because she was a very vibrant, aggressive fighter pilot, and she was doing exactly what she wanted to do, and understood these risks, and could handle the situation very well." Mariner's experience has led her to believe about 80 percent of the men she has worked with are neutral.[68] They just want to see qualified people perform well. Ten percent are extremely supportive, another two percent are "jerks", and eight percent are prone to jerk behavior. She thinks the jerks are just looking for someone or something upon which to place blame.

ADM Stanley R. Arthur, former Commander of the U.S. Seventh Fleet, says that Hultgreen was qualified. "Her death is a tragic reminder that naval aviation is a dangerous business."[69]

The Navy issued two reports, the first of which was its public report released in February 1995, the Judge Advocate General (JAG) investigation report. CDR Robert J. Spane, Naval Air Force, U.S. Pacific Fleet, stated that the left engine malfunctioned, probably because of engine stall. It was not clear if the crew realized the left engine was malfunctioning. The correct response was not chosen, possibly because the pilot thought it would put the aircraft in danger of hitting the carrier. An analysis of Hultgreen's records indicates she was qualified. Other parts of the public report indicate additional long-standing problems, for example, the inherent problems of the F-14's TF-30 engine and its susceptibility to stalling in any flight regime.[70] Two weeks after the anonymous faxes circulated, the second mishap investigation report, which is not usually released to the public, was anonymously placed on Military City Online and made accessible to the public.[71] MIRs demand freedom of expression in order to learn from crashes and train pilots; therefore errors are stressed.

According to the MIR, Hultgreen ranked number one in defending the fleet from simulated attacks by enemy aircraft and in air refueling and ranked second in tactics to evade enemy aircraft. The report criticizes her for over-

shooting the "center line" of the carrier and says she lost "situational awareness" but was well within her "envelope" except for the ejection. The MIR is a
very technical report. I was lost in its technicality, my concentration faltering,
when my eyes fell upon the sterilely stated words: "Souls on board, two." It is
in Hultgreen's mishap that many of the issues of women in combat surface.

Those service individuals who test equipment are often at great peril, but
the risk they take lessens the overall risk for the greater number who will, in
the case of carrier aviation, fly the aircraft in warfare. Gillcrist writes about
going down as a test pilot:

> Every thing was black out in front of me. I thought about the cold
> water down there.... As I grabbed the face curtain handle and yanked
> down hard, I thought about what the baby-sitter would do when I
> didn't show up. Would I ever see my kids again?[72]

Gillcrist ejected at 9:17. He did see his kids again, but not without tremendous
skill and good fortune. Gillcrist's parachute's shroud lines that connected the
parachute canopy to his shoulder harness wrapped around his neck and the seat
pack. The two-hundred-pound ejection seat was tangled in the shroud lines
approximately 15 feet above his head.[73] The opening jerk had not worked; he
saw no life raft below him. Although he was able to cut those shroud lines, below
him there was no sound of the carbon dioxide bottle inflating the raft. He
thought he had timed the release of his shoulder harness. Surprised at how far
below the surface of the water he went, he found the right shoulder harness had
not released. The ejection seat was now 15 or 20 feet below him and the shroud
lines were wrapped around his ankle. He was going down. His flotation vest
was barely balanced by the ejection seat below. He freed himself of the shoulder harness, but when the ocean swelled, the parachute pulled him under. He
clawed and kicked his way to the surface several times. He finally cut away most
of the shroud lines wrapped around his right ankle and could float higher. He
reached for the shroud cutter, but got the wrong end of it and it sank to the
floor of the ocean. He pulled his survival knife and freed the shroud lines while
being pulled under every 15 seconds by the swell. Gillcrist got into the rescu-
ing horse-collar backwards, and a swagged cable-fitting ripped a two-inch gash
into his bicep. He went into shock, but his rescue was successful.

Sometimes testing and training do not deal a lucky card, and life is snuffed
out. "Eject! eject!" may have been the last words Lt. Kara Hultgreen, U.S.
Navy, heard.[74] The lessons learned are the sacrifices many military people
make in training, sometimes including their life.

Conclusions

Military women are indeed on their way to being allowed to serve where
they are the most qualified. Many military women interviewed say that the new

combatant woman will know what they were denied, to be a soldier first. In spite of the disadvantages in war, women served willingly, bravely, and with a great sense of duty to their country. We honor their historic legacy of valor.

The definitions by policy still hold serious research implications, such as why women cannot yet serve in some units. This restriction will be examined more fully throughout the book, but particularly in Chapter 5. What constitutes a battlefield as well as the nature of military strategy and doctrine has forever changed and will affect a growing proportion of the military personnel.[75] The battlefield is not an arbitrary line. Combat support people are in danger; and I would add for all to remember that combat support includes both men and women. If the enemy disrupts the combat support, they will be less concerned about destroying the soldiers in direct battle. Definitions in policy have to change in order for training to continue changing; thus enabling military men and women to defend our country properly.

Chapter 3

Evolution of Women's Involvement in War and Combat: The Historical View

Ah, what honor to the feminine sex!
—Christine de Pisan[1]

Women Warriors

"The woman warrior," says Francine D'Amico, "has been viewed as distressing, intriguing, and compelling."[2] D'Amico discusses these images within the framework of the antifeminists and three types of feminism—radical, liberal or equal rights, and critical feminists. The antifeminists believe the woman warrior destroys the family and fabric of our society and decreases military readiness. They think the genders are "naturally" different. The radical feminists view the warrior as a symbol of power for governance and thus freedom from patriarchy. According to D'Amico, equal rights feminists see the warrior as evidence of equality with males. The critical feminists think the woman warrior promotes martial and masculine values and allows women to be militarized but not empowered. D'Amico states, "Military institutions and their needs (not women's needs) determine women's role in the armed forces." We must deconstruct the "warrior mystique," D'Amico concludes, and in its place build a positive concept of citizenship and equality.

The Woman Warrior in Ancient Greece

CAPT Rosemary Mariner, USN (Ret.), points out that 400 years before the birth of Christ, Plato's *Republic* identified many of the central issues of women serving in combat. The defining characteristic, "thymos" or spiritedness, of a warrior clan protecting the Just City was found in both genders. Plato argued

45

that "what has to do with war, must be assigned to women also, and they must be used in the same ways." It had nothing to do with equality or feminism, but with what was considered just and the best defense. Plato concluded such a state could not exist, however, until "philosophers became kings, and kings became philosophers."[3] Mariner maintains that now, 2400 years later, "what is really being argued is not the nature of war, but the nature of [wo]man."[4]

Aristotle viewed women as "unfinished men" who were not the equals of any men in any sphere.[5] Mariner maintains that the Aristotelian view has been more commonly held in America than Plato's view. In the past 30 years, however, the interpretation of the Aristotelian view has changed dramatically because of the women's movement.[6] Thomas K. Lindsay says that Aristotle's conclusion concerning equality and justice is sobering.[7] It is easier, Aristotle concludes, to hit on the truth than it is "to persuade those who are capable of aggrandizing themselves. The inferior always seek equality and justice; those who dominate them take no thought for it."[8] Lindsay points out that Mary P. Nichols in *Citizens and Statesmen* invites us to consider seriously whether Aristotle sees elements of the tragic in politics, that is, in political questions. Darrell Dobbs argues that Aristotle's remark that the female is a "disabled male" must be placed in the context of the rest of his sentence, "and her catamenia is *sperma*, though not pure *sperma*—there is only one thing that it does not have, the *archē* of soul."[9] Dobbs says that "the only 'disability' Aristotle finds in the female is her inability to ignite a pregnancy."[10] From Aristotle's reasoning that the male *sperma* has the capacity to set the female residue into motion, therefore, imparting to the embryo "the very notion that is active in the male *sperma*." A possible expectation is that all offspring will be born male. Thus, the generation of a male is typical, and the generation of a female is a departure from type.[11]

Both Aristotle and Plato, according to Mariner, agreed that a prerequisite of full citizenship was membership in the guardian class. Mariner reminds us that from the time of the Old Testament's description of Deborah's leadership on the battlefield[12] to Joan of Arc to Margaret Corbin in the Revolutionary War to MAJ Marie T. Rossi in the Gulf War, women have taken up arms and fought.

Women as Men

In different periods in history, women have taken up arms and fought, but sometimes they have fought in the guise of men because it was the only way they would be allowed to fight. Women served in the guise of males during the Crusades in the twelfth century. Queen Eleanor of Aquitaine led an entire group of women dressed as men during the Second Crusade.[13] In the seventeenth century, Queen Jinga of Angola (Jinga Mbandi) led her people as a male. She was involved in guerrilla warfare against Portuguese occupiers.[14]

It is unusual for a poet to portray a woman in combat, according to Helen Solterer, who has investigated various representations of the woman warrior in medieval times. Although Reina Pennington's book *Military Women Worldwide: A Biographical Dictionary* provides us with "literally hundreds of examples of women who participated in siege warfare throughout history,"[15] Solterer's analysis is based on a little-known group of four thirteenth-century narratives, *Li Tournoiement as dames* (The Ladies' Tournament). Most specifically, she studied the version attributed to Pierre Grencien.[16] Changing situations for women in high medieval society changed the very means of textualizing them. Solterer believes that what is represented as comedy or sheer fantasy belies a backhanded admission of the prospects for female militancy by dramatizing a plot of combat and victory. These stories may not be so ludicrous after all, she concludes. Convention is jarred by simply substituting women for men in the central fighting role. While the duality signals the crux in representing the female military activism during the thirteenth century, she argues, the superficial conventionality of the *Tournoiement* creates the means whereby the phenomenon of female militancy is addressed.

Solterer discovers more than the "sensibility" of women warriors for combat and victory. She boldly examines the critical reticence surrounding the homoerotic dimensions of the tournament "because it compounds the silence about the male and female homoeroticism" typical of many medieval narratives. She notes that in a way almost parallel with contemporary times, only recently has there been discussion of homoeroticism, male or female, in the interpretation of medieval chivalric customs. "In a society," Solterer continues, "where male jousting entails one significant mode of social relations, this silence bespeaks the discounting of homoerotic impulses as strongly as it does the privileging of heterosexual ones."[17] As in any type of contemporary military analysis, Solterer believes that the force underlying the aggression between male warriors can be interpreted as homoerotic, with women spectators sharpening it further, and that it can also be interpreted heterosexually, with men's fighting accentuating the erotic charge between men and women. Either way, she says, women occupy a key position as instruments of men's desire for each other or representation of heterosexual desire.

To what extent does women's prominence change the rules? Solterer says the rules remain undisturbed.[18] Even as warriors, women continue to be subject to the scrutiny of men, vulnerable to the same power play. "The simple change of position does nothing to alter the nature of conflict." Ironically, the switch of gender roles can serve to vindicate the norms of society rather than undermine them.

Solterer documents the position that women's militarism in the Crusades was present but ambiguous.[19] Women were equally committed to martial effort and were intent on proving publicly their fitness as combatants. They dedicated this unified, powerful force to the service of their husbands and lords.

When women are allowed the right to leave their household, their possible choices increase. They can aspire to the military role, and they can behave as warriors. Thus the woman warrior who claims association with her male counterpart gains greater independence. She is depicted by some as being beautiful and possessing military skills and by others as being desexed. Solterer concludes that *Tournoiement* describes sexual identities that continue to have a strong afterlife in the ongoing debate over the female combatant.

Nancy Caciola views gender attributions in the Middle Ages as trans-sexual. Women saints were heroically described as virile. The "virgo militans" struggled with an element specifically constructed as masculine. The value of recent work on gender as performative is that it strikes a balance between individual and cultural constructions of identities.[20] Gender identities are not enacted in a vacuum; the reception and evaluation of actions as masculine or feminine are part of a cultural dynamic. Gender identities are constructed by many individuals, their communities, and their representatives, such as writers and painters. Gender characteristics are, in part, a reflection of the primary male authorship of texts. Caciola is correct in her premise that writers, painters, etc., are representers of individuals' communities within a culture. Power in Western societies has been male dominant. In the United States, Congress (presumably reflecting societal wishes) and the military (making and interpreting policy) determine whether a female can serve in combat. Many in the military may not support having women in combat but are obliged to carry out a congressional mandate. Whether Congress disallows women in combat as it did in 1948[21] or allows women in some positions but not others as in 1991 and 1993,[22] the gender definition is largely created by males. Military policy, particularly on ground combat, reflects congressional guidance and the predominantly male upper echelon of officers and congressmen.

In the Middle Ages there were women warriors who were admired as saints or denounced as witches. Jeanne La Pucelle, known as Joan of Arc only after her death, wore men's clothing, bore arms, and successfully led the battle of Orleans in May 1429.[23] She was unsuccessful, however, in an attempt to deliver Paris from the English. In May 1430 she was captured by Burgundian soldiers allied to the English during her attack on Compiègne. The Burgundians sold her to the English, who kept her in captivity for one year before burning her in 1431 at the stake in Rouen at the age of 19.[24] Controversy abounded whether Joan was a saint or a witch. James L. Matterer believes that symbolically Joan of Arc probably served as a divine substitute for Charles VII. She most likely donned men's clothing because men-at-arms would feel more at ease following someone into battle who was in armor, not in a dress. "The reality of the situation," he continues, "suggests that she dressed as a man out of necessity and to fulfill the requirements of a soldier, not of a witch." If Joan of Arc had to wear men's clothing in order for men to follow her into battle this would illustrate Caciola's premise that gender performance is part of a cultural dynamic. It is only a perception within a given culture that a woman cannot lead men and that men cannot follow a woman. The ideology for not supporting women in combat masquerades in reasoning that women are not physically qualified, they are mothers, they will get pregnant, they will be a distraction, they present hygiene problems, and so forth.

Eric Jennings points out that the legend of Joan of Arc has been long exploited to evoke strong emotions and to defend diverse causes.[25] Joan's testimony at her trial suggests she never claimed any such complexity. She perceived her purpose as a straightforward one: "to obey Saint Michael's voices and rid France of the English." It was her dramatic death, Jennings believes, that ensured her myth would live on. Jennings notes that Joan was "enterprising, childless, combatant, defiant and, even more notably, had dared to intrude into many fields traditionally reserved for men. She had thereby successfully blurred gender boundaries."[26]

Although Frances Gies thinks modern male historians disparage or minimize Joan's military talent,[27] Leonard Cohen's song is a tribute that shows Joan of Arc remains an admired figure: "Something in me yearns to win such a cold and lonesome heroine."[28]

WOMEN AS MEN IN AMERICAN WARS

During the American Revolutionary War (1775–83), Deborah Sampson Gannett disguised herself as a man, Robert Shurtleff, to join the Massachusetts Regiment of the Revolutionary Army. Although she treated her own wounds twice, a doctor discovered her gender at the time of her third wound.[29] According to the Women in Military Service for America Memorial Foundation (WIMSA), there are many stories of women like Sampson who served alongside men to defend freedom, but it is difficult to find them in the history books.

RMC Roxine C. Hart has found a number of women who served as messengers in the Revolutionary War and risked their lives. In 1781, Emily Geiger rode 50 miles through enemy territory to deliver a message to General Sumter. She was captured, searched, and released because the enemy found nothing. She had memorized the message. Madeline Moore, "the Lady Lieutenant," followed her lover into combat, acquired a fallen soldier's uniform, got commissioned, and led men into battle in western Virginia.[30]

Women also served as men during the American Civil War (1861–65). "The history books," says Col. Kelly Hamilton, "credit the women of the Civil War era as camp followers, but give little recognition to those who chose to serve disguised as men."[31] The Civil War echoed medieval heroines masquerading as males. Sometimes women were not discovered unless they were ill, wounded, or captured. These women were discharged. Jennie Hodgers, alias Albert D. J. Cashier, was not discovered until years later.[32] There were others.

Sarah Emma Edmonds served as Private Franklin Thompson.[33] Loreta Janeta Velazquez, who was married to a Confederate officer, dressed as a man and joined the battle. According to Richard Hall, she served under the name Harry T. Buford. Steve Clark states two sisters, Mary and Molly Bell, passed for male soldiers as Tom Parker and Bob Martin for about two years in the Confederate Army under Gen. Jubal Early in the Shenandoah Valley. A Civil War exhibit at the Museum of the Confederacy in Richmond tells their story. After they were discovered, the *Richmond Examiner* ran an article that began, "Pants versus Petticoats."[34]

"Pvt. Lyons Wakeman was not what 'he' seemed to be," says Lauren Burgess. "He was actually Sarah Rosetta Wakeman, a young farm girl from central New York State."[35] Burgess says Wakeman was not the only woman who disguised herself as a man; hundreds did. Their gender remained hidden and their reasons for enlisting were the same as those of their male counterparts. Private Wakeman enlisted to help support her family. Linda Grant De Pauw, of The MINERVA Center, says that in the Civil War, Rosetta Wakeman was a "typical soldier. She was buried in New Orleans along with her secret. She remains a man on her service record. We honor the hardships of men in the Civil War. We would do well to remember that hundreds and perhaps thousands of them were actually women."[36] In 1996, I asked De Pauw what progress had been made in identifying women who had served as men in the Civil War. She replied: "Scholars Deanne Blanton and Lauren Burgess are currently researching women (officers as well as enlisted) who served in the Civil War. There is a tendency to research only women who formally were women in order to get documentation, that is, official documents from official archives. Those women who fought without being enlisted are the most hard to find. Women fought alongside men."[37]

Cathay Williams, a black woman, served after the Civil War as William Cathey from 1866 to 1868. Her gender remained concealed until she applied for a pension as an invalid in 1891; the pension was denied.[38] Regardless of under which guise a woman served, we do know they served (see Chapter 4).

WOMEN WARRIORS: WOMEN AS WOMEN

In many wars, women served in the military as women. During the Revolutionary War, Margaret Corbin took over a cannon when her husband was killed. Mary Ludwig Hayes, known as Molly Pitcher, served seven years alongside her husband.

According to Kathryn Sheldon, records, journals, and diaries indicate a number of women served not only during the American Revolution, but during the War of 1812 as well, although their service is not well documented.[39] The log of Commodore Stephen Decatur's ship contains the names of nurses Mary Allen and Mary Marshall on board the *United States*.

Women have always been allowed in military intelligence. Military intelligence is a combat support role, and requires a great deal of bravery and skill. During the Civil War, Belle Boyd, a notorious spy, befriended Union officers and passed on military secrets to the Confederates. Boyd began as a nurse but is well known for her thirty-mile ride to bring information to "Stonewall" Jackson.[40] She was commissioned as a captain, reported as a spy about thirty times, arrested about a half dozen times, and imprisoned twice.[41]

Two women who actually served as women in the Civil War were Margaret Edwards Walker, a surgeon for the Union who received the Congressional Medal of Honor, and Clara Barton, who served as a medical aid.

The majority of women in the Civil War served in support roles such as nursing and laundry work. Mattie E. Treadwell notes that the Civil War revealed the need to organize support efforts.[42] Women who openly went to war during the Civil War were thought of as guardian angels. These women, according to Hall, were nurses, water carriers, cooks, laundresses, etc.[43] According to Hall, one postwar commentator called them "half-soldier heroines" because while following the male soldiers they sometimes took up arms and shot back.

"There is a paradox," notes C. Kay Larson, "that the exigencies of war usually demand more of women than what regulations state or what politicians spout."[44] Larson says that to find out what women do in war, we have to look at what they do in the field during war. What actually happens in the field during the war may be different for men and women alike from what their training was. Regulations have to be adapted to meet necessity. Hall puts it another way: in the heat of combat, artificial distinctions tend to vanish. In the Civil War, he explains, nurses, daughters, and wives did battle. This kind of adaptation occurred in other wars and conflicts.

Black women, Sheldon states, served in many of the same ways as white women—nursing, domestic duties in medical settings, laundry, and cooking.[45] One account of the first black soldiers chronicles island people—men, women and children—who came to drill with soldiers. One mother collected all the latest news of rebel movements for her son, who was a scout.[46] When large numbers of freed black men enlisted, female family members sought employment in their units. Five black nurses served on the *Red Rover*, a Navy hospital ship; four have been documented: Alice Kennedy, Sara Kinno, Ellen Campbell, and Betsy Young.[47] Other black nurses served in Union hospitals. Approximately 180 black female and male nurses served in hospitals in Maryland, Virginia, and North Carolina.[48] Susie King Taylor was a nurse and laundress for an all-black unit, the South Carolina Volunteers. Sheldon reports that King was never paid for her services. The black men did not receive pay for 18 months but were finally granted full pay along with back pay.[49]

In World War I, Flora Sandes, a nurse, served undisguised and moved through the Army ranks from private to sergeant to commander. She was severely wounded, recovered, and returned to the front for the rest of the war. She was honored as a national heroine.[50]

CAPT Rosemary Mariner, USN, says that mental outlook for the soldier is important. Most know that if they serve, restrictions will be lifted in times of necessity. Mariner believes one should not fall into false security because a soldier may be called upon at any time in a crisis. "If you think you will use the training, whether it is SERE [Survival, Evasion, Resistance, and Escape] training [or a similar type of training], take it for real. Life is episodic and we don't know when we will use it [the training]."[51]

It is beyond the scope of this book to detail the women from other countries who have served in combat and noncombatant positions, but some combat positions have been opened in Belgium, Canada, Denmark, the Netherlands, Norway, and the United Kingdom, according to Mady Segal.[52]

Women: From Noncombatant to Combatant

Women served informally as nurses as long ago as the Revolutionary War. The U.S. Army Center of Military History (CMH) chronicles the beginning of women nurses during the Revolutionary War "shortly after" June 14, 1775.[53] The Second Continental Congress authorized the Continental Army. Maj. Gen. Horatio Gates reported to George Washington that the ill needed good female nurses. Washington asked Congress for "a matron to supervise the nurses, bedding" and for nurses "to attend the sick and obey the matron's orders." Even Martha Washington nursed the wounded.

By examining rations allowed for soldiers, John Rees concluded that women numbered about 3 percent of the Continental Army, or one woman for every 30 men.[54] Some women served as washerwomen to keep the soldiers clean. Wives of soldiers campaigning with the Army performed practical tasks but also "provided some semblance of home life for men in the army." Rees thinks any study on the number of women in this eight-year war suggests many lines of potential research. How were the Revolutionary War women treated? Were they always allotted tents for shelter and hospital care? One thing is clear: women in the Revolutionary War influenced the logistics of the Army.

The contributions of women who have participated in the military have been largely unrecognized and unrecorded, but, according to Sheldon, black women have faced the double burden of race and gender.[55] She notes that no documentation of black women's military service in the American Revolution has been discovered. They probably served alongside black men.

THE NONCOMBATANT NURSE

The formal journey of women in combat zones began nearly 100 years ago.[56] Women have officially served in the Army uniform since the Army Nurse

Corps was established in 1901. The establishment of the Women's Army Corps (WAC) and an opening of career fields followed. Even before the Army Nurse Corps (ANC) was established, Dr. Anita Newcomb McGee had recruited over 1,500 nurses for the Spanish-American War, which began in 1898.[57] The Navy Nurse Corps was established in 1908.[58] In 1918 the Army School of Nursing was founded.[59] The Air Force did not establish a nurse corps until 1949, however.[60]

The record of the women who served during the Spanish-American War paved the way for the formal establishment of a permanent nurse corps.[61] More than 1,500 Army contract nurses served stateside, in Hawaii, Cuba, the Philippines, Puerto Rico, and on the hospital ship *Relief*.[62] Twenty nurses died in the huge epidemics of typhoid and yellow fever in the Spanish-American War, according to Sheldon. Women's bodies have been found in excavated battlefields.[63] Thirty-two black women were recruited in an effort by the Surgeon General's Office to recruit "immune" females (women who had survived the epidemics). Most of the black women were sent to Santiago, Cuba, in 1898 to handle the worst of the epidemics. Two of these women, T. R. Bradford and Minerva Trumbull, died from typhoid fever.[64] Sheldon estimates that as many as 80 black women may have served in the Spanish-American War.

In 1899, Harriet Camp Lounsbery, secretary and treasurer of the Order of Spanish-American War Nurses, published a letter seeking eligible members. Many nurses believed uniting war nurses would form closer bonds. Others praised the wearing of the cross as a high honor. The order also sought to form an honorary membership composed of "noble women" who worked for the soldiers, but were not nurses, such as the Red Cross Auxiliary No. III. The order proposed to take whatever money was left of the 25 cents each nurse sent for expenses to erect a memorial tablet in Arlington National Cemetery or some other suitable place.[65]

In 1918 by Armistice Day, 21,480 nurses had entered World War I and 10,000 had served overseas.[66] It was not until shortly after the armistice that 18 black Red Cross nurses were offered assignments in the ANC. They served at Camp Grant, Illinois, and Camp Sherman, Ohio, had separate living quarters, and cared for prisoners of war and black soldiers. Ultimately, the force reduction led to their discharge in 1919.[67]

NURSES IN THE COMBAT ZONES IN WORLD WAR II

Nurses have often deployed with combat troops in time of war.[68] The selfless service of nurses in all conflicts is well documented. Some died of illness or in plane crashes, and many shared danger as the following account illustrates:

> Early in the morning of 8 November 1942, sixty nurses attached to the 48th Surgical Hospital climbed over the side of a ship off the coast of

North Africa and down an iron ladder into small assault boats. Each boat carried five nurses, three medical officers, and 20 enlisted men. The nurses wore helmets and carried full packs containing musette bags, gas masks, and canteen belts. Only their Red Cross arm bands and lack of weapons distinguished them from fighting troops. They waded ashore near the coastal town of Arzew of D-day of Operation Torch with the rest of the assault troops and huddled behind a sand dune while enemy snipers took potshots at anything that moved.[69]

The 77th Evacuation Hospital was often under fire, and in February 1943 the nurses moved the hospital when they heard the German army had broken through the Kasserine Pass in Tunisia. According to the head nurse of the 48th Surgical Hospital near Gafsa, the hospital was situated between two primary targets for German bombers—an ammunition dump and an airfield. The nurses performed their duties under hostile fire.

Although under the terms of the Hague Convention, hospital ships could only carry patients and appropriate medical personnel and were clearly marked with large red crosses, they were subject to enemy inspection and were not always spared in bombing. Some nurses were wounded and others killed. Flight nurses were at greater risk because their planes doubled as cargo planes and therefore could not display the markings of the Geneva Red Cross to protect them from enemy fire. Seventeen flight nurses lost their lives in World War II.[70]

One of the most famous incidents happened on November 8, 1943, when severe weather forced down a C-54 with 13 flight nurses and 13 medical technicians of the 807th Medical Air Evacuation Transport Squadron flying from Sicily to Bari on the east coast of Italy.[71] Partisan guerrillas took the Americans to a nearby farmhouse. In order to conceal their presence in the area, the flight crew set fire to the plane. The partisans then took the Americans on a two-month, 800-mile hike to safety. All nurses except three arrived safely behind Allied lines. A German unit trapped those three and kept them for several months in Berat, Albania. Obtaining Albanian identification, the nurses left Berat and traveled for five months behind enemy lines to reach safety.

In World War II, 87 Army and Navy nurses were held for three years by the Japanese as prisoners of war (POWs). Sixty-seven Army nurses were liberated after a three-year imprisonment in Santo Tomas Internment Camp. In total, 201 Army nurses died in World War II.[72] MAJ Mary E. V. Frank, Army Nurse Corps historian, reports that two days after the Japanese attack on Pearl Harbor, December 10, 1941, five Navy nurses on Guam were taken prisoners of war.[73] They were repatriated on August 25, 1942. Eleven other Navy nurses assigned to the Canacao Naval Hospital were also taken as prisoners. Only one Navy nurse escaped. All eleven nurses were working as Japanese prisoners when they were liberated on February 23, 1945. Sixty-seven Army nurses, three dietitians, one physical therapist, and one nurse in Germany were also POWs.

The first nurses to be assigned to the field in World War II were the nurses of Bataan, who were taken prisoners. Frank states, "Although they tortured the men, the Japanese kept their distance from the women. The Japanese commander allowed the hospital to function as it had been, but curtailed their time outdoors to one hour per day." Margaret Nash, who was stationed in Manila at Canacao Naval Hospital, says, "we were right in the middle of a military target."[74] For three years, Frank continues, the women were tortured by their own fears, had to bow to their captors, suffered the petty harassment of roll call and long lines, and endured malnutrition and the loss of freedom. Nash agrees that they were not mistreated, beaten, or tortured in the strictest sense, but that Japanese guards would walk into their quarters at any time during the day or night. Not knowing when this might happen caused the women much distress. If anyone escaped, Nash reports, the nurses had to watch an unmerciful beating and shooting of the escapee. Elizabeth Norman and Sharon Eifried say that because the Japanese had no precedent to follow, they grouped the Navy women with civilians. The decision added to the nurses' chance of survival because the mortality rates in the military POW camps exceeded 50 percent.[75] The 56 Army nurses stayed in two rooms and shared one toilet and shower. Their confinement allowed them to sleep, recuperate, and bond, all of which contributed to their survival. Their mission, work, and faith kept them going.

According to Norman and Eifried, the prisoners came under the supervision of the Japanese military War Prisoners Department and a General Miromoto in 1944. Within six weeks, access to outside hospitals was denied. Roll call happened twice a day. Food supplies decreased and disease increased. The nurses had no military training on how to survive in captivity. Their nursing training helped, however, because it taught hard work, duty, and responsibility. They understood nutrition. "They were a self-selected group of confident, mature women who traveled around the world in an era when most American women married and stayed home," state Norman and Eifried. When they were liberated on February 3, 1945, they returned home to a vastly changed world, as Frank notes.

The Army Nurse Corps had grown from 7,719 to 44,802, and the Navy Nurse Corps had reached 8,896. Both units had commissioned status. The nurses were no longer simply women in the armed forces, but were members of the Women's Medical Specialist Corps (WMSC), the Women's Army Corps (WAC), Women Accepted for Voluntary Emergency Service (WAVES), Women Marines and SPAR (Coast Guard), Women's Air Force Service Pilots (WASP).

Medical personnel in warfare are unarmed and therefore are not supposed to be targets. According to MAJ Lillian Pfluke, USA (Ret.), bearing arms is "the essence of warfare. The Geneva Conventions lays it out. It is fundamental to being a soldier."[76] Sharon Wildwind, a nurse during the Vietnam War, provides insight into this complex issue. "If nurses arm themselves, they have to give up the sanctity of being a nontarget. Sometimes the sanctity is eroded and all kinds of people are attacked. Most doctors and nurses that I know would not use a weapon, because if they are armed, they become a *legitimate* target"[emphasis added].[77] Medical personnel are special people serving a special purpose. Many are "the silent heroes," not only in warfare, but in civilian life as well. Their bravery in warfare makes it especially important that they not be considered legitimate targets but their exposure to hostile fire makes the issue of legitimate target provocative.

In their internment of nurses in 1942, the Japanese absolved themselves from the responsibility of feeding the prisoners by declaring them to be civilians under protective custody rather than declaring them to be POWs.[78] In addition, in the words of Margaret Nash, a World War II POW, "On January 5, 1942, the Japanese came to talk with our commanding officer, Capt. [Robert G.] Davis, Medical Corps (MC), and told him we were prisoners of war (POWs). Capt. Davis mentioned the Geneva Convention about POWs, but the Japanese replied, 'We didn't sign it.'"[79] An enemy nation that does not sign an agreement may think that any part of our military, direct or indirect, is a legitimate target.

NONCOMBATANT WOMEN SUPPORT PERSONNEL

It was in World War I that women actually enlisted in the U.S. military for the first time to free men to fight, Sheldon says. Women enlisted in the Navy and Marine Corps as yeomen, masters-at-arms, mess attendants mostly assigned to clerical duties, and telephone operators. The Red Cross war-relief women numbered 4,600, while nurses numbered 10,000. Three hundred fifty American women doctors served overseas.[80] Four black women and 3,476 white women were YMCA volunteers.[81] One can clearly see that the struggle of the black woman to be a legal part of the nursing corps is analogous to the present struggle of military women to be admitted into all combat positions. In both cases the difficulties of arranging proper quarters and mess facilities have been cited as major problems.[82] However, "World War II would, indeed, make it practical to enlist black nurses," as Sheldon notes. The YMCA, YWCA, Salvation Army, and American Women's Hospitals also worked to care for the soldiers. AT&T recruited over 200 bilingual women telephone operators who worked with the U.S. Army Signal Corps.

World War II saw not only more white women participating, but more doing so officially, and the Army permitted black women to serve in the nurse corps, with a quota of 56.[83] In 1941, President Franklin D. Roosevelt issued Executive Order 8802 that created the Fair Employment Practices Commission (FEPC), which was to alleviate discrimination in defense. In 1944 the quota for black nurses was dropped, and in 1945 the Navy dropped its color ban.[84] Two thousand black students were enrolled in the Cadet Nurse Corps (civilian nurse training) before the quota was dropped. About 512 black Army nurses served both at home and overseas during the war. About 6,520 black women served in WAAC/WAC, but they were totally segregated except for officer candidate training, and the black women receiving this training still lived in segregated quarters. In 1944, black women were allowed in the WAVES, and 72 served under integrated conditions. Although the Coast Guard allowed blacks in their women's unit, SPAR, in 1944, few black women enlisted.[85] About 800 Native American women as well as Asian American women served. Carmen Contreras-Bozak was the first Hispanic woman in the WAC. Women served as nurses, in intelligence, and were translators, interrogators, and interpreters.[86]

In World War II, 400,000 American women served in nearly all occupations except direct combat assignments, and 458 died. Over 80 military nurses were held POWs. At the end of the war, the number of military women dropped to a postwar low of about 14,000 around 1948.[87] After World War II, hostility existed from men at all levels toward women in a support status other than nursing, says Hart. As the military reorganized and as women performed well, however, the military leaders in the European theater began to praise their efforts. At the same time women in the southwest Pacific were treated with contempt. They were not awarded earned medals because it enraged men. Men labeled these women "lesbians" or "whores" and believed women were assigned only for the "morale" of the troops. Hart says an Army investigation revealed that not only male soldiers but many wives back home started and perpetuated the resentment. The attitude at this time, she says, had a devastating effect on policy for years to come.[88] Women's programs emphasized higher quality than for men of the same service and established double standards for women for the next 40 years. Women were caught in a "time warp" that did not lift until 1967, according to Hart.

WOMEN'S SERVICE IN KOREA

In 1950, at the beginning of the Korean conflict, 22,000 women were on active duty, constituting less than one percent of the total force. One third were in health professions, and in general only nurses were on active duty in Korea. Those women who were on active duty performed administrative, communication, medical, or intelligence work. About 540 women served in the combat zone.[89]

WOMEN'S SERVICE IN VIETNAM

In Vietnam, nurses deployed in the largest number ever (6,600). Eight service women died in Vietnam, five in the line of duty. Women's roles were legally limited to token roles, says Sheldon. The first woman Marine, Sgt Barbara Dulinsky, served in a combat theater. CAPT Elizabeth Wylie was the first female the Navy deployed in Vietnam.[90] In 1964, Margaret E. Bailey became the first black nurse to be promoted to lieutenant colonel and later colonel in the ANC. In 1979, Hazel W. Johnson was the first black woman general officer and Chief of the ANC.[91] Mary L. Haynes reports that nine Army nurses died on active duty.[92] During the eleven-year period between March 1962 and March 1973, only one nurse died in Vietnam as a result of hostile fire; she was LT Sharon A. Lane, of Canton, Ohio.[93] She died of shrapnel wounds during an enemy rocket attack in 1969 while on duty at the 312th Evacuation Hospital in Chu Lai. The Bronze Star Medal and the Purple Heart were awarded to her posthumously, along with the Dr. Anita Newcomb McGee Award presented by the National Society of the Daughters of the American Revolution.

Although there were no WAC deaths in Vietnam, Specialist Fifth Class Sheron L. Green received the Purple Heart, the only WAC to have received it since World War II. In 1970, Anna Mae Hays, Chief, ANC, and Elizabeth P. Hoisington, WAC director, became the first women to be promoted to brigadier general. For the WACs, Haynes notes, the Vietnam War was the last conflict in which they would participate as members of a separate branch of the army.

In 1971 the Air Force promoted the Women's Air Force Director, Jeanne M. Holm, to brigadier general, and in 1973 she became the first female major general. In 1972 the director of the Navy Nurse Corps became the first female admiral. In 1973 six Navy women, including Captain Mariner (see Chapter 2), were the first to earn military pilot wings. In 1974, 1LT Sally Murphy, U.S. Army, became the first military helicopter pilot.[94]

LAW AND WOMEN IN THE SERVICES

Following World War II, the number of women in the military decreased. Congress passed the *Women's Armed Services Integration Act of 1948* (PL 625), which gave women permanent status in the military. Sheldon notes that although this was a milestone for women, it was discriminatory. It imposed a two-percent ceiling on the number of women in the military, restricted promotions, and limited the number of women who could serve in some command positions to ten percent. Women could not attain any rank above lieutenant colonel in the WAC or above commander in the Navy. Women could be discharged without cause and could not fly aircraft or be assigned to ships engaged in combat.[95] In 1967, Public Law (PL)90–30 eliminated the ceiling and promotion cap, and thus repealed parts of the *Integration Act of 1948*.[96] Some restrictions on assignments were also removed, such as the legal ceilings on women's promotions that had kept them out of the general and flag ranks.[97] President Lyndon B. Johnson believed that the underutilization of women was a waste we could no longer afford.

In 1969 the Air Force became the first branch to open its Reserve Officer

Table 3.1
Number of Women Who Served in Military Conflicts

Military Conflict	Number of Women Who Served
Civil War	Not known
Spanish American War	1,500
World War I	33,000
World War II (era)	400,000
Korea (era)	120,000
Vietnam (deployed in theater)	7,000
Grenada (deployed)	170
Panama (deployed)	770
Desert Storm (deployed)	35,000
	(7% of total U.S. force deployed)
Haiti	120+
Bosnia	700+

Source: Women in the Military Service for America Memorial Foundation, Inc., Arlington, Virginia, with information courtesy of the Departments of Defense and Veterans Affairs. VA data as of July 1, 1995.

Training Corps (ROTC) to women. In 1972 women officers in the Army were integrated into male officer courses and could be assigned to all positions but combat arms. In 1972 the Equal Rights Amendment (ERA) cleared Congress and focused the nation on the issue within the military. The service secretaries thought it was time to review policies rather than risk court interference. In 1973 the draft ended. The Department of Defense studied its manpower programs to determine how it could best utilize women. It concluded women were less physically capable, so laws and policies prohibiting them from serving in combat were kept in place. The DOD study concluded they could increase the utilization of women 22 percent without impacting combat effectiveness, but the military did not increase its number of women dramatically.[98]

In 1973 the Supreme Court ruled in *Frontiero et vir v. Richardson, Secretary of Defense, et al.* (hereafter referred to as *Frontiero v. Richardson*) the first significant case involving women in the military, that a military woman with a spouse could receive the same entitlements as those offered to a military man with a spouse without the requirement that the woman prove the dependency of her spouse.[99] Also in 1973, women became eligible to command men except in combat, and tactical units and flight training opened to women in the Army and Navy.[100]

In a newspaper article that I wrote in 1996, I noted that the military had made some progress in allowing women into combat positions and I said, "We have to give the military credit for their 'beginning.'"[101] I spoke with Joseph McCullough, a former infantry service person and retired anesthesia nurse, who told me: "I'd like to offer you another point of view. In 1942 male nurses didn't get commissions in the Service, only women did. In 1951, Congresswoman Mrs. Frances P. Bolton from Ohio introduced a bill [H.R. 911] to allow male nurses commissions. In 1955, the Army started commissioning men [PL 294, 84th Congress, signed by President Dwight D. Eisenhower]. It wasn't until 1959 that the Air Force did so. The Navy did so in 1964. I served three years in the infantry division and then went to anesthesia school, but the Army still did not admit men into nursing. Here we are now, our women want in combat. Things take a long time."[102]

Many female veterans know that women have served in a variety of difficult positions and received no credit or benefit. BGen. Wilma Vaught, U.S. Air Force (Ret.), says that women who earned their stripes on the World War II battlefields were passed over for promotions, which were given to less-qualified men. "These were women who started their careers in the military, who answered the call. They really gave of themselves and they didn't receive the appointments that should have been theirs. I felt I owed it to them that I should give a part of my life to recognize and honor them."[103] In 1987, General Vaught began raising money for the Women in the Military Service for America Memorial (WIMSA). Congress approved the memorial in 1986 but allocated no funds. The memorial is complete and stands at the gateway of Arlington National Cemetery to honor the 1.8 million women who have served in the armed forces.[104]

With the memorial in place to remind the nation of the women who served willingly, bravely, and often without recognition, we are ready to move ahead to give the military woman her rightful place as a soldier in today's and tomorrow's world.

Chapter 4

Evolution of Women's Involvement in War and Combat: The Contemporary Scene

She's not the girl next door. She's a soldier.
—Mary Whitley, former U.S. Army captain

Background

THE 1970S

As I noted in my previous book, *Power and Gender*, "Women have served in the military since the beginning of our country. Whatever their task, wherever their placement, service women were subject to many of the same dangers of war as the combat soldier."[1] By law and policy, however, women were not permitted to serve in combat. Only recently have women been assigned to combat positions. Movement to open more assignments for military women accelerated in the 1970s.

When the Vietnam War ended, women comprised less than two percent of active duty personnel and less than two percent of the National Guard and Reserve.[2] Women who served did so in traditional roles such as administration and medicine. In a time of peace, military women secured a meaningful place, points out Kathryn Sheldon. In 1973 the military draft ended and the All-Volunteer Force (AVF) began. Only 1.6 percent of the military services were women in 1973 compared to 8.5 percent in 1980 and 13.1 percent in 1996.[3] Sheldon notes that women also began serving in nontraditional jobs, sailing on ships, attending service academies, and training to be pilots.

In 1976 the Air Force flight program opened to women. In 1977 the Air

61

Force began to train women as members of Titan missile launch crews.[4] In 1977 the army issued a combat exclusion policy that opened assignments for women to most of the brigade level positions, medium and high-altitude air defense artillery and missile and rocket field artillery slots in battalions and batteries, and to all aviation positions except aerial scout and attack helicopter pilot. This policy vacillated somewhat, and some of the positions changed over the next ten years.[5]

In 1977 the Coast Guard began a successful mixed-gender crews program.[6] In 1978 women ceased to be managed in separate units in the military.[7] The Women's Army Corps deactivated, and the members integrated into basic branches. LT Colleen Nevius became the Navy's first woman test pilot.[8] In 1978 a class-action suit charged that the Navy discriminated against women by not allowing them to serve aboard ships. Congress amended Section 6015 of Title 10 of the U.S. Code to allow the Navy to assign women permanently to duty aboard noncombatant ships and temporarily to duty aboard combat ships for periods not to exceed 180 days. In 1981 in *Rostker v. Goldberg* a ruling was made by the U.S. Supreme Court, however, that the male-only draft was not discriminatory.[9]

The Carter administration advanced the utilization of women in the military, and the number of women increased during this period. The Army, however, resisted Carter's proposal for further increases. A new definition of combat made no mention of boundaries and distance, but referred to a person's or a unit's primary mission. Following Carter, the Reagan administration saw what Hart called a "womanpause."[10] The Army froze its percentage of women at about nine even though there was no law regulating the percentage of women the Army was allowed. The Women in the Army (WITA) policy review group was established. WITA concluded that the Army's policy did not exclude anyone from combat, but it did limit job opportunities for women without providing women with protection from danger. "The result of the Army's 1978 definition was that women could not serve in specialties primarily responsible for killing the enemy, but they could serve in specialties that exposed them to an equal opportunity of being killed."[11] WITA's efforts created the Direct Combat Probability Coding (DCPC). Direct combat became interchangeable with close combat, and the definition in effect as we know it today was born. It was during this time that physical strength requirements were developed (see Chapter 8).

THE 1980s

The Air Force reduction in the number of females recruited led Congress to monitor the Air Force in 1985. The Reagan years saw the military services try to minimize the gains of the Carter administration. In 1985 the Army reopened most job categories it had closed and by 1988, the percentage of women was about eleven. The Direct Contact Probability Coding eroded. The role women took in Panama, says Hart, caused the Army to take another look at its policy. In 1984 the Air Force reopened the security policy field and assigned women to the Airborne Warning and Control System (AWACS) aircraft. In 1985 it opened the Peacekeeper missile field, and in 1986 it opened reconnaissance aircraft and electronic countermeasures aircraft and began to assign women to Minuteman missile crews. Except for three percent of its positions and four career fields, the Air Force opened all positions to enlisted females. All officer career fields opened. Transport aircraft jobs opened, and thus women could participate in airdrop missions on transport planes if the transport was included in the fleet. In 1992, positions in combatant aviation opened.

In 1984, the Navy allowed women to serve in military detachments on civilian ships that deployed with the Navy battle group. Still restricted were assignments in Mobile Logistics Support Force (MLSF) ships because they fit the combat definition of 1978. In 1987 the ships were renamed Combat Logistic Force (CLF). By 1988 more women were assigned to aviation units and P-3 Orion aircraft. Oilers, ammunition ships, and supply ships were opened to women. The navy changed its definition of combatant to include units, ships, aircraft, and task organizations which have as their primary mission to seek out, reconnoiter, and engage the enemy. In 1978 only one of these tasks had to be satisfied; the new definition required all three be satisfied not just for the task force, but for the individual unit.

The Marines made some progress. In 1984 deployment with amphibious forces with headquarters units and air combat elements of the Marine Amphibious Brigade opened for women. Weapons training opened in 1987.[12]

In 1988 the Task Force Study Group on Women in the Military devised the Risk Rule. "Noncombatant units could be closed to women 'provided that the type, degree, and duration of risk is equal to or greater than that experienced by associated combat units.'" DACOWITS's recommendation to assign women to the naval mobile construction battalions in 1988 was also defeated.[13]

GRENADA (1983) AND LIBYA (1986)

Over one hundred women deployed in Operation Urgent Fury in Grenada in 1983.[14] In the attack on Libya in 1986, Air Force women served as pilots, copilots, and boom operators of the KC-135 and KC-10 tankers that refueled the FB-111s.[15]

OPERATION JUST CAUSE, PANAMA 1989

Over 770 women deployed in Operation Just Cause. In Panama the lines of combat became even more indistinct. Three female Army helicopter pilots came under heavy enemy fire. Army CPT Linda Bray, commander of the 988th Military Police Company, led her soldiers in a firefight against Panamanian Defense Forces. "In doing their jobs," says Sheldon, "the combat line had been crossed."[16]

OPERATIONS DESERT SHIELD AND DESERT STORM 1990–1991

By 1991, women could be pilots in all services except the Marine Corps. Civilian women served on civilian ships that deployed with battle groups. Similar assignment on Navy ships opened. The Coast Guard has had all positions open since 1978. In time of war, the Coast Guard is no longer under the Department of Transportation but becomes part of the Navy. In that case, its positions would be limited consistent with the Navy's policy.

In 1991, Army women served in the forward-support areas of the battlefield, while the women in the Marine Corps served in rear area personnel and administrative posts. The effects on policy of Desert Storm had not yet taken place.[17] The Marine Corps's first female brigadier general, Margaret A. Brewer, now retired, says that during Operation Desert Storm: "Initially, there was some question as to whether female Marines would deploy with their units. This question was soon resolved and more than 1,200 female Marines served ... as integral members of their units."[18]

The Persian Gulf War was a watershed. The largest single deployment of women in history, 35,000, occurred. Military women made up seven percent of the forces. They served as aircraft pilots and in logistical support, in supply units, in repair units, and on hospital ships. Although women were not "officially" in combat, the lines were blurred because of long-range artillery and surface-to-surface missiles. MGen. Jeanne Holm points out that the "unisex weapons" did not distinguish between combat and support troops.[19]

Carolyn Becraft, who was then with the Women's Research and Education Institute (WREI) and now is Under Secretary of Defense for Family Issues, notes that the Persian Gulf War was the first large-scale U.S. military operation since the establishment of the All-Volunteer Force.[20] Approximately 537,000 men and women served, including about 100,000 reservists. An additional 128,000 reservists were also activated. Military women numbered over 33,300 in combat support positions. They served in important assignments, and their numbers reflect the record proportions that women have reached in both the active and reserve components since 1973. In 1991, military women numbered 378,550. A look at the statistics reveals the tremendous support women gave in the Persian Gulf War. Not only were their numbers greater than ever before, but many women participated in combat and combat support operations. Twenty-six thousand Army women deployed to the Persian Gulf (Table 4.1).

Army women participated in the initial invasion into Kuwait and Iraq and

Table 4.1
Women in the U.S. Armed Services in the Persian Gulf War

	Army	Navy	Marine Corps	Air Force	Coast Guard
Positions open to women	52%	59%	20%	97%	100%
Deployed	26,000	2,500	1,000	3,800	13
Active Duty	83,200	57,100	9,300	73,600	2,600
	11%	10%	5%	14%	7%
Reserve	63,100	23,100	1,800	16,000	1,750
	21%	14%	5%	19%	15%
National Guard	31,500			15,500	
	7%			13%	
Lost Lives	11				
POWs	3				

Source: Based on Carolyn Becraft, "Women in the U.S. Armed Services: The War in the Persian Gulf," Women's Research and Education Institute, Washington, D.C., March 1991.

served with U.S. Patriot missile battalions. Two women commanded battalions, while others were in command of companies, aircraft squadrons, and platoons and squads in various units. Eleven Army women lost their lives. Five of the 122 U.S. troops killed in action were Army enlisted women.

According to Becraft, 2,500 Navy and 1,000 Marine women deployed to the Persian Gulf. These women served on hospital, supply, oiler, and ammunition ships of the Combat Logistics Force and also on repair ships. Women Navy pilots flew helicopters and reconnaissance aircraft, and they served in Navy construction battalions, fleet hospitals, and reconnaissance squadrons. Some were public affairs officers.

The Air Force deployed 3,800 women to the Persian Gulf. They served in military airlift, airlift terminal and cargo management, aerial refueling, communications, intelligence, firefighting, aeromedical evacuation, and support activity. Air Force women pilots flew and crewed strategic transport, tactical transport, tankers, reconnaissance, and aeromedical airlift aircraft. Thirteen Coast Guard women were deployed and served in port security positions.

Becraft notes that four other allied nations deployed women in the Persian Gulf War: Canada sent 150 women, or 3 percent of the total it deployed; France, 13 out of 10,000 total; Great Britain about 800, or 1.5 percent, 52 of whom served on combat ships; and Kuwait, 9 out of 250 volunteers.

In Desert Storm, two women were taken prisoners of war. According to the Women in the Military Service for America Memorial Foundation, these two prisoners were MAJ Rhonda Cornum, a doctor, and Specialist Melissa

Table 4.2
**Number of Military Women Held Prisoners
of War (POWS) in Military Conflicts**

Military Conflict	_Assignment_	_Number of_ _Women POWs_
World War II	All officers, all nurses	88
Desert Storm	One doctor; one was the first enlisted woman	2

Source: Women in the Military Service for America Memorial Foundation, Inc.,
Arlington, Virginia, with information courtesy of the Departments of Defense and
Veterans Affairs. VA data as of July 1, 1995.

Rathbun-Nealy, a heavy equipment transport driver. For comparison, the 88
women taken prisoner in World War II were both officers and nurses (Table
4.2). MAJ Marie Rossi, an Army helicopter pilot, was one of five women killed
in action in the Persian Gulf War.

It is little wonder military women have labeled the Gulf War as the watershed for women being allowed in some combat units. At the time of the Gulf
War, there were no statutory restrictions for the assignment of women in the
Army, but actual policy was restrictive. The statutory restrictions were in place
for the Navy, Marine Corps (as part of the naval service), and the Air Force.
The Persian Gulf War contributed in a major way to lifting the ban on women
in combat (Table 4.3). It was a historic mark for women in the military. It is
little wonder that the war in the desert brought about major change in the military woman's role, but there were other significant incidents that also contributed to the climate of change.

TAILHOOK '91—CATALYST FOR CHANGE

Women officers were among the targets of attack by Navy and Marine
carrier airmen at the Tailhook Association Convention in 1991.[21] Tailhook '91
had a tremendous impact on the military. LT Paula Couglin, a female Navy
helicopter pilot, formally complained that she had been physically and inde-
cently assaulted by a group of naval officers at the 1991 Tailhook symposium
at the Las Vegas Hilton. Indirectly, her courage was a factor in causing the
Navy leadership to move. Not only did all services reexamine policy on sexual harassment, they also, along with Congress reexamined combat exclusion
law.[22] Tailhook raised broader concerns about the process of changing how the
military culture views the role of women in the armed forces. Specifically, the
issue of sexual harassment and discrimination in the military was the focus of
the House Armed Services Committee report, sometimes referred to as the
Aspin-Byron Report.[23]

Table 4.3
**Statutory Combat Restrictions at the Time
of the War in the Persian Gulf and After the War**

	Persian Gulf	*After Persian Gulf*
Army	No statute, by policy, according to Title 10 U.S. Code § 3012	
Navy & Marine Corps	Title 10 U.S. Code § 6015	Repealed 1993
Air Force	Title 10 U.S. Code § 8549	Repealed 1991
Coast Guard	Defense statutes do not apply. Coast Guard is part of Department of Transportation.	

Source: Based on Carolyn Becraft, "Women in the U.S. Armed Services: The War in the Persian Gulf," Women's Research and Education Institute, Washington, D.C., March 1991.

The 1992 hearings of the Military Personnel and Compensation Subcommittee and Defense Policy Panel of the Committee on Armed Services of the House of Representatives investigated sexual harassment complaints and other issues related to opportunities for women in the service.[24] The Committee recommended the services approach the problem of sexual harassment in the same way they have handled the problem of illegal drug use and the integration of blacks into the military. The most notable change in the military after Tailhook '91 was the integration of women into previously male-dominated domains such as some combat duty.[25]

The purpose of the 1993 hearings on women in combat was twofold. First, they examined how the services planned to implement Secretary of Defense Les Aspin's decision to allow women to compete for assignments to combat aircraft. Second, they considered the Department of Defense request that the statutory exclusion for combatant ships be repealed.[26]

At the time of the combat hearings in 1993, over 200,000 women served on active duty, comprising 11.5 percent of the active force. The number of women in the selected reserve increased to over 140,000, or 13 percent of the force. Women in the military not only increased in number, but they were offered wider career opportunities. Eighty-seven percent of skill categories were open to women before the hearings, representing over one million jobs.[27] The U.S. military strength was at its lowest levels since the Korean War. Aspin predicted that by the end of 1994 our active force would be over 25 percent smaller than it was in 1987.

Secretary of Defense Aspin's decision on April 28, 1993, directed all services to allow women to compete for assignments in aircraft, including combat missions, directed the Navy to open additional positions aboard ships, including combat vessels, and directed the Army and Marine Corps to study opportunities for women to serve in additional ground positions, including those in field artillery and air defense artillery.[28]

One qualification was that women not be assigned to positions involved in direct ground combat. Department of Defense (DOD) policy change was reported in February 1994. Ground combat assignments began in January 1994 when the Secretary of Defense repealed the Risk Rule and promulgated a definition of direct ground combat. This permitted the assignment of women to all positions for which they were qualified except those below the brigade level whose primary mission was to engage in direct combat on the ground. The most prominent restraint deals with direct ground combat. The unending challenge of the direct ground combat exclusion will be examined in detail in Chapter 5.

Conflicts After the Repeal of Exclusion Laws

At the time of the UN's Operation Restore Hope in Somalia in 1993, 1st Lt. Jeannie Flynn of the U.S. Air Force entered combat pilot training. Congress repealed the ban on women serving aboard combat ships. In 1993, servicewomen deployed to Somalia with UN forces and to Bosnia with UN forces and NATO Operation Joint Endeavor.[29] Sergeant Allison Hanley, a Fort Monmouth Military Police (MP) soldier, returned home from Bosnia in the early summer of 1996 after being there six months. Hanley served as a team leader with the 536th MP Company; she was in Tuzla Main for the first four months and then moved on to Camp Lisa, about five miles outside Serbrenicia, near Serb headquarters. While there, she helped provide security for the investigation of mass grave sites. Hanley dealt not only with the weather, mud, and uncertainty, but also with being the only woman in her platoon: "I lived with nine men for seven months; that was the biggest challenge. I think I can get along with any man now, but they (the male soldiers) were professional and treated me like an NCO."[30]

In 1994 in Rwanda, women again deployed with UN forces.[31] That year Navy women also boarded the USS *Eisenhower*. During Operation Uphold Democracy in Haiti in 1994, women served on combat ships temporarily or permanently (law 6015 had been repealed in 1993).[32]

In December 1998 in Operation Desert Fox, Navy LT Kendra Williams became the first female combat pilot to fly a strike mission. Williams flew her F/A-18 Hornet fighter bomber from the deck of the carrier USS *Enterprise* in a bombing run over Iraq. Two other female pilots, LT Lyndsi Bates and LT Carol Watts, also flew F/A-18s over Iraq.[33] LT Andrea Quy was one of eight women flying the F-14 Tomcat.[34] These missions marked the first time female pilots put bombs on target in war, Navy officials say.[35] The Air Force identified

Table 4.4
Number and Percentage of Women in
the Military, 1996, by Service and Rank

Service and Rank[1]	*Number of Women*	*Women as a Percentage of Total Personnel*
Total Armed Forces	195,635	13.1%
Officers	31,193	13.4%
Enlisted	161,276	13.2%
Army	68,610	14.1%
Officers	10,526	13.0%
Enlisted	58,084	14.3%
Navy	51,109	12.4%
Officers	7,869	13.6%
Enlisted	43,240	12.2%
Marine Corps	8,573	4.9%
Officers	750	4.2%
Enlisted	7,823	5.0%
Air Force	64,177	16.7%
Officers	12,048	15.8%
Enlisted	53,129	16.9%
Coast Guard	3,166	9.3%
Officers	568	8.0%
Enlisted	2,598	9.6%

[1]Officers include warrant officers.

Source: U.S. Department of Defense, Defense Manpower Data Center, September 30, 1996, in Georgia C. Sadler, Annette M. Wiechert, and Dina A. Warnken, *Women in the Military: Statistical Update 1997*, Washington, D.C.: Women's Research and Education Institute, 1997.

its first female combat flier as 1st Lt. Cheryl Lamoureux, an electronic warfare officer, who flew on a long-range B-52 mission against Iraq from the U.S. base on the Indian Ocean island of Diego Garcia.[36] Operation Desert Fox was a milestone in military women's progress toward full involvement in combat.

Recent Progress

In 1995, Lt. Col. Eileen Collins, U.S. Air Force (USAF), became the first female pilot of the space shuttle. In 1995, BGen. Marcelite Harris, USAF, became a major general, the first black woman to do so. As of April 25, 1997, most of the highest ranking females in each of the services were three-star generals or admirals, but all of those had been promoted within the last year (Table 4.4).

Table 4.5
Percentage of Black Women Among
All Women in the Military, 1996

Service	Officer	Enlisted
Army	20.6%	47.3%
Marine Corps	9.7%	25.0%
Navy	9.4%	29.8%
Air Force	10.5%	24.8%
Coast Guard	5.8%	14.8%

Source: U.S. Department of Defense, Defense Manpower Data Center, September 30, 1996, in Georgia C. Sadler, Annette M. Wiechert, and Dina A. Warnken, *Women in the Military: Statistical Update 1997*, Washington, D.C., Women's Research and Education Institute, 1997.

In 1997, military women served in many jobs. "Although the proportion of occupations open to women is above 90 percent in each of the services, only about two-thirds of positions in units are open to women in the Army and Marine Corps because infantry, armor (tanks), and field artillery remain closed to them."[37] The Coast Guard's positions are 100 percent open to women, with the Air Force following with 99 percent. "Women make up 13.1 percent of the military ranks with 195,635 women on active duty as of September 20, 1996"[38] (Table 4.5).

Black women make up a significant percentage of the women in the services. The highest percentage is in the Army (47.3 percent of the enlisted women) and the lowest percentage is in the Coast Guard (14.8 percent) (Table 4.6). With a high concentration of black military women in the Army, far-reaching research implications are apparent. If the ground combat exclusion policy is ever legally changed to permit women, will it affect black women the most? If so, why? Will they be called to serve in ground combat because they are superior in skill or because of discrimination?

Peacekeeping, Today's Military—
Is It Really More Innocuous?

MAJ Angela Manos, U.S. Army, and David R. Segal underscore that you cannot understand today's Army if you do not understand yesterday's Army. Today's Army has more adult dependents other than spouses, more civilian male spouses, more sole parents, more dual parents and more women. The number of women has risen from 2 percent in 1973 to 13 percent in 1995. The Army has moved from being an Army of short-term, drafted single males to

Table 4.6
**Highest Ranking Females Active Duty in Each
of the Services, as of November 1998**

<u>Service</u>	<u>Highest Ranking</u>
Army	LTG Claudia Kennedy, Three Star
Navy	VADM Patricia A. Tracey, Three Star
Air Force	MGen. Susan L. Pamerleau, Two Star
Marine Corps	Lt Gen Carol A. Mutter, Three Star

Sources: *NBC Nightly News*, transcript, "Newly Appointed Three-Star General Claudia Kennedy Comments on Her Life in the Service of the Army," June 20, 1997; Federal News Service, "Prepared Statement of Vice Admiral Patricia A. Tracey, U.S. Navy Chief of Naval Education and Training Before the Senate Armed Services Committee Personnel Subcommittee," June 5, 1997; *Montgomery (Alabama) Advertiser*, "Ex-Maxwell Instructor Promoted to Major General," September 16, 1997; *CBS This Morning*, transcript, "Major General Carol Mutter of the U.S. Marine Corps Discusses Her Career and Her Nomination to Become Lieutenant General," March 29, 1996.

an all-volunteer force of men and women who are married with spouses working outside the home.[39]

There are 125,000 soldiers permanently based overseas, and 34,000 soldiers deployed in more than 90 countries. The missions are varied and take place in peace and in war and at home and abroad. Soldiers may provide disaster relief in time of hurricanes, earthquakes, floods, or forest fires. It is not likely that there will be another world war, but our soldiers have been involved in conflicts in Panama, Bosnia, Somalia, Korea, Rwanda, Haiti, Iraq and Kuwait.

The Army has been reduced in strength by 450,000 and has closed almost 400 overseas bases and 33 major installations in the continental United States. Manos and Segal say that "as we move toward the twenty-first century, our nation will have to respond to a world that is increasingly unpredictable. And it is very important for everyone to remember that the Army does not get to choose its wars—or its peacekeeping operations or humanitarian aid missions."[40] Manos, a former member of the Army Chief of Staff Group for GEN Gordon R. Sullivan, reports:

> In Somalia—wherever you go, you must be ready to soldier. This may mean providing first aid, operate a radio, or provide force protection. The distinction is not whether a person is in "combat" but whether a soldier is ready to do what needs to be done. If we can get our organization to see everyone (whether it be women, blacks, Hispanics) to see us all as soldiers first, and as soldier, female or soldier, black or soldier, Hispanic second, then you will begin to see less and less of these issues. It is all about Command Climate, and our values. It is about dignity and respect, not gender and race.[41]

"This is a very different Army," Manos and Segal maintain. "In 1979 an air defender soldier and 'his' family probably spent their lives in Fort Bliss, Texas, and Karlsruhe, Germany, if 'she or he' came in 1989, she or he probably deployed three or more times to Saudi Arabia or Korea, leaving the family behind."

Major Manos spent time in the field interviewing our soldiers and found them proud to serve but eager to share their concerns. A common question from a majority of soldiers deployed on operational missions was, "Will we get the combat patch?" These soldiers served in what they perceived to be high-risk areas but were not getting the combat patch because they accomplished the mission in an area that had not been declared a combat area. They do not understand the criterion, especially because Somalia was the only operational mission that soldiers knew about that resulted in the awarding of the combat patch. It was apparent that for whatever reason, no one had explained the difference to them. They wanted to know why.

Second, they asked, according to Manos and Segal, "Why are we staying?" Unless someone tells them, the soldiers do not understand that their task is to support the military operations whatever those are for however long it takes. "Of course if you do not understand why you are still there, the next question becomes, 'Why are we here in the first place?'" The most challenging question was, "When can I go home?" Without knowing this, Manos and Segal continue, soldiers simply cannot plan. The date may not be known, and that is understandable, but leaders must tell the soldiers that they honestly do not know; otherwise the soldiers will think their leaders are not telling them the truth about that or anything else.

Soldiers also talked about their realization that they have the ability to remain neutral while on peacekeeping missions and that they can maintain their combat readiness. A resounding message Manos and Segal heard from family members was that "peacekeeping is no less stressful than war making." Despite these and other things soldiers talked about, Manos and Segal report that 80 percent of the soldiers and spouses say they will stay in the army.

Women in the Academies

In 1975 the Stratton Amendment to Title 10 of the U.S. Code provided for the admission of women to previously all-male service academies.[42] President Gerald Ford signed Public Law 94–106, which established the admission of women, and in July of 1976, women were allowed to enroll in military service academies. One hundred nineteen women entered West Point, 81 entered the U.S. Naval Academy, and 157 enrolled in the U.S. Air Force Academy. Women also entered the Merchant Marine in 1974 and Coast Guard academies in 1976.[43]

The principal place for training military leaders is at the service academies. Women at the academies were in a combat training environment, points out Hart, and since women were not allowed in actual combat, objections surfaced.[44] The most common complaint by male cadets and midshipmen was the lowering of physical standards. Allowances such as privacy and class substitutions also disgruntled male cadets. GEN Andrew Goodpaster, the superintendent at West Point, made sweeping changes on the basis that mental pressure should be academic, not abusive and demeaning. The female cadets and midshipmen had no choice, however, but to accept hazing, says MAJ Lillian Pfluke, member of the first graduating class of women at West Point, "because we got it every day. We had to accept it. It happened."[45]

At West Point the proportion of women graduates doubled from 7 percent in 1980 to 14 percent in 1995 with a female as the top graduate, Rebecca Marier of New Orleans.[46]

In 1980, BG Joseph Franklin, Commandant of Cadets, agreed that the combat restriction could pose a serious problem for the women and for the Army. He said, "Five or 10 years from now, ambitious, aggressive women may feel stymied because the combat path is closed to them. It is possible a large number will leave. Combat is where the action is. It's like having to sell computers when what you want is to design them."[47]

Armored Ceiling

The "armored ceiling" was firmly in place at the time of gender integration of West Point, Annapolis, and the Air Force Academy. The armored ceiling was perhaps so named because, according to MAJ Lillian A. Pfluke, "You can't even see through it."[48] In spite of the difficulties, the first female cadets have excelled, making the way easier for the women who follow. In fact, it would appear that the first female cadets crashed through the armored ceiling, although MAJ Pfluke says: "No we haven't crashed through the 'Armored Ceiling.' The Academy is not the ceiling, it is the floor."[49] Yet the accomplishments of some of the first female cadets are impressive. MAJ Carol Barkalow, USA, participated in Operation Desert Storm. Naval flight officer Kathryn Ozimek has flown over the frozen Antarctic aboard a high-tech communications aircraft.[50] Lt. Col. Select Susan Desjardins, who was in the first group of women to graduate from the Air Force Academy, became Deputy Military Assistant to the Secretary of the Air Force. In 1974, Nancy Wagner, now a captain for the San Francisco harbor pilots, was one of the 16 women admitted to the Merchant Marine Academy.[51]

United States Military Academy, West Point

The women admitted to West Point in 1976 graduated in 1980 as part of the first class of women to finish the academy.[52] Women in the first class at

West Point have a pioneering story to share. "Women who are in military training to be an officer are not the girl next door or your mother or your sister. They were among the top athletes in college. Military women are just like men who become airborne—he is not your average guy—he's the top five percent," says former CPT Mary Whitley, a 1980 West Point graduate who was the first woman officer to serve in the Supply and Transport Battalion at Fort Stewart, Georgia, and was formerly in the Army Transportation Corps. "Society has a mental image of her as the girl next door and she is not. For example, MAJ Lillian Pfluke is a world class triathlon, biking and downhill skiing athlete."[53] The women of the class of 1980 know how it was, and thankfully, how it has changed, as Pfluke notes: "West Point has changed. It is a success story. Now in addition to teaching duty, honor, and country, it teaches consideration of others. It [the teaching and consideration of others] has been extraordinarily effective."[54] One example Pfluke cites to demonstrate that wrongdoing has not been accepted by the institution occurred in 1994, when West Point football players turned in some teammates for groping female cadets as they ran past during a pep rally. But through it all, the nebulous American public has perhaps not always had an accurate perception that military women are highly qualified to defend our nation. Perhaps nowhere has the misperception been so apparent as in the struggle of the academies to admit women to be among the military leaders of tomorrow.

MAJ Carol Barkalow acknowledges that she has a successful career in the Army, but she wanted to be an infantry officer. She believes that the Army should open more combat fields to women and that women will not make the upper ranks unless the fields are opened. Most cadets, Barkalow says, didn't mind women, but there was "a vocal minority that sometimes made it hell."[55] Barkalow's book, *In the Men's House*, describes her experiences. In 1976, 119 females arrived at the Academy of about 4,000 men and by all accounts the women were anything but welcome.[56]

MAJ Mary Finch, USA, who was a 1983 graduate of the U.S. Military Academy, says: "There will always be a problem at the academies. The guys come from civilian life and West Point is macho. He looks at the woman in uniform next to him and comes up with reasons not to accept her. She isn't doing what I'm doing—etc.,—until they get in the real world, this is how they see it."[57] Finch characterizes her experience at West Point as very challenging, developmental, and at times heartbreaking. "But over all," she says, "it was a wonderful experience that I wouldn't trade for anything. It (along with my parents' influence) made me who I am today."[58]

Most of the women of the first graduating class at West Point whom I interviewed told me they did not realize it was going to be as difficult as it was. MAJ Jane McKeon, a former behavioral science and leadership instructor at West Point and member of the first graduating class of 1980, best reflected their innocence when she responded to a question a reporter asked her in 1976—"How will the men react to women at West Point?" McKeon says that her answer was the most naive thing she has ever said: "We know they [the men] may be upset, but Congress has passed a law and I'm sure they will accept us in a professional manner."

McKeon says it was the most difficult at first:

> When we first arrived at West Point, the male cadets thought we would all be either loose women or lesbians. It was very difficult for them because we didn't fit in either category. Eventually, the male cadets would come around as they got to know us as individuals. They would say, "You're O.K., but I don't like the rest of the women." They thought they were paying us a compliment. We saw it as a very slow process of overcoming their ignorance one woman at a time.

At their West Point class reunion, McKeon says, many men apologized to the women for being such jerks 20 years ago. "Some guys can see the part they played in the discrimination towards the first few women at West Point." She adds, "The fact that they now understand prejudice will have a positive impact on the way they raise their sons and daughters."

McKeon was 17 years old when she entered West Point and was the oldest of six children. "I grew up with the belief that you can be whatever you want to be. Work hard and it will happen. I was looking for ways to grow and develop intellectually, emotionally, and physically, as well as pay for my own education."

Major McKeon had many challenging and exciting jobs during her career in the military. As a lieutenant, she served in Germany as a platoon leader, executive officer, and battalion adjutant in a truck battalion forward deployed to support the Third Corps. She returned to the States and worked one year as a captain in combat developments. She made decisions that influenced the design of future military organizations. "It always amazed me to see the level of responsibility assumed by relatively junior officers in the Army. My civilian counterpart in the corporate world would not have comparable responsibility in terms of personnel, equipment or budgeting." McKeon commanded as a captain in Virginia and then later again in Korea as a major within missile range of the North Korean border. "It was estimated that it would have taken only 40 minutes for the enemy to overrun the city where my husband and I and our five children lived." McKeon's unit managed the flow of fuel, food, equipment, and personnel in and out of Korea by rail, air, and highways. Her unit worked closely with Korean nationals and often contracted services to supplement U.S. Army assets. Prior to her assignment in Korea, MAJ McKeon was sent to the University of Richmond to acquire a master's degree in psychology to prepare her to return to West Point to teach in the Department of Behavioral Sciences and Leadership. She was the first female graduate to teach, mentor, and counsel cadets in that department.

In 1980, West Point Cadet Sonya Nikituk said that in the four years she attended the Academy some resistance remained, but that she had seen a change in the men's attitudes since her freshman year. During that first year, a male upperclassman had told the women that his goal for the year was to run them all out. According to Victoria Irwin, writing in the *Christian Science Monitor*, "None of the company's women left that year, and only one left before graduating."[59]

What was it like for the first class at West Point and how did the first cadets feel? Irwin found that both men and women cadets were tired of the spotlight and that there was some misunderstanding surrounding the type of training women received compared to men. Women received the same military training, attended specialty schools, and took combat training.

In 1996, when I asked Pfluke about a cadet needing to keep a low profile, she replied, "Of course, a woman by definition has a high profile, you can't hide, everyone knows you." A support group was formed and open to both men and women, but most of the women were not active. COL Barbara Lee felt that the group may have gotten a "feminist" label to which "most men have a visceral reaction.... Women have to adopt masculine values, because those are related to competency."

Writing in 1980, reporter Irwin noted that women were constantly reminded of their gender through ribbing. The members of the first graduating class at West Point told a story that was amazingly consistent when they were interviewed 16 years later in 1996. It was not easy breaking the gender barrier. Danna Maller, a former U.S. Army captain and helicopter pilot, said that fortunately, West Point is doing better now, with 80–90 percent of entering women eventually graduating versus 52 percent of the first class. "It's not perfect, but it is better. My approach was to take it one day at a time. It was difficult."[60] Although Maller says the opposition was a very vocal minority, the majority were more concerned with their own survival. "Some guys said, 'Girls! What's so bad?' They did not stand up for women to the guys who didn't accept." Maller said that she knew there would be opposition but didn't understand its nature and depth or how difficult it would be to overcome. "Everyday we were reminded we weren't supposed to be there by a look or a comment. At first my attitude was, 'I understand where this is coming from'—I thought that when they saw we were doing a good job—they would accept us. They didn't."

As a captain in the Army, Maller was a platoon leader. She was responsible for 10 Hueys (transport helicopters) and 20 pilots. "The Hueys transported troops or supplies and were used for noncombat missions. Women were not allowed to fly 'combat helicopters.'"

Maller, who in 1996 was executive vice president at Llama Asset Management, credits her success in part to her tough experiences while a cadet at West Point. Maller says serving in the actual Army was easier than attending West Point. "West Point," she says, "was so intense and constant."

"All of the women in the class," says Maller, "have an interesting story to tell. Attending West Point was not something we had planned to do. The decision to admit women did not occur until December of 1975 and we entered the Academy in July of 1976—it all happened very quickly."

MAJ Mary Finch, USA, and a member of Bush's Presidential Commission, says: "We all struggled with 'what do I need to do to get accepted?' I decided that, 'no matter what I do it won't please them—so I'll please myself.' It was a load off my mind. It helped me the rest of the time I was there. I was lucky. I was good at leadership and in athletics. I had that advantage over females that didn't [have those skills]."

Maller said her main interest was her own survival with mental health intact. "I was aware that if I had to sacrifice too much it's not worth it. It is emotional and physical, with acid pressures. I know my limitations. I enjoy achievements. I didn't feel like I had to be at the top of my class."

Finch agrees with the first class of women West Point cadets, "It is an intense environment. You know you're not wanted. Men would say, 'Women cadets are this, this and this, but not you.' This was their way to try to control us. Some women didn't figure it out. I just felt these guys had the problem, not me." Finch also believes that West Pointers changed a lot after she graduated. She recalls a former cadet who sat by her on a bus trip later in life. He was one of two men she had turned in to protect other women. He praised her. She asked herself, "What is this? Has he gone through a time warp?" People do change. At the 10-year reunion, the other guy she had turned in was nice. He said he had changed. Finch thinks, "They get out in the real world; get families, and over time change."

"The Academy," says Maller, "wanted to spread the women out as much as possible among the 36 companies. The first year only 12 of the 36 companies had women and there was a distinct difference in attitudes between those companies and the ones in which there were no women. Because the women were spread out, it was not easy for them to be supportive of one another. Their main concern was trying to blend in as much as possible with their male colleagues, and their relationships with each other at times took on a secondary role. Maller says that she never personally saw physical harassment, but verbal harassment happened all the time, "You have to remember ... things happen."

Whitley gives additional insight:

> I did not understand *enmity*. I was a minority [before entering West Point], I was always a majority. You know you can do it in your heart— the institution didn't make structural changes to accommodate women, for example, gang showers and the windows. There were shades only on the windows of the females' rooms. I could view males. They put a bunch of us in, but sprinkled us around. They didn't expect us to last. But we did.

Whitley says the women spent a lot of time trying to blend in. By the end of the second year, she said, the women thought they needed to get together. The last two years there was more networking. It was, she says, a nonwelcoming place—the cadets didn't want her there. Whitley notes, however, that although West Point was full of discrimination, she did not find it in the Army, even though she was the first woman assigned to her battalion. West Point is not the Army; West Point is very strict—"weed out the weak." West Point is supposed to identify those who are not going to be good officers. Maller echoes Whitley's sentiments: "We had so much to deal with at West Point, the Army was easier. West Point was so intense. At Ft. Ord and as time went by, men seemed to accept women in leadership roles."

In 1996, James Vesely wrote in the *Seattle Times*, about how difficult it was when the service academies opened their doors to women:

> Before a woman was First Captain at West Point, a post held by Pershing, MacArthur and Westmoreland before her, the U.S. Military Academy struggled with the presence of women in the cadet ranks. The service academies at Annapolis, Colorado Springs and New London, Conn., faced the same obstacles but survived. It wasn't easy for women in the service academies, but frankly, it's not easy for anybody. But the essential question—whether women can succeed in the U.S. service academies, is now moot.[61]

The women in the first graduating class at West Point not only were successful in that they beat the odds and did graduate, but they are successful women in their own right. Perhaps as an institution, West Point believed it had reached its major goal, to train an officer. It is interesting to note that in delivering the Supreme Court's opinion on the Virginia Military Institute (VMI), Justice Ruth Bader Ginsburg recognized that women had graduated at the top of their classes from each of the federal military academies and were serving successfully in the military,[62] an accomplishment that indicated that Virginia's fears concerning VMI's future might not be solidly grounded.[63]

"Predictably," writes Rosemary Yardley in 1996, "the windows rattled at tradition-encrusted West Point, Annapolis and the Air Force Academy. But the service academies worked diligently to create an atmosphere of fairness that would help women succeed, not fail.... In 1995, the top graduate at West Point was a woman."[64]

Members of the first class of women to graduate from West Point became a part of the class-action suit against the all-male Virginia Military Institute. Seventeen women filed a legal brief siding with the Justice Department against VMI's all-male policy. Among those 17 were LTC Rhonda Cornum, Army flight surgeon and POW, BGen. Evelyn P. Foote, USA (Ret.), Maj. Alison Ruttenberge, Colorado Air National Guard, and Kristine Holderied, top graduate of the U.S. Naval Academy class of 1984.[65] In 1995, MAJ Lillian Pfluke asked, "Is VMI dangerously out of touch with their mission: educating leaders for our country and for society?"[66] In 1996, Pfluke stated that the armed forces of today have no place for someone who grows up in a leadership environment so hostile to women that a federal judge has to assign U.S. marshals to protect a cadet.[67] Pfluke says that being a part of the group that filed the lawsuit has a special resonance for her: "We already did this!... Women shouldn't have to fight this one all over again." She also believes that the current single-sex leadership environment produces leaders that have no place in the Army.[68]

Lawyer Anita Blair argues, however, that VMI was an alternative to the military academies and not intended to "mimic" them or to produce military officers. She believes single-sex public education has a value.[69]

AIR FORCE ACADEMY

In 1976, the cadet oath was taken by 157 women, and four years later 97 of those women graduated. Twenty years later, in 1996, that same oath was taken by 228 women and those that graduate will be the class of 2000.[70] The first class of women entered the Academy in 1976 through a granite arch that bears the legend, "Bring Me Men." All freshmen were called "doolies" (Greek for slaves) and had to go through basic cadet training called "beast" barracks. Women ran the same obstacle course but did the flexed-arm hang in the place of pull-ups; they were not allowed in flight training.

Col. Warren Simmons, the Air Force Academy admissions director, noted: "These are not the kind of women who are going to be satisfied with administrative jobs. They want to go out and do all the physical things. The Air Force has never gotten a group of 98 women with their qualifications." The desire of women to compete for flight training, previously an exclusively male preserve, was the major bone of contention, says Theresa Armbruster, who was a cadet in 1980.[71]

Capt. Alison M. Weir, U.S. Air Force Academy (USAFA), admits there are some problems for women, but offers solutions as well:

> One of the reasons, as I see it, that women are treated as they are is that they are not a large enough force to be anything other than a dismissable minority. The USAFA, the opinion of many of the female cadets is that they "don't want to stand out" and as a result attempt to melt into the woodwork. Until women in the military are willing to identify themselves as such and recognize that despite all attempts to the contrary that they naturally "stand out," they will continue to be treated as a dismissable group.... When cadets who were not born when the first women entered the academies 20 years ago feel that they can still object, I realize that we still have a great deal to do to make our presence felt.[72]

The 1996 commencement speaker, Gen. Ronald Fogleman, Air Force Chief of Staff and 1963 USAFA graduate, said that when he graduated there were no women, three blacks, and two Asians in his class. In 1996, however, 62 women, 70 blacks, 62 Hispanics, 28 Asian Americans, and 9 American Indians graduated.[73]

NAVAL ACADEMY

In 1976, surveys showed three-quarters of male midshipmen opposed the admission of women. It is little wonder, say journalists Shane, Daemmrich, and Bowman, given two centuries of male tradition.[74] James H. Webb, a 1968 U.S. Naval Academy (USNA) graduate who later served as Secretary of the Navy, claimed in a 1979 controversial article in the *Washingtonian*, "Women Can't Fight," that the presence of women poisoned the training of combat leaders. His claim did not foster a positive reception of women at Annapolis.

The first 55 female graduates were legally restricted from participating in combat. Twenty-six of the original members of the 1980 class did not graduate. The female dropout rate was 6 percent higher than for men. The women spoke of their years at Annapolis as difficult, but not overwhelming. Janie Mines had the impression that the Naval Academy was less difficult than West Point. Sandy Irwin said that at times it got pretty bleak and she felt like walking out but didn't.[75]

Opposition remains, say Shane and his fellow journalists. A 1990 survey found half of the male midshipmen still opposed the presence of women. In 1996, 26 percent of the graduates surveyed said the program is not successful. Women, say the authors, are partially responsible in that they just want to "fit in." Women cadets are more likely not to be isolated if their performance is above criticism.

According to Daemmrich and Shane, if the women at Annapolis thought they had found loyalty, they found out otherwise when they testified against a male classmate accused of rape. Their initial bad treatment had not disappeared, it had just gone underground.[76] Daemmrich notes, however, that despite sexual harassment and rape problems at the Academy, Capt Duska Pearson, USMC, assured her "gung-ho" all-female students: "It's no longer a few good men." Opportunities are the same for women as for men. Sexual harassment videos and seminars are now commonplace, and women compete for jobs previously closed.[77] Banter flows easily now between women and men, but this was not always the case. A Delta Air Lines pilot, Chrystall Campbell, graduate of the first class in 1980, echoes the first women graduates of West Point: "Not one day in four years went by that someone didn't say something nasty to me." Campbell says she was naive and had no idea the degree of resistance that would be there. It was easier in flight school and in the fleet than in the Academy.

In 1989, Laura Herath took the midshipmen's oath. Her first year was a pivotal one for the Academy because of the incident when 19-year-old Gwen Dreyer was handcuffed to a urinal. Prohibition of hazing and zero-tolerance policy resulted. LT Herath says the atmosphere changed for the better in the years she attended. If harassment occurred, women were more likely to put a stop to it or report it. The most significant change was Congress lifting the ban on women in combat. Herath changed her career plans from becoming a civil engineer to flying.[78]

In February 1994, three female midshipmen who chose surface warfare qualified for oceanography along with four men. Six women were among the 27 midshipmen who chose surface nuclear power training. In addition, 9 women were among the 136 midshipmen who chose to be Navy pilots. Three women were among an additional 56 midshipmen who chose careers in naval aviation and will become naval flight officers.[79]

Linda Grant De Pauw has followed the history of women at the Naval Academy since they first entered. "Studying the history was what lead me in search of a good fantasy: my novel *Baptism of Fire* set in a Navy of the future in which 'gender prejudice has disappeared from memory.'[80] I've been pleased to discover that men seem to enjoy the adventures of Maggie Steele (Annapolis class of 2080) as much as women do."[81]

De Pauw believes that even in the future it will be difficult for many people to accept the concept of women as warriors: "As we approach the turn of the third millennium, it is hardly rational to pray for a war as those who wished to prove themselves in combat did in earlier times. Ironically, as those with actual experience of combat (the old fashioned kind) disappear from the military, the symbolic importance of 'war' as a proof of masculinity overshadows historical reality and hostility toward the concept of woman as warrior grows shriller."[82] On the other hand, Pearson thinks the situation will get better. Women are at the point of full integration in the Navy.[83] The involvement of women in war and combat begins in the academies with the training of our leaders. Pearson believes there will be a time five or ten years from now when women will be among the top leaders of the academies.

COAST GUARD ACADEMY

In 1980 a total of 14 women and 142 men graduated from the Coast Guard Academy in New London, Connecticut.[84] In peacetime the Coast Guard is the humanitarian arm of the Transportation Department, policing American waters and performing rescue missions. It is the smallest of all services. In wartime it becomes part of the Navy. According to *U.S. News and World Report*, the Coast Guard Academy was just as rigorous and just as hard on its first group of women as were the other academies. Twenty-four of the 30 women who enrolled in 1976 quit before graduation.[85]

Virginia Military Institute (VMI)

On June 26, 1996, the Supreme Court ordered the Virginia Military Institute (VMI) to open its doors to women or lose its state funding. Generations of VMI alumni felt a sense of loss as tradition gave way to social change.[86] The school had the option to become a private institution or shut down or comply with the court's ruling. Traditionalists viewed the ruling as the end of single-sex education in the United States. The *Washington Post* pointed out that it would be a costly undertaking to make the school private. Alumni would have to raise tens of millions of dollars to purchase the land in the Shenandoah Valley, replace the $11.6 million the school gets in taxes each year (one third of VMI's annual operating budget), and increase the subsidized tuition rates.

The Wilmington, North Carolina, *Morning Star* commented on the momentous change in an editorial showing a flair for humor touching inmost in the soul:

> From wherever he went after crossing over the river to rest under the trees, Stonewall Jackson must be marveling. What in the name of Robert E. Lee has happened to VMI?
>
> They call it progress, General.
>
> We freed the slaves not long after you left us, and we're in the final stages of freeing women.[87]

Admiral Stanley R. Arthur, former Vice Chief of Naval Operations, said the biggest mistake made in the debate was to include the service academies in the discussion:

> VMI and the Citadel have a minority of their students enter the military. They use a military environment to provide the discipline, the stature to their program, and encourage military service, but they are not an adjunct to the service academies. The service academies did change as they admitted women and they needed to since they were training officers for a military career that included leadership of an increasing number of women in expanding roles.... Over the years, the service academies have been wrestling with the charges of double standards. This is an indication that changes have been made. Necessary changes in my mind, because men and women are in fact different and a "one standard fits all" ignores this basic fact.[88]

Admiral Arthur understands the court decision applies to publicly funded colleges, but he also believes there is still a place for single-sex education. He knows, however, that VMI and the Citadel will change to accept women, thereby dropping those male-only characteristics that made them unique.

> Both VMI and the Citadel have designed their programs to reduce each new entrant to a state of complete vulnerability and then build

them up to a state where they are completely supportive of one another and owe their well-being to maintaining this close alliance. Their methods are very much a throwback to a time that is not recognized by most in our society. When you include women, the process must change because the methods are not acceptable for mixed genders, [for example], showering [in groups] ... This does not mean there are not ways to accomplish the same end, but they will be different and thus the culture will change, probably for the better but a change nonetheless.

Maller believes that VMI will be a better place:

I am very happy and relieved that the Supreme Court made the decision to open the doors of VMI to women as long as they remain a public institution. In my mind, it was the only logical decision that could have been made, but things don't always follow a logical course. I believe that VMI will be a better institution as a result and the education that these young men (and women) will now receive will be much more appropriate for a society in which men and women are supposed to be equal partners. These young men will now learn to interact with women as colleagues and I believe they will learn to have more respect for women as a result.[89]

Pfluke echoed Maller: "I'm happy because it's the right decision, proud to have played a role both directly and indirectly, but still amazed that after 20 years (we entered West Point on July 7, 1976) this kind of thing is still an issue."[90]

In September 1996, VMI voted to admit 34 women beginning in the fall of 1997. In December 1996, VMI complied with the Supreme Court decision, filing its first quarterly report on assimilation of women. The report contained basic standards for uniforms, haircuts and physical training. Uniforms (except on special occasions, when women could wear skirts) and haircuts would be the same for men and women. Physical fitness tests would be the same for everyone but were not considered tests for admission or graduation. VMI will begin integrating women into individual sports and phase in team sports, but will initially ask for a waiver from the NCAA as it builds its team sports.[91] This request hits at the heart of Title IX which requires that women be given equal opportunity in athletics. The VMI report addressed sexual harassment and fraternization generally. It indicated that construction would begin for modifications of toilets and showers and outside security lighting would be added.

In January 1997, VMI announced a mentor program that would involve women in administrative and staff positions.[92] According to the *Richmond Times-Dispatch* of March 13, 1998, *VMI* admitted 30 women and 394 men in the fall of 1997.

CITADEL

On July 30, 1996, the Citadel ended its 154-year-old tradition of admitting men only and the Citadel Board of Visitors submitted its assimilation plan.[93] The Citadel's decision was in response to the U.S. Supreme Court's 7-to-1 vote on admitting women to VMI. The Citadel's decision to admit women also followed a legal battle with Shannon Faulkner. Faulkner, a female from Powdersville, South Carolina, sued the Citadel in 1993 in order to become the first woman admitted. She won her case, but dropped out after one week, citing reasons of stress and heat. Nancy Mellette, a 17-year-old resident of Irmo, South Carolina, continued the lawsuit.[94]

"Officers and gentlemen they [the Citadel cadets] were not," wrote Rosemary Yardley in the Greensboro, North Carolina, *News and Record*.[95] When Faulkner was admitted, a sign near the campus read, "Die Shannon." A T-shirt in Charleston read, "1,952 bulldogs and one bitch." When she resigned, some cadets let out whoops and hollers of hysterical jubilation and some did push-ups in the rain.

Some said Faulkner did not succeed. Pfluke did not agree, "None of us do it alone, we all walk in the footsteps of those women who went before us."[96] Faulkner did the "court thing." Each person involved in removing the obstacles for women make unique contributions.

The plan that the Citadel Board of Visitors submitted in July 1996 for the assimilation of female cadets addressed fairness in promotions, the adequacy of female role models in leadership positions, efforts to get the entire corps to support a coed system, facilities, dress code, sexual harassment training, sports' policy, inclusion of females in the Citadel's various programs, privacy, showering, discipline, teaching methods, latrines, and billets.[97]

In August 1996, four women joined the ranks of Citadel plebes, Jeanie Mentavlos, Kim Messer, Nancy Mace, and Petra Lovetinska. All four made it through Hell Week, but only months later in January 1997 two of the Citadel's first four female cadets announced they wouldn't return for the spring semester because of sexual harassment and hazing.[98] According to CNN, the hazing included physical abuse and death threats from some of the Citadel's 3,600 cadets. According to Tim Kulp, who represents female cadet Jeanie Mentavlos, the hazing included a number of things, but the primary concern was that the women were set on fire using a nail polish remover solution and a lighter on more than one occasion.[99] Roger Cossack, the host of CNN's *Burden of Proof*, stated that the horrible allegations included "being butted with a rifle, being burned, having part of their clothing burned, having—almost being strip-searched at one time."

Citadel president Maj. Gen. Clifton Poole explained to CNN that the Citadel had a hazing regulation that provided punishment for offenders. Prior to the allegations, the Citadel had expelled six cadets for hazing other male cadets. Poole said he suspended two people in connection with the hazing incidents involving the female cadets. He elaborated that hazing at the Citadel would be a problem even if there were no women at the institution.[100]

Webster's defines the verb *haze* in these terms: "1. in nautical usage, to oppress, punish, or harass by forcing to do hard and unnecessary work. 2. to initiate or discipline (fellow students) by means of horseplay, practical jokes, and tricks, often in the nature of humiliating or painful ordeals."[101] Not all hazing is serious, according to Dorothy Mackey, a former Air Force captain, who offers as an example "old school pranks [of] putting Vaseline on door knobs."[102] The type of hazing at the Citadel, says Mackey, is more serious. She sees it as a message from the Citadel leadership. The government forced women upon them. They must abide or lose funding and the school. Mackey asserts, "Until the head leadership is held accountable for the safety of its entire school's actions, they will by covert means do anything to keep women out."

The Citadel's investigation resulted in 120 penalty tours and confinement to the barracks, which Gene Moser says are "no fun, ... especially if it happens to be the second semester of your senior year."[103] The punishment also included loss of rank, according to Cybill Fix of the *Charleston Post*. The Citadel dismissed one accused cadet, restricted nine, and exonerated one. Two cadets left the school.[104] The assailants are also subject to possible criminal punishment from state and federal law. Along with Mentavlos, Kim Messer also charged that she had been harassed. Both women did not return for the second semester. In May 1997, Nancy Mace and Petra Lovetinska appeared on the news to say they had successfully completed the year. One incident of inappropriate behavior happened to each, for which they "got an apology."

U.S. V. VIRGINIA

The Supreme Court case *United States of America v. Commonwealth of Virginia* (hereafter referred to as *U.S. v. Virginia*) received national attention. The Virginia Military Institute at Lexington, Virginia, and the Citadel in Charleston, South Carolina, were the only two state-operated, male-only schools in the country. According to Joan Biskupic in the *Washington Post*, the schools were the last of a kind "building discipline and loyalty through the 'adversative' method, which relies on arduous physical routines and constant humiliation."[105]

Writing in the *New York Times*, Linda Greenhouse said that the case presented two questions.[106] First, did the exclusion of women violate the equal protection guarantee of the Fourteenth Amendment? The Justice Department charged that it did and sued the State of Virginia in federal district court in Roanoke in 1990. Second, if the Supreme Court found the all-male admissions policy unconstitutional, was the alternative women's program enough to remedy the violation? The case had a complicated history in the lower courts (see

Appendix A). In 1995 the Fourth Circuit Court of Appeals in Richmond answered yes to both questions. The appeals court reasoned the admissions policy deprived women of equal protection but argued that the Mary Baldwin College program in Staunton, Virginia, was "sufficiently comparable" to a VMI education.[107] Thus the problem was supposedly solved. The appeals court said that for women to take part in rigorous military training would destroy "any sense of decency that still permeates the relationship between the sexes." The appeals court also thought that the Spartan type of life in the barracks and brutal "rat line" screaming and harassing of first-year cadets would be detrimental to female cadets.[108]

The Supreme Court reversed the *U.S. v. Virginia* Fourth Circuit Court of Appeals decision based on the separate but equal philosophy.[109] Chief Justice William H. Rehnquist concurred in the Supreme Court decision, but disagreed with the Court's analysis. Rehnquist agreed Virginia violated the Equal Protection Clause by maintaining the Virginia Military Institute's all-male admissions policy, and establishing the Virginia Women's Institute for Leadership program did not remedy that violation.[110] Chief Justice Rehnquist stated, however, that it was unfortunate the Court had introduced an element of uncertainty respecting the appropriate test for sex discrimination analysis.[111]

The media provided coverage of the varied reactions. The VMI cadets around for summer school did not want the decision, but they knew they had to accept it. Some alumni were not too happy.[112] The *Richmond Times-Dispatch* conducted a poll, and 75 percent of more than 200 people who responded opposed the Supreme Court ruling.[113] Most of the callers opposed were women who wished to keep the school's tradition. Supporters, however, called it a "social breakthrough."

NORWICH UNIVERSITY, NORWICH, VERMONT

Frank Griffis, dean of admissions of Norwich University, which was founded in 1819 and is the nation's oldest private military college, stated: "Today's military is not a single-sex environment. Our students learn how to work with and report to women, which is the kind of situation they will face in the real world."[114]

MERCHANT MARINE ACADEMY
AT KINGS POINT, NEW YORK

The United States Merchant Marine Academy at Kings Point, New York, accepted women in 1974. According to Linda McAffrey, who attended the Academy as part of its second class, Kings Point provides merchant officers but also allows graduates to serve out their obligation as U.S. naval officers. Many midshipmen use the latter option.[115]

The debate rages on concerning the issue of whether men and women should be trained together in the academies or as recruits. Such gender issues will be addressed in Chapter 11.

The repeal of the ban on women serving in combat represents a cultural change that has been reflected in the law at a time of great movement in the history of women in the military. The legal struggle involving the Citadel and the Virginia Military Institute has also increased the opportunities for women.

Chapter 5

Law and Policy

Rest in reason and move in passion.
—Kahlil Gibran

Overview

Women's role in the military and combat has been determined by a combination of law, policy, and practice. Internal military legal opinions have also contributed to the evolution of law and policy about women in combat.

LAW

Because women had proved of great value to the war effort in World War II, Congress gave them a permanent peacetime military duty role in the armed services. In 1948, Congress passed the *Women's Armed Services Integration Act* giving women permanent status in the military. A provision excluding women from combat was incorporated into the statute.[1] This original combat exclusion statute stipulated that women in the Navy and Marine Corps could not be assigned to ships or aircraft that engaged in combat missions and Air Force women could not be assigned to aircraft engaged in combat missions. There are no statutory limitations on assignment of Army women. A military female puts it another way, "The law is silent on the assignment of Army women." By law the Secretary of the Army was given the statutory discretion, says Milko.[2] The combat exclusion laws did not apply to the Army, but the Army based its combat exclusion policies on the perceived intent of Congress.[3] It was not until 1956 that the Combat Exclusion Law was codified in Title 10 U.S. Code § 6015,[4] which stated:

> The Secretary of the Navy may prescribe the manner in which women officers appointed under section 5590 of this title, women warrant officers, and enlisted women members of the Regular Navy and the Regular Marine Corps shall be trained and qualified for military duty.

The Secretary may prescribe the kind of military duty to which such women members may be assigned and the military authority which they may exercise. However, women may not be assigned to duty in aircraft that are engaged in combat missions nor may they be assigned to duty on vessels of the Navy other than hospital ships, transports, and vessels of a similar classification not expected to be assigned combat missions.[5]

The limitation to "women officers appointed under section 5590" was inserted to avoid application of the section to personnel with a medical corps specialty and to women appointed in the medical, medical service, and dental corps.

In 1992 the Committee on Military Affairs and Justice of the Association of the Bar of the City of New York issued a report that stated, "DOD's failure to allow women to compete for aviation combat positions probably violates equal protection guarantees under the Fifth Amendment. Even if the DOD's refusal to allow women to compete is not arguably a violation of this amendment, its blanket refusal to allow women to compete for combat aviation positions is wholly inconsistent with the DOD's prior public positions: 1) welcoming the repeal, 2) stating that military women should be allowed their full potential, and 3) stating that if the law was changed, the DOD would change its policies to be consistent with the new law."[6]

According to public law provisions within the now repealed 6015, women could not be assigned permanently to combatant vessels but could be assigned temporary duty aboard those vessels to get necessary warfare qualification. "Anything 179 days or less is a temporary assignment."[7]

Title 10 U.S. Code § 8549, applicable to the Air Force, which provided that "Female members of the Air Force ... may not be assigned to duty in aircraft engaged in combat missions" was repealed by the *National Defense Authorization Act for Fiscal Years 1992 and 1993*.[8]

Public Law 90-30 of 1967 eliminated the two percent strength ceiling and promotion cap of the *Integration Act of 1948*.[9] The *Defense Officer Personnel Management Act* of 1981 (DOPMA), "made officer personnel management uniform for both men and women, eliminated separate promotion categories for women and abolished restrictions that prevented women from receiving an equal opportunity for assignments and promotion."[10] Milko notes that the Department of Defense Task Force Report on Women in the Military stated that the definitions of combat and risk thresholds varied among the services and during change of technologies.[11] In 1988 the Task Force established clear standards for evaluating a noncombatant position for women that resulted in the opening of 31,000 positions.[12]

In 1992–93 the *Defense Authorization Act* repealed exclusion laws regarding combat aircraft. In 1994 the Secretary of Defense modified the DOD Risk Rule (see Chapter 2). He defined direct ground combat and an associated assignment rule. Women are now allowed in all positions "except those units whose primary mission is to engage in direct ground combat. Generally speaking, this means that Armor, Infantry, Ranger, Special Forces and Field Artillery Battalions remain closed in the Army. In the Marine Corps, the infantry regiment and its associated elements remain closed."[13] Since 1993, women have been eligible for some 260,000 additional military positions, many of which involve combat.

According to the Committee on Military Affairs and Justice of the Association of the Bar of the City of New York, when the Equal Rights Amendment and sexual stereotyping came under constitutional attack in the courts in 1991, the resulting debate influenced the services to examine themselves. The changes in the law evolved with great drama and much individual effort and sacrifice.

CASE LAW

Seven major Supreme Court decisions are reflected in these words from *Goldman v. Weinberger,*

> The military is, by necessity, a specialized society [separate] from civilian society.... "The military must insist upon a respect for duty and a discipline without counterpart in civilian life," in order to prepare for and perform its vital role.... The essence of military service "is the subordination of the desires and interests of the individual to the needs of the service."[14]

This chapter is designed to portray the legal elements leading up to and including that powerful time of legal development around the period of the Gulf War.

Before the repeal of combat exclusion laws, case law was closely examined for possible litigation that could result from the ban. Little controversy existed until the 1970s when the emergence of the women's rights movement sparked criticism of the exclusions.[15] Further, the federal courts were the "ultimate catalyst" in revising existing discriminatory policies. Milko cites five cases but notes that because few constitutional challenges to exclusions exist, when the exclusions are addressed in litigation, the courts have relied on these decisions for support in upholding other issues. In 1975, *Schlesinger v. Ballard* upheld a discriminatory mandatory discharge statute, 10 U.S. Code § 6382(a), which requires that male officers who have not been promoted in nine years be discharged from service. The appellee said that if he had been female he would have been entitled to 13 years before discharge. The court reasoned that because females were restricted from compiling similar sea duty, and the longer period was consistent with the goal of providing women fair opportunity for promotion, the law was fair.[16] *Campbell v. Beaughler* in 1975–76 involved hair length regulations; it held that Marine Corps regulations setting different standards for men's and women's hairstyles do not offend equal protection law. Enlisted Marine reservists challenged the policy that women could wear hairpieces but men could not and asserted that this stipulation interfered with the uniformity of combat units. The military argued that the hairpieces were a safety hazard with gas masks and with the earphones used in mine detecting units, but because of combat exclusion rules, female marines do not wear gas masks or operate mine detectors.[17] *Kovack v. Middendorf*, 1976, entailed allocation of military scholarships. The district court reasoned that the Navy policy setting stricter requirements for women and granting a higher number of Navy Reserve Officer Training Corps (NROTC) scholarships to men was based on greater need for males than females because of the exclusion law. The court upheld the constitutionality of disparity because it was necessary to maintain the Navy and was therefore a "legitimate government purpose."[18] *Lewis v. U.S. Army*, 1988, upheld the principle that the Army's setting of higher service entrance requirements for female enlistees does not violate due process or equal protection on the basis that men and women are not "similarly situated" because of exclusion policy.[19] While gender discrimination in the military is subject to judicial review under the Constitution's Fifth Amendment Due Process Clause, *Rostker v. Goldberg*, 1981, upheld the male-only selective service registration law.[20] The purpose of the draft was to prepare for combat, and women were not eligible for combat; therefore, due process had not been violated.[21]

Contrary to the comment in *Hill v. Berkman* in 1986, the court has found no challenge to exclusionary statutes in reported case law.[22] In 1978, however, *Owens v. Brown* did challenge the constitutionality of § 6015.[23] As a result, Congress in 1978 amended the statute to make it less restrictive.[24] The issue of women lacking physical strength for close combat is addressed in *Chandler v. Callaway*, 1974; *U.S. v. Yingling*, 1973; *U.S. v. Cook*, 1970; *U.S. v. St. Clair*, 1968.[25] *Crawford v. Cushman* held that women have the right to remain in the service after bearing children.[26] *Kovach v. Middendorf* held "that disparate classifications of men and women mandated by section 6015 do not violate female plaintiff's equal protections rights."[27] In 1970, *U.S. v. Dorris* found that the gender-based classification did not violate due process because it was justified by the government's interest to provide for defense.[28] Jeanne Liebermann notes that in 1970 in *U.S. v. Clinton* the court used the "rational basis" test. The court stated that although gender-based discrimination "may be unconstitutionally arbitrary in some contexts, congressional chivalry in drafting men only to comprise an army has a sufficiently rational basis to avoid constitutional condemnation as mere chauvinism."[29] Thus, courts have held some classification is permissible.[30] The art lies in determining the line between permissible and prohibited classifications. The courts have traditionally "sustained a government classification if it is reasonable rather than arbitrary."[31]

There is some inconsistency in application.[32] According to an Air Force analysis in 1992, "It appears that a governmental statutory or regulatory scheme utilizing sexual classifications must meet three tests, namely: (A) is the objective or purpose of the statutory or regulatory scheme lawful or permissible; (B) if so, is that objective or purpose important to the government; and (C) if so, is that objective or purpose met by the classification or could it be met by a less discriminatory classification without substantial damage to the important governmental interest."[33] In conclusion, the analysis states that "Federal statutes, regulations, or policies governing the armed forces may not violate the equal protection rights of military personnel guaranteed by the Due Process Clause of the Fifth Amendment."

In 1991 Congress considered a repeal of the law against women in combat assignments with a provision that the services could implement regulations on the subject. Since the services could restrict women through policy, the navy examined the legal standards for gender-based assignments and classifications. In the past, gender-based classifications were upheld on the basis that there was a statutory ban on women in combat. Removal of the bar could generate extensive litigation. Title VII of the *Civil Rights Act of 1964* is federal legislation prohibiting sex discrimination in employment.[34] There was concern that Title VII could be used to challenge any Navy policy containing gender classification. *Hill v. Berkman* held that uniformed members of the military were covered by Title VII so that Title VII was the exclusive judicial remedy for claims of sex discrimination brought by a member of the uniformed services. However, the court noted that "because combat risk is an occupational qualification mandated by statute, it is an appropriate bona fide occupational qualification exception to Title VII ... further ... the standard of review is the 'clearly erroneous' standard when a military decision is challenged under Title VII, in order to allow the military to have the necessary flexibility to make changes and alter policies."[35] On the other hand, *Roper v. Department of the Army* found Title VII did not apply to uniformed military members.[36] After reviewing these precedents the Navy analysis concluded there would be risk of Title VII suits challenging the Department of the Navy exclusion regulations, depending on which circuit heard the case. This was in addition to the risk that any policy might be challenged based upon the Equal Protection or Due Process Clauses of the Constitution. There was concern that, in reviewing such cases, deference would not be accorded to military policy determinations of gender-based classifications as had been accorded congressional statutory determinations enacted into law. It was noted that any action by Congress to ease the exclusion increased the Navy's litigation risk because the Supreme Court in cases such as *Sollorio v. U.S.* had relied upon Congress's "plenary" power under the Constitution to regulate land and naval forces.[37] Thus the conclusion was drawn that more scrutiny would be applied to the Navy's regulations should the law be repealed.

In 1996, Justice Ruth Bader Ginsburg delivered the opinion of the Supreme Court in the Virginia Military Institute (VMI) case, *United States v. Virginia*, which states in part:

> A prime part of the history of our Constitution, historian Richard Morris recounted, is the story of the extension of constitutional rights and protections to people once ignored or excluded.[38] VMI's story continued as our comprehension of "We the People" expanded.[39] There is no reason to believe that the admission of women capable of all the activities required of VMI cadets would destroy the Institute rather than enhance its capacity to serve the "more perfect Union."[40]

Further, Ginsburg observed that Virginia, while maintaining VMI for men only, failed to provide any "comparable single gender women's institution."[41] Instead, it had created a Virginia Women's Institute for Leadership (VWIL) program that Ginsburg identified as a "pale shadow" of VMI in terms of the range of curricular choices and faculty stature, funding, prestige, alumni support, and influence.[42]

Ginsburg gets to the heart of gender discrimination. She says that it may be assumed that most women would not choose VMI's adversative method.[43] Ginsburg cites Fourth Circuit Judge Diana Gribbon Motz's dissent from the Court of Appeals' denial of rehearing *en banc*. Motz says that it is also probable that "many men would not want to be educated in such an environment."[44] Education, she explained, is not a "one size fits all" business. The issue is not whether "women—or men—should be forced to attend VMI" but whether the State of Virginia can constitutionally deny to women who have the will and capacity the training and attendant opportunities that VMI uniquely affords.

Further, Ginsburg attacks generalizations about "the way women are," and she provides the following critique of VMI's position:

> Estimates of what is appropriate for *most women*, no longer justify denying opportunity to women whose talent and capacity place them outside the average description.... Virginia never asserted that VMI's method of education suits *most men*.... Virginia accounted for its failure to make the VWIL experience "the entirely militaristic experience of VMI" on the ground that VWIL "is planned for women who do not necessarily expect to pursue military careers." By that reasoning, VMI's "entirely militaristic" program would be inappropriate for men in general or *as a group*, for "[o]nly about 15% of VMI cadets enter career military service."[45]

Justice Sandra Day O'Connor, the first woman to serve on the Supreme Court, authored the 1982 precedent-setting decision, *Mississippi University for Women v. Hogan*, that held unconstitutional the exclusion of men from a state-supported nursing school, Mississippi University. Ginsburg explained that *Women v. Hogan*[46] was the closest guide.[47]

Ginsburg said the justification for distinctions based on sex should be genuine and free from generalizations, not hypothesized or invented after the fact in response to litigation. When the lower court of appeals held that VMI's program for women was comparable to what the men received, it ignored the standard of searching scrutiny in sex discrimination cases and invented a standard of its own. Ginsburg flatly states, "Today's skeptical scrutiny of official action denying rights or opportunities based on sex responds to volumes of history." She reminded the Court that "our Nation has had a long and unfortunate history of sex discrimination."[48] "We the People"[49] did not include women voters until 1920. "And for a half century thereafter," Ginsburg eloquently brings home, "it remained the prevailing doctrine that government, both federal and state, could withhold from women opportunities accorded men so long as any 'basis in reason' could be conceived for the discrimination."[50]

In 1971, for the first time in our nation's history, in *Reed v. Reed*, the Supreme Court ruled in favor of a woman who complained that her State had denied her the equal protection of its laws.[51] According to Ginsburg, the Court held unconstitutional the Idaho Code prescription that among "several persons claiming and equally entitled to administer [a decedent's estate], males must be preferred to females." Since *Reed*, the Court has repeatedly recognized that neither federal nor state government acts compatibly with the equal protection principle when a law or official policy denies to women, simply because they are women, full citizenship stature—equal opportunity to aspire, achieve, participate in and contribute to society based on their individual talents and capacities.

According to Ginsburg, the Court has in post–*Reed* decisions carefully inspected official action that closes a door or denies opportunity to women (or men). Ginsburg summarizes the Court's "current directions for cases of official classification based on gender":

> Focusing on the differential treatment or denial of opportunity for which relief is sought, the reviewing court must determine whether the proffered justification is "exceedingly persuasive." The burden of justification is demanding and it rests entirely on the State.... The State must show "at least that the [challenged] classification serves 'important governmental objectives and that the discriminatory means employed' are 'substantially related to the achievement of those objectives.' ... The justification must be genuine, not hypothesized or invented *post hoc* in response to litigation. And it must not rely on over broad generalizations about the different talents, capacities, or preferences of males and females."

Justice Clarence Thomas did not participate in the decision because his son was enrolled at VMI. Justice Antonin Scalia dissented because he thought the Court took its analysis too far: "This [decision] is not the interpretation of a Constitution, but the creation of one."[52]

An editorial in the *Washington Post* said that Scalia was accurate in that his question is yet to be answered as to whether "this ruling sounds a death knell for private single-sex colleges, for special public school programs for boys and for any other gender distinction in the law that cannot withstand the strict scrutiny review now applied to race distinctions."[53] According to the *Post*, the Supreme Court created the same test for evaluating gender laws as those that make distinctions based on race. These laws are subjected to "strict scrutiny" and "narrowly tailored" to serve a "compelling" state interest in order not to violate the Equal Protection Clause of the Constitution. In gender distinctions, the more flexible standard of "intermediate scrutiny" was used and the law had only to serve "important" government objectives and be "substantially related" to their achievement. In the VMI case the additional qualification was added that gender-based action can be sustained only if the defenders demonstrate an exceedingly persuasive justification.

Judith Lichtman, president of the Women's Legal Defense Fund, believes that the Supreme Court's opinion did not make new law, but did forcefully apply the existing standard. The standard meant different things to different appeals courts.[54]

The Navy and Title 10 U.S. Code § 6015

To fully understand the case law, it is helpful to review the history of Title 10 U.S. Code § 6015 and case law's application to the pros and cons of the repeal of §6015. Navy documents indicate an ongoing struggle with the interpretation of § 6015. In 1974 the Judge Advocate General (JAG) of the Navy concluded, "It is legally permissible to assign women to aircraft of VR (fleet tactical support) squadrons which are not 'engaged in combat missions,' and which do not have as an assigned mission the landing on vessels which go to sea, except hospital ships and transports."[55]

The original combat exclusion law was part of the 1948 *Women's Armed Services Integration Act.* (In 1956 it was codified as § 6015.) The 1978 amendment to § 6015 permitting the temporary assignment of women to combat vessels resulted, in part, from *Owens v. Brown,* holding that the exclusion of women from all but hospital ships and transport ships was overly broad and therefore unconstitutional under the Due Process Clause of the Fifth Amendment. Controversy surrounded the hearings on the 1978 amendment because temporary duty on combatant vessels and potential assignment to all noncombatants (vis-a-vis only hospital and transports) would be allowed under this amendment. Congress again examined the restriction in 1980. The Secretary of the Navy recommended repeal and wanted Congress to authorize the

Navy to regulate the combat restriction. In 1981 it was again viewed and the Navy proposed a repeal. In both cases the Navy was opposed to women in combat assignments, but their position on the repeal was different.[56]

In 1985 the issue arose whether a female Navy judge advocate could be assigned as the legal officer on the USS *Independence* while it was undergoing maintenance in a shipyard. It was decided that she could be assigned temporary duty aboard the ship for not more than six months.[57]

In 1974 the Deputy JAG wrote that he was confident that the JAG's opinion concerning women landing and taking off from combatants was on "sure footing," but he added, "It is evident that we've been drawing some fine lines in this area."[58] The complete text of the JAG opinion states that it is quite clear from the House subcommittee hearings on the *Women's Armed Services Integration Act of 1948* that Congress knew very well that women had performed as pilots and crew members of aircraft and acquiesced in their continuing to fill that role. The only limitation was that women could not be assigned combat missions.[59] RADM H. B. Robertson, Jr., USN, Acting JAG, says, "The precise meaning of the phrase engaged in combat missions, however, was not made explicit by Congress."[60] The Navy JAG had previously concluded that the phrase referred to "flights in which the aircraft are ordered to employ offensive ordnance or weapons or any kind against a hostile force, known or potential; in which they may otherwise be reasonably expected to become engaged in the employment of ordnance against such forces; or in which there is reason to believe that the aircraft may be attacked or threatened by hostile forces."[61] If an aircraft mission involved any of these three circumstances, it was considered a combat mission and § 6015 was applicable.

The same opinion addressed whether assignment to crew duty on an antisubmarine patrol aircraft could be classified as combat and thus be proscribed by the statute. If a female was killed or injured, could she or her heirs sue? The JAG opinion stated that the propriety of such an assignment would be dependent upon the exact nature of the mission of the aircraft. If it involved any of the three circumstances set forth above, then it was a combat mission and the prohibition applied.[62]

Owens v. Brown challenged the constitutionality of § 6015.[63] The Washington, D.C., Federal District Court invalidated § 6015 not because of the combat exclusion, but because of its prohibition against assigning women to sea duty. The overly broad restrictive language of § 6015 was not reasonable under the Fifth Amendment because it barred women from any duties at sea, even noncombatant.[64]

BGen. G. L. Miller notes that the *Owens* case and the recognition that the blanket restriction of § 6015 prevented the use of highly trained women in many skill areas motivated Congress to amend the law in 1978.

According to Miller, the congressional hearings on the amendment were very controversial and both the Secretary of the Navy and the Chief of Naval

Operations "supported a full repeal of the exclusion in favor of tailor-made service regulations. Members of Congress, however, feared that a full repeal would give the impression that Congress endorsed the idea of placing women in combat." Therefore Congress rejected the proposed legislation to repeal all combat restrictions and passed the amendment to the original law. The amendment authorized Navy and Marine women to be assigned to temporary duty aboard combatant ships and to permanent duty on vessels with a classification similar to that of hospital ships and transports that would not be expected to be assigned combat missions.[65] The Navy began to allow female civilian engineers and technicians access to sea trials of surface ships because the Equal Employment Opportunity Commission found the navy liable for sex discrimination under Title VII.[66]

In 1980, President Jimmy Carter recommended that Congress amend the *Military Selective Service Act* (MSSA) to register and conscript women as well as men. Congress held hearings, but rejected the proposal. In 1981 in *Rostker v. Goldberg*, the Supreme Court implicitly upheld the combat exclusion laws. Although the case did not challenge the combat exclusions laws, the Court found that Congress was justified in rejecting the proposal that women register because women were not eligible for combat anyway.

In 1990, largely as a result of the performance of women in Panama, the combat issue resurfaced. Representative Patricia Schroeder (D-Colo.) proposed legislation that would require "the Army to conduct a four-year test program that would allow women (at their option) to enter all occupational fields, including combat arms."[67] Hearings were held by the Military Personnel and Compensation Subcommittee of the House Armed Services Committee, which rejected the legislation.

The Department of Defense opposed the bill. The Secretary of Defense said the bill would countermand the intent of Congress that military women not serve in combat. The Secretary of Defense argued that the proposed test program was in conflict with budget and personnel reductions and provided "no conclusive evidence of mixed gender unit performance under actual combat."[68]

After Desert Storm ended, Congress again held hearings. According to Miller, proponents were initially lobbying for a modification of § 6015 but subsequently had expanded their agenda to include the repeal of all statutory restrictions. The Defense Advisory Committee on Women in the Services (DACOWITS) supported the repeal, claiming it would benefit the armed forces by giving them greater flexibility to utilize fully all qualified personnel. The Department of the Navy was again concerned about possible litigation and noted that "the repeal of the combat exclusion law could result in a diminution of judicial deference to military actions regarding women assignments." Traditionally, the courts have tended not to override congressional and executive actions with regard to military actions. If there was no statute, the courts might be inclined to enter into the issue of women's combat roles. Thus combat exclusion decisions by the services will be seen as *not* reflective of the will of the American people (as demonstrated through Congress)."[69] Therefore litigation and differing results among the services could follow.

The Navy was also concerned that the repeal could "result in a successful challenge to the male-only draft/registration provisions." Thus the use of combat exclusion in *Rostker* as the basis of excluding women from draft registration would no longer be valid.

The Navy point paper said that if some combat units were open to women, the exclusion of women from the draft would be more difficult to defend.[70] Could drafting only males withstand an equal protection challenge? Other discussion centered around structural adaptations of ships, physical standards, risk, budget, and impact. The paper concluded that repealing the exclusion was an issue involving mission effectiveness, and if the law was repealed, the services should have a plan to meet that goal.[71] Another point paper expanded on possible policy implications such as personal privacy (berthing and submarine configuration and operations), rating qualifications and advancement, recruiting quotas, assignment policies in sea and shore rotations, interrogations and searches policy, and involvement of DOD.[72]

Since combat policy was gender classified, some information papers indicated judicial scrutiny would be more detailed. Most military policies needed only to be related to a legitimate government interest to withstand judicial review (*Kovach v. Middendorf*), and this test was easy to meet. "Gender based classifications must meet a tougher test. They must be *substantially* related to an *important* government interest." Combat, clearly an important government interest, made the challenge "to articulate reasons for excluding women from combat, in whole or in part, that are *substantially related* to combat effectiveness."[73]

The Association of the Bar of the City of New York completed a study of the combat exclusion laws and policies and recommended their repeal.[74] The study focused on the federal laws prohibiting women from serving in Air Force and Navy combat positions, and on the Army's voluntary policy.

In 1991 the House Committee on Armed Services noted that because women had served in all phases of the war effort in the Gulf, much of the then current statutory law restricting women's role in combat was an "anachronism." Further, the Committee recognized that women in the military will be exposed to combat whether or not they are on the front lines. Thus, the Committee argued for repeal of the restriction on flying combat missions in the Air Force, Navy and Marines. They also noted that lifting the restrictions "would not mandate that women perform such missions. That decision would rest with the Secretaries of the Air Force and Navy."[75]

In 1993, prior to the repeal of § 6015, the House Armed Services Committee made its report to accompany bill H.R. 1378.[76] The House considered and passed its bill on May 11, 1993, and seven days later on May 18, the Senate did likewise.

The Air Force and Title 10 U.S. Code § 8549

Congress prevented not only Navy women but also Air Force women from being assigned to duty on combat aircraft.[77] The exceptions to the prohibition are for women in medical, dental, veterinary, medical service, nursing, medical specialists, judge advocate and chaplain functions in 10 U.S. Code § 8067.[78]

In 1973 the Judge Advocate General of the Air Force published an opinion regarding the assignment of women as aircrew members on a Strategic Air Command (SAC) airborne command post. The opinion stated: "A distinction between combat and combat support activities is consistent with the history and intent of 10 U.S. Code § 8549 and would permit female aircrew members to serve on a SAC airborne command post, so long as that aircraft did not engage in active combat missions within a war zone."[79] The Air Force JAG was in all probability responding to the DOD draft of the Defense Officer Personnel Management Act (DOPMA), which would have repealed Navy and Air Force exclusion law.[80]

Essentially the Air Force designated aerial combat as "(1) delivery of munitions or other destructive material against an enemy or (2) aerial activity over hostile territory where enemy fire is expected and where risk of capture is substantial."[81] Women also could not be assigned "where there is probability of exposure to hostile fire and risk of capture."[82]

The Army and Title 10 U.S. Code § 3013(g)

UNITED STATES CODE AND RESULTING ARMY POLICY

In 1988, the Secretary of the Army issued the following combat exclusion policy:

> Women may not serve in Infantry, Armor, Cannon Field Artillery, Combat Engineer, or Low Altitude Air Defense Artillery units of Battalion/Squadron or smaller size.[83]

Milko notes that "The Army, reading the Navy and Air Force statutes as signifying congressional intent to bar women from all combat, promulgated internal regulations prohibiting women from combat assignment."[84] Title 10 U.S. Code § 3013(g) provides, "The Secretary of the Army may ... (1) assign, detail, and prescribe the duties of members of the Army ... and (3) prescribe regulations to carry out his functions, powers, and duties under this title."[85]

The changes which resulted in the military from the 1991 and 1993 legislation were not achieved without a struggle, particularly in the Army. The 1994 hearings attest that sharp conflict and resistance prevailed over women being allowed in ground combat. Interviewees acknowledge the struggle and recognize that the gains, though slow, must be consolidated for continued steady progress. MAJ Lillian Pfluke, USA (Ret.), says, "The legislation passed following Desert Storm eliminated any legal restrictions on assigning women to combat positions, but [it] established some administrative restrictions."[86]

In part the law states that except in cases covered by law, whenever the Secretary of Defense proposes to change personnel policies "in order to make available to female members of the Armed Forces assignment to any type of combat unit, class of combat vessel, or type of combat platform that is not open to such assignments, the Secretary shall, not less than 30 days before such a change" notify Congress of the proposed change.[87] If the Secretary makes a change in the ground combat exclusion policy, a 90-day notice to Congress is required by law.

THE PRESIDENTIAL COMMISSION

In 1992, President George Bush appointed a commission to study the issue of assignment of women in combat. At the time of the Commission's vote against assigning women to combat aircraft, Congress was initiating repeal of the restrictive laws and assignment policies. MAJ Mary Finch, USA, who was a member of the commission, points out, "The fact that the Commission could not come to the same conclusion as the Congress and Secretary of Defense is disturbing and gives some indication as to why it was so controversial."[88] Finch says that the issue of ground forces is by far the most complex one with which the Commission dealt. Little time was spent examining ground forces, Finch believes, because the commissioners pictured combat only as infantry and armor, and paid little heed to investigating other areas that restricted women (military intelligence, engineers, artillery). Because not many qualified women would be available for the infantry and armored units and very few women would be both physically qualified and interested, Finch agrees these units should remain closed for the time being, but she also believes there were many positions unnecessarily closed in field artillery, air defense artillery, engineers, and noncombat branches based on the Risk Rule. The Risk Rule, says Finch, is unworkable on the modern battlefield, particularly since combat aircraft laws and policies were repealed, allowing women into combat where they are exposed to a high risk of capture. (The Risk Rule was rescinded in 1994 by Secretary of Defense Aspin.) The commission stated:

> The DOD Risk Rule was never designed to prevent women from being placed in harm's way. The chaotic environment of war precludes this from occurring. While the DOD Risk Rule has been used to guide

planning in the past, the reality of combat, the fluidity of the modern battlefields, and the war fighting doctrine of the U.S. Armed Forces bring into question the validity of such a rule. Lethal and sophisticated weapons have greatly expanded the size of the battlefield to "over the horizon" fighting. Front lines are losing their meaning in an age of fluid battles and highly mobile forces. Military combat support and combat service support personnel, such as logistical, technical and administrative services, are increasingly at risk of injury, capture or death regardless of their location."[89]

Finch concludes that our own war doctrine recognizes the lethality of rear areas where support personnel work. After Desert Storm, the Marine Corps awarded 23 women the Combat Action Ribbon. The Scud attacks exposed women to danger, and two army women in combat support and service support positions were captured and taken prisoner.[90]

THE JOINT STAFF DISCUSSION OF "COMBAT"

The appointment of the Presidential Commission prompted the Joint Chiefs of Staff to consider the meaning of the term *combat*, in preparation for their testimony before the Commission. The Joint Chiefs believed women "would be thrust into 'combat' as a matter of circumstance."[91] They reasoned that combat takes place at many levels and *combat* is a broad term connoting an environment more than an event. Placing their rationale against the backdrop of history, they cited examples such as the Iraqi Scud missile hitting the U.S. barracks in Dhahran during the Gulf War and support units throughout the Cold War being every bit as much in harm's way as the combat units alongside or just to the rear.

Using Webster's Third International Dictionary's first definition of combat as a point of departure, "A fight, encounter, or contest between individuals or groups," the Joint Chiefs pointed out that there is a more direct sense of combat defined by Webster, "Actual fighting engagement of military forces as distinguished from other military duties or periods of active service without fighting."[92]

"This sense of direct combat," they write, "is captured in Joint Pub 1-02's definition of 'combat troops': 'Those units or organizations whose primary mission is destruction of enemy forces and/or installations.'" They conclude it is this direct sense that is more germane to discussions: "combat is engaged in by those who close with and destroy the enemy by fire and maneuver." This is the "piece of the combat pie" on which they thought discussion should focus. A definition common to all services is "increased and sustained danger, a high degree of stress, frequent actions in a more difficult and challenging physical environment, and an increased emphasis on both individuals and units." Having said this, the Joint Chiefs were urged to use visual depiction of direct combat as it applied to their service, for example, films from wars since World War I.

Pfluke notes that the distinctions concerning direct ground combat are as clear as mud in Bosnia. The guiding principle at work, she says, is the definition of ground combat which determines which units and which positions are open to women. She asks the reader to consider that definition— women may not serve in units that engage an enemy on the ground with weapons, are exposed to hostile fire, and have a high probability of direct physical contact with the personnel of a hostile force[93]—in the context of the average soldier in Bosnia right now. Every soldier in Bosnia carries an individual or crew-served weapon on his or her shoulder. Every soldier is trained and ready to use that weapon. There is a high probability, she writes, that a soldier will use his or her weapon. The only part of the definition missing is exposure to hostile fire. But is it, Pfluke asks, really realistic to think that only the infantry and armor units will be engaged in hostile fire? She thinks not. "If there is direct ground combat in Bosnia, women soldiers will be involved, despite the Army's convoluted assignment policy.... The Army's policy on the assignment of women is muddled, and no place is that better demonstrated than in Bosnia right now." Pfluke's explanation should make every citizen, from small-town American to the U.S. congressperson, more aware of the complexities of the Bosnian situation:

> The closed [to women] combat units are conducting reconnaissance patrols on the roads, in the villages, and throughout the countryside. But women truck drivers drive up and down these same roads every day. (If you were going to attack someone, would it be an Abrams tank or a five ton truck full of diesel fuel?) The closed combat units man checkpoints on the Bosnian roads (but so do some military police units with women. Do the men get the "dangerous" ones? How do you tell?). The closed combat units that man these checkpoints need food, fuel, water, and maintenance support every day; all brought to them by units with women. (Do we just hope that no direct ground combat occurs during lunch hour?)[94]

Linda Grant De Pauw has an answer similar to Pfluke's, but it may not be one the Joint Chiefs could totally accept. De Pauw believes women are very good at sneaking up and killing and carrying out terroristic activities:

> Women have the advantage because women can appear and nobody pays attention, and then they can set off a bomb. Women can fly now. Bosnia is largely air strikes. Women will be there. Women cannot operate tanks, but women can operate trucks loaded with gasoline. The enemy is not as likely to attack a tank, as it is to attack a gasoline truck

and therefore expose all other vehicles, including the tank. Combat exclusion preserves the image that only men do the killing.[95]

SECRETARY OF DEFENSE LES ASPIN SETS NEW POLICY

In 1993, two years after Congress repealed the Air Force combat exclusion provision of the law that prohibited women from being assigned to combat aircraft and shortly before the Navy statute was repealed, Secretary of Defense Les Aspin stated it was time to address the remaining restrictions on the assignment of women.[96] New policy opened combat ships and aircraft, and the Army and Marines were directed to study opportunities for additional assignments. (The repeal of the statutory restriction on the assignment of women in the Navy and Marine Corps became PL 103–160 on November 30, 1993.)[97]

A STUDY AND IMPLEMENTATION OF ASPIN'S POLICY

The "implementation committee," reported John Lancaster in the *Washington Post*, "completed a draft policy document that would bar assignment of women to units that 'co-locate' with ground combat units.... Other units, positions or billets will be closed to women when the probability of their engaging in direct combat on the ground is equal to or greater than that of closed units that engage in direct combat on the ground."[98] Lancaster stated that the panel contained ample representation by the military services but lacked civilian oversight to meet the Clinton administration initiative. Resistance was "stiff" from the Army and Marine Corps. A senior military officer described the proposed policy as a potentially "catastrophic" setback for women seeking wider career opportunities. The officer thought that if it were adopted, we wouldn't have women in Somalia, Bosnia, the Persian Gulf or anywhere. "It's a retrogression."

Lancaster concluded his article by saying: "It was one of those panels, chaired by Marine Lieutenant Colonel (Lt Col) Eugene D. Brindle, that recommended an expansion of the 'risk rule' under which women are excluded from certain combat specialties." The proposed policy recommended that women be excluded not just from direct combat jobs but from any unit with "a high probability of direct physical contact with the hostile force's personnel."[99]

KEEPING THE BALL IN PLAY

Pfluke points out that the study was conducted in utmost secrecy with no women involved.[100] Things were going badly. The leak to Lancaster resulted in a vicious search for the leak source and security was tightened. Pfluke thought that the Army had been the most progressive of the four services since 1974, but these events raised "the specter of the Army falling far behind the Air Force and Navy in its treatment of women, and cast doubt on whether the Army will ever welcome women into its 'core' leadership and organizational culture."[101] The Navy and Air Force acted speedily and in good faith to open their combat aircraft to women, including special operations and aircraft in close support of ground combat operations, says Pfluke. The Army sent some women to learn to fly some attack helicopters, but the Army also unilaterally announced that women would remain barred from special operations aircraft and from assignment as pilots in calvary units. "Why," Pfluke asks, "would air cavalry flight operations be ground combat, while other Army combat aviation operations and the Navy and Air Force close air support missions are not? Are some people just clinging to obsolete and arbitrary distinctions?" Pfluke considered these questions controversial, but she had more. "What about the increased roles for women the Army is supposed to be studying? This study is being conducted in utmost secrecy, deciding the fate of the careers of many women without public debate, and apparently without Army women involved in the process."

The real issue, Pfluke contends, is that women in the Navy and Air Force had the opportunity to rise to the highest positions in the service, but without being able to advance in field artillery, air defense artillery, and engineering units, army women would fall far behind. To achieve most political goals, the art of the possible lies in the art of compromise, step by step. Pfluke believes qualified women should be in direct combat, but the reality of political forces has to be dealt with, so one works to strike a balance.[102]

ASPIN PUTS A HOLD ON STUDY RELEASE

In 1994 the study was ready for release but was put on hold by Aspin. Lancaster wrote that Aspin expressed a concern that it wouldn't sufficiently expand job opportunities.[103] The policy was heavily influenced by the Army and Marine Corps, which had long resisted opening combat jobs to females, especially in ground units. Officials said the policy would continue "to exclude women from most jobs in field artillery, short-range air defense, military intelligence, combat engineering, air cavalry and 'special operations' aircraft." Aspin, who was distracted by budget and other problems, was told by his aides to take another look at the policy. As formulated, it was not what Aspin would have wanted. Or as Pfluke puts it, "The study was ready for release, but put on hold by Aspin: not good enough."

On January 12 and 13, 1994, GEN Gordon R. Sullivan, Army Chief of Staff, and Togo D. West, Jr., Secretary of the Army, named eight units they intended to open to women soldiers: maneuver brigade headquarters, division military police companies, chemical companies (reconnaissance and smoke platoons), mechanized smoke companies (smoke platoon), divisional forward support battalions (forward maintenance support teams), engineer companies (medium girder bridge and assault float bridge), collection and jamming companies (military intelligence battalions), and Washington ceremonial units. The rationale used for opening the units "is that they are only rarely part of cavalry, armor or infantry battalion task forces."[104] The decision opened approximately 7,000 additional positions to women on active duty, 1,000 in reserve, and 10,000 in the National Guard that translated, according to the memo, into an increase from 60 percent to 67 percent of active component positions open to women.[105]

DIRECT GROUND COMBAT DEFINED:
RISK RULE RESCINDED

On January 13, 1994, Aspin stated the "policy should allow U.S. servicewomen to serve in some combat support jobs from which they are now excluded because the service is rescinding the risk rule, which barred women from noncombat units where the risk was as great as that in combat units. As of today, the Risk Rule is being replaced by a less restrictive ground combat rule"[106] (see Appendix B). Women were still barred from direct ground combat. Women could not serve in units that (1) engaged an enemy on the ground with weapons, (2) were exposed to hostile fire, and (3) had a high probability of direct physical contact with the personnel of a hostile force. Now the services were to use the direct combat rule as a guide to what positions would be open.

CONTINUING EFFORTS

Pfluke does not deny that Aspin did great things, "but it comes down to how the Army and Marine Corps choose to interpret this." Major Pfluke was "very disappointed" that artillery jobs remained restricted.[107] "Army women fully expected to be allowed in Multiple Launch Rocket Systems (MLRS)," she said.[108]

SHALIKASHVILI KEEPS SPECIAL
FORCES AVIATION CLOSED TO WOMEN

GEN John Shalikashvili, the Chairman of the Joint Chiefs of Staff, successfully kept Special Operations Forces (SOF) Aviation closed to women. This directive affected approximately 1,250 positions.[109] Shalikashvili reasoned that these missions require low-altitude flights and landing, they often remain deep behind enemy lines, and the aircrews are fully integrated with ground forces in direct combat. The basis of his recommendation is physical location. Interpreting policy in this way is disconcerting if there are numerous women serving secretly in the Special Forces who get no credit or recognition for their contributions.[110]

Pfluke has pointed out that "Fifty years ago, the world was thrust into the atomic age in a brilliant flash over Hiroshima, Japan."[111] This technological advance changed our lives forever. Back in the United States, however, the cavalry still owned more than 60,000 animals. In an atomic age, Pfluke asks, "Whatever for?" Pfluke reminds us that because the horse cavalry was slow to go, it is one of the best examples in all military history of the danger of rigid thinking. The Army was unable to "recognize and respond to tremendous technological, social and cultural change."

Pfluke's analysis does not differ from what women in other branches of the services have told me. Women have been flying airplanes since the beginning of the century and they flew every type of aircraft in World War I. Women taught top fighter pilots but were not themselves allowed to fly. 1st Lt. Faith Richards, U.S. Air Force Reserve, affirms that WASPs trained men during World War II. RADM Paul Gillcrist, former U.S. Navy fighter and test pilot, agrees with this assessment in his book *Spindrift*. His wife, LT Nancy Murtagh, trained at Pensacola, Florida, where she became the first woman aviation physiologist in the Navy. Her first assignment was at the Naval Air Station in Alameda, California, where she was in charge of training all Pacific Fleet naval aviators in water survival, low-pressure chamber, night vision, ejection seat escape, and survival equipment.[112]

Women fly attack helicopters in combat aviation brigades, Pfluke points out. But in calvary units, those same trained, competent, and skilled pilots cannot fly those same helicopters. The same can be said about the Multiple Launch Rocket System (MLRS). With the rescinding of the Risk Rule, Pfluke thinks "it's tough to find any rationale for keeping those units closed to women."[113] Maybe, she writes, it is because the "combat of precision deep strike battle featuring the Multiple Launch Rocket System and the Army Tactical Missile System are edging uncomfortably close to the heart of the Army's core competency ... and we can't have women do that!" Like other interviewees, Pfluke remains optimistic, thinking this will all change, including ground combat, when new and younger leaders take over who will hire the person for the job and therefore increase readiness.

SECRETARY OF THE ARMY TOGO WEST'S
PROPOSALS TO THE SECRETARY OF DEFENSE

Togo D. West, Jr., Secretary of the Army, proposed recommendations to Secretary of Defense Aspin to open MLRS, SOF aircraft, and the air cavalry troop and its associated support positions to women. Basically, West said that the issue was not whether women would be in combat: "Women are, today, in the fight. The issue is whether obstacles have been placed in their path, preventing them from reaching their full potential. Women should be assigned to any job they can perform. We reviewed your [Secretary of Defense Aspin's] request [for a list of all units and positions closed to women and their proposed status based on implementation of the new policy] in such a light."[114]

West believed that opening the positions was a consistent application of the definition of ground combat and a demonstration of the army's commitment to expand opportunities for women. Readiness would improve because there would be a larger pool of quality soldiers, and the demonstration that the Army valued the talent and commitment of female soldiers would enhance its ability to attract and retain the highest quality women.[115]

West said the most difficult element of the definition of direct ground combat to meet was that the unit must have a "high probability of direct physical contact with the hostile force's personnel." According to West, "It is unlikely that this part of the definition is met in the case of air defense artillery, field artillery, and air cavalry." Second, West chose to use the significant flexibility provided to define the term *collocation* in a narrow sense to avoid keeping positions closed unnecessarily. West's policy recommendations included this statement: "'Collocation' [should be used] as a reason for keeping units closed only when they operate in such close proximity to direct combat units that they are almost indistinguishable from direct ground combat units—in terms of the physical demands on the soldier, source of support, physical contact, etc. If we use collocation as the rationale for keeping a broad range of positions closed, we are in essence returning to the previous 'location on the battlefield' criteria for closing positions." Third, West thought that although the air cavalry troop is assigned to the same squadron as the ground element, the aviation element operates separately.

Specific issues Secretary West addressed were combat engineering units, field artillery, air cavalry, Washington ceremonial units (which he said should be open because they have no contingency mission to deploy), and SOF units. Combat engineers' primary mission, he maintained, "is not to engage in direct ground combat, and the battalion headquarters do not routinely collocate with maneuver battalions (they operate independently or from the brigade headquarters)."

In air defense artillery, West said that the argument by the leaders of the Forward Area Air Defense (FAAD) Artillery that it should remain closed because their units engage in direct ground combat fails on two points. The definition of ground combat includes "engaging the enemy *on the ground*" along with a "high probability of direct physical contact with hostile force's personnel." The primary mission of the air defense, West wrote, is to engage the enemy in the air. The possibility of direct physical contact with the enemy exists, but it is not a part of the primary mission.

The most significant reason given for restricting the assignment of women to field artillery was the inability of these women to serve as direct support officers because these assignments mean collocating with direct combat units. West points out that there is no requirement to serve as a fire support officer (FSO), but the restriction will hamper women in field artillery. He is quick to note: "Not *all* men can serve as FSOs because there are not enough positions. In addition, the MLRS units do not provide fire support personnel to the maneuver units. The decision to restrict the assignment of women on the basis of career obstacles is a matter of personnel policy, not an issue of the direct combat rule. I believe women should be given the facts upon which to make an informed decision and have the opportunity to choose. There is no reason to close field artillery on the basis of the DOD policy."

West applied a similar logical reasoning to the air cavalry. It is assigned to the same squadron as the ground cavalry but does not experience a "high probability of direct physical contact with the hostile force's personnel" and does not collocate with direct ground combat units.

Special Operations Forces (SOF) and Ranger units engage in direct ground combat, but again, the aviation positions are not in direct ground combat units and for the most part do not appear to operate in a significantly different way than do similar conventional aviation forces such as the attack helicopter and air assault units. Although the probability of direct physical contact with the personnel of a hostile force may be higher than it is for other types of aircraft, the Joint Chiefs have not demonstrated that it is significantly so. There is also no doctrinal requirement presented for aviation units remaining with Ranger or Special Forces units to participate normally or routinely in the operation as part of the ground force. "Sharing danger does not, in itself, constitute collocation." The pilots' and crews' mission is to maintain a rapidly accessible aviation capability for a possible or future portion of a mission. Inherent in this purpose, West writes, is the avoidance of enemy detection or physical contact on the ground.

Unfortunately, West's no-nonsense and logical recommendations were not adopted. Sensible policies that remove artificial barriers for women often are not accepted. According to Pfluke, West's paper was leaked to the press and led to the disastrous results of an embarrassing and public standoff between the Secretary of the Army and the Chief of Staff of the Army. West was forced to withdraw the document, and the Secretary of Defense told the two to "work it out."

Assistant Secretary of the Army Sara E. Lister, a proponent for women but also a pragmatist, says that she and her staff sought to preserve combat effectiveness while expanding the accessible pool of high quality talent. Lister believed she understood the burden of combat and the argument that "the infantry to include special operating forces and armor units which will carry the fight directly to the enemy must inherently remain all male."[116] She argues that the same cohesion may take place in mixed-gender units, but it "would constitute an unwarranted risk to combat effectiveness of the Army." Even though women have already proven their value, bravery, and willingness to share the dangers of war, Lister says, history has demonstrated it works best this way. Lister does, however, apply West's reasoning to air defense and field artillery (cannon), and she agrees with his reasoning regarding field artillery (MLRS) and army SOF aviation positions.

General Sullivan reported that the Army review of positions resulted in the recommendations to open approximately 32,000 additional positions, increasing the total number of open positions.[117] Sullivan did not support the assignment of women to Combat Engineer Battalion Headquarters, Artillery Battalions and Batteries and Forward Area Air Defense Artillery Batteries. He reasoned that the Combat Engineer Battalion had a "mission to clear obstacles, establish breaches and crossings, demolish fortifications, and perform other close combat." Its secondary mission was "to fight as Infantry when necessary." Combat engineers "fight attached to or in support of Infantry or Armor units, generally preceding other units on the battlefield." The current doctrine, he said, indicates they fight under their own command, therefore he did not believe that women should be assigned there and, in particular, as commanders.

Currently, women are trained to use weapons, including rifles, pistols, machine guns, and hand grenades. According to Sullivan, "They [women] are fully aware that this is not just for sport target practice! There were women in advance of the ground combat units during the sweep across Iraq in the Gulf War."

MGen. Jeanne Holm, USAF, writes of several women who served in the so-called "behind the front of war lines" of the Gulf War. Army SGT Theresa Lynn Treloar's classified assignment "put her closer to the battlefront than any other American woman on the ground in Iraq."[118] It was probably an assignment so close to the front lines that it would have been considered against army policy. The camp was only a few miles from the front and was within range of Iraqi artillery. When Army LT Phoebe Jeter, the African American commander of an all-male Patriot Delta Battery of "Scudbusters," faced Scuds coming into her area carrying either chemical or conventional warheads, she ordered thirteen missiles fired, destroying at least two Scuds. "The ultimate irony, of course," says Holm, "was that by the Army's Humpty Dumpty definition, Jeter and her men had not been in 'combat.'"[119]

In a memorandum to West, Sullivan said that even though the 1988 Department of Defense Risk Rule allowed the army to expand opportunities for women, the new DOD direct ground combat definition and assignment rule had "not significantly changed the Army's combat exclusion policy. The very nature of the Army's mission, ground combat, limits the application of the new DOD assignment rule."[120]

On January 28, 1994, General Sullivan wrote that the Army had responded to the Secretary of Defense's Policy guidance.[121] More than 9,000 positions were opened to women; four women aviators completed AH-1 (Cobra) training, three completed the AH-64 (Apache) courses, and the first woman graduated from OH-58D (Kiowa Warrior). Some Special Operations Forces aircraft and some air cavalry units remained closed to women, however, because they deploy with and are assigned to ground combat units.

THE EFFORTS OF 15 CONGRESSWOMEN

The saga reached what Pfluke calls "a desperate point" when, within 72 hours of General Sullivan's statement, the proponents of opening more units in the Army were successful in getting a letter to Secretary of Defense William J. Perry that was signed by 15 congresswomen.[122] The letter stated that it was vital that the policies across services be comparable. "No service should be allowed to fall behind another in allowing women equal opportunity. Specifically, recommendations to exclude women from any aviation assignments, particularly Special Operations aircraft, are unjustifiable in light of the rescission of the risk rule and the new opportunities for women in combat aircraft." Further, they hoped that Secretary Perry would oppose attempts to exclude women from indirect ground combat, including rocket and missile artillery like MLRS and air defense.

The great effort by military and congressional women had a disappointing conclusion. The action was finally resolved on July 27, 1994, but West's recommendations to Perry were discouraging. Although some positions were to be opened to women, West stated that some units and skills should not be opened "because they meet either the direct ground combat definition or one of the exclusion provisions."[123] The units that were to remain closed were Infantry, Armor and Field Artillery Battalions, Special Forces Battalions, the Ranger Regiment, Ground Cavalry Squadrons, FAAD Artillery Batteries, and Ground Surveillance Radar Platoons (Military Intelligence). Thus an additional 32,699 positions were to be opened, and 348,301 were to remain closed.[124] The Army justified not opening some positions because "they meet either the direct combat definition or one of the exclusion provisions." In all, 67.2 percent of the army positions would be open to women.

On July 28, 1994, Secretary of Defense Perry approved each service's proposal to open additional positions to women.[125] In a letter to Senator Sam Nunn (D-Ga.), chairman of the Senate Committee on Armed Services, Perry reported actions taken to expand the roles of women in all the military services.[126] The Army, he wrote, would have open 91 percent of the career fields and 67 percent of the positions. He listed again the units that would remain closed. Previous ground combat exclusion policies prohibited assigning women to the closed units, and under the new policy these same career fields remained closed. "Therefore," he concluded, "we have not opened any positions closed by the Military Services' Ground Combat Exclusion Policies in effect on January 1, 1993." This letter signified that the remaining exclusions were intact and were being forwarded to Senator Sam Nunn for possible congressional action.

SECRETARY WILLIAM J. PERRY'S PRESS RELEASE

On July 29, 1994, Secretary of Defense Perry said that "by increasing the numbers of units and positions to which women can be assigned, the Military Services gain greater flexibility in the development and use of human resources."[127] Perry also noted that the policy changes would further enhance the already high state of readiness of the armed forces while simultaneously expanding the opportunities for women in the military.

On September 19, 1994, MAJ Christine Hallisey, USA (Ret.), and BG R. Dennis Kerr, USA, provided information on women in the Army which indicated progress with respect to the data Sullivan had released in January.[128] At the end of July 1994, women comprised 12.9 percent (71,351) of the active Army, 7.9 percent (31,606) of the Army National Guard, and 21.6 percent (49,767) of the Army Reserve. Downsizing was not expected to impede female accession or progression. As of October 1994, new defense policy resulted in 91 percent of all Army career fields and 67 percent of all Army positions being open to women. Women would be allowed in 87 percent of the enlisted military occupational specialties, 97 percent of the warrant officer specialties, and 97 percent of the officer specialties. Between April 1993 and July 1994, additional positions that opened for women numbered 41,699. On April 28, 1993, the Department of Defense had directed the services to open more specialties and assignments to women. Women were specifically admitted to combat aviation assignments.

According to an information paper, "The Direct Combat Position Coding (DCPC) System implemented the Army's policy. DCPC is the classification of each position according to the probability of direct combat. Female soldiers assigned to positions coded 'open' are subject to the same utilization policies as male soldiers and deploy with their units to perform their assigned mission."[129]

The information paper concludes that the army will open new units, positions, and specialties on October 1, 1994. "The Army assignment policy will be rewritten to reflect the new assignment rule. Women will be eligible for assignment to these newly opened units and Military Occupational Specialties (MOSs) in October 1995. Twelve women have completed aviation training and are assigned to combat helicopter units."[130] MAJ Pfluke says that when she retired in September 1995, almost one year after new units were to have been opened, many of the promised units had not yet been opened to women.[131]

LTC Karen McManus, USA, offers another version of the official story in a March 1996 article in *Army Women's Professional Association*.[132] "Today," she writes, "707,000 positions (67%) are coded open in the Total Army. The female population in the Army is 146,500 or 13.4% of the active force and fill 21% of the active Army positions open to the assignment of women. Women comprise 22.5% of the Reserves and 8.2% of the National Guard." The lower percentage in the National Guard occurs because more positions in the Guard are infantry and armor, which are closed.

McManus points to the confusion about whether women can be in combat units and serve in combat. Women have and continue to serve in combat units and deploy. She reminds us that there is no statutory restriction. She cites the 82d Airborne Division as an example where women are allowed in a divisional military police company, combat aviation brigade, division headquarters, and all brigade headquarters, but women are not allowed to serve in the infantry units below the brigade level.

McManus notes that an October 1995 visit by DACOWITS to Fort Polk, Louisiana, discovered women had not yet been integrated into positions of observer/controller. In 1996, McManus states, there were six women, officer and enlisted, filling those positions. Holly K. Hemphill, the 1996 DACOWITS chair and a civilian political appointee, says a high DACOWITS priority is checking to see that appropriate units are properly integrated. "We consolidate the gains. We try to make sure women in the jobs are not just on paper."[133] Hemphill says that DACOWITS's project is to inquire about the 250,000 jobs which are open and evaluate what they find.

POLICY EFFECT ON WOMEN: THE CASE OF THE MULTIPLE LAUNCH ROCKET SYSTEM (MLRS)

Major Pfluke says that changing the army's employment concept of the Multiple Launch Rocket System (MLRS) operations is an example of the Army's desperation to keep women out of ground combat.[134] As to the issue of collocation, Pfluke says, "How can something with a max effective range of 30 kilometers, and a minimum effective range of over 10, be considered the front line?"[135] The MLRS field manual of September 1992 says the MLRS unit is usually assigned a general support (GS) or general support reinforcing (GSR) mission. These GS or GSR assignments force artillery headquarters to accommodate the MLRS unit limitations by modifying the standard tactical mission. Further, "A mission of direct support (DS) is not appropriate for an MLRS unit because of the system characteristics and the unit structure."[136]

The Multiple Launch Rocket System employment concept was changed on September 30, 1993, however, to state that, regardless of the tactical mission, MLRS units are positioned and fight well forward and MLRS units move with the maneuver forces they support. In defense, MLRS units move laterally along the forward line of our own troops (FLOT). This allows MLRS units to take maximum advantage of their range to protect maneuver units from the destructive effects of the enemy's indirect fire systems. The range of the MLRS provides commanders with a deep strike option which translates into: "MLRS units are positioned close to the FLOT to engage the enemy at maximum ranges and to continue to attack him throughout the depth of the battlefield. Forward position is critical to accomplishing these deep missions."[137]

The significance of the changes in the Army's manual in the proper positioning of the MLRS may exclude the woman soldier. In September 1992 the manual read, "Whenever possible, MLRS battalion and battery HQ elements should position out of range of enemy artillery." This positioning, it states, can keep the enemy from determining the MLRS mission or location.[138] In September 1993 the manual was revised to state, "the MLRS units fight forward, positioned as close to the FLOT as possible, to maximize the system's ability to attack deep."[139] Fighting forward, it states, increases the risk to the soldiers because MLRS units have limited ability to defend themselves against ground attack. When the MLRS unit fires, it increases the vulnerability of all elements in the immediate vicinity to enemy fires. MAJ Pfluke is correct that the manual could be interpreted to keep women out of the MLRS unit because under the change, ground combat includes the field artillery. Pfluke pointed out that field artillery is the key to the culture of the Army. "The MLRS is a sacred cow that must remain closed at all costs. The manual itself did not keep women from the MLRS unit, it was symbolic."[140] So she concludes that, as in all conflicts, women are allowed in restricted units during necessity and when the crisis passes, women are not allowed in those units. And, I would add, since they are not "assigned" to these units, it is not likely they will be in a position to receive the recognition, honor, pay, or promotions that go with being a permanent part of the "combat elite." In 1998, DACOWITS did not accept the Army's reasons for barring women from MLRS units.

POLICY UNDER REVIEW

COL Barbara Lee, Office of the Assistant Secretary of the Army, explains:

"We are doing a complete look. We used to think women could be assigned anywhere.... We [the Army] meet with and destroy the enemy. In Saudi Arabia, when we [the Army] worked with the Saudi Defense (National Guard), women were not allowed in their buildings. The cultural norms of Saudi Arabia did not make women desirable soldiers. We'd be setting a female up for a failure, so we exclude women [in a situation like that]. Looking at positions to be opened is an ongoing process. It is a bureaucratic paper drill. We have to be fair to the Army at large and at the same time, not impede career paths."[141]

According to Lee, many positions are now open. She explains that from a practical point of view, if only 14 percent of the Army is women and the Army allows women in 90 percent of the positions, there won't be the number of women needed to fill these positions.

All things considered, Lee thinks that women are doing very well and that the integration of women is a long-term change. It takes 15 to 20 years to develop a battalion commander, which means that interested soldiers must begin this path early in their career. Lee concludes: "There is a lot of desire to maintain the status quo. It takes a lot of effort. It isn't all fixed, but we are on the road. We could do better, but we are doing pretty good, give a high mark."

History demonstrates progress, states Lee. The first graduating class at the U.S. Military Academy that included women was in 1980, and ROTC was graduating women in 1976. Lee believes that women are being trained in the same way as their male peers. If women don't have training, they don't get the position, and women are getting the training.

Major Pfluke agrees that considerable progress has been made since 1976 when she began her long journey in support of women in the army. She says that if she had been able to foresee the future back in 1976, she might have gotten discouraged because progress has been slow. But her dedication to the military is unmistakably positive: "The military service is a tremendous opportunity. The only limitation is by ability. It is a way to make something of yourself. It is a better opportunity to do so than in society because the military provides a person with a fair chance. You start even."[142]

In the fall of 1996, the press released an August 1995 Pentagon message intended to spur units to code properly their Tables of Organization and Equipment (TOEs) to open positions for women.[143] This Pentagon release referenced messages related to expanded roles for women in the Army. The Pentagon stated that the assignment process would begin based on the August 1995 message that the Army could open three new military occupational specialties (MOS) and over 32,000 positions in over sixteen different types units. As a result, 91 percent of the career fields and 67 percent of the army's positions were to be "gender neutral."[144] Specific units to be opened by October 1995 included division military police companies, chemical reconnaissance and smoke platoons (chemical companies), smoke platoons (mechanized smoke companies), engineer bridge companies, military intelligence collection and jamming companies, forward support teams of forward support battalions, a military police platoon attached to the 3d Infantry (Old Guard) Regiment, regimental aviation squadrons of the armored cavalry regiments, and the air cavalry troops of the divisional cavalry squadrons.

The following military occupational specialties (MOS) would also open: engineer bridge crewmember—12C, combat engineer senior sergeant—12Z, and field artillery surveyor—82C. Women would also be eligible for assignment to all MOSs and areas of concentration (AOCs) in the following headquarters (HDQRS): Maneuver and Separate Brigades, 3d Infantry (Old Guard) Regiment, Armored Cavalry Regiments, Headquarters and Headquarters Company (HHC), 160th Aviation Group, Special Forces Groups, Chaparral Air

Defense Artillery Battalions, Divisional Air Defense Artilleries, Corps Avenger Air Defense Battalions, and Combat Engineers.

The units that were not to be opened because they met either the direct ground combat definition or one of the exclusion provisions were Infantry Battalions, Armor Battalions, Field Artillery Battalions, Special Forces Battalions, the Ranger Regiment, Ground Cavalry Squadrons, FAAD Artillery Batteries, Combat Engineer Companies, and Ground Surveillance Radar Platoons (Military Intelligence.)

Guidance provided to clarify the assignment of women to aviation unit maintenance organization was three-pronged: "A) All positions within aviation squadrons organic to armored cavalry regiments, to include the aviation maintenance troop, are open to women; B) All authorized positions of the aviation unit maintenance troop organic to the 101st Airborne Division are open to the women; and C) The aviation unit maintenance units assigned to division cavalry squadrons organized with ground and air troops remain closed to women."

Guidance provided to clarify assignment of women in combat engineers stated: "The positions of commander, executive officer, and operations officer in the Combat Engineer Battalion Headquarters are open to women, as are all positions within the Combat Engineer Battalion Headquarters and headquarters to companies. This includes regimental and brigade engineers assigned to separate engineer companies of Armored Cavalry Regiments and separate brigades. Only the combat engineer line companies remained closed to women."

Finally, the message directed that army policy on the assignment of women be rewritten (AR 600–13) to reflect the new policy. Further, as the assignment opportunities for women were expanded, the Army was to have gender-integrated basic training. Career opportunities for women were to be expanded while simultaneously maintaining combat readiness of the force.

In 1993 a message intended to clarify Army policy on coding of Tables or Distribution and Allowances (TDAs) explained that except for a few positions, all positions in TDA units would be coded gender neutral. According to the message, "Since TDA positions are not established for missions involving direct combat, TDA positions should be open to females in most cases."[145]

The message also provided instructions for coding positions: "TDA positions may be coded gender specific (male only or female only) if there is a valid need for such coding. That the MOS is closed to females is not sufficient reason to code the position closed to females." Even if a TDA position required a MOS closed to females, it would still be coded interchangeable unless gender specificity was approved by headquarters.

Based on the data I have obtained, I have been unable to determine whether there are any women in the new positions opened in 1994, including the Combat Engineer Battalion Headquarters, Armored Cavalry Regiment

Table 5.1
Women in New Positions in U.S. Army, July 1996

	Number of *Women Assigned*	*Percent of* *Open Positions* *Filled by Women*
Combat Engineer Battalion Headquarters	163	5%
Armored Cavalry Regimental Headquarters	68	35%
Special Forces Group Headquarters	24	7%
Air Defense Artillery Battalion Headquarters	98	10%

Source: LTC John S. Westwood, USA, Chief, Leadership Division, letter to Rosemarie Skaine, November 14, 1996.

Headquarters, Special Forces Group Headquarters, and Chaparral Air Defense Artillery Battalion Headquarters. In November of 1996, I wrote a letter to Secretary of the Army Togo West to find out the current status of the units newly open to women in 1994. I asked if they are in fact open to women, if women are being assigned to them and if women are currently serving in them?[146]

LTC John S. Westwood, USA, Chief of the Leadership Division, explains, "The authorization documents that list all Army positions provide a code which identifies whether a position is open or closed to the assignment of women or men."[147] In October 1995, the coding was completed. Westwood says that authorization documents and "gender" codes are periodically updated to reflect organizational structure changes. There are units comprised of career fields open to women and career fields closed to women. According to Westwood, "The positions that should be coded open are indeed properly coded on the authorization documents. These documents are reviewed quarterly to ensure execution of policy. The quarterly review also includes a report on the number of women actually assigned to these newly opened positions."

To answer my question regarding the assignment of women, Westwood supplied the data listed in Table 5.1. Westwood stresses that these figures only reflect a "snapshot in time" and could be higher or lower on any given day. He concludes, "As of July 1996, the active Army had 36 female battalion commanders and seven female brigade commanders. In 1997, women will take command for the first time of an Aerial Exploitation Battalion and a Field Artillery Battalion."[148] In October 1997, RAND found that women held only 815 of more than 47,000 additional jobs opened to women over the previous three years. Dana Priest said that the Army's approach was intentionally slow and nonconfrontational according to the December 28, 1997, *Washington Post.*

Chapter 6

The American Public*
by James C. Skaine†
and Rosemarie Skaine

In the controversy surrounding women in the military and women in combat, the opponents contend that the American public does not want women in combat and that having women in combat runs counter to deeply held values of the American public. Over the years, the appeal to the public's beliefs and values has been a powerful one for those who argued that women should be restricted to noncombat roles. Two questions must be considered: who is the American public and what does the American public believe about women in combat?

WHO IS THE AMERICAN PUBLIC?

The question about who the American public is can be answered in several ways. One way to answer is to say that each of us is a part of the American public. As citizens of the United States of America, we are the American public. But, are we a meaningful part of the voice of American public? We are not always sure. It is difficult to draw definitive conclusions about what is or what is not amenable to the American public. In 1993, Congressman Roscoe Bartlett (R-Md.), a member of the Subcommittee on Military Forces and Personnel of the House Committee on Armed Services, said the question of who the American public is has always puzzled him.[1] Does the Congress as a representative of the public reflect the wishes of the American public and speak

* *Appreciation is expressed to Surendar Yadava, Department of Sociology, Anthropology, and Criminology, University of Northern Iowa, for statistical assistance.*

† *Professor James C. Skaine, Communication Studies, University of Northern Iowa, has served as president, chief negotiator, and academic freedom and professional rights chair for United Faculty, the faculty union.*

for it? Is the American public represented by those people who speak to Congress?

When he was asked, "Is the American public only those voices speaking through Congress? Do we know who is the American public?" ADM Stanley R. Arthur, USN, replied, "I think of the American public as the parents, grandparents, brothers and sisters, husbands and wives of our service members and potential service members."[2] He does not believe Congress is the American public.

In 1992, Mady Segal and Amanda Hansen examined the issue of what part of the American public consists of those who speak to Congress at hearings. They analyzed the explicit values expressed in congressional testimony on laws governing American military women from 1941 to 1985.[3] They concluded that more research is needed to analyze other forms of public discourse such as the media that also reflect and affect cultural norms. Testimony at hearings reflects the political culture of a particular time but is not necessarily representative of the larger society. In that case, testimony at hearings is part of the American public concept.

Segal and Hansen have analyzed the characteristics of the speakers, who testified before Congress. Most speakers, 69 percent, were male. The number of women testifying was highest during periods of greatest activity; for example, 41 percent of the speakers testifying in the 1980s were women. Second, the policy positions that speakers advocated dealt mostly with what assignments should be open to women. None of those who spoke in the 1940s, 1950s, or 1960s advocated assigning women to combat. "It was simply not an issue," say Segal and Hanson. Not until the 1970s did it become an issue. The draft issue surfaced in the 1940s and the 1980s. In the 1940s, 4 out of 33 speakers favored drafting women. In the 1980s, 11 speakers favored drafting women, but 48 gave statements that were negative toward women's military participation. Third, testimony of speakers was evenly divided during all decades on "whether their arguments appealed to military effectiveness only, to citizenship rights and responsibilities only, or to both." Those who testify at congressional hearings of course constitute a part of the American public, but only a part.

CPT A. Dwight Raymond, USA, answers the question "Who is the American public?" by examining the role of all its parts with the help of *A Theory of Justice* by John A. Rawls. Government institutions reflect interpretations of just principles. The institution's political legitimacy is not absolute, and moral legitimacy is a separate issue. The "final court of appeal is not the court nor the executive nor the legislature but the electorate as a whole."[4] In other words, says Raymond, the leaders are legitimatized by the institution and the institution is politically legitimized by the will of the people. Popular opinion offers guidance about what is politically legitimate but not moral legitimacy. Raymond draws upon the work of Peter Berger to say that the masses can be wrong, society is not as democratic as it should be, it tends to reflect what people think.[5]

THE POLLS AND SURVEYS OF THE AMERICAN PUBLIC

A January 1990 CBS News/*New York Times* poll asked 1557 adults nationwide whether women members of the armed forces should be allowed to serve in combat units if they want to. Seventy-two percent said women should be allowed to do so, while 26 percent said they should not.[6] In January 1990, in the aftermath of the invasion of Panama, Congresswoman Patricia Schroeder (D-Colo.) proposed a four-year experiment in which women would serve in army units such as the infantry and tank corps. In February 1990, Schroeder and *McCall's* magazine conducted a survey of 755 American women on whether they approved of combat duty for women. Seventy-nine percent said they approved of combat for women in general and 60 percent said they would not oppose it for their daughters. In the poll, 83 percent of women between 18 and 45 said they favored combat for women, while 74 percent of those over 45 approved of the idea. *McCall's* said, "It is time for any barrier to women's full acceptance in the military to be shed. It is time for the ban on women in combat to be lifted.[7]

An NBC News/*Wall Street Journal* poll in September 1990 asked the question, "Do you feel it is acceptable or unacceptable for the United States to send women on military missions where they may be involved in combat?" Seventy-three percent said it was acceptable, and 23 percent said it was unacceptable. Seventy-one percent of the men and 74 percent of the women said it was acceptable.[8]

On February 5, 1991, the *Orlando Sentinel Tribune* reported the results of its telephone poll of 1,626 callers to the newspaper. The majority, 878 (54 percent), said women should be allowed to serve in combat zones and 748 (46 percent) said they should not be allowed to do so.[9]

THE U.S. PRESIDENTIAL COMMISSION'S POLLS AND SURVEYS

The U.S. Presidential Commission on the Assignment of Women in the Armed Forces as part of its mission had polls and surveys conducted to determine the attitudes of a range of populations.

The Commission's survey research produced mixed results. Dr. Charles Moskos, commissioner and military sociologist at Northwestern University, and Laura Miller surveyed soldiers to determine whether they agreed that women should no longer be excluded from combat roles.[10] MAJ Mary Finch, a commissioner, believed that the survey was biased, but that it did appear to clarify a major argument, "the belief that it is only a few women officers who are in favor of expanding the roles for women in the military to further their own careers."[11] Testimony before the Commission agreed with the finding. Miller and Moskos found that 70 percent of female officers, 77 percent of female noncommissioned officers, and 75 percent of enlisted women believe that women should be allowed to volunteer for combat roles.

The Presidential Commission hired the Roper Organization to conduct two polls. CAPT Georgia Clark Sadler, USN (Ret.), has analyzed the results of these surveys (see Table 6.1). One survey, the Roper Organization Survey of the American Public, was a random telephone survey of 1,700 adult Americans, and the second, the Roper Organization Survey of the U.S. Military, was a written survey of 4,422 active and reserve military personnel. In general, the American public was more supportive of women in combat than was the American military, with the Navy and Air Force leading the way in favor and the Army opposing and the Marine Corps adamantly opposing.[12] Both civilian and military polls demonstrated support for drafting women even if an ample pool of young men were available. As for assigning women to direct combat, the public was evenly split, but the majority of the military opposed it. The navy was the only service in which a majority supported assigning women to direct combat. If women were given a choice, the public and the military favored women in combat, although the military was less supportive of women in ground combat.[13]

Sadler notes that the Roper poll revealed three main trends in the 1990s. First, both the public and the military support women serving in combat, but the military did not support direct ground combat. Both said that it would not have a negative impact on national security, but they believed men and women with young children, especially single parents, should not serve in combat.[14] Seventy percent of the public and 57 percent of the military thought the effect would be positive or neutral.[15]

On the issue of prisoners of war (POWs), 51 percent of the military compared to 44 percent of the public responded that women shouldn't be subjected to the same possibility of capture as men. Again the Navy expressed the least concern, with 40 percent, and the Marine Corps the highest, at 67 percent.[16]

On the question of whether the presence of women would erode bonding, 54 percent of the military said it would, but only 41 percent of the public did.[17] A consistent response was that most Navy personnel agreed with all seven reasons for women serving in direct combat and most marine personnel disagreed with all seven.[18]

Both the public and the military thought women should not serve in direct combat if pregnant, two-thirds of the public thought single mothers should be excused and one-half to three-fourths of the military thought so. Fewer military respondents than public respondents would excuse the married mother. Half of the military and half of the public thought single male parents should be excused, but 43 percent of the public and 14 percent of the

Table 6.1
Roper Poll Concerning the Assignment of
Women to Different Types of Combat Situations

Type of Assignment	Not Assign	Voluntary	Require
Assign to Combat Ships?			
Public	17%	51%	29%
Military	29%	39%	30%
Assign to Combat Aircraft?			
Public	18%	53%	25%
Military	30%	43%	25%
Assign to Ground Combat?			
Public	27%	45%	25%
Military	49%	30%	19%

Source: CAPT Georgia Clark Sadler, USN (Ret.), "The Polling Data," *Proceedings of the U.S. Naval Institute* 119:2 (February 1993): 52.

military thought a married male parent should be excused. Regarding dual military couples, 55 percent of the public and 65 percent of the military thought the wife should be exempt from combat, but only two percent and one percent respectively thought the husband should be exempt.[19]

The Commission's survey of retired flag and general officers found that most did not favor assigning women to combat roles.[20] According to MAJ Finch, opponents of women in combat argued that the only experts on the issue are military and particularly retired senior officers because they have "real" combat experiences.[21] Finch notes that "this group is also the oldest, had the least exposure to women in the military and the most stereotypical views of women in general."[22]

OTHER STUDIES OF WOMEN IN
THE MILITARY AND COMBAT[23]

Pamela Conover and Virginia Sapiro conducted a study that drew on the American National Election Study 1991 Pilot Study. They found gender bases are more complex than many theorists have thought.[24] Their study showed women are more afraid of the prospects of war and more wary of foreign involvements, but when given justifications, they are as willing as men to ponder the use of force.

For questions concerning the Gulf War, the distance separating women and men grew, and on every measure, women reacted more negatively. The gender differences were most pronounced for emotional responses such as fears about hypothetical wars and distress over the Gulf War. This suggests gender differences are socially constructed and contextually driven. Early in life girls learn to put off the use of violence until later in the course of conflict and then they escalate more slowly and are more emotionally upset by the situation. Women would thus react more to "real" situations.

The most intriguing difference in male and female attitudes that Conover and Sapiro found is the greater impact of partisanship on men's attitudes about militarism and war. On six of seven dependent variables, partisanship was a significant predictor of men's attitudes, but for women it was insignificant in every case. It could be, Conover and Sapiro say, that men's reactions to the use of military force may be more available for politicization, for being organized by the agendas of institutionalized politics, than are women's. They did not find, however, the difference carrying over to domestic issues involving violence. This could mean that women's partisan ties are weakening. Disheartened by Republican rule and skeptical about Democratic promises, women may just be relying less on partisan cues. Conover and Sapiro believe that if this is the explanation, we would expect to find gender differences in the effects of partisanship on a wide range of issues, not just issues of violence. More research is clearly needed.

Conover and Sapiro also say the stereotype is that men are militaristic and perpetrators and women are pacifist and victims.[25] In the latter part of the twentieth century, women have been less supportive of militarism and U.S. involvement in World War II, Korea, and Vietnam by an average margin of 7 to 9 percentage points.[26] Recently women have been less likely to support defense spending.[27] Conover and Sapiro conclude that American women are hardly pacifists but are less militaristic than men. In summary, there is a gender base to the orientations. There is a need to recognize the subtle ways these gender bases interact with other attitudes to shape foreign policy stances. The UN finding that women are underrepresented and unrecognized in decision-making positions and should be empowered politically and economically and represented at all levels of decision-making demonstrates one of the subtleties.[28]

A Study of College Student Perspectives

We conducted a survey of college students as a significant aspect of the American public. We surveyed 889 college students in six universities and colleges in the midwestern and eastern United States. The respondents provided demographic data on age, classification (freshman, sophomore, etc.), marital status, and gender. They also provided information on whether they had served in the Reserve Officers Training Corps (ROTC) or in the military (Tables 6.2–6.7). The typical respondent was a female who was 20 years old, a sophomore, had never married, had no military service, and was attending a large midwestern university.

Table 6.2
Gender of Respondents to Skaine Opinion Poll

Gender	Number	Valid Percent
Female	486	55.3%
Male	393	44.7%
Total	879	100.0%

Missing Cases: 10

Table 6.3
Age of Respondents to Skaine Opinion Poll

Age	Number	Valid Percent
18 or under	181	20.5%
19–21	523	59.1%
22–26	122	13.8%
27–35	26	2.9%
36 and over	33	3.7%
Total	885	100.0%

Missing Cases: 4

Table 6.4
Classification of Respondents to Skaine Opinion Poll

Classification	Number	Valid Percent
Freshman	369	41.9%
Sophomore/Junior	367	41.7%
Senior	101	11.4%
Graduate	22	2.5%
Unclassified	22	2.5%
Total	881	100.0%

Missing Cases: 8

The survey contained items on a range of issues concerning women in the military and combat. On the items "In the workforce, males hold the higher positions" and "In the military, males hold the higher ranks," 64.1 percent and 82 percent respectively of the respondents agreed and 27 percent and 8.9 percent disagreed (Table 6.8). The respondents clearly believe that men hold the higher positions in the workforce and by a higher margin believe that it is men who hold the higher ranks in the military.

The respondents indicated that they believe that neither men nor women

Table 6.5
Marital Status of Respondents to Skaine Opinion Poll

Marital Status	Number	Valid Percent
Single, never married	797	91.9%
Married	51	5.9%
Divorced, separated, widowed	19	2.2%
Total	867	100.0%

Missing Cases: 22

Table 6.6
Service in ROTC of Respondents to Skaine Opinion Poll

Served in ROTC	Number	Valid Percent
Yes	61	6.9%
No	818	93.1%
Total	879	100.0%

Missing Cases: 10

Table 6.7
Service in the Military of Respondents to Skaine Opinion Poll

Served in Military	Number	Valid Percent
Yes	47	5.4%
No	820	94.6%
Total	867	100.0%

Missing Cases: 22

want to go to war. When presented with the statements, "Most males do not want to go to war" and "Most females do not want to go to war," 61.2 percent of the respondents agreed that most men do not want to go to war and 13.2 percent disagreed. Seventy-five percent (75.1 percent) agreed that most females do no want to go to war and 7.4 percent disagreed (Table 6.9).

The results of questions relating to military families appear in Table 6.10. Seventy percent (70.3 percent) said that military life is equally hard for the mother and father and 12.2 percent said that it was not. Similarly, the respondents said that parenting in the United States is considered to be the responsibility of both the father and the mother. Seventy-eight percent (77.6 percent) agreed and 14.1 percent disagreed. The percentage of the respondents that

Table 6.8
Skaine Opinion Poll Concerning Higher Positions in Workforce and Military

Survey Item	SA* No. %	A No. %	N No. %	D No. %	SD No. %	Total No. %
Workforce males hold the higher positions.	169 19.1	402 45.5	162 18.4	93 10.5	57 16.5	883 100.0
Military males hold the higher ranks.	403 45.6	321 36.4	81 9.1	43 4.9	35 4.0	883 100.0

Missing Cases: 6

*SA—strongly agree; A—agree; N—neutral; D—disagree; SD-strongly disagree

Table 6.9
Skaine Opinion Poll Concerning Desire to Go to War

Survey Item	SA* No. %	A No. %	N No. %	D No. %	SD No. %	Total No. %
Most males do not want to go to war.	183 20.8	355 40.4	225 25.6	79 9.0	37 4.2	879 100.0
Most females do not want to go to war.	311 35.4	349 39.7	153 17.5	43 4.9	22 2.5	878 100.0

Missing Cases: 10 and 11

*SA—strongly agree; A—agree; N—neutral; D—disagree; SD—strongly disagree

agreed dropped on the item "In the United States, other than the biological act of birth, the mother and father are asked to take equally responsible parenting roles," and the number of respondents who disagreed increased: (55.6 percent) agreed that the roles were equally responsible and 31.5 percent disagreed.

Some opponents of women in combat argue that placing women in combat positions affects a woman's fertility. The college students we surveyed clearly do not agree. Only 11.5 percent agreed that "allowing females in combat threatens the fertility rate," and 68.2 percent disagreed (Table 6.10).

In the all-voluntary force, the draft is not an issue at this point but registering for the draft still is. Currently, only males are required to register for the draft. More college students agreed than disagreed that if men are drafted,

Table 6.10
Skaine Opinion Poll Concerning
Military Life, Parenting, and Fertility

Survey Item	SA* No. %	A No. %	N No. %	D No. %	SD No. %	Total No. %
Military life is equally hard for the mother and father.	225 25.8	388 44.5	153 17.5	90 10.3	17 1.9	873 100.0
Parenting in U.S. is considered to be responsibility of both the father and the mother.	418 47.6	263 30.0	73 8.3	90 10.2	34 3.9	878 100.0
In the U.S., other than biological act of birth, the mother and father are asked to take equally responsible parenting roles.	189 21.6	297 34.0	113 12.9	221 25.3	54 6.2	874 100.0
Allowing females in combat threatens the fertility rate.	37	64	178	337	261	877

Missing Cases: 16, 11, 15, and 12

*SA—strongly agree; A—agree; N—neutral; D—disagree; SD—strongly disagree.

women should be also. (Table 6.11). Forty-four percent (44.1 percent) agreed and 33.5 percent disagreed. Forty-seven percent (47.0 percent) agreed, and 32.3 percent disagreed that if men are required to register for the draft, women should be also.

The military does not assign women to all combat units. Even after the combat exclusion provisions were repealed, policy remains which restricts women from being assigned to specific combat units. In response to the statement "Congress should lift all restrictions on women serving in combat," 46.4 percent of the survey respondents agreed and 28.3 percent disagreed. They were even stronger in their response to the statement "women should be allowed only in noncombatant military positions." Only 22.6 percent agreed but 51% disagreed (Table 6.11).

The relationship between serving in combat positions and rising to the highest ranks in the military has been a strong one over time. The response of college students in our survey to the statement "Admitting women to combat opens for them the coveted ranks within the military" shows that they understand this relationship. Fifty-seven percent (57.4 percent) agreed with the statement, and only 14.6 percent disagreed (Table 6.12).

The treatment of women in the military has been a subject of controversy

Table 6.11
Skaine Opinion Poll Concerning
Draft and Combat Restrictions

Survey Item	SA* No. %	A No. %	N No. %	D No. %	SD No. %	Total No. %
If men drafted, women should be also.	154 17.9	225 26.2	192 22.4	168 19.5	120 14.0	859 100.0
If men required to register for draft, women should be also.	158 18.4	245 28.6	178 20.7	161 18.7	117 13.6	859 100.0
Congress should lift restrictions on women serving in combat.	157 18.3	240 28.1	208 24.3	139 16.2	112 13.1	856 100.0
Women should be allowed only in non-combatant positions.	79 9.4	111 13.2	222 26.4	264 31.4	165 19.6	841 100.0

Missing Cases: 30, 30, 33 and 48

*SA—strongly agree; A—agree; N—neutral; D—disagree; SD—strongly disagree.

over the years. The sexual harassment and abuse charges in connection with the Tailhook Convention of navy personnel in 1991 and the Aberdeen Proving Grounds in 1996 are two notable examples of negative treatment. One cause of the wrongful treatment of military women may be resentment that women are being admitted to combat positions. Forty-nine percent (49.7 percent) agreed that the wrongful treatment of women in the military is the result of remaining resentment of women being admitted to combat, and 25.2 percent disagreed. By a 3–1 margin (40.7 percent agreed to 13.2 percent disagreed), the respondents agreed that "eradicating sexual harassment should increase military readiness" (Table 6.12).

Opponents of women in combat raise the issue of women being taken as prisoners of war (POWs) if they are placed in combat positions. They invoke the cultural value that men should strive to protect women from harm. Their argument conflicts, however, with another cultural value: we should not betray our country by providing information to the enemy, thereby committing treason. In our survey, two statements, "Men will provide information to an enemy who threatens to torture a female POW" and "Women will provide information to an enemy who threatens to torture a male POW," found half of the students responding "neutral" (49.2 percent and 50.9 percent respectively) (Table 6.12). On both statements, however, more students disagreed than agreed. Twenty-three percent (23.5 percent) agreed but 27.2 percent disagreed that men would provide information to the enemy. Nineteen percent (19.2 percent) agreed and 29.9 percent disagreed that women would do so. The results are

Table 6.12
Skaine Opinion Poll Concerning Bonding and Treatment of Men and Women

Survey Item	SA* No. %	A No. %	N No. %	D No. %	SD No. %	Total No. %
Admitting women to combat combat opens coveted ranks within military for them.	105 12.3	386 45.1	240 28.0	83 9.7	42 4.9	856 100.0
Wrongful treatment of women in military is due to remaining resentment of women being admitted to combat.	97 11.3	329 38.4	215 25.1	158 18.5	57 6.7	856 100.0
Eradicating sexual harassment should increase military readiness.	67 7.9	278 32.8	390 46.1	80 9.4	32 3.8	847 100.0
Men will provide information to enemy who threatens to torture female POW.	35 4.1	166 19.4	420 49.2	181 21.2	52 6.1	854 100.0
Women will provide information to enemy who threatens to torture male POW.	29 3.4	135 15.8	435 50.9	196 23.0	59 6.9	854 100.0
Pledge men and women make to give their lives may be bond that leads to equality.	126 14.7	372 43.4	209 24.4	113 13.2	37 4.3	857 100.0

Missing Cases: 33, 33, 42, 35, 35 and 32

*SA—strongly agree; A—agree; N—neutral; D—disagree; SD—strongly disagree.

not conclusive, but they do indicate that more college students do not believe that either men or women would provide information to the enemy under such circumstances than believe they would. The data do not support the position of those who say that women should not be in combat because men in the military would provide information to enemy to prevent a woman from being tortured or that women would provide information to protect men from harm.

One statement in the survey that focused on what might be the basis for men and women in the military to bond and reach equality was "the pledge that men and women make to give their lives may be the bond that leads to equality." Fifty-eight percent (58.1 percent) of the respondents agreed and 17.5 percent disagreed (Table 6.12). This response offers hope that the young men and women who are part of the population that will join the military believe that men and women in the services can bond and be equal as they serve.

The American public is dynamic as it moves through time. A cherished position in one era is discarded for another. The public has not always supported women in the military. Today it does. The public has not always supported women serving in combat positions. Today it does.

Chapter 7

Sociological Theory and the Evolution of Combat

Vive la différence!

A slender, young male ended his presentation at a women's conference by saying that "vive la différence" may be the only generalized difference between women and men. And these days, as one military male put it, "la différence" is openly admitted to exist between members of the same gender. So what are the general differences between the genders when it comes to qualifying for combat in armed conflict? If there are differences, can they be generalized? Can we apply all differences unilaterally for all women and all men? "Vive la différence" has taught us otherwise. Differences clearly exist among all people.

Whatever the gender issue, can a woman break down her existing self-concept, a process that, according to Louis Zurcher, makes it possible to instill a new one?[1] Do the smoke-screen issues surrounding the assignment of women in combat such as pregnancy or hygiene functions, for example, mean a definite no? Zurcher focuses on the discontinuity of socialization in naval boot camp. As an example of Ervin Goffman's "total institution," the camp translates into isolation from the outside world.[2] The recruits' physical needs and activities are planned. Boot camp challenges civilian values such as freedom, privacy, integrity, and even the ability to determine one's own appearance. In fact, Zurcher states, the Navy assaults these values as a means of breaking down the assumptions and experiences of any former life. The recruit is told when to eat, sleep, take care of bodily functions, write a letter home, where and how to store his bedding and gear. The boot marches in formation wherever she or he goes unless special permission is given. The recruit must come to attention in a special position. The list goes on.

Zurcher points out that responses from civilian life are no longer appropriate, whether one was a student, son or daughter, sweetheart, or part-time

grocery clerk. The authority figures in these former roles are compartmental-
ized. Any staff person in the recruit's service branch can correct the recruit at
any time. The recruit will replace old responses with new as he or she learns
what Goffman calls the institutional privilege system.[3] Zurcher's application
of Goffman's theory relates to the military of today. Language that might have
been forbidden in civilian life is not off limits in the military. Obscene language may become simply the language of the group.[4] In the heat of armed
conflict, more explicit salty language may be acceptable in mixed gender units.
It may not be acceptable in some circumstances in either military or civilian
life. The focus of this book, however, is combat.

Which of Goffman's four ways would a female recruit react while undergoing role dispossession-repossession within a total institution: situational
withdrawal, intransigent role, colonization, or conversion?[5] In 1995, after a
two-and-one-half year court fight to become the first female cadet at the
Citadel, Shannon Faulkner quit after less than a week.[6] She was overweight,
and she was worn-out from her legal battle. Five male cadets landed in the
infirmary from heat-related illness. According to Rosemary Yardley, no one
faulted the physical condition of the 23 male cadets who also quit, nor were
there cheers when the male dropouts left.[7] Faulkner was a lone 20-year-old
woman in a very hostile institutional environment. Some asked, "Did she leave
the Citadel totally because of heat exhaustion?" Implied in their question is
another question: "Did she withdraw from the situation because she was not
able to be repossessed within the total institution of the Citadel?" If she left
because she was unable to be repossessed and was physically qualified, then,
in all probability, she experienced situational withdrawal. Bionic men and
women do get sick. They also get well. She could have stayed, lived through
the heat exhaustion, gotten well, and converted to Citadel life. According to
Zurcher's boot camp analogy, Faulkner did not "find a home in the Citadel."
Faulkner, for whatever reasons, found that the Citadel challenged her civilian
self-concept. A military woman said, "Why I would have been the meanest,
toughest recruit." If Faulkner had done what this military woman would have
done, she would have converted.

Anne-Marie Hilsdon says that for the female recruit there is the double
transformation ritual: civilian to military and female to male. "The sense of
exclusivity of the military force is bolstered by the inferiorisation of civilians
and women. Military women however, present an internal contradiction to this
process. How is their differential embodiment produced?"[8] Hilsdon's research
based upon the armed forces of the Philippines examines "how gender and sexuality are transmission belts for the inculcating of military discipline, and vice
versa." Military institutions, she says, "are saturated with a masculine culture
of technologies."[9] Through the process of discipline and punishment, women
learn "to be 'tough'—control emotions, to act ruthlessly and to take orders."[10]
Male trainers insisted the women were men because the women entered a

"male" course. Hilsdon explains that crying, for example, was viewed as inferior, female, forbidden, and civilian. Treatment of women as men was curtailed during meetings, administering punishments, and social gatherings, where women were looked upon as children. The complexity of female soldiering increased, says Hilsdon, when women were required to retain civilian forms of gender and sexuality such as acting as an entertainer at a military social. Regardless of the context, "civilian" appearance and behavior belied expectations of military propriety. Thus, she concludes, "The feared 'disorder' of female sexuality was controlled effectively through invoking military discipline."[11]

Hilsdon notes that the military disciplinary discourses and mechanisms are specifically gendered, and she offers dress as an example. Female soldiers contradict military or masculine representation in oppositional relation with civilian women and children, but soldiering in a male body remains different from soldiering in a female body. The soldier is always produced as male. Females are often defeminized as lesbians, which separates them from other women, or deprofessionalized, which distances them from men.[12]

Nonetheless, practically speaking, Shannon Faulkner made a difference in her pre–Citadel fight. In allowing her to become the first female to be admitted to the all-male bastion, the Citadel broke with its own tradition. Other women have accepted the challenge of entrance with more ease because of Faulkner, their foremother, and have become repossessed and converted to the sanctioned (and changing) role the Citadel offers.

But progress seldom follows a straight line forward. In 1996 two female cadets filed a complaint of hazing. As a result one male cadet was temporarily expelled and five others were suspended. Two of the four women enrolled alleged that upperclassmen had sprayed their clothes with a flammable liquid and lit it in a hazing incident. The four female cadets study with 580 males. Maj. Roger Poole, interim president of the Citadel said the lighting of a flammable liquid was not a prank cadets had to endure. Hazing is illegal in South Carolina.[13]

Times are changing, says Dirk Johnson, with the Navy now having mixed-gender training divisions. The new approach is to mix the number of men and women. Whenever a minority is created, so is the potential for problems. The Army and Air Force sprinkle women into training units in smaller percentages. The Marines do not mix women and men in basic training, but do mix in recruit training. CAPT Cory Whitehead, the first woman to serve as the commander of the Great Lakes Naval Training Center, now the Navy's only boot camp, does not rule with the traditional fear and intimidation approach. Mixing men and women was done mainly for logistical reasons, but many modifications have been made to change explicitly the atmosphere of intimidation that could lead to sexual harassment.[14]

Captain Whitehead makes boot camp more humane. She assigned a chaplain to each training ship and told commanders that psychological services are available for recruits, and said the commanders should come to her for help. The obstacle course is now called the "confidence course."

When the soldier leaves the military as well as when she or he enters it, the rules governing daily lives change abruptly.[15] Killing once again becomes homicide, and foraging, theft, incendiarism, arson, and strong, salty language become incorrect. Linderman writes that combat overthrew the original views of Union soldiers during the Civil War, while initial conceptions of the war by people at home remained unchanged. Returning soldiers tended to resist the expectations to discuss combat because it was painful and they were readjusting to civilian life. Civilians wanted to know how much the foe had been damaged, but soldiers could not always provide this information, even if they wished because intense combat produced a narcotic effect. Their perceptions of what they had done from one battle to the next blurred. Combat's painful nature, combined with the need to convert to societal expectations, made the Union soldier isolate his "military self." Civilian life was now his "total institution," translating into isolation from the military world, except in some cases when he associated with other veterans. At departure from the military, the soldier's environment is society at large, which challenges her or his military self-concept. Society asks soldiers to depersonalize their combat experience. They are dispossessed of their military role. Society offers them the sanctioned role, "their concept of a military individual returning and living in civilian society."

Cpl Timothy Sexton, a young Marine who served in Desert Storm, says: "The Marine Corps trains you, 'Once a Marine, always a Marine.' This means the way you perform in life—take the attributes that the Marines taught you to be successful and apply them in life."[16] Sgt Maj Charlene K. Wiese, USMC, Headquarters, Barstow, California, says the military teaches conduct that reflects in soldiers 24 hours a day; teamwork, honor, and commitment can be taken back to civilian life.[17] Interviews demonstrate the consistency of military philosophy across the ranks. ADM Stanley Arthur, former aviator and Commander in Chief, U.S. Pacific Fleet, Pearl Harbor, and Deputy Chief of Naval Operations, observes: "The total institution is in your mind. The military will always be within you."[18] The military trains its people to have a sense of order and discipline translatable to any type of life, including life in society.

Does the military remain a total institution at the time of departure? Sexton and Arthur say that the total institution is military, but the military training provides attributes that are workable for any type of life. Sexton adds that society has certain expectations because you were a Marine. He says that as a Marine he upholds the welfare of society. He also believes that in society's view, if he doesn't take on that kind of commitment, he is in someway diminishing the societal expectations of a Marine. Sexton was at a basketball game when the ball got stuck in the rafters. Sexton is candid: "I'm afraid of heights.

I have to overcome the fear—do what is expected. What would the civilians think of the Marines as a whole, I have to consider that."

Arthur explains that the military gives a transition course for people who have been with the military either for a career or for the young sailors who return from a six-month cruise. Lessons on driving and safety are examples. "We were finding deployments bring a large number of injured and dead sailors. The west coast California highway patrol gave five days of lectures to our sailors. The chaplain lectures on the family and changes they will meet, e.g., the wife is now used to paying the bills and don't walk into [your home] and get upset with the kids, because the kids are asking her first." It is true that society is not soldiers' total institution upon departure, according to Arthur's and Sexton's views, but the military institution does prepare service people to live successfully in society.

Conflict Theory: Does It Apply to Women in Combat?

THE ORGANIZATION AS AN EXTENSION OF SELF
AND SACRIFICE FOR THE GOOD OF THE ORGANIZATION

The mission of our military to protect and defend the constitution must not be forgotten. Georg Simmel distinguishes between giving up personal interest in favor of a collective orientation.[19] The distinction adds to the "respectability" of a conflict when, as in the case of war, the collective success orientation is approved by the normative system. The self-sacrificing soldier plays what Simmel calls a "representative" role. Parsons restricts it to leadership roles. We care about the things for which we sacrifice, and thus our loyalty increases to an organization for which we have made sacrifices. An individual who relinquishes some personal interest for the sake of a group feels as if she or he has invested in the group and will then project herself or himself into the group through the group's purpose and power. Thus the group becomes an extension of her or his own personality. "Under these conditions, threats to the group touch the very core of her or his personality."

According to RADM Paul Gillcrist, USN (Ret.), a combat aviator veteran and test pilot, "One or the other is greater than the sum of his parts. One fellow threw himself on a grenade to save a life. Survival becomes overshadowed by the organization."[20] Gillcrist asks, "Is this dependent on gender—this ought to be explored."[21]

The Gulf War demonstrated that women are willing to die, and some women, according to Holm, say that if there is going to be a hit, let it be me, not the man.[22] Women in combat do and will sacrifice for the good of the entire organization, and in some cases, some women would rather take the bullet.

Role Theory

PARENTING

Globally, women soldiers represent 456,840 out of a total of 25,381,960, according to Elisabetta Addis, an international scholar. The United States has the highest number of women soldiers, 216,000 (out of 2,117,900 in the total force), followed most closely by China, which has 136,000 females with a total force 3,030,000 males. Great Britain, France, and Cyprus follow, with other countries having fewer than 10,000 soldiers each.[23]

According to Addis, most NATO countries admit women as volunteers instead of draftees because their young children need them. Some people think that the fertility rate would be threatened by the service of young women in the military. Many women choose to be mothers rather than soldiers, and Addis believes that men, if they had a choice, would choose to stay home to be fathers rather than soldiers.

Pay appears to be the same for men and women at the same rank in all nations. The key issue, Addis admits, is whether women are prevented either directly (grade or seniority) or indirectly (combat) from attaining senior grades. Pay is determined by grade or seniority and combat service and is the key point in understanding the economics of the woman soldier.

In Addis's opinion, military life is harder on the mother because of the different parental role she is asked to take, but I take issue with Addis. A female is only biologically bound to bear the child physically. In the United States, the responsibility to rear a child, that is, parenting, is equally bound to both the female and the male. Other than the biological act of pregnancy and birth, parenting is ideally a shared responsibility. Strong differing opinion exists, however, on this subject.

Addis also argues that men are more acclimated to the idea of rank. Sophisticated modern technology requires, however, a more educated personnel and a more continuous flow of information both up and down on the hierarchy. Thus the military may be evolving toward a less authoritarian model that will be more compatible with feminine perspectives.

The conclusions Addis reaches are insightful. The existence of a force comprised either exclusively or mostly of men creates and perpetuates economic inferiority among civilian women. However, if there is a choice for women, whatever choice is made, both kinds of choices help the military to function and both entail heavy costs to the women who fulfill them. According to Addis, the choice to be a soldier often brings with it suffering, as in the Tailhook scandal. The military is still a good choice for women because of gains made in economic status and independence. Economic gain is an important step towards a world in which women's freedom will be more than a freedom to choose the lesser of two evils.

In researching Marine history, it is clear that some female parents performed extremely well in the Gulf War, according to Maj R. S. Lenac, assistant Chief of Staff.[24] Capt K. E. Foss, permanently assigned to the USMC Air Station, Camp Pendleton, deployed to Southwest Asia in January 1991. She left her son, who was less than five months old, in the care of her husband, also an active duty captain. Maj R. S. Lenac notes that Foss was "extremely fortunate in having a husband who can successfully handle a Marine Corps career, part time graduate school, and a small child. Capt Foss' confidence in his abilities had allowed her to concentrate on her duties in Southwest Asia."[25] The Fosses are an excellent example of parenting being the responsibility of both parents.

Of course, responsibility cannot be shared if there are not two parents. Lenac cites the case of Cpl P. L. Foster, a single parent with a three-year-old child who "volunteered for duty" in the Gulf War and quickly made arrangements to leave her dependent daughter with her sister. "Carrying the same workload as her male counterparts," she completed all tasks assigned to her. Aside from the normal anxiety produced by long-term separation, Foster "maintained a cheerful and positive outlook," although she was eager to return home soon.

Family roles remain at the heart of the controversy over whether women should serve in combat. One military man told me that a woman can serve in combat but she cannot be the primary shooter. Part of the reason some men believe this "primary shooter" mentality is that for whatever reason, religious, macho, or acculturation, the end result is the same. Women are mothers, and therefore, according to Linda Grant De Pauw, the prospect of women at war is faced by some with unease.[26] In an interview, De Pauw was even more blunt in contradicting the conventional wisdom:

> Women and children are killed in vastly greater numbers as civilians than are soldiers in war. But society accepts that because it does not contradict the image of women as victims.... The horror of women in body bags is not a horror of a dead woman. It's that the woman was a warrior, that she is not a victim. American culture does not want to accept that women can be both warriors and mothers, but conjures for itself an ultimate horror—the murdering mother. To accept women as warriors means a challenge to patriarchy at its most fundamental level.[27]

Mady Segal points out that cultures sometimes see the mothering role as being diametrically opposed to the warrior role because giving life in childbirth is the opposite of taking a life in war. Segal says that the more movement that occurs away from traditional family norms, especially from the nuclear family, the greater the representation of women in the military. "This does not mean," she says, "the demise of family values."[28] Structural support such as parental leaves or community-supported child care can be provided.

Women will have more opportunity in the military as society supports diverse family forms.

Francine D'Amico agrees that "War has been perceived as men's domain, a masculine endeavor for which women may serve as victim, spectator or prize. Women are denied agency, made present but silenced."[29] The antifeminists, however, believe that the woman-warrior image destroys the family and fabric of our society and decreases military readiness. They believe the genders are "naturally" different. D'Amico thinks, however, that women's participation in the Gulf War did not challenge traditional gender roles and constraints. She reminds her readers of the "many unidentified women who were among the 'collateral damage' of the precision bombing and Iraqi occupation."

CPT Sharon Grant Wildwind, a U.S. Army nurse in Vietnam, suggests that as we arm women, we are dealing with a archetypal attitude because in the minds of some, we are looking at the destruction of the breeding population.[30] She believes that if medical scientists could develop an artificial uterus, the face of war would change. I agree that this archetype exists, but I would add that we are really looking at the destruction of the breeding population when we place women anywhere in a war. We are not preserving women's lives in support positions. Many of the same dangers exist in noncombat zones. Wildwind adds two more dimensions we are addressing when we arm women: a mystique and the Church:

> A high percentage are from the South, black, or Spanish American. Therefore, we are also dealing with the blacks' view of females, and the Hispanics view of church as well as their view of women. Most troops are Black Americans, Hispanic, lower income and southern. The church played a major role in the attitudes toward the nurses of the 60s. Women went directly from high school to nursing school. [Nursing schools] had a strong religious background. The schools were run by religious orders or had a history of religious orders and encouraged that background. Nurses were used to taking orders. The Army was but an extension of Nursing School with all of its regulations.... The nurses today do not have as religious [a] background as their predecessors.

When asked what message she would like to offer to readers of this book, Wildwind said, "Give women a chance to make all the contributions that they can." It seems clear that in order for military women to use their full potential, we must lessen or remove the archetype, address the mystique, and approach the Church.

PREGNANCY

Having a baby is the one thing a female can do that a male cannot. Pregnancy should not be viewed as a disease, according to De Pauw, who says,

"They used to keep out women who had hysterectomies. Women had hysterectomies so that it wouldn't be a problem having a career. Applying the pregnancy argument to all females, sterile and celibate, makes no sense. Moreover, women and children get hit in war. Soldiers keep themselves safe. They may be socialized to protect, but biologically they do not. Biologically the tendency is to save yourself."[31]

Mady Segal says certain theoretical factors will affect women's military participation. First, and most important, the military's need for personnel will expand women's military roles. Other relevant theoretical factors are the social structure and the cultural values supporting gender equality.[32] "Perceptions are socially constructed," says Segal. "The saliency given to specific arguments about women's military roles, is not based on objective reality, but rather on cultural values."[33] Segal believes there is a process of "cultural amnesia" that occurs in the aftermath of war so that the contributions women made are reconstructed as minor or nonexistent, allowing culture to retain its myth that men fight and women stay home. When a new emergency arises, rediscovery takes place. Segal contends that when national security makes it necessary to increase the roles of military women, that need will override unsupportive cultural values.

Feminist Theory

MOTHERS

In 1993, Conover and Sapiro found the more common view is that early differential socialization and experiences, that is, socially constructed gender, make females more pacifist than men.[34] Feminist theory focuses especially on the experiences of mothering and being mothered. Women do more parenting than men, and are therefore more empathetic, nurturing, and other-centered. A minority of men parent.

Conover and Sapiro term these feminists "maternalist thinkers." They believe that Sara Ruddick shaped the clearest theoretical links between mothering and attitudes toward militarism.[35] Ruddick argues that mothers develop ways of thinking and acting that are more likely to serve as the basis of peace politics. The "mothers" concept is closely related to the philosophy presented in the UN's 1995 Plan of Action for Armed Conflict (see Chapter 1). According to this document, women often work to preserve social order in the midst of armed conflict when a community has collapsed; women are peace educators, and education is essential for lasting peace.[36] Ruddick differs in that the "mothers" concept is not totally based in gender because men also assume a mothering role. The UN's Plan of Action supports the female gender for furthering peace even though males should benefit as well.

The tie between maternal thinking and antimilitarism, according to Conover and Sapiro, is that a primary ideal of maternalism is nonviolent peacemaking, although materialism sometimes supports militaristic purposes. It is the feminist mothers who are most likely to seek peaceful strategies. Ruddick, say Conover and Sapiro, holds that feminist mothers help account for the foreign policy gender gap. The United Nations 1995 Conference in Beijing reinforces the belief that there is a gender gap. Its platform on military conflict states that women's role of preserving the social order in the midst of armed conflict is important but unrecognized (see Chapter 1).[37]

"Civic" Feminists

The other feminist theorists, according to Conover and Sapiro, emphasize peace politics.[38] They are "civic" feminists. Politics rather than gender or mothering makes them more pacifist. Civic feminists can be male or female, but are usually female. Whatever their gender, civic feminists tend to be less militaristic in policy. Females espousing civic feminism are greater in number and their antimilitaristic views open the gender gap.

Civic feminism opposes militarism and commits to democratic values. These values renounce hierarchy, domination, force, and exploitation and identify the military as a bastion of sexism. Therefore, Conover and Sapiro argue, civic feminism shapes the link between itself and militarism. Feminists believe women are more pacifist than men because they are biologically so or are acculturated to be so. The maternalist feminists say the women who are mothers will be less militaristic than both women who are not mothers and men.

Conover and Sapiro's study found no support for the positions of either type of feminists, the "mothers" or the "civics"[39] (see Chapter 6). They discovered that men's and women's thinking differs fundamentally. Men's attitudes are more partisan, and women are more afraid of war in both the abstract and the concrete because of early socialization.

Feminist Ethics Theory

Rosalyn Diprose is aware of the current emphasis on identity politics, but frames her discussion around the maternal body and the general distinction between men and women.[40] She does not believe that any sexed-identity escapes contamination by the dominant discourse which privileges heterosexuality and subsumes women under a general category as man's "other" and as potential, actual, or failed mothers. She believes that the focus of ethics should be on particular kinds of women rather than particular discourses.[41]

Diprose argues that the standard approach to ethics both perpetuates the mechanisms of the social subordination of women and remains blind to them. She believes the mechanisms entail an "injustice against women that begins in the ways in which social assumptions about sexual difference constitute women's embodied existence as improper and secondary in relation to men." According to Diprose, moral codes may maintain a semblance of order but at the expense of justice for women. The new feminist ethics try to take sexual differences into account. Diprose does not believe one injustice can be displaced by another. In 1993, in Australia, a male won a beauty contest that allowed him to compete for the Miss Australia Awards. Some judges were female, and different judging criteria were used for men. Many feminists opposed beauty contests, but the Australia contest existed without any male oppressor, the judgment was made and endorsed by women. Diprose asks, "If a man can be judged more meritorious on criteria developed specifically for, and therefore presumably favourable to, women's modes of embodiment, what does this say about the evaluation of sexual differences in general?"

Ethics is not just a study of the logical status of our moral judgments or setting universal principles for regulating behavior. It is also about location, position, and place. Or as Diprose states, "It is about being positioned by, and taking a position in relation to, others."[42]

Diprose is no less provocative in her insistence that surrogate mother-hood, in forgetting the body and citing universal rules, relies on an unsuitable model of the relation between a person and her body and misconceives the nature of the relation between the person and others.[43] If ethics is to allow sexual difference, then embodiment and the nature of identity and difference must be rethought. The issue of the pregnant body illustrates the problems that arise in attempts to govern the relations between the parties involved in a surrogate birth by contracts based on universal ethical considerations, despite what appears to be the insignificance of embodiment.

The report on surrogacy presented by Australia's National Bioethics Consultative Committee (NBCC) is Diprose's guide to what is typically to be the nature of the individual and what relations should exist between individuals in biomedical ethics based on autonomy, justice, and the common good.[44] Autonomy means having the right to make one's own decisions. Justice requires that arrangements between people should not be exploitative and should serve the best interests of all involved. The principle of the common good requires that the entire community must be considered in an arrangement between individuals.

In most cases, women and men have the right to do with their body as they please.[45] A woman does not have the right, however, if her body is pregnant. Diprose believes that universalist contractarian ethics cannot fairly accommodate sexual difference. Therefore, pregnant embodiment and the ethics of reproduction are omitted. Diprose thinks it is necessary to examine feminist ethicists for our "epoch," which has its own problems in adequately addressing sexual difference.

If we apply the NBCC's three criteria not to the issue of surrogacy but to the issue of pregnancy in the military, one could conclude that a female service person could elect to get pregnant. Whether her pregnancy would bring harm to others may not be easily answered. The principles of justice and the common good raise tough ethical questions, especially when, according to Diprose, pregnancy and reproduction ethics are not adequately developed.

One ongoing argument against women serving in combat is a possible loss of time because of pregnancy. According to the 1993 congressional hearings, some men see pregnancy leave as an inequity, but is the absence of a soldier because of pregnancy any different from the absence of a soldier because of an attack of appendicitis? In 1993, B Gen Thomas V. Draude, USMC (Ret.), a member of the 1992 Presidential Commission, stated:

> No mixed gender ship ever failed to sail on time or missed a commitment because of personnel readiness ... The results of a Navy multi-year study on lost time [showed] when pregnancy and convalescent leave after childbirth were excluded, women averaged two days lost per year compared to three days for men. When time lost for pregnancy, childbirth, and convalescent leave are considered, women lost 12 days per year. Finally it was noted that the percentage of Navy women nondeployable for Desert Shield/Desert Storm was 5.6. The percentage for male Marines was 8.8. (However, no one believed that the high rate for male Marines was cause for concern).[46]

Some who testified in the 1993 hearings thought that pregnancy affected cohesion, particularly when it was perceived as a way to escape from combat duty.[47]

Diprose draws upon the work of new feminist ethicist Carol Gilligan, who takes sexual difference into account in her ethics of care and its derivatives. The ethics of care is based on recognizing a fundamental connection between self and other.[48] Gilligan challenges moral theories which privilege justice and rights, theories where maturity is measured in terms of the ability to solve moral dilemmas using universal ethical principles derived from the contract model of social change. Gilligan says there are differences in modes of moral reasoning between some men and some women. Diprose asks whether these differences are natural or socially constituted. Gilligan's care ethic is based upon women serving as a complement to a masculine ethics of justice, a risk of gender stereotyping which some feminists believe is responsible for continuing oppression of women.[49]

Luce Irigaray says we live in complex and difficult times and calls for a revolution in ethics and a well-developed sense of irony. Diprose believes that any revolution of ethics begins with the ethics of ethics. If women are to have a "fairer deal" and a wider range of possibilities for living, there must be an ongoing questioning of ethics.[50]

In 1984 Genevieve Lloyd argued that intelligence or rationality is automatically equated with masculinity. Diprose points to the abundance of examples in transsexual literature of how male to female transsexuals perform male ideals of feminine bodily behavior better than women. She concludes it may be little wonder that a man could win a woman's beauty contest, as it happened in Australia, on criteria of bodily behavior and shape.[51]

Diprose cites Moria Gatens's 1991 theory "that the evaluation and regulation of sexual difference in patriarchal social relations is implicitly based on the valorization of a particular kind of male body.... Moral, legal, industrial and interpersonal evaluation of sexual difference is productive: it produces the modes of sexed embodiment it regulates." According to Diprose, "a key argument throughout this book is that any injustice experienced by women begins from this mode of production and maintenance of sexual difference."[52]

Michel Foucault and Irigaray claim that social identity is sexed and embodied, and they argue that identity is socially constituted in relations to others. "If universalist ethics regulates social exchange through which sexed identity and difference is produced and if this perpetuates injustice against women, then ethics needs to be understood as the problematic of the constitution of embodied, sexed identity."[53] There are two parts to their ethics. First, how one's embodied ethos is constituted by social discourses and practices, including ethics. Disciplinary power articulates the ways in which embodied identities are constituted, normalized, and marginalized. It also helps explain why injustice is difficult to locate and correct. Surveillance and moral regulation of the maternal body is reassessed here in terms of its consequence for the normalization of the social body as a whole. Hilsdon has applied Foucault's theory that military discipline and mechanisms are specifically gendered.[54] Other possibilities of Foucault's ethics, according to Diprose, lie in aesthetics of self, that is, recreating the self as a corporeal work of art, without reference to the disciplinary moral code. Feminist ethicists would find a problem with aesthetics of self because the male body is already considered a work of art in comparison to women's modes of embodiment. The value and status men have in patriarchal social relations is generated through the constitution of women's modes of embodied existence as other to the norm.

Diprose defines ethics on the basis of Foucault and Irigaray "as the examination and practice of that which constitutes our embodied place in the world,"[55] and she also relates ethics to how one's identity is constituted in relation to others. Feminists disagree about the extent to which this production of sexed identity and difference involves the overvaluation or degeneration of women's modes of being. It is, argues Diprose, this productive evaluation of women's embodied existence in terms of virtue or shame which provides the basis for women's exclusion from social change.[56]

Ethics

THE OBJECT OF ETHICS

Daniel Callahan believes that "We argue about ethics because it is so fundamental, and because how we ought to live our lives is a very difficult problem."[57] Teaching ethics, according to Callahan, can mean dealing with indifference or outright hostility. The field of ethics is disturbing and controversial, and it is often avoided. But if ethics is taught well, it forces a confrontation with professional goals and daily practices and makes us examine the goals for which we are living, working, and leading our professional lives. Many people do not want to confront those questions because they realize they may not like what they find.

Ethics is meant to stimulate people to behave as well as they can, notes Callahan. Ambiguity and uncertainty accompany ethical decisions and force people to question their goals. Some people object to arguing that ethics will make a military person less competent. Callahan points out, however, that one does not sit down and think about Aristotle during battle or ponder moral dilemmas in the midst of a crisis. If a person has given thought to ethics in advance of difficult moments or, as the military say, seconds, she or he will be more prepared for a crisis and hard decisions.

COMPETENCE AND ETHICS GO HAND IN HAND

Further, Callahan says, ethical problems do not arise out of a vacuum but are part of institutional arrangements or structural elements. The basic goal of a person who is trying to be ethical is to avoid ethical dilemmas in the first place. The problems would not be as likely to arise if institutions were more ordered and managed. People will ask the basic theoretical question, "Why should I be moral?" Other questions are also posed: Where do we get our moral rules? How do you justify moral obligations? How do you develop notions of what are appropriate virtues for people? Although Callahan believes the answers lie in a theoretical foundation, he maintains that the questions are very old and very tough and have no easy answers. Addressing ethics is better, however, than avoiding it.

Diprose writes that the object of ethics is to undermine rather than repeat the normalizing, discriminatory, and totalizing effects of dominant discourses which privilege heterosexuality and subsume women under a general category as man's other and as potential, actual, or failed mothers.

ETHICS THEORY

Diprose defines ethics "as the study and practice of that which constitutes one's habitat" or the authorization of one's embodied place in the world.[58] Ethics recognizes a constitutive relation between one's world, or habitat, and one's embodied character, or ethos. Ethics is about taking a position in relation to others. It is also about identity and difference. Simply stated, ethics is concerned with moral principles, moral judgment, location, position, and place.

ETHICS AND NATIONAL DEFENSE

Some people say to me, "Now that the U.S. is engaged in peacekeeping, it may be okay for women to serve." Others say, "Combat uses more stand off weapons now, but why blow up the female half of our civilization?" During our 1991 intervention against Saddam, one soldier interviewed on the news said: "Now that we have Patriot missiles, it's okay for women to serve in combat. You know, even men feel better that you are saving a life rather than taking it."

Whether one is dealing in small conflicts or nuclear warfare, the American just-war tradition, though changing, continues to guide policy and attitudes. This tradition has prevailed in past wars and is applicable now.[59] The concept of the justice *of* war, *jus ad bellum*, involves deciding whether war is moral, whereas the concept of justice *in* war, *jus in bello*, concerns fighting cleanly, explains MAJ H. F. Kuenning, USA. The Western ethics of violence is based on the just-war tradition. Is violence justified and if violence is justified, what is permitted and prohibited? The justice of war contends just cause, proper authority, right intention, proportionality (aggregate sense), last resort, and the aim of peace. Justice in war also addresses proportionality (proximate sense) and discrimination (or noncombatant immunity). One must consider the interplay, according to Col. Michael O. Wheeler, USAF, among the aggressor, an innocent victim, and an onlooker.

Desert Storm and Desert Shield were responses to President George Bush's call for an all-volunteer force to counter Saddam Hussein's invasion of Kuwait. President Bush, as the proper authority, contended Iraq should not overrun or possess Kuwait; thus the American position involved the right intention, just cause, and proportionality (aggregate). Moreover, since Iraq's invasion was viewed as an act of aggression, it would appear that our involvement was the last resort and had a peaceful aim.

Wheeler's conclusion that there is no simple distinction between defense and offense is illustrated by the Gulf War efforts. Defense has no moral superiority over offense on the face of it, whether one is engaged in general defense or defense against nuclear weapons.

Kuenning believes the traditional and deeply ingrained American values of *jus ad bellum* and *jus in bello* are both in trouble because war has changed and the shifts are traumatic. The justice of war standards "outlaw" war. In fact, he says, Western attempts, especially American efforts, to eliminate war have only made war more destructive and brutal. The growing tendency is to take the war to entire enemy populations. Nuclear weapons could mean rapid and worldwide destruction, which conflicts with our values. Any justification for war is seen for what it is, in Kuenning's words, a move toward a holocaust, and is therefore, immoral.

Kuenning also maintains that the justice of war is under attack by humanitarian and apolitical ideals proposing a natural state of peace among men. This antiwar concept of peace is based in the United States on our geographical security and 200 years of liberal democracy. Americans have another tradition according to Kuenning, a distrust of government and of the military. Antiwar sentiment did not begin with the Vietnam War but dates back to the eighteenth century.

According to Kuenning, the standards revealed in slogans such as Wilson's "Make the world safe for democracy" and the Grenada justification "Protect the vital national security of the United States" are impractical and they decouple. Justice in war standards also change. Noble warriors supposedly face an evil enemy in an action that is viewed by the United States as "a legitimate war with a quick decisive, punitive victory." As humanitarians, Americans then sanction extreme measures that can backfire, such as indiscriminate tactical and strategic bombing, massive use of artillery to preserve American lives, and an attitude of no restraint on combat operations.

The UN Conference Plan of Action is in agreement with Kuenning that it is appalling that our forces operate in highly political limited wars without regard for the impact of their operations on the societies for which the contest is being waged. With crusading rhetoric, a United States president convinces Congress and the public that a war is justified. The public uses its idealistic priorities. The key, Kuenning says, is the link between the justifications of war and *in* war. Military leaders, he says, can only ensure *jus in bello*, the morality of strategy and tactics so that the United States forces fight effectively for low-key sustainability and resolution, and moral criticism of American intervention is minimized.

Most interesting is Kuenning's discussion of moral logic in small wars. Moral relativism is often seen in the argument that no rules exist in war. The law of war does authorize reprisals, but not in kind. It is illegal for a soldier to execute or torture helpless people under any circumstances. Unfortunately, because of parochial attitudes, some members of the American fighting forces tend to treat foreign people in war, friend or foe, with disgust and contempt. Although we value human life, strategies such as massive, high tech fire power are used to protect American lives. The "sliding scale" moral logic or judgment varies depending on the size of the war.

According to Kuenning, there are some problems that occur in the military in small wars. The warrior ethic is a tradition in the officer corps, an arm of the executive (civilian) government. The goal of these officers is national security and a life of service. Kuenning would agree with Zurcher and Sexton that the actual "warriors" become apolitical and withdraw from civilian ways of thinking. The warriors view their role strictly as military. Combat with victory is the warriors' goal, which is fulfilled through the preservation of the nation. They leave the questions of when and why to fight to civilian leaders. To them, they, the warriors, are the answer to political military problems.

The warriors' second problem is the nature of the enemy. The enemy may be unprofessional and uninformed, may operate outside of convention, and may integrate messy social values into her or his approach that dismay the apolitical professional. The use of air forces in small wars is questionable because it optimizes combat power, not political or ethical sensitivity.

The forces are extensively trained in military and technical skills for a short mission but moral questions do not receive much attention during this training. Instead, the law provides guidance. A war crime is any violation of the law of land warfare, and a list of black and white rules exists to answer World War II's problems. War crime law has defined some moral problems and has established punishment for violations. International laws usually treat problems from the last war. Terrorist acts of violence seek political ends, but are dirty and indiscriminate military acts.

Although the forces have little training in ethics, theory, or morality, the oath soldiers take is the codification of their loyalty. The U.S. Army officer swears:

> I (NAME), having been appointed an officer in the Army of the United States, as indicated above in the grade of (RANK) so solemnly swear (or affirm) that I will support and defend the Constitution of the United States against all enemies, foreign and domestic, that I will bear true faith and allegiance to the same, that I take this obligation freely, without any mental reservation or purpose of evasion; and that I will well and faithfully discharge the duties of the office upon which I am about to enter; SO HELP ME GOD.[60]

"The oath should be viewed as the foundation to which the soldier's loyalty is ultimately tied," notes CPT A. Dwight Raymond, USA. If the moral grip of the oath can be loosened, he says, then some cases of treason may be examined for their moral justification. The oath is more than words and must be placed in the context of certain presuppositions and tacit understandings. It is grounded in divinity, but more firmly in justice. The soldier should not be blamed for being loyal even if popular belief, comrades, or history might indicate she or he should have committed treason.

James H. McGrath sheds a new light on the oath which he sees as a voluntary public vow by which a soldier consents to be bound by others.[61] In his survey of both historical and contemporary institutions that are similar to the armed forces, McGrath points out that the soldier's oath is much like the oath an FBI agent takes. Today the oath is viewed in a more casual way.

According to Raymond, the soldier gives the benefit of the doubt to the state and to the law. Soldiers can assume that the war their country is fighting is just and that they should follow all just orders. A soldier can also have an independent judgment. If war seems immoral, the soldier should resign. Treason is a risk, but when motivated by concerns for justice it is sometimes permissible in order to prevent a great wrong. Soldiers should be free, however, to concentrate on their duties and should be free of moral guessing games. Citizens have a right to have a reliable military. The soldier should be free to be loyal. West Point's motto, "Duty, Honor, Country," is an ethical standard whose parts can compete and thus give tension to the soldier's loyalty.

Sexton says the tradition and history of the Marine Corps dictates how the enlisted person's role is different from that of an officer who is not on the battlefield and is above the level of sergeant.[62] The enlisted person and the officer have two different agendas. The loss of a battlefield leader is seen as just an expenditure. The battlefield soldiers are pawns in a chess game. "We are taught to respect officers. They [leaders] stress you are a team: [The Marine Motto] *Esprit de Corps, Semper Fidelis*—a link has been taken out and you are a little weaker, but you have to overcome." During active duty in Desert Storm, Sexton was a rifleman and chaplain's assistant. He had to have strength to help the others to overcome adversity and uphold the philosophy of the Marines. Sexton, who is now a trainer of recruits in the Iowa National Guard, thinks the military has gotten too involved with the needs of the soldier and should return to the edict of President John F. Kennedy, "Ask not what your country can do for you, but what can you do for your country." Sexton points to the "Code of Conduct" and the "Soldier's Creed" as guides to help one understand the standards of ethical conduct the soldier is required to follow (see Appendix C).[63] The last point in the Code of Conduct perhaps says it best,

> I will never forget that I am an American, fighting for freedom, responsible for my actions, and dedicated to the principles which made my country free. I will trust in my God and in the United States of America.

As a guardian of the public trust, the soldier places loyalty to the Constitution, laws, and standards of ethical conduct above any personal gain. A military officer once told me, "A soldier will do what she/he is told even at her/his own peril."

Consideration of ethics thus would appear to be compatible with the military. A study of ethical problems ahead of time should help military personnel, not hinder them. CPT Thomas J. Begines, USA, believes that a personal morality of ethical egoism, even enlightened egoism, is not compatible to the military officer.[64] The officer is required to act for the "common good," for vague but collective "national interests," and for "the welfare of the soldiers." Any moral dissent has to occur only within the ranks of the military and not go against the decisions of civilian authority. The officer does not, however, have to obey orders which he or she believes immoral. In this case, she or he should resign or refuse to obey, but not take actions contrary to a superior's orders. Begines believes that moral theory should be taught in military schools and institutions. If we take morality seriously, he says, we must embrace a conception of special trust and confidence that requires and permits morally based dissent within the bounds he has described. Disturbing as the field of ethics may be, it appears to me that it must be a strong consideration in training the military of tomorrow.

SEXED IDENTITY AND DIFFERENCE

Diprose credits Hegel with taking seriously the idea that sexed identity and difference is constituted through, rather than prior to, social exchange. She dislikes Hegel's legitimizing of the subordination of women: Woman is man's complement and her difference transparent and reducible to man's identity.[65]

Deconstructive feminists argue that ethics is based on a "gift" idea as opening other possibilities for women's existence beyond those which position women as "other" to men. Diprose argues that a move too quickly to the "gift" idea will make it more likely that means of discrimination will be left in place.[66]

ECONOMY OF REPRESENTATION OF SEXUAL DIFFERENCE LIMITS WOMEN

Nietzsche's philosophy is used as a basis to explore a more direct analysis of social constitution of embodied existence. Sexed bodies are constituted within an economy of representation of sexual difference which limits possibilities for women.[67]

Like Nietzsche's philosophy, existentialism demonstrates how injustice begins with the ways in which women's bodies are constituted as improper in relation to men by social discourses and practices. Existentialism considers the ethics of reproductive practices in the light of intervening analysis.

SOCIOBIOLOGY

In 1993, Conover and Sapiro reported that some radical feminists, who believed gender differences were rooted in biology, interpreted the differences as indicators of the female's innate moral superiority.[68] It is fitting to conclude this chapter with a discussion of biomedical ethics and the role of biomedical science because it is the ultimate discourse on the body. For that reason alone, biomedical ethics and science are of utmost importance. Diprose demonstrates who dictates which embodied existences, how they can be transformed and by whom and to what end. This is the point, she concludes, where comparisons are made, values born, and not all bodies are counted as socially viable. Most applicable to the military's mission of readiness is her statement, "the privilege of a stable place within that social and political place we call the 'common good' is secured at the cost of denigrating and excluding others."[69] Maintaining that this view is neither negative or positive, she argues: "We are the embodied products of regimes which regulate sexual difference, these regimes support our existence. Thus, there is no back door to freedom via anarchy or solitude." We all become the subject and object of ethics, she concludes. Without ignoring the injustices against women, it is also necessary to pay attention to the mechanisms which ground injustice and make it possible.

In order for women's place in the military to continue to change, the values and mechanisms of the military must continue to change as well.

Chapter 8

Readiness

> Leaders in combat have to be competent and qualified in
> order to accomplish the mission. My goal in the process
> of picking soldiers for leadership roles is to base the deci-
> sion on quality so the Army gets the very best. I wouldn't
> want my sons and daughters fighting under someone
> picked solely on the basis on gender or race.[1]
> MAJ Jane McKeon, U.S. Army (Ret.)

What Are the Real Issues of Readiness?

Gen Charles C. Krulak, Commandant of the Marine Corps, says that the most important long-term investment in combat readiness is the professional military education of our leaders.[2] A consistent struggle exists between maintaining necessary forces and modernizing them. Provided funding is adequate, the services can provide what Krulak calls operationally ready, well-trained, and versatile forces. Readiness will depend on continuous training and education, the outfitting of soldiers with the best technology on the battlefield, and sufficient numbers in our forces.

Readiness is key to forward engagement, according to ADM Stanley R. Arthur, Vice Chief of Naval Operations, and budget is basic to readiness. Studies to measure and manage readiness have been done by the General Accounting Office (GAO), Congressional Budget Office (CBO), and Secretary of Defense William J. Perry's Task Force. In its efforts to develop a comprehensive assessment system, the Navy concluded that "there is no singular measure of readiness which fully captures the broad spectrum of components which go into the overall readiness measure for any particular force or individual unit."[3] Like Krulak, Arthur says that no matter how we measure readiness, we can never lose sight of our most precious readiness resource, the men and women of today's Navy. The Navy's surveys have shown that insufficient compensation is the main reason why people leave the Navy. Quality of life issues are also paramount.[4]

MAJ Lillian Pfluke, USA (Ret.), says the reason why the old rules changed can be answered in one word, readiness. Pfluke says that Secretary of Defense Perry's overall goal is to maintain a high quality, ready, and effective force. By increasing the number of positions to which women can be assigned, the services gain greater flexibility in the development and use of human resources.[5]

The readiness issue becomes very complex when the people element is introduced. Terms such as *cohesion* surface. What makes a unit of military people work effectively together for a common good? Physical ability, mental and psychological adeptness, and good leadership? What is good leadership? The answers to these questions and more are addressed in the chapters that follow. Cohesion, how well a unit works together for the "common good," affects readiness, the degree to which our forces are operationally ready, well trained, and versatile.

The process of attaining a cohesive unit is fraught with cultural biases, but many of these biases are beginning to give way. Biases center primarily around the issues of gender, ability, sexual behaviors, and opportunity. Readiness hinges on how the cohesion issues are addressed by force command.

In October 1997, the RAND study found that gender integration is perceived to have a relatively small effect on readiness, cohesion, and morale. According to the study, a majority of both sexes preferred integrated training, and leadership is regarded as the overwhelming influence on unit morale.

GENDER ROLES ASSUMED IN COMBAT

Most of the literature reviewed and people interviewed agree with Mady Segal that if there is a need to defend our society, women will not be defined in a societally constructed gender role, and even if they are, that constructed role will be overridden and they will be helping the war or peace effort.[6] The concepts that "necessity is the mother of invention" and that modern warfare weaponry no longer demands the physical strength (specifically upper body strength) once needed for tasks demonstrate why women are serving and will serve in combatant assignments. Air power, nuclear technology, and smaller weapons contribute to the possibility of women serving in combat. ADM Arthur believes the military of today can accommodate women in more roles than in the past. He says that if we don't accommodate women, we must use the available source of male manpower. Women not only have great stamina, they have knowledge and talent that will be especially useful as we continue to be more high tech.[7] Segal points out that technology has enabled women to control reproduction. Women can control when and how many children they will have. The current trend is to marry later, to have fewer children, and to have them later. Thus women will have more military opportunity, and it is more likely they will ascend to the higher ranks.[8] According to Segal, it is a simple supply and demand equation. If there are not enough men, women will serve. The war in the Gulf demonstrated the importance of the U.S. reserves to the active component, and the reserves contain a larger percentage of women.

The real issues of assigning women in combat are not gender constructed, therefore, but are based on qualifications. And, as many of my interviewees said, assignment should be based on the simple adage "the best person for the position." Dr. Bernard D. Rostker, Assistant Secretary of the Navy, says, "In both the Navy and Marine Corps, recruiting, as well as occupational and training standards, are gender neutral."[9]

Dorothy Schneider and Carl Schneider found half of the men are going to perform well under high stress situations and half will not. It is going to be the same with women. Ability differences exist within a group of men or a group of women. As Schneider and Schneider say, in a mixed group whose members are similar in ability, some will perform well and others will not.[10] Whether a person is qualified to perform combat duty should be the criterion.

The issue of the mixed-gender unit becomes entangled with the issue of the unit's readiness to perform its military mission. In the past, one of the most visible figures in opposition to assigning women in combat was Elaine Donnelly. Donnelly, a member of George Bush's Presidential Commission on the Assignment of Women in the Armed Forces, has testified frequently at congressional hearings. In 1993, Donnelly said, "We [those writing the alternative view section of the Commission's report] found as our deliberations continued, the question of violence against women and the risk of capture caused the Commission to give serious thought to the nation's cultural values: Would the use of women in combat be a step forward for our civilization, or a step backward?"[11] Donnelly found a cultural dissonance with the concept of violence against women in armed combat.[12] The point Donnelly may have been missing is that women, as noncombatants, are at risk of capture or violence. For example, nurses have been captured and have been at risk, as was Rhonda Cornum, a physician who was a prisoner of war during the Gulf War. Both men and women were sitting in a dining hall when a Scud missile hit. Being assigned in a technically defined noncombatant role does not protect a woman from violence and violation. In 1994 and 1997, Donnelly again spoke against women serving in combat roles, but this time in her capacity as president of the Center for Military Readiness (CMR).[13]

Brian Mitchell believes that women do not belong in combat and views women as a "weak link."[14] His primary arguments against women in combat center on women's effect on readiness. He argues that women are smaller and not as strong as men, take more time off, produce a higher turnover rate, are more likely to be discharged for homosexuality, have more injuries, and are more likely to suffer emotional distress. Mitchell believes women are basically rights-oriented and pacifistic, thus forcing out discipline, replacing it with leadership, and ultimately eroding the spirit of combativeness, aggressiveness, an eagerness to fight, a willingness to die, or the courage to kill.[15]

Although Mitchell's arguments sum up the usual position against women in combat, there are other reasons some people oppose women serving in direct combat. CDR John Calande, Jr., U.S. Naval Academy, class of 1963, says, "The best way a woman can serve this country is to stay home and provide a strong family core. This is desperately needed. The political competition generated between men and women by the feminists is ruining the foundation of our country."[16] Joe Helmick, a 1986 West Point graduate, who served for four years as a cavalry officer in the 3d Armored Division in what was then West Germany, says that his "opinions on women in combat reflect my overall philosophy of roles and responsibilities of the sexes outlined in Christian heritage and scriptures."[17] In a more practical sense, he points out, that in any war women are in combat in the roles of supporting men. "This role is consistent with the purpose of women. God created woman to be a 'helpmate' for man. During war, more than any other time, men need help in the capacities of healing, caring for the wounded and dying, logistics, supply, and other support capacities." Helmick believes that women are less fit than men and are not designed to carry out physical demands of life in the field.

ALL-VOLUNTEER FORCE (AVF) VS. CONSCRIPTION

One issue raised in combat debate is conscription, the drafting of women for the services. At present, the United States has an all-volunteer force (AVF) and is involved primarily in peacekeeping missions. Some say we will never be involved in a major conflict again. Others say we will be, but not for many years. Others say the smaller conflicts around the world will lie just beneath the surface before a larger conflict erupts. Pfluke says while we have not had a draft since 1972 and no prospects for another one soon, "When this country needs women to be drafted, it will draft women, and at that point we will have many more serious problems to worry about than if that is the correct thing to do.... The U.S. would have drafted women (primarily nurses) in World War II if it had gone on a few more months."[18] No matter which view a person holds, the issue of readiness forces us to address the conscription of women.

Readiness is the most dominant issue when the issue of women in combat is discussed, so dominant that members of the Presidential Commission were sharply divided on how women in combat would affect military readiness, according to MAJ Mary Finch, USA, a member of the Commission.[19] In 1993, Finch reported that members in favor of women in combat argued military readiness is enhanced by a larger pool of applicants because the military can choose the best qualified individual for a given position. Members who opposed having women in combat argued politics would dictate unavoidable quotas, thus permitting less qualified women in key positions and weakening our readiness. The opponents also argued that there is no present military necessity to open combat positions to women.

The Presidential Commission concluded that women should not be required to register for the draft or be drafted.[20] President Jimmy Carter would not have agreed with this decision. In 1980 he proposed that women be registered for the draft.[21] Although polls in general showed four out of five Americans supported Carter, and polls of the 18- to 24-year-old age group reflected Carter's position favorably, Congress was opposed. The House approved draft registration for men, but not for women.[22] The only two of the seven members of the Senate manpower subcommittee who favored women's registration were President Bill Clinton's Secretary of Defense, former Senator William Cohen (R-Maine), and Senator John Culver (D-Iowa).[23] Carter had proposed the registration of women when the Russians invaded Afghanistan in December 1979. In 1993, Finch said women should be subject to conscription and be used as the Congress and armed services see fit, whatever the assignment, and thereby contribute to national security. It would be unfair to expect males to cease their pursuits and not expect the same of females, adds Finch.

ADM Stanley Arthur says that readiness is primarily a people issue and there are limits we have to acknowledge.[24] The images of World War II, for example, the pictures of Marines storming the beach and getting mowed down by the enemy, are horrific to watch. The public does not want that to happen to women. If a woman goes down in a plane in combat, it does not bother the public as much. In response to my question "Is this image a cultural perspective?" or "Is it just how a woman dies?" Arthur replied, "It is how she dies." It is a cultural viewpoint.

On another aspect of the issue of women in combat, Arthur had this to say, "If you have a 6-ft., 200-pounder, to carry a 50-pound machine gun, you will choose the 6-footer over the 5-foot woman." In response to my question, "What if the woman is a 6-foot, 200-pounder?" Arthur replied, "If she is a vision of [the] six-foot woman, [she] is not the vision of the American public." Arthur says we have to learn how to assign and accept women in the military better than we have, but we have limits. It is clearly a delicate issue for the American public. Arthur points out another difficulty: "Our most expensive product is our people. Expanding rapidly is a concern for everyone. Congress says to enhance women in the military, but no draft. [This is] an interesting contradiction in view. If Congress would say register all 18-year-olds, then make the decisions. It would be the right way."[25]

BGen. Wilma L. Vaught, USAF (Ret.), president of the Women in Military Service for America Memorial Foundation (WIMSA), says: "Invoking the draft isn't just that you need more people, but you need people with certain skills, armory and artillery. What do you do about women? The reason goes out the window and we take men that shouldn't be in those positions either. The issue is the survival of the U.S. as a nation. You use people the best way you can."[26] She believes there will not be as many women assigned to specific categories such as the Navy Seals, Infantry, Artillery, or Armor Battalions.

In 1993, LTG Thomas P. Carney, Deputy Chief of Staff for Personnel, Department of the Army, said that when we talk about conscription of women, we are talking about conscription of women into ground combat because there are enough people that volunteer for the other areas of the military. Therefore the Army and the Marines are the ones who would have to deal with conscription of females.[27] Lt Gen Matthew T. Cooper, Deputy Chief of Staff, Manpower and Reserve Affairs, USMC, noted that the Marines have traditionally been a volunteer force and they would not voluntarily assign women into direct combat units unless specifically directed to do so because of a policy decision. Cooper did not believe conscription would be required to fill marine grades.[28] Capt. Patricia A. Gavin, USAF, Maxwell AFB, Alabama, says, "Since the end of the draft and the beginning of the All-Volunteer Force with its 'shrinking manpower pool' women have been making up the void in the services that has been left by the end of the draft."[29]

In 1996, ADM Arthur said that Carney's conclusion was "predominately right. Not everyone is conscripted—not into a combat role." Senator Arlen Specter's (R-Pa.) view that everyone drafted would be going to war is not necessarily so. "The primary reason for the draft is to have enough manpower."[30] In 1995, Mady Segal said that an alternative to conscription might follow the examples of Canada and Sweden. Women can volunteer for combat jobs.[31] Israel conscripts both men and women, but only men have long reserve obligations and serve on active duty. Women's duty time is shorter and ends when they become mothers.

James D. Milko says the Persian Gulf War led to the repeal of the 1988 amendments to the Navy and Air Force public laws prohibiting women from serving in combat assignments. While the repeal is positive, he says further action is needed to open combat positions to qualified women on a volunteer basis. Opening positions on a volunteer basis would not lead to overturning the male-only draft registration law.[32]

DRAW DOWN

Historically, women have had a much lower propensity to enlist than men. Will the number of women who want to serve supplant the number of males or will their number be smaller than males? Is the military (particularly the infantry) usually short-handed, as it was in Vietnam and the Korean War?[33] Segal, Jones, Manos, and Rohall say that Western armed forces are asked to do more with less.[34]

BACKGROUND

Women's military roles become more important when national security is at stake. Few nations conscript women, and if they are drafted, their responsibilities differ from men's. According to Mady Segal, France, Greece, Norway, Germany (civilian jobs only), and the United Kingdom conscripted women in World War II. The United States did not conscript women, but did assign women to positions in the military. When World War II was over, women's military jobs were again limited. Women are seemingly treated as reservists in both civilian and military life.[35]

File papers entitled "Department of Defense (DOD) Response to Draft Registration Questions by Senator Sam Nunn (D-Ga.)" discuss the question of "How the Supreme Court would ultimately rule on the legality of male-only draft registration if Congress repealed the combat exclusion laws and the DOD implemented a gender neutral assignment policy for combat duty."[36] The Supreme Court decision in *Rostker v. Goldberg*, a case discussed in the context of the file papers, upheld male-only draft registration. The Court held that it was constitutionally permissible for Congress to conclude "that there would be no practical reason to draft women" and therefore "no reason to register them." Since the purpose of the draft would be to raise combat troops, women were simply not similarly situated with men for the purpose of draft registration. Second, by statute and DOD policy, women were not permitted combat assignments.

The file papers concluded that any future Supreme Court decision on the constitutionality of an all-male draft registration would closely examine any expression of congressional intent in amending or repealing the combat exclusion laws. Such a decision would also be a principal factor in determining the constitutionality of any future DOD combat exclusion policy. This paper held that if the laws were repealed and if DOD policy changed, "the underlying basis of the *Rostker* decision would be substantially eroded, if not removed. Thus, the male-only draft registration law would be subject to challenge."[37]

Col. Kenneth A. Deutsch, USAF, Director, Officer and Enlisted Personnel Management, wrote in a memorandum to CAPT Keating, USN, that Senator Nunn had also raised two other questions about the impact of a possible repeal of the combat exclusion policy on the draft and whether all males would be subject to assignment in combat.[38] Senator Nunn explained that the Supreme Court decision in 1981 relied heavily on policy.[39] If the DOD removed the combat exclusion in all services, would the Court rule that all women would have to be registered and subject to the draft? Nunn also raised the issue that it is probably service policy that all males are subject to being called into combat no matter what their classification—truck drivers, cooks, or mechanics—while women are not. Does this, he asks, set up a legal challenge by men saying they are not treated fairly because they are subject to go into combat? Would the services also subject all women to being called into combat?

A draft point paper on 10 U.S. Code § 6015 raises the same issue, "Could a draft/registration policy for men only withstand an equal protection challenge if § 6015 is repealed?"[40] The paper made four major points. First, the precedent-setting case, *Rostker v. Goldberg*, 453 U.S. 57 (1981), held there was no violation of equal protection in registering men only because the disparate treatment served an important government objective. The case resurfaced when President Carter requested a transfer of money from the DOD Selective Service to register men and women. Members of the executive branch and the military testified in support of that decision, but Congress allocated funds only to register males. The Court reasoned the purpose of the draft was to raise "combat troops." Since women were excluded from combat under statute and regulation, they could be excluded from the *Selective Service Act*. The Court articulated that Articles I and II of the Constitution vest authority in Congress and the executive branch that provides great latitude in determining the needs of the military. Therefore, if Congress and the executive branch thought noncombatant positions held by women could be filled by volunteers and if administrative burdens to process women as draftees through a different channel were too great, the Court would defer.

The majority of the judges relied heavily on the in-depth study made by Congress and statements to the effect that "our people" believed that women should not "intentionally and routinely engage in combat."[41] The draft point paper on 10 U.S. Code § 6015 asks the reader to compare the view of Congress with House Armed Services Committee report language on the proposed amendment to § 6015:

> Much of our current statutory law restricting the roles of women in combat appears to be an anachronism. Society is recognizing that in the wars of today and in the future, women will be exposed to combat regardless of whether they are on the front lines and that they deserve to be treated equally with their male compatriots.[42]

Second, the point paper stated that if some "combat unit" positions were open to women, the exclusion of women from the draft or registration would be more difficult to defend. A valid distinction could be made, however, on the degree of exposure to direct combat or the physical requirements for the positions for which women were to be drafted.[43] Third, the issue of including women in registration and the draft could be raised at any time if the law is amended or appealed. The last point made was that no draft of men or women can be conducted without congressional approval.[44]

Francine D'Amico noted in 1996 that *Rostker* ruled a male-only draft was constitutional, that is, it was not a violation of the Fourteenth Amendment for equal protection. The purpose of the draft was to raise troops for combat, which was not open to women. According to D'Amico, the rescinding of § 6015 and § 8549 after the Gulf War merely shifted discretion to the services.[45] Marian Neudel says, "This is all true as far as it goes, but all *Rostker* stands for is that Congress had the 'right,' if it 'chooses,' to draft only men. It does 'not' imply that Congress has ever 'lacked' the right to draft women."[46]

DISTRACTIONS

One important goal of the military is to keep distraction at a minimum for soldiers. Most people would not list the family as a distraction, but it can be if the military is not appropriately responsive. Soldiers, male or female, are more effective when they know their families are being taken care of while they serve their country.

Thus, gender is not the only distraction from military readiness. Some argue it is not a distraction. Others say it depends on what you mean by distraction. Do you mean that men and women cannot get along in a crisis or do you mean that attraction of the sexes is a distraction and therefore men and women cannot fight together?

When Col. Kelly Hamilton, USAF (Ret.), senior female pilot in Desert Storm and Assistant Director of Operations for Strategic Planning, Air Mobility Command, returned from the war, she was heavily involved in changing the Air Force's Combat Exclusion Law. "The argument," she said, "that it [mixed gender groups] was going to affect esprit de corps is a peacetime issue. Wartime people understand."[47]

When asked, "Do you think women are a negative distraction in combat of any kind?" ADM Arthur responded that it would depend on the situation.

> In the Navy and on a ship [women would be a] distraction anytime [whether] pleasant or unpleasant. The times in-between is when the distraction would be more important. During long periods of loneliness all of a sudden you are involved in a short time. Not so much on a ship because you are assigned an exact place.
>
> Military combatant personnel are in training most of the time. We also have to account for the fact that we are not at war very much of the time. Thus, the importance of training and peacetime become critical times to train how not to respond to any distraction.

Physical strength may not be as much of a factor on a ship, according to Arthur, who notes: "On a ship if one person is hurt, a lot of people are hurt and there isn't much you can do about it. There are occasions when we carry people.... In the field, during ground combat a wounded soldier may ask can she carry me off the battlefield."

Would either gender "take a hit" or leave someone behind? RADM Paul Gillcrist finds the question troublesome because the issue is always there whether someone will take a hit or leave someone behind *regardless of gender*. "Is it harder for a male to leave a female, or in the four or five seconds he would get killed while he ponders whether to leave?" Gillcrist asks.[48] "Air combat doesn't present this problem. One or the other is greater than the sum of his parts. One fellow threw himself on a grenade to save a life. Survival becomes overshadowed by the organization." Gillcrist asks, "Is this dependent on gender? This ought to be explored."[49]

At the crux of what Roxine C. Hart lists as a sociological issue is group interaction. The argument favoring women is that they may have a skill a male might not have, so they may very well complement one another. The other side argues that men may become inhibited in the presence of women, openly rebuff them, compete with them, or compete with other men for their attention.[50]

Experts testifying before the Presidential Commission stated there is a perception in combat units that women are incapable of accomplishing the physical demands of combat or may become pregnant to avoid combat.[51]

PSYCHOLOGICAL DIFFERENTIATION
BETWEEN "REAL WORLD" AND COMBAT

Col. Hamilton stresses that "the goal in war is to get the job done, be prepared, keep it light, so people don't dwell on what's coming."[52] Hamilton says that "keeping it light" helps psychologically. No doubt a sense of humor helps soldiers not only to differentiate between the two worlds of combat and peace, but also to be "ready" when the time comes.

PREGNANCY

The Presidential Commission found that, on the average, women are available only one hour a month less than men because of maternity leave. Women have a lower absence rate than males when pregnancy and postpartum convalescent leave are excluded. When pregnancy and convalescence are included, females have four times as much lost time as males. Finch reports, "The issue of pregnancy and its effect on deployability became a key concern for the Commission."[53] Finch thinks that women in the military are "here to stay," only women bear children, and the military must plan for pregnancies. The Commission, according to Finch, recommended that each unit be designated with a deployment probability code. A woman who became pregnant in a high probability coded unit would be transferred to a lower probability coded unit.

The General Accounting Office (GAO) reported that the DOD found non-deployables were not a serious problem in the Persian Gulf because the services could replace them. If the number of women increased, however, there is a potential for a deployment problem.

PREGNANCY EARLY IN LIFE

CAPT Sadler, USN (Ret.), and Patricia Thomas say that it is important to know how many women are pregnant at any one time in order to address effectively the impact of pregnancy. Citing the Navy Personnel Research and Development Center (NPRDC) survey of enlisted women in May 1988, 1990, and 1992, Sadler and Thomas report pregnancy rates for enlisted women ranged from 8.4 percent to 8.9 percent.[54] Pregnancy, they say, is manageable and "the solution is not to control or reduce the number of women in commands, but to reduce the number of unplanned pregnancies."[55] NPRDC found 68 percent of the pregnancies of junior women were unplanned. Over half the women were not using contraceptives. Times have changed, they conclude, and the Navy should deal with pregnancy through education that will help the Navy accomplish its missions without penalizing women, men, or commands. In February 1995, Secretary of the Navy John H. Dalton signed a new Navy policy on pregnancy affirming that pregnancy is a natural event and is not a presumption of medical incapacity.[56]

Pregnancy is most prevalent among women who have enlisted for the first time, and it peaks at the seaman apprentice and seaman pay grades. In 1992, 70 percent of the men who fathered the babies of women in the military were themselves in the military. Sadler and Thomas state that one possible reason for the higher rate among junior women is that they are at a very fertile period in their lives. The Navy pregnancy rate and civilian birth rate for the prime childbearing years of 20 to 29 are about the same. Other reasons they give for the pregnancy rate are that the women are often away from home for the first time with no support system, are outnumbered nine to one, and may not be able to deal with the resultant sexual attention.

Pregnancy rates are not higher among women assigned to sea than to shore. "The percentage of pregnant women who were assigned to a ship *at the time they became pregnant* was lower than the percentage who were ashore."[57] Between 1988 and 1993, the annual pregnancy rate on ships dropped by approximately 25 percent.

Although pregnancy is the primary reason women leave the Navy before planned, it is not likely to have a meaningful impact on separation rates within command. In the entire Navy, pregnancy ranked seventh as a reason for leaving and represented only four percent of all premature separations. Punitive reasons and personality disorders represented 25 and 24 percent, respectively, of the reasons for separation.[58]

The Navy requires pregnant women be transferred from ships no later than the twentieth week of pregnancy, but Sadler and Thomas maintain that pregnancy is not an unanticipated personnel transfer that could affect mission accomplishment. The date of the "impact," they explain, is known and should not be as disruptive as other losses. The 1991 NPRDC survey showed that ship vacancies resulting from pregnancy averaged 2.6 months, whereas vacancies from other causes last 5 or 6 months.[59]

Contrary to misconceptions, the survey showed that women did not get pregnant to avoid deployment, newly reported pregnancies did not peak right before deployment, and the percentage of time men and women were available for duty was about equal. The NPRDC results did show, however, that most respondents thought other personnel have to work longer and harder because of pregnant women. Sadler and Thomas contend that the mission is accomplished nonetheless and "just as a command copes when a man is in the brig or an unauthorized absentee, it also makes adjustments for a pregnant woman."[60] Some males feel a sense of inequity, however, because they hold the burden to deploy.

PRISONER OF WAR (POW)

Brig. Gen. Mike Hall testified about the POW issue before the Commission on the Assignment of Women in the Armed Services:

> The issue of gender with regard to [being a] prisoner of war (POW) is a non-issue to me. I see that as a human issue. I have read reports of male prisoners being repeatedly raped, military prisoners being repeatedly raped, as part of the process to break their self-esteem and to render them in a situation of absolute powerlessness. The crime of rape is a human crime, not a gender crime. It's a crime of power, and certainly can be as devastating to either gender.[61]

Hart indicates that training experience has not shown that women POWs would be more likely to give information to the enemy, accept special favors, fail to keep faith with other prisoners, or fail to follow orders. Therefore he concludes it is not likely that military women POWs will adversely affect national security any more than male POWs would.[62] RADM Gillcrist asks: "Is this [the female POW issue] really still a concern? It bothered me before the Gulf War. We watched it happen in the Gulf War and the women survived, came home, and told their stories."[63] All of war, he adds, is horrible.

One woman who talked about her experience as a POW was Rhonda Cornum. Cornum, a 37-year-old flight surgeon, said that it was unpleasant and there was a "phenomenal amount of focus on this for women but not for men." Men suffered more abuse. Maj. Jeffrey S. Tice, USAF, was tortured with jolts of electricity that caused a tooth to explode from its socket. Specialist (SPC) Melissa Coleman (Rathbun-Nealy) was sexually molested by Iraqi soldiers in the Gulf War. According to the Pentagon, 19 American POWs in the Gulf War were sexually abused.[64]

Like Cornum, Hamilton says that the possibility of becoming a POW is not limited to those whose assignment is technically labeled combat. She notes that it is significant Cornum's capture and Rossi's death highlighted the "Catch-22" of the Combat Exclusion Law, 10 U.S. Code § 8549, because these women were considered noncombatants. "The argument that the Combat Exclusion Law existed to protect women was clearly flawed. In the twentieth century war scenario, the definition of battlefield and combatant had blurred."[65] Hamilton also points out that because the media attempted to show the grimness of what could happen, the result was an "unexpected lesson in history." Women POWs of World War II and the Korean War were now willing to tell their remarkable stories.

Finch says the possibility of women becoming POWs was a key issue to the Presidential Commission. There appears to be a greater likelihood of sexual molestation and rape of women POWs than of men POWs. Finch agrees with Hamilton that "the fact that two women could be captured and taken prisoner while not serving in combat positions shows how dangerous the modern battlefield really is and that all service members are in danger of capture regardless of position."[66] In a follow-up interview in 1997, Finch noted, "Although one of the two women taken prisoner during Desert Storm admitted to being sexually molested (it is likely the other woman also was), 26 women in Desert Storm reported being raped by U.S. Army forces (their fellow soldiers) during the withdrawal of forces from the Gulf."[67]

Hamilton wrote home during the Gulf War: "The POW situation is, unfortunately, just what the Air Force has prepared us for, the inhumanity and insanity of war. Having to review the data on your 'rescue card' prior to each flight has a really sobering effect. The information contained on the card is one set of data you must truly commit to memory. Under the highest stress your answer must be the correct one in order to facilitate a rapid rescue."[68] Hamilton was well aware that a combat aviator cannot divulge secrets and wrote home, "Now, on the subject of operating location, I must stand by my favorite old quote, 'I could tell you where I am, but then I would have to kill you.'"[69] As a graduate of military flight training, she took water and land survival courses. "Alongside our male counterparts we endured the rigors of Survival Training and Prisoner of War camp in which we were taught to escape, evade, and if captured, how to resist and survive."[70] The POW training was very realistic. It included periods of intense interrogation using a variety of techniques that were intended to create psychological and physical distress and strip captives of their self-esteem. "These were not classroom courses where you go home at night to a warm bed," she adds. Hamilton feels the training, while not something she would want to experience again, taught her something about herself and her strengths and weaknesses as well as how to recognize and control her fears. Most importantly, she gained a deep and abiding appreciation of her commitment to the United States.

The second issue often raised is that the judgment of male POWs will be adversely affected because women are present, causing them to take an incorrect course of action. Critics of women in combat also believe that the enemy will capitalize on the situation by torturing the women to break men's resistance.[71]

The President's Commission reviewed existing studies, listened to expert testimony, visited on-site training, and interviewed experts. According to Finch, instructors in the Air Force's Survival Training course (SERE) found that male prisoners had a more highly protective response to their fellow women prisoners than to their male counterparts. Instructors testified that such a response can be trained out of men because heightened reactions increase the likelihood that captors will abuse the women prisoners. Finch concludes, "If they really are concerned with protecting the women, the best thing they can do is to control their reactions."[72]

Opponents of assigning women in combat, says Finch, have argued training that desensitizes males would contribute to the decay of society. Even though the Roper Survey produced some evidence that the American public is supportive of women in combat, 44 percent of those surveyed believe greater protection should be offered to women. Finch believes it is unknown whether mistreatment of women POWs would destroy or increase the American will to fight.[73]

Since the percentages of air crew members captured in both the Vietnam and Gulf wars were less than one percent, Finch does not think that opening up combat roles to women will increase the likelihood of women being taken prisoners. It is not a major stumbling block, she concludes.

Conclusions

Pfluke is hesitant to say we are dealing with a cultural value because culture holds diverse opinions. There is no one element to a culture.[74] Although some issues surrounding readiness may be a result of our acculturation to the belief that women should not be assigned to ground combat because they are not qualified, it does not make the issues any less real for those people struggling with the change. I do believe that those issues are peacetime issues and in the heat of combat, military necessity prevails. Our military leadership and our armed forces will deal with their mission to protect and defend our Constitution in a ready manner by making use of available talent to ensure our very freedom.

Chapter 9

Cohesion

We will fight like lions. Until the last [wo]man is killed.
—French soldier calling from the darkness
during the American Revolution[1]

Effective military leadership deals with factors affecting cohesion, real or perceived. Forces that do not help soldiers work together for the common good affect the protection of our country. With a variety of examples illustrating a lack of cohesiveness in academies, military schools, and training grounds, effective leadership to address cohesion in training is a current concern. Some people argue, however, that some of the perceived issues will not surface in a combat situation. MAJ Mary Finch, USA and a member of the U.S. Presidential Commission on the Assignment of Women in the Armed Forces, states, "Clearly the most complicated and still undecided issue is how women in combat units will affect cohesion."[2] At the time the Commission was deliberating, all cohesion research was limited to all-male combat units, notes Finch.

PRIVACY

Practicality and privacy in care of bodily functions where there is a "zero privacy" environment on the battlefield may affect cohesion, according to some.[3] RADM Paul T. Gillcrist says that the article written by James H. Webb, Jr., while he was a professor at Annapolis caused him some embarrassment when he became Secretary of the Navy because he concluded in the article that women cannot fight.[4] Webb reasoned that because latrines were exposed in a combat zone, women could not fight. Latrines were exposed so service people would not get killed while attending to their bodily functions.[5] In 1996 a young female officer speaking to a ROTC class said, "What's the big deal? Pull a tarp over your head and squat." Still some, M. C. Devilbliss, for example, argue that feminine hygiene poses a cohesion problem.[6]

In 1996, Col Paul Roush, USMC (Ret.), and a 1957 Naval Academy professor, noted, "Webb's views against women in combat roles perpetuate 'the politics of resentment' and breed cynicism among midshipmen and the military
at large."[7] Roush said there is plenty of data to show women can fly planes and
serve on ships. He believes that Webb's article "'has been the single greatest
purveyor of degradation and humiliation' for women at the academy. The stress
women suffered is greater than 'an infinite number of beatings with a cricket
bat.'" Webb was repeatedly struck with a cricket bat until it broke to help prepare him and other academy cadets to be combat officers and withstand the
rigors of capture by the enemy. As a result, Roush continued, those women are
"more prepared to be a warrior than all of their male counterparts."

BONDING

Michael Rustad believes it is a mistake to blame problems of women
solely on the attitudes of males. Excerpts Rustad pulled from the *Final Report*
of the Army Administration Center in 1978 revealed many of the same spe-
cious arguments why women would create tension. It was suggested that women
would interfere with male bonding and inappropriately bond with men.[8]

MAJ Paul Christopher, USA, says that another fallacious argument is that
a disparity exists between men and women in that women are more nurturing. Some observers who believe in this disparity think the nurturing characteristic will interfere with women's ability to place mission before people.
Women are unsuited for combat in their opinion because they cannot make
tough battlefield decisions. Christopher does not agree with the assertion that
no feasible tool exists for measuring emotional capability and that because nurturing is known to be a feminine quality, there is no choice but to exclude
females from combat.[9] Are women more innately nurturing and if so, will it
necessarily interfere with their service in combat? Christopher restates the
premise, "It is affirmed that women are innately more nurturing than men in
their relationships with members of the same sex and or in their relationships
with members of the opposite sex." Examining homogeneous relationships
first, it seems highly questionable that women develop with other women
alliances that are any stronger or more nurturing than the relationships that
men develop with other men. It is reasonable to believe bonds of friendship
that develop between members of the same sex are no different for women than
they are for men. "There is no reason to believe that the female 'bonding' that
occurs through normal association is any stronger than the male bonding that
is said to occur. And even if some instances of exceptionally strong ties between
females were documented, it is not reasonable to suppose that such relationships are based on some innate disposition. If women are more nurturing, it
must encompass their relationships with the opposite sex." It is interesting to
note that Christopher believes that in most male-female relationships—hus-

band and wife, girlfriend and boyfriend—it is the man, not the woman, who is usually considered to be the more protective and nurturing. In fact, he says, this contention that men are more protective of women than they are of other men forms the basis for a separate argument on why women should be excluded from combat roles. If some women are more nurturing in some relationships, the same can be said of men. Christopher concludes, "Therefore, women are not naturally disposed to be more nurturing than men are in their relationships with others of the same or opposite sex." He rejects the idea that women have an innate biological disposition to nurture that extends beyond their relationship with their children.

BGen. Wilma L. Vaught, USAF (Ret.), president of the Women in Military Service for America Memorial Foundation (WIMSA), states: "Bonding is grossly overstated. Bonding occurs when people have a job to do and a stake in the outcome. Bonding has less to do with ethnicity and gender. When the chips are down, we bridge those differences. I have been trained to help women. On the battlefield, helping your buddy has nothing to do with gender."[10] Vaught believes the answer to the issue of service in combat is being able to do what one is trained to do.

BGen. Mike Hall, New York Air National Guard, Adjutant General of the State of New York, and former theater air liaison officer to the Central Command in Operation Desert Storm, testified before the Presidential Commission that cohesion is a leadership issue. "It has to do with what values you affirm, and that's cultural. It's not an easy thing to change cultural values."[11] Hall stated that the services should not maintain segregated units because they lead to behaviors that society as a whole judges inappropriate, such as the misconduct at Tailhook '91. He does not believe we would see the kinds of things that hurt the military deeply as a result of Tailhook, "if you had more women in more units, because there would no longer be a situation of what is classically referred to as male bonding."

Male bonding is not always positive; it can produce devastatingly negative results, as Hall notes:

> I remember, as a youngster about eight years old, listening to my grandfather tell me a story of his youth in Tampa, Florida, when a group of white males, incensed that a black man had allegedly raped a white woman, tied that person to the back of car, dragged him around town, and left his carcass in the black neighborhood as an example, to prevent others from creating the same kind of crime. That's classic male bonding, and it doesn't belong in our society.[12]

Hall lived in segregated dormitories. Women's dorms were some place else, some place you might like to sneak into. After he graduated, the dorms became coed and a whole new culture was formed. What he and his contemporaries had found titillating "just became everyday life for people in that experience." Hall says that in a public service such as the military, members are asked "to check our personal beliefs and our inappropriate behaviors at the door when we enter, and that is an issue of discipline." An enlightened leadership will view bonding as a manageable issue, adds Hall.[13]

MAJ Mary Finch says:

> The general concept of women in the infantry is that the squad bonds. If women train with their units, the members will know she can and will do her job. That's all that matters. The guys will accommodate her. As with mixed gender noncombat units, the squad will be cohesive or not based on a number of factors to include mission, leadership, and quality of soldier.
>
> I have seen men take great pride in the women in their units. The same thing will happen [in combat units]. Some men, particularly older men, see women soldiers as their wife or daughter, and can't relate to her as a soldier. They want to take her under their wing—to protect her. These guys are getting more exposure. It's going to get better.[14]

MGen. Holm supports Zimmerman's concept of men and women bonding in the Persian Gulf War.[15] Men and women shared the agony of anticipation in the Persian Gulf War because long-range artillery and surface-to-surface missiles were unisex weapons. Holm underscores the bond by explicitly titling a section of her chapter on the Persian Gulf War, "Death Did Not Discriminate." Thirteen women, notes Holm, did not come home alive. The first women to die since Vietnam and the first enlisted women to be killed in action, they perished with 25 males on February 25, 1991, when a Scud missile hit their barracks near Dhahran.

Holm reports on peoples' reactions to the deaths of those thirteen women[16] A former employer of SPC Beverly Clark, a recent high school graduate, said, "There's been a lot of tears [here]."

David Fairbanks, fiancée of SPC Christine Mayes, 22, tells us, "She didn't really want to be over there any more than the rest of them, but that's what she got paid for; that's what she did."

Some ways people die are harder to take than others. SPC Adrienne L. Mitchell, 20, wanted to finance her own education under the G.I. Bill. She wrote home to her parents that she was not afraid and the Scud missiles were the only thing service people worried about. Three days later she died. Her father, Frank Mitchell, a retired Air Force Chief Master Sergeant noted that he served 30 years and did not get a scratch, while his daughter died after five months.

Holm dedicates her book to one of the women who died, MAJ Marie T. Rossi, 32, pilot and Commander of B Company, 18th Army Aviation Brigade.[17] MAJ Rossi and three men in her crew were killed on March, 1991, the day after the Persian Gulf War ceasefire. Her helicopter hit an unlit tower at night in bad weather. Warrant Officer Ken Copley, helicopter pilot and veteran of the Vietnam War, paid Rossi the ultimate pilot's compliment: "She was one of the most respected pilots I have ever known." Rossi had flown several times into Iraq facing hostile fire.

On February 24, 1991, on the eve of the massive ground assault into Iraq, Rossi stated her philosophy in a CNN interview. She said that what she was doing was no greater or less than the man who was flying next to her or in back of her. She clearly saw women as soldiers. Sometimes a person has to "disassociate" how she feels personally about the prospect of going to war, she said, and see the death that is going to be out there. Yet she also knew it was the moment that everyone trains for and she was ready to meet the challenge.

Capt. Terry VandenDolder, an Air Force Reserve pilot who flew 22 bodies home, said there was great sadness and grief for the lives lost, but no more for the women than the men. These few faces from Holm's research of women who died in combat convincingly show that it is a bond because death and the willingness to die is an equalizer.

Most women and men I interviewed told me that if I were to ask most men whether they wanted to go to war, they would say they do not. Dorothy Schneider and Carl Schneider point out that half of the men are going to perform well under a high stress situation and half will not. The same is true with women. The interviews revealed that some people believe if women are allowed to fight when they have to, why not when they want to? The enemy knows that killing women in war, whether combatant or noncombatant, is a morale factor for their opponents, who view the accomplishment as one which the enemy uses in their favor. "Get this word to the front and back home that they've killed a number of women."[18]

Some service women are against combat, say the Schneiders. Some interviewees offered comments such as: men are born warriors, I'd freeze up, I don't want to be there, we have cycles. Among the reasons service women advanced for having women in combat were the following: women feel cheated, I'd rather go than not, it made me feel good to have the commander put it in writing that he had confidence in me.[19]

Lt Col Greg Morin, USMC, says that in combat soldiers will bond regardless of their background or gender.[20] Danna Maller, a former Army helicopter pilot, thinks that men can bond with women. "When the situation is intense, your main concern is getting the mission accomplished. You tend to forget personality differences. It is a very high-pressure environment and you focus on getting things done."[21]

Conclusions

In armed conflict, men and women not only will bond, but have been bonding throughout time. Legal changes that have occurred affect policy and both law and policy affect behavior. In conflict, what matters is the successful completion of the mission by whomever is qualified to work on it. It is a leadership challenge, but not an unfamiliar one. Not all people of the same gender are necessarily going to have the ability to form a cohesive group. Mixed gender groups are working now, not without challenge, but they are working for the common good of keeping our nation safe.

Chapter 10

Ability

The meaning of gender is socially constructed.
Mady Segal[1]

Male-Female Abilities

A discussion of ability in the military almost always provokes questions about whether women can "measure up" to some specific standard in some specific test whose consequence will be apparent at some specific time. The congressional hearings of 1993 and 1994 and the Presidential Commission's report are filled with effective argumentation to fit any position and to support any argument. They include statements that it is not physical characteristics but cohesion and absolute trust that are more important.[2] The Presidential Commission recommended that the services should retain gender-specific physical fitness tests and standards to promote the highest level of fitness and wellness in the armed forces. The Commission was more divided, however, when it discussed occupational physical requirements, basic training standards, and precommissioning standards. It voted 14–0 that the services should adopt gender-neutral muscular strength and endurance and cardiovascular requirements for those specialties for which they are relevant. The purpose of the 1994 hearing of the Military Forces and Personnel Subcommittee of the House Committee on Armed Services, titled Assignment of Army and Marine Corps Women Under the New Definition of Ground Combat, was to evaluate the impact of changes in assignment policy for women on the constitutionality of an all-male military selective service and the need to establish gender-neutral physical performance standards for military positions being opened up for both sexes. What do all of these multitudes of tests and positions mean? Most interviewees say, "Assign a military position on the basis of a person's qualifications, not gender." As CAPT Rosemary Mariner, USN, has said, "A Soldier Is a Soldier." Unfortunately, if physical qualifications are approached on the basis of gender, then qualifications will not have to be closely examined. Thus, rather than present every physical test that I can find and present every single argument for or against a certain aspect of physical testing, I have chosen to present some reasoning to support CAPT Mariner's concept, "A Soldier Is a Soldier."

GENDER AND STRENGTH, STAMINA, AND OTHER BIOLOGICAL DIFFERENCES

Division of labor may have been useful in earlier times, but it is less so now. Technology, as Mady Segal points out, has decreased the importance of physical strength and reproduction. How society deals with gender differences is very important. Women's roles in the military are a cultural interpretation of gender. Cultures can stress gender equality or gender differences, and stressing either will have an effect on the military woman's role. Segal maintains, "The greater the emphasis on ascription by gender (and thereby the less the emphasis on individual differences), the more limited women's military role."[3]

LT Michael J. Frevola, an attorney who is a member of the U.S. Naval Reserve, agrees with Segal that with the advent of modern weaponry, Congress's concerns that women will be overpowered are misplaced. It is more important now to have superior technical skill, intelligence, and training. Even the Army and Marine Corps are mechanized in some fashion and possess automatic and lightweight weaponry.[4] Some specialties such as Special Forces still require uncommon physical strength, but their numbers are small and their requirements prohibit an "overwhelming majority of men and women from becoming members." Frevola's research shows, however, that the Department of Defense no longer supports the idea that women cannot fill the position of a front-line infantryman successfully. According to Frevola, military sources have said that military institutions have not altered their physical readiness requirements to accommodate women except where absolutely necessary. The Navy and Marine Corps acknowledge that a service member who successfully completes basic training can fill any line position, but in 1996 the Army and Air Force still utilize strength testing for same jobs. Frevola believes there is always a "gender overlap"—the strongest and largest women will be stronger and larger than the smallest men eligible for combat duty. If strength requirements for graduating basic training for men and women were the same, the weakest women in the ranks would not be weaker than the weakest man and thus any worse off than some of her fellow male soldiers. Strength requirements should be decided by position, he concludes, and not by gender.

B Gen Margaret A. Brewer, USMC, (Ret.), believes that military women could appropriately be assigned to all occupational fields except the direct ground combat specialties. These specialties generally require a high degree of physical strength. She adds, "If, at some future time, a decision is made to assign women to direct ground combat specialties then valid definitive performance standards should be established for men and women. The establishment of such physical strength standards would help to ensure that anyone, male or female, who does not meet the standards would not be assigned to that combat specialty."[5]

Ability of Women to Carry Their Weight

THE INFANTRY

Before the Army froze the recruiting of women at about nine percent during the Reagan administration, GEN Edward C. Meyer, Army Chief of Staff during the Carter Administration, established the Women in the Army Policy Review Group (WITA) which was charged with reviewing the issues involved and formulating policy. The direct combat definition became official, and the issue of physical capabilities surfaced. WITA established physical strength requirements for each military occupation specialty (MOS).[6] The General Accounting Office (GAO) also recommended gender-free strength testing of potential recruits. WITA agreed, saying, "The Army cannot be assured of accomplishing the ground combat mission if women are randomly accessed into positions with physically demanding tasks exceeding their capabilities." The Air Force developed similar tests. A test to measure strength and endurance, MEP-SCAT (Military Enlistment Physical Strength Capacity Test), was developed but never implemented. In 1985 the Air Force dismissed WITA's findings "because there was no proof that those who lacked the strength to perform their assigned tasks actually degraded unit effectiveness."[7]

MAJ Paul Christopher, USA, maintains that if assignments to combat units are restricted based on physical standards, those standards must be applied equally to both sexes.[8] To apply them only to women is unreasonable and discriminatory, he adds. He rejects the arguments that try to exclude women from combat based on an alleged physical difference.

Physical fitness tests, referred to as PT tests, determine individual physical fitness, not qualification, for combat readiness, says MAJ Pfluke.[9] Gender and age norming is the only way to measure physical fitness accurately. "This is NOT to say that the physical qualifying standards for jobs should be gender or aged normed," clarifies Pfluke. Using physical fitness tests as a reason to exclude women from jobs that they are qualified for is a wrong use of the tests, and these tests can sometimes affect morale. Pfluke proposes more education within the services as to the true purpose of these tests.

Some observers argue that certain women would be strong enough to be in the infantry, but they would be such a minority that their numbers in the infantry would not reach critical mass, in the psychological sense. In 1993 the Canadian infantry found that when they opened to women, they got one volunteer. She was a very lonely infantry person. LTG Thomas P. Carney, Deputy

Chief of Staff for Personnel, USA, says that for reasons of unit cohesion and other issues he doesn't see the Army voluntarily or involuntarily placing women into infantry roles.[10] The question we have to ask Carney and others who hold similar positions is, do we reach critical mass of needed numbers with all men? (See Chapter 8.) Another argument posed is that men are more aggressive. But as Helen Rogan asks, how do women feel about being in combat with men who are not adequate to back *them* up?[11]

J. Michael Brower says, "One of the oldest myths surrounding the question of women in the military has been that females simply lack, in general, the physical stamina to sustain the most demanding tasks, including combat."[12] Army researchers have destroyed the myth with a new study that indicates women can develop adequate strength if trained correctly. In May 1995, the training began, ninety minutes a day, five days a week. More than 75 percent of the 41 women studied were found fit for traditional male military duties. Before the training 25 percent of the women could perform the tasks. The women ran a two-mile wooded course wearing a 75-pound rucksack and performed squats holding a 100-pound barbell on their shoulders. Women are not allowed, however, to compete for many jobs involving heavy lifting, says Brower. This study along with one carried out by the Ministry of Defence in Great Britain with similar findings should help dispel the myth of women's physical incapacity.[13] Brower reminds us that "without the proper credentials, military women can never be full partners with their male counterparts."[14] Only a small percentage, he continues, of people assigned to combat actually are ever exposed to direct enemy fire, but combat is a necessary assignment for military men and women whose goals are the top military positions. Twenty-five percent of all recruits are female, adds Brower, but without a combat assignment, top key positions will not be available to them.

Brower says that the military's "separate but unequal policy, like the proverbial house divided against itself, cannot long stand the batterings of social progress at work on its bigoted superstructure."[15] The military's most prestigious and meaningful positions are within the combat arms. These positions, says Brower, are not available to women because their job tracks remain restrictive. "High rank may be conceded, but it is the *position* that females are permitted to retain that truly measures their progress within what is still popularly perceived to be a males' game, despite the presence of more women under arms than ever."[16] Many of the arguments against assigning women to combat positions, according to Brower, are a smokescreen, reflect a double standard, and "are as flat as decanted champagne today."[17]

RMC Roxine C. Hart notes that the biological issues, especially strength and endurance, are among the debatable questions concerning women in combat. The usual arguments concerning women's biological capability involve their potential to perform physically and that is affected by prior athletic activity. If women continue to increase their participation in athletics, then they will be more capable. Second, the real issue is how strong does a woman have to be? If we acknowledge that not all men are physically capable for some combat assignments, we should also acknowledge that some women are physically capable. In contrast, opponents say that body composition, size, mass, fat distribution, and structure contribute more to strength, explosive power, speed, throwing and jumping abilities. Cardiorespiratory differences also favor men in size of heart, lungs, oxygen content and uptake, hemoglobin content, body temperature, and sweat gland functions.[18]

MENSTRUATION AND PREGNANCY

Many believe that field duty is no place for a pregnant woman unless there is an absolute way to utilize her. Hart, however, maintains that pregnancy and menstruation are not unfavorable if the enormous range of individual differences concerning what women can and cannot do while pregnant is considered. What must also be considered is the range of types of combat jobs. Women are pregnant for a small portion of their lives, some women never are pregnant, and most people in combat jobs do not spend the majority of their time in combat. Hart adds that pregnancy is not likely for a prisoner of war (POW). Stress and poor diet would probably cause women prisoners to experience amenorrhea and thus be incapable of becoming pregnant. Perhaps the most convincing argument Hart gives is that military nurses have endured menstruation without a reduction in their ability to perform their wartime duties.[19] Hart says that the real problems of menstruation in the field are probably those having to do with privacy and cleanliness.[20]

Pregnancy is the only temporary disability that service members inflict upon themselves without fear of punishment. As ADM Stanley R. Arthur points out: "There is no penalty for getting pregnant and not deploying. The stats are basically no different in amount of lost time, they are about the same. The issue comes to a head in deployability. There are always a few people who find an excuse not to deploy. Those people are usually trying to take advantage, but you can deal with it directly."[21] Arthur raises the issue of whether some women get pregnant so they don't have to deploy. Because there is a ratio of 15 percent females to 85 percent males, the loss of a female is more apparent. It is not necessarily clear, however, whether a pregnant woman has planned her pregnancy. And a pregnancy can happen whether the person is single or married. "It will take care of itself eventually, but will always be a sticky point," Arthur concludes.

The Navy

BACKGROUND

The Navy's progress has not been without a struggle. In 1974, *Parade* magazine featured a female pilot, LT Judy Neuffer. The picture caption reads,

"The Navy issued Judy a man's uniform, but they didn't require her to meet the same physical fitness tests that men must go through to became pilots."[22] Neuffer was the first of eight women admitted into the Navy's flight program. The caption is harsher than the contents of the article, but it led to an internal examination by the Navy of the physical qualifications of women naval aviators.[23] R. E. Smith, Ph.D., based his concerns upon the Supreme Court decision *Griggs v. Duke Power Company*. He believed the selection requirements for pilots were not job related or they were discriminatory against some males. "If a male who meets the same physical standards as a female is rejected because higher standards are required of males, this would constitute a clear case of sex discrimination in employment."[24]

CAPT Larry G. Parks, Assistant JAG, indicated the report concerning the waiver of physical qualifications was accurate, but that standards had been revised so they were currently the same for all personnel. *Griggs* in fact dealt with the application of Title VII of the *Civil Rights Act of 1964*, which was not applicable to the Department of the Navy.[25] The proposed response to Smith from the Judge Advocate General's Office states that Congress itself has in some instances created distinctions in law based on gender. Title 10 U.S. Code § 6015 is "particularly relevant," the letter continues, because it prohibits the assignment of women to aircraft engaged in combat missions. The letter also pointed out that "the Supreme Court recently upheld [*Schlesinger v. Ballard*] the validity of the statutes which treat men and women officers differently for purposes of discharge."[26] According to the letter, the Court had relied partially upon Congress's rationale to compensate women with regard to tenure for their lesser opportunity for promotion.

The letter notes that the standards for a program of physical conditions have been revised; approaching gender norming, a policy several women interviewers say should be implemented today.[27] "The capability which is measured is that of the whole person. Women as well as men are evaluated from the standpoint of a rigorous overall performance standard."[28] Policy changed even though *Griggs* was not applicable. It was an institutional beginning.

It was only a beginning, however. According to some military women who lived through the institutional struggle, policy didn't change until the law changed. And other military women think the policy has not changed enough. The potential of these women is not fully utilized.

CAPT Rosemary Mariner, a naval aviator, says that because of hydraulic controls, upper body strength is not a factor in airplanes. Ejection seats are also designed to accommodate lightweight soldiers. Mariner notes, "We've had a number of lightweight women, as we do lightweight men, eject successfully over this 22-year period."[29]

LT Carey D. Lohrenz, F-14 Tomcat pilot and squadron mate of LT Kara Hultgreen (see Chapter 2), is the pilot who was referred to as "Pilot B" in the aftermath of Hultgreen's fatal crash. In 1994, Lohrenz and Hultgreen were the first female pilots to complete F-14 training and to be assigned to squadrons on the West Coast. According to James W. Crawley of the *San Diego Union-Tribune*, critics of the Navy have questioned both aviators' training:[30]

> A report by the Center for Military Readiness, a group opposed to women in combat roles, stated that both Hultgreen and another female pilot, called "Pilot B," were given preferential treatment during training at Miramar. Although the report did not name "Pilot B," she is described as an F-14 pilot assigned to the *Lincoln*. Lohrenz was the only female F-14 pilot aboard the *Lincoln*, Navy officials acknowledged.

According to Crawley, Elaine Donnelly, director of the Center for Military Readiness (CMR) and a member of the Presidential Commission, said that the Navy had created a double standard in training women as combat pilots.

On April 22, 1996, Susan Barnes, WANDAS (Women Active in Our Nation's Defense, Their Advocates and Supporters), filed a lawsuit in Washington, D.C., District Court against Elaine Donnelly, CMR. According to the Center's own newsletter, *V.I.P. Notes*, "CMR had previously identified LT Lohrenz as 'Pilot B' to protect her identity to the greatest extent possible, but will cease doing so because LT Lohrenz has now publicized her name with the lawsuit and a personal appearance on national television."[31]

In a "CMR Friend" letter in February 1997, Donnelly writes,

> The information was so specific and disturbing that CMR brought it to the attention of the Senate Armed Services Committee. Four months later, after a series of meetings with high-level Navy officials we learned two things:
> • Kara Hultgreen and the second female aviator really did receive extraordinary concessions in training to fly the F-14; and
> • Due to perceived political pressures being brought to bear on the Navy, nothing substantive would be done to acknowledge the problem, much less correct it.[32]

The letter also states that "Actual training records indicated that the women were simply not allowed to fail" and that the Center for Military Readiness later acted out of concern for both men and women when it "published a 25 page *Special Report: Double Standards in Naval Aviation* in April of 1995, accompanied by 105 pages of training records and evidence of extraordinary concessions extended to the two women during their training."[33]

From 1992 to 1995, Navy statistics show that 128 pilots and flight officers, including 7 women, were brought before field naval aviator evaluation boards. The Navy had 11,693 pilots and flight officers, says Crawley. Of the 128 evaluated, 56 were grounded permanently and 72 were approved for flying. Of the 7 female pilots, 3 have been permanently grounded by evaluation boards since October 1992. In 1992 the Navy had 287 female pilots and flight officers.

According to Crawley, the CMR distributed training records obtained from anonymous sources which indicated Lohrenz had received three downs (serious mistake affecting flight safety), two signals of difficulty (less serious but needs to be corrected), and two unsatisfactory grades that were either changed or not recorded on the official records. Two or more downs result in an evaluation board hearing and possibly the end of an aviator's career.

In February 1997, VADM J. R. Fitzgerald, the Navy Inspector General (NIG), reported that the Navy did not discriminate against and did not give preferential treatment to the first group of female combat naval aviators. Some unskilled male leadership annoyed women and angered men who viewed the leadership as either showing favoritism or being condescending.

RADM Paul Gillcrist, an F-14 aviator, has commented upon this case:

> These weren't all landing grades. I do not know if there is a written policy in the Pacific Fleet. A down is when the pilot has to go back and refly. A Training Squadron Human Resource Board evaluates and says the pilot has to refly, but first if we go down again, we go before an official Naval Board by Card Office. They may decide if they are going to terminate the flight status or recommend to terminate flight status. The Skipper of the Training Squadron may decide either way. In the case of the two females' allegation, were they especially lenient? That may be; that I don't know, but it's one thing to say you can go back and try it again under carefully monitored conditions, than to say she is safe, when she is not, is another thing. They may send the female back again and again and it is not criminal, but it is wrong. It may be that they gave her more chances, but it is another thing to declare her safe. To give her more chances in a monitored situation is not criminal. To say she is safe in an unmonitored situation would be criminal.

Gillcrist says he had been sent back and then he would come back and do better. But he says that if he had been sent back ten times by some Landing Signal Officer (LSO), he would have thought the situation was silly, forget it. "Is nine, eight, seven or six too many times?" asks Gillcrist. "It is a judgment call, but not to be implied as morally wrong, it is a monitored situation."[34]

When asked whether he thought female pilots were given extra training and their unsatisfactory performances were redesignated afterward as practice flights to a greater extent than has been done for men, Gillcrist says that the Navy has done this for men, that is, given extra training. He cites the example of the French pilots who came over to get ready to fly the F-8 in the late sixties and early seventies. There was always a concern whether these Frenchmen understood English and special American phrases well enough, so the LSOs were careful on the radio. When they said such things as "wave off," they would make sure the French pilots knew what "wave off" meant. Gillcrest observes, "French pilots got more chances than American pilots, which was deemed appropriate because of the language differences. Were the French guys any better? No, but they got preferential treatment. We made an exception. Again the LSOs wouldn't clear unless the pilots were safe. The LSOs reputation is on the line when he approves someone."

"Is there really a double standard?" I asked.

"Maybe LSOs were told to give the young females a fair shake and bent over backward and gave her more chances, but standards were not changed, just the opportunity to get to the standard *may* have been more. There is nothing wrong, this is not unsafe. Senior officials might acknowledge that they tell LSOs this," emphasizes Gillcrist, "They were either safe or not safe." Gillcrist doesn't think any woman deemed by an LSO to go to a carrier is unsafe. "The LSO's not going to do it. He's not going to risk his own life to say that."

Admiral Arthur would agree: "As a naval aviator for 37 years, I can assure you there is no quota policy when it comes to earning the Navy's 'Wings of Gold.' Those charged with training young men and women to fly know that the student naval aviator they train today could be their wingman tomorrow. No one involved in this training would push through a pilot who was unsafe or unqualified."[35]

In February 1996, Susan Barnes, who identified herself as "the attorney for the surviving F-14 pilot (the infamous 'Pilot B' who was vilified along with Lt. Hultgreen in a 'report' issued by a right wing organization opposed to women in combat)," posted comments about the case on H-MINERVA's "List for Discussion of Women and the Military and Women in War". Barnes noted that she had "actually read many of the records on which the 'report' is allegedly based and ... become very familiar with the training environment in which the women were required to operate."[36] According to Barnes, "the report, entitled Double Standards in Naval Aviation, is allegedly based on training records that were stolen by a fellow officer of Hultgreen and Pilot B in violation of federal law. More importantly, the Report MISREPRESENTS the content of those training records. I know. I have read the Report and have compared it to the content of the training records."

According to Barnes, the Center for Military Readiness is not a genuine "think tank" in the usual sense. "It is a radical right front for a woman named Elaine Donnelly who has a long, and very public, record of opposition to military women."

Barnes is an "advocate for military women who greatly admires their willingness to serve their country in a variety of unique, difficult and challenging roles." At the time of this post, Barnes could not answer the following questions she posed because of client-attorney restrictions:

> Before you come to a conclusion as to the competency question wouldn't you like to know: whether the "scores" by which the competency of the female combat pilots are measured are based on an objective scoring system or subjective system? I.e., is the scoring "system" something that can be observed with objective criteria that apply to all or is it

more like scoring a figure skating competition where the perceptions of the scorer color the outcome? How the scores of the women—all in their first year in the fighter aircraft—compare with the scores of their male aviators AT THE SAME LEVEL OF EXPERIENCE? What the background and experience is of the guys who are grading carrier landing performance? Whether there are any extraneous factors (prior involvement in Tailhook scandal, promotion being held up, history of public or private opposition to admittance of women to their exclusive club—the fighter jock community) that affect their ability to judge the women fairly? Would you like to know how many of the 22 were still at Miramar when Hultgreen and Pilot B arrived there and how many of them had the opportunity to grade Hultgreen and Pilot B on their performance? Would you like to know the actual facts as to how young male aviators in circumstances similar to those of the women are treated in the training command and in the squadron? And how about the safety record of the F-14? How many accidents in the last several years? When a male pilot totals a multi-million dollar aircraft and survives, how does the Navy respond? More training and keep flying or removal from flight status? How does the training the women really receive compare to the training of the men?

Barnes's questions pose far-reaching research implications beyond the resources of this author, but my support and interest follow her, for I too am not an unbiased observer. The military woman presents us with an opportunity to honor her service in unique, difficult, and challenging roles.

According to Evan Thomas and Gregory L. Vistica in *Newsweek*, there is a still-secret draft of an inspector general's report questioning whether women of Air Group 11 were given adequate support on the USS *Abraham Lincoln*. All new carrier pilots need extra teaching and training. Thomas and Vistica assert, "Aboard the *Abraham Lincoln*, the women were left to sink or swim."[37] The experiences of female fliers aboard the ship show that some deep prejudices will have to be overcome before they can succeed, say Thomas and Vistica. In March 1997, Lohrenz had a desk job at Miramar. The June 1997 *NIG* report on Carrier Air Wing 11 returned Lohrenz to flight status, but only land-based aircraft.

In 1996 several jet accidents occurred in the Pacific; there were seven crashes in all.[38] In February 1996, the General Accounting Office (GAO) reported naval aviation was safer than ever before. Gillcrist says that he knows nothing about certain types of aircraft, but that, "There is nothing sinister. You have an accident. You don't like them. The three F-14s in the course of five days is what concerned people. The possibility of pilot error is always there, but it is necessary not to prejudge the investigation. The bothersome thing is the pilot involvement," says Gillcrist, "because you have to ask if the pilot had the means to prevent a crash by a simple act of discipline."[39]

STRENGTH ABOARD SHIPS

A female soldier who lacks strength poses a risk of creating a crisis and bringing danger or death to other soldiers.[40] The USS *Constellation* suffered fire at sea, but upper body strength and endurance turned out not to be a problem.[41] Some believe men suffer from a double standard. Do we use the same standard for men and women?[42]

It is often inaccurately asserted that women lack this or that qualification. BGen. Wilma L. Vaught, USAF (Ret.), believes the idea that women cannot handle the stress involved in combat is not necessarily so. "Women handle more stress than men do in a lifetime. Women may express stress differently, but it doesn't mean they don't handle it better."[43] In the 1980s, the Danish Navy, says Vaught, decided that men and women ought to train and fight together to have a stronger force. Women reacted immediately and well in this situation.

Conclusions

In interview after interview, military people told me that the basic consideration in dealing with ability, whether we are evaluating a woman or a man, is the use of gender and age norming. "Gender and age norming are important to ensure the overall fitness (wellness) of service members," according to MAJ Mary Finch.[44] Finch explains that "all service members in a particular specialty should have to pass the same physical tests, so long as the tests are based on skill and real strength *requirements* for the job, not on old tests that were designed to challenge men and which are not relevant to required strength." The intent of the Army physical fitness test is not to determine qualification for combat.

Finch was asked how would she respond to the statements "Women have an inherent disadvantage because gender norming avoids the real problem (that is, the disadvantage)" and "Since the disadvantage is inherent, women can never be equal to men in the military; therefore we are putting lives in danger, the women's lives and the males who serve with her." She replied: "What is required for the job? Make all soldiers meet those requirements—disadvantage or not. Just make sure there is an honest broker checking that the strength/endurance requirements are based on real requirements for combat."

BGen. Wilma L. Vaught, gets to the heart of the issue: "We shouldn't have women or men in a situation where they are not trained or capable of doing the job. So if we are not physically strong enough to do the full scope of the jobs in the infantry, then we shouldn't be there."[45] Further, Vaught believes that ability should be assessed by what someone can do for a thirty-day period, not just a one-day period. "Physical strength and stamina over a sustained period of time [are the criteria], for example, 40-pound shells. I can do it three hours, but can I do it all the time in defense? If a person can't, he or she shouldn't be assigned to that job specialty." She also contends we should ask the question, "Should the job be done that way?" In the late 1970s, she says, "It was felt that women shouldn't lift X amount. As a matter of fact, men couldn't lift certain amounts either. They would get a friend. Men developed low back problems. So we have to ask, 'Is the job being done right in the first place?' And 'Are the standards what they should be?'"

Because women are entering additional nontraditional specialties, particularly combat-related ones, President Bush's Presidential Commission on the Assignment of Women in the Armed Forces concluded physical tests should be established for all service members because women tend to have less upper body strength and cardiorespiratory endurance than men.[46] Finch explains that if the Army decided to create specific tests for nontraditional specialties and combat assignments (there are presently no such tests or qualifications), these tests should not be gender or age normed, but should be based on the job requirements.[47] Finch points to the experience of Pfluke, who testified to the Commission that she would accept a transfer to the infantry tomorrow, "only nine weeks after delivering her second son" (see Introduction). Finch concludes that she is not sure whether the small numbers of women who would be interested and qualified to join the infantry women would be worth its opening up to them. She reports unanimous agreement, however, that women in combat assignments should meet the same requirements as men. Women who testified and were eager to be assigned to combat units were the most concerned that standards not be lowered.

BGen. Mike Hall testified before the Presidential Commission about his experience in 1990, when he was assigned to the Central Command as the theater air liaison officer in Operation Desert Storm. During that time he saw men and women sharing the common bond of living in deprived conditions on a daily basis in order to do something worthwhile for their nation.[48] Hall believes that if women are allowed in direct combat-related assignments, they would perform the air liaison role with ground forces well. Capt. Jackie Parker, the first woman to graduate from Test Pilot School, flew the F-16 in school, but after she graduated, she was restricted by assignment to heavy aircraft. Hall testified that Parker was a fully capable pilot. Parker went to Test Pilot School, something Hall did not have the opportunity to do. She had achieved more by age 31 than he had by that age, but he had more opportunities ahead than she. Poignantly, he testified, "And all that opportunity was there for me, it's not there for her, and the difference is I've got the Y chromosome."[49]

Hall testified that the Army physical test (PT) is slightly more sophisticated than the Air Force PT in that it requires sit-ups and push-ups in addition to a timed run. In the fighter business, he says, they have built an aircraft that makes us capable of approaching human limits and can specifically measure qualification for G-tolerance in the centrifuge. There is a significant difference in individual tolerance, but Hall does not believe there is any gender basis for discrimination. "The real issue is whether you, as an individual can pass that test."[50]

HOW MUCH HAS THE IDEA THAT WOMEN LACK THIS OR THAT QUALIFICATION BEEN EXPLORED?

Is the gender thing a red herring? Major Pfluke says that it is. We don't call age norming a double standard.[51] Differences in physical ability exist between the genders, but some of those same differences exist within each gender. The differences within one gender are the crux of the issue. Interviewees never denied that males help their friends who may be a little less physically able. Add to this fact that there are women who are more able than many men or other women and the issue of women in combat becomes heated rather quickly. Some military interviewees believed that addressing gender issues would prevent me from getting to the real issue, that a female in the military is a soldier first. "The concept of a woman soldier will get lost," one military woman said.

A 1993 USMC study found that proper training enabled women to perform sit-ups to male standards and to improve on other performance. Lt Col Greg Morin, Department Director, Military Police, says that combat is an individual thing for men and women. "We are individuals. Some women and men would fit and others would not. Yes, some could, some couldn't."[52] Morin believes it takes time for change. People who do accept women in combat will be in the higher ranks in the future. "The Marine Corps," he notes, "has overcome some major challenges. I think we can overcome that. The military is moving in the direction of women integrating."

Morin also says, "the rapid progression of technology has detracted from the 80-pound pack and 8-mile [test] as a prerequisite for combat. Technology has made it possible for women to fight a battle as well as men. Light vehicles that can move and maneuver make it less necessary for the hike and walk. It is becoming easier," he concluded, "for a woman to be in combat."

In April 1997, the Marines were leading the challenge with their very own pioneering moment. Another barrier limiting the role of women in the military fell. "Enlisted women for the first time shot live ammunition from heavy weapons in the Marine combat training that follows boot camp,"[53] says Michael Janofsky. "One of the women, Pvt Cynthia Martinez, 20, and other women like her reflect the scale of change in the centuries-old military assumption that women could not be warriors." In 1995, Gen Charles Krulak, Commandant of the Marine Corps, overhauled Marine training. Training with 305 men and a "gender-integrated chain-of-command," 54 women were among the first to endure the grueling "Crucible" combat training after boot camp.[54] The other services conduct mixed-gender recruit training, but Krulak ordered men and women to learn combat skills together. Krulak says Marine recruit training will remain separate.

Admiral Arthur believes the military will never return to zero:

> Women will reach top ranks easier than their male counterparts. With all that has been developed, this [progress] has to move forward so a talented female will be moved forward. But if put in measuring units, for example, race,—how much of the female population will be in control of arms. It will never reach parity. Maybe 50 years from now with a new generation raised in a unisex way [it's possible]. But the way we raise our kids and grandkids today, women will not go to the fox holes. Women will gravitate to what they do best. A few will [go to fox holes] but [numbers of women doing that] will not grow significantly.[55]

Arthur thinks it isn't within our cultural beliefs to assign women in direct combat.

Progress is taking place. The early nineties saw the ban lifted on the assignment of women in some combat positions. Policy is modifying, and a beginning is taking place. To the women working for the cause, more change will come, but slowly. At any rate, the assignment of a soldier to any position within the military should depend upon his or her qualifications, physical ability, and mental and psychological wherewithal for the position. These criteria will give our forces the best state of readiness and our nation the best defense.

Chapter 11

Sexual Issues

If you tell your guys to respect women, they will!
—A young female commander

The Commander's Challenge

Training. If one word exists to sum up the solution to the military's current problems with sexual issues, that word is *training*. But then we have to ask, "Training who and what?" RADM D. M. Williams, USN (Ret.), says, "If we expect men and women to work and fight together in combat units, I cannot imagine anything worse than training them separately. That idea is gaining currency in the nation's capitol."[1] Perhaps Gen. Charles Krulak, commandant of the marines, had similar thoughts; he introduced The "Crucible" as a requirement for women as well as men recruits.

In November 1996, female soldier trainees at the Army's Aberdeen Proving Ground in Maryland complained about being forced into sex by two drill instructors, one company commander, and other staff. "Particularly offensive," MG Robert D. Shadley, Commander of OC&S, said, "is that the charges represent an abuse of power by leaders toward those who are trained to obey them," *Army Link News* reported November 15, 1996.

The problems that the Aberdeen Proving Grounds had with sexual behavior is one framework for discussion. Writing about the Aberdeen situation in the *Washington Post*, Richard Cohen says, "the Army has mixed together some awfully impressionable young women and some awfully tough men and tried, in the name of a wonderful ideal, to make things work."[2] Cohen concludes that it is possible the Aberdeen event is "a warning to the brass and the civilian leadership that they are attempting the impossible—a fight not against a few bad men but against a more formidable foe: human nature."

In order to agree with Cohen's conclusion, one would have to believe that a female recruit has the right and the strength not to obey a superior officer. One would also have to believe that it was all right for the drill sergeants to

187

vie with one another to see who could have sex with the most recruits and to hold trysts both on and off base, some of which were rape, but all of which were against the rules. The commander had the power, or in military terms, the rank to make certain his or her orders were carried out. We also have to ask then: Is rape human nature?

In July 1997 the Army briefed Congress about its unreleased findings, "that many drill sergeants are unprepared to handle the absolute power and control that comes with their position." The Army also said their background checks on drill sergeants were lax. In September 1997, a "scathing report" was issued acknowledging sexual harrassment and discrimination. The Army charged 12 Aberdeen staff members with sex crimes ranging from inappropriate sexual comments to rape. On November 23, 1997, *Army Link News* stated that, determined to stop those problems acknowledged in the ranks, the Army also noted that some male leadership had been delayed in acceptance of having more women in the ranks.

Following the Aberdeen event, a 22-year-old Army veteran, SGM Brenda Hoster, accused the Army's senior enlisted soldier, SGMA Gene C. McKinney, a 29-year-old veteran, of having sexually assaulted and harassed her when she worked for him as a public affairs officer. McKinney denied the allegations, but then retired. In March 1998, McKinney was found not guilty according to *Time* on March 23, 1998.

At any rate, the Aberdeen Proving Grounds event, could, as Williams suggests, provide a framework for useful political debate in our country about integrating women into the military and combat units.[3] Debate often brings a collective consciousness, which is part of what is needed in a changing institution such as the military. Training, however, remains the critical element. Training men and women to work and fight together is the commander's challenge. General Krulak's "Crucible," according to B Gen Margaret Brewer, USMC (Ret.), is a "grueling 54 hour training event consisting of physically and mentally demanding challenges conducted during the 11th week of recruit training for male and female recruits."[4] "Values training" is taught under the new "transformation" schedule along with the Crucible.[5] While the Marines are the only branch of the armed forces that has separate gender training, they do bring the recruits together for the Crucible.

In March 1998, CNN reported that Secretary of Defense William Cohen said the services could continue to mix the sexes in basic training, but that they must house them in separate areas.

Although some movement is underway in Washington to revert to barring women from certain assignments, that would be a mistake. By reverting, we also remove the opportunity for men to view women as equals and as colleagues. When women are equal in training, skill, opportunity, and rank, the power element is reduced. LT Michael J. Frevola, attorney and Navy Reservist, concludes that the continuation of any exclusion will perpetuate the stereotype that women cannot succeed in the military and will foster tokenism, sexual harassment, and resentment. Congress should see through to its conclusion gender integration within the United States armed forces.[6]

During research for my first book, *Power and Gender*, I sometimes talked with men who resented women going forward and reporting wrongful sexual behaviors. Many times I responded, "As society changes and more women get in positions of power, we are going to hear men say something quite different than what you are saying. We are going to hear, 'Hey this female boss did this or that sexual thing to me.' As the balance of power begins to tip, we are beginning to see some examples. As I write this chapter, the Air Force is threatening to court martial its first female B-52 pilot, a 26-year-old graduate of the USAF Academy, 1st Lt. Kelly Jean Flinn. Who told? The male, Marc Zigo, who told Flinn that he was legally separated and had filed for a divorce from his wife, an enlisted woman based in Minot, North Dakota.[7] She allegedly had a brief fling with an enlisted male as well. The charges against Flinn were adultery, conduct unbecoming an officer, making a false official statement, and fraternization. Zigo testified against Flinn. Although Flinn sought an honorable discharge, the Air Force gave her a general discharge. Air Force Secretary Sheila Widnall said Flinn's "lack of integrity" and her "disobedience to orders" were more serious than the adultery charges. "It is primarily those allegations that made an honorable discharge unacceptable," Widnall said.[8]

The National Organization for Women (NOW) analysis argues that gender bias exists, because most service members who are guilty of sexual misconduct, lying and fraternization have received "nonjudicial punishments," not court martials.[9] NOW points to the 140 naval and marine aviators who were referred for disciplinary action for sexual misconduct (including indecent exposure) and for the sexual assault of 90 individuals. Fifty-one of the 140 military aviators were found to have lied during the investigation. None of these pilots or navigators received a court martial. All received nonjudicial punishments such as verbal and written reprimands and fines.

NOW also points out that in November 1996 in Germany a USA staff sergeant and a private first class were discharged from the army in lieu of court martial for lying, adultery, and having sex with a 12-year-old girl (the daughter of an Army sergeant). The girl became pregnant.

According to NOW, a total of 12 cases were referred for prosecution for sexual misconduct in the Air Force during the first months of 1997. Of those cases, 42 percent (5) were women, even though women comprise only 16 percent of the Air Force. Further, NOW reports that a lieutenant colonel at Minot Air Force base, where Flinn was stationed, had sex in 1996 with his secretary, which constitutes adultery and fraternization, and was given only a reprimand and a fine. Flinn had an affair with a civilian and was up for a court martial, facing up to 9½ years in prison if convicted.

The responses of Col. Robert E. Reed, chief of the Air Force's military justice division, on the May 11, 1997, CBS *60 Minutes* program made me think that anyone with common sense and knowledge of human behavior would not agree with his assessment that in all of the years he served he could not think of any guys who engaged in adulterous relationships. The double standard is the norm and norms are difficult to break.

On June 7, 1997, Reuters reported that Air Force Gen. Joseph Ralston, top candidate for chairman of the Joint Chiefs of Staff, came under criticism for an adulterous affair 13 years ago. Secretary Cohen responded to questions whether adultery is treated the same for both genders and all ranks by creating a panel to review the issues.

SOCIETAL SEXUAL BEHAVIORS

Members of the Bush Presidential Commission believed that possible sexual activity between unit members could have a detrimental effect on cohesion and that it would take some time for males to view females as people rather than as sexual beings.[10] MAJ Mary Finch, USA, and a member of the Commission, states that the Commission found males in combat units had a higher likelihood of supporting expanded roles for women in combat. This support, she says, is explained by the fact that males' experiences have shown them the capabilities of female coworkers, making it easier for them to view women as individuals. Opponents argue that males are against expanding the roles of women because they do not believe women can meet the requirements.[11] A relationship exists between societal sexual behaviors toward women, a woman's occupational position in society, and a man's background and belief system.[12] It is no different in the military. As the military includes more women as commanders, men will have more opportunity to view them as colleagues and this interaction should reduce unacceptable sexual behavior.[13]

HETEROSEXUAL AND HOMOSEXUAL ATTRACTIONS: ARE THEY A PROBLEM?

A common argument voiced by some opponents of women serving in combat goes something like this: "Heterosexual attraction is bad, but homosexual attraction is not a problem because the homosexual ban should be upheld. Homosexuality is not accepted so it does not cause the problems that heterosexual attraction would." Does this mean that when something is banned, it is not a problem? MAJ Mary Finch would agree that any kind of attraction between service members in the same unit affects "good order and discipline" and "unit cohesion." "Homosexual or heterosexual activity, innuendo, and gaming are all contrary to good order and discipline and if they are not handled properly, cohesion problems can occur. Good, strong leadership is required. There are plenty of regulations to back up the commander in disciplining offending soldiers. There will always be attractions between individuals on the job, but professional soldiers should behave professionally on duty. The leadership fails when units find themselves having all kinds of resentment and cohesion problems because soldiers of the opposite sex are carrying on in an unprofessional manner and nothing is being done to stop the behavior. A strong commander makes all the difference."[14]

Being selected for a command is a great accomplishment and responsibility, according to Finch. A mixed-gender unit has its unique challenges. "When the gay ban is no longer upheld, commanders will have to rise to the challenge of ensuring that soldiers are professional on duty time." Finch, like others, points to the civil rights era when commanders rose to the challenge of getting angry white soldiers to deal fairly with black soldiers. "This is a leadership issue, plain and simple!" Finch concludes.

"Gender issues, i.e., distraction, homosexuality, etc., only exist when you don't have combat," says Linda Grant De Pauw. "You have young people trained to do violence and school is out. What do you do with them? Prostitution, common law wives, men having relationships with men exists, but it is not a problem in combat.... If people think their heads are going to be blown off, they don't do it."[15] Distraction is a failure in leadership and a discipline problem, says De Pauw. It is the commander's challenge. "You don't want them playing with guns or drugs either. What are you going to do with these guys in a dangerous situation?" she asks.

LTC Timothy A. Rippe, USA, University of Northern Iowa professor of Military Science–ROTC, says that as a commander he would want to avoid gender attractions for a unit in combat. He believes in qualified equal opportunity so that more soldiers will come back alive:

> You can not regulate away gender attraction. Just like the racial problems that still exist today, laws, policies and regulations have been implemented with the intent of eliminating racism or sexual harassment, but the services are still composed of men and women who join its ranks with all the prejudices and unethical behaviors they developed prior to serving. It is true that education and military discipline can temper much of this negative behavior, but it will not all be eliminated. Consequently, these problems still exist in units. The notion that combat will cause soldiers to self-regulate their behavior because of the mission at hand is utterly false. When it comes to gender attractions, soldiers will find whatever means it takes to engage in sexual relations. My point is simply this: Combat is stressful, chaotic, and violent as it is. Why create an environment that encourages gender attraction and all the ensuing consequences of sexual relations for the leaders who just want to get the mission done and bring home as many of his/her soldiers alive. Do you really want to give the commander one more problem to deal with that would draw his/her attention away from this goal in the name of social equality?[16]

ADM Stanley R. Arthur, U.S. Navy, (Ret.), says, "All share the fear. We are brought up that the opposite sex is a distraction. At the right moment, we might not be distracted, but again we might."[17]

FRATERNIZATION

When asked, "Do you believe there are any gender differences which would prevent women from serving in combat roles," CAPT Rosemary Mariner, replied with a simple no. At the time of this interview, she was the proud parent of a 15-month-old baby. "Parents must control the behavior of their children," she said. "In the military it is how you control behavior of your people [that matters]. There are strict fraternization rules regarding such behavior as undue familiarity between juniors and seniors, whether males or female. Whether these rules are fairly enforced is important." Mariner says, however, that leadership won't eradicate all inappropriate behavior. She recalls that while she was on duty on her first ship, there were more homosexual discharges than male and female misbehavior discharges. "This was a real eye-opener to me," Mariner explained. "Homosexuality is the reason why strong rules on fraternization go back to the Greeks."[18]

"Mixed-gender ships," says Mariner, "are a far more normal environment. A mixed-gender ship is no longer an esoteric issue. Females have deployed. We have lots of experience doing it successfully. This is not [sic] a red herring. There are no 'mad dogs' and drunken macho fights."[19]

Arthur believes that females are more tolerant of homosexuality than males. "For a male, homosexuality presents the same problem as does the mixed-gender group. Here the male has shared a part of himself that he doesn't want his buddy to know. In the case of the mixed gender problem, we deal straight or ignore it. For homosexuality 'The don't ask—don't tell' is the mode."[20] A woman I interviewed said that she believed homosexuality is less of a distraction. When I asked Arthur his view, he said, "Yes because of policy and because in most cases we deal with it with an automatic response. The mechanism for terminating it is there more than it is not. Heterosexual behavior can surprise a soldier. It is a natural feeling."[21]

Commissioner Sarah F. White testified she had received a letter from an Air National Guard pilot who served in Saudi Arabia who wrote that fraternization and sex took place regularly. Enlisted women were quietly sent stateside to face charges of prostitution. The pilot argued integration of women into combat positions would only assure greater distraction and hinder the military's mission. BGen. Mike Hall, New York Air National Guard and Adjutant General of the State of New York, said he did not share the view represented in the letter and believes there are human failings in any situation.[22]

Regarding the issue of homosexuality, Major Finch explains: "Everyone hangs on a spectrum of sexuality. What some men (particularly homophobics) are really afraid of is that they are too close to center (bisexual) than they are comfortable with. They fear, perhaps, that if tempted, they may find themselves behaving in ways which are against all the teachings they have been exposed to. They are scared of how they might behave. Some heterosexual guys find this too close for comfort."[23]

FAVORS

Some argue women should be excluded from combat because of the likelihood of sexual involvement and competition for sexual favors; that men and women live together for extended periods, so sex is inevitable. The involvement might lead to jealousy, animosity, or even hatred—emotions that would severely detract from readiness. MAJ Paul Christopher, USA, asks, "Is it really true that sexual involvement results in increased animosity in an organization?"[24]

Christopher's own response to this question should offer a boost to the beleaguered military academies of today. The cadets at the U.S. Military Academy live and work together in a restricted environment with women comprising about 10 percent of the corps. If negative emotions did result, Christopher contends they would be magnified in organizations where there is more competition for sexual favors. He has not found this to be the case at West Point or any other military academies. Many people who believed there would be increased animosity in the beginning of mixed gender in the academies have found this is not the case.

Christopher says this has not happened in combat support units either. Citing civilian police and fire departments as examples, he concludes that women do not loosen the bonds of camaraderie between workers but have become an important part of the social infrastructure. There is no reason, he concludes, that it will be any different in military combat units.

SEXUAL HARASSMENT, RAPE, ASSAULT

It is difficult to tell if inappropriate sexual behavior takes place more in the military than in civilian society, but history demonstrates that the behaviors do occur against the military woman.[25]

In 1995, results of the first of three surveys of the DOD indicated that since 1988 sexual harassment reports declined. The second survey produced a higher rate, 43 percent of active-duty military (78 percent of women and 38 percent of men) indicated they had experienced sexual harassment). No results were calculated from the third survey conducted for "research purposes."

In 1996, in the *Duke Law Journal*, Madeline Morris said the peacetime rates of rape by American military personnel are actually lower than civilian rates, but in the combat theater, military rape rates were several times higher than civilian rates.

Sexual harassment can potentially happen anywhere, but if it is happening in the military training setting, then it is possible it could happen in a combat situation. In November 1996, the Army brought charges of rape and sexual harassment against military trainers at the Army Ordnance Center at Aberdeen Proving Ground.[26] There were more than a dozen victims, according to the Pentagon, all females in their second eight-week period of training.

MAJ Lillian Pfluke, USA (Ret.), thinks that to understand why harassment occurs one has to look at life in the barracks. "Recruits and drill sergeants are young people thrown together at a time of their lives when sex is much on their minds. Meanwhile, the Army's male-dominated, combat-oriented culture exacerbates the tensions."[27] Pfluke spent 15 years in the Army and knows as long as women are not treated as equals, the Army will continue to have two classes of soldiers. Men will keep treating women disrespectfully, even though both wear the uniform. Without equal jobs in ground combat, women cannot be equal in the Army. Pfluke believes it may be harder to change the Army's core culture because having separate castes provokes tensions; unless you are allowed in the combat-arms branches you cannot become a senior leader. Pfluke believes the basic core of the Army culture must change.

In July 1996, the twentieth anniversary of the opening of the service academies to women, an anniversary that followed the Supreme Court decision that opened the Virginia Military Institute and the Citadel to female cadets, MAJ Pfluke, West Point alumna, and Cadet Leticia Gasdick, West Point senior, appeared on National Public Radio. Pfluke said that harassment is a part of plebe year, but the harassment she experienced was beyond what is acceptable. "It went from little things—like when you see an upper-class cadet, you salute and say, 'Good morning, sir,' and he would say, 'It was a good morning 'til you bitches got here.' You would have stuff thrown at you, out the windows, anonymously—eggs, tomatoes, and things. You would have your room vandalized regularly with anything from shaving cream to people coming into your room when you're not there and actually beating off in your underwear." When Noah Adams asked, "Cadets masturbating in—in the underwear—in your underwear?" Pfluke responded yes.[28]

When Adams asked Cadet Gasdick if she were surprised or shocked at what happened 20 years ago at West Point, Gasdick said that even though she had heard about it happening, she was shocked, and it was not occurring now. Pfluke says change takes a long time and attributes the change to hard-hitting policies from above so that everyone down the chain of command gets the message that women are here to stay and attitudes start to change.

Gasdick says she didn't feel the need to form support groups with women because most cadets associate, whether male or female, through their sports or academic-year company. Gasdick says you may hear a comment now and then and there may be a few cadets who have difficulty in accepting women. The response to those few is, "Hey—what are you thinking? You're going to have to wake up. You're going out in the Army two years from now, and things are going to be different."[29]

Rape is not sufficiently documented in the literature whether our own troops or other nations' troops commit it. In her explanation of the "logic of silence," Ruth Seifert points out that is because historians have been predominantly male.[30] Yet one can come across references such as Zimmerman's analysis of the Gulf War and Copelon's analogy that the United States military in Vietnam raped Vietnamese women and established brothels, relying on dire economic necessity rather than kidnapping to fill them. The reasons motivating the Americans, according to Seifert, were similar to the reasons the Japanese military industrialized sexual slavery of women in World War II. The Japanese used rape to motivate and reward their soldiers.[31]

Capt. Patricia A. Gavin, USAF, offers a provocative last word on the all-volunteer force and how women pay. Women have been making up the void since the end of the draft. But "why?" she asks. "In essence, women have been taking the 'beating' the gays who lied about their sexuality or managed to get through military physicals once received under the draft." Gavin explains, "The end of the draft meant homosexual men no longer would be 'outed' by military selective service screening officials who would ask them about their sexual orientation. This meant 'gay' ... men could avoid the ... draft and being outed with the end of the draft." She asks provocative questions such as "How many males have been raped but are too ashamed to talk about it?" It is possible, she says, that some gays now avoid service because of the end of the draft and young women take up the slack.

The consequences when women are "raped in the ranks" are much more severe. Gavin's questions continue: "What does the commander do if he suspects such a crime has occurred but can't prove it? What if the service member who has been raped has been threatened and told to remain silent? What about the child she carries if she becomes pregnant?" When a complaint is filed, you are only entitled to back pay and reinstatement, no punitive or compensatory damages. Gavin does not believe the military is the best use of the talents of females in the United States because of the problems of integrating the ranks and the sexual harassment issues today and resulting monetary cost.

Rape, Gavin points out, is not something that just happens to women—the consequences for women are just more telling if they become pregnant. She asks, "Are you beginning to understand that power sharing and intimacy are synonymous and that no matter your sexuality or that of your comrade in arms, you can be compromised if someone wants to get rid of you because of what you know or don't know?"[32]

Someone's sexual orientation should not be a negative factor. SGT Sharon F.

Daugherty II, USA, founder in 1990 of Gay, Lesbian, Bisexual, and Transgendered Disabled Veterans of America, says that people have to be reminded constantly that there are service members in our armed forces of various orientations:

> Somewhere near our faded ribbons you'll find our pride.
> We are the veterans that may not have fired a shot,
> but are important too. We are the veterans that didn't have a voice,
> we feared the witch hunts. Though it wasn't always easy and it wasn't
> always fair,
> when freedom cried we answered, we were there.
> Still, through it all, we are the veterans that may never be the same...
> we served proudly in silence.[33]

VIOLENCE TOWARD OUR WOMEN BY OUR OWN TROOPS

RADM Paul T. Gillcrist, USN (Ret.), says that violence perpetrated by our own troops happens now without women: "People in the platoon get in a fight. There is a set of nerves. People get jittery over an upcoming battle. It is silly not [sic] to *think* mixed gender would be any different."[34]

In an alternate view, Elaine Donnelly cites Tailhook '91 to justify not exposing women to the violence of combat. The risk of capture is like saying street crime against women is wrong, but organized crime is okay.

VIOLENCE OF OUR TROOPS AGAINST ENEMY WOMEN

The issue "women of the enemy—spoils of war" is part of what Tailhook was about according to Zimmerman. The young pilots did not have the spoils of war like the past pilots because the enemy kept their women hidden.

Violence against women committed by our own troops is a difficult issue that has probably not been extensively researched. One person said to me, "How can someone advocate putting women in combat and be against violence towards women?" We have but to return our attention to the Linda Grant De Pauw interview, the UN Conference in Beijing, or the Bosnian genocidal rapes to know that violence exists toward women whether or not they serve in combat.

Some societal sexual behavior can improve as men grow accustomed to working with women and viewing them as equals. The negative sexual behavior is in most cases a societally constructed role. As more women are trained and allowed into the same roles when qualified, some of the negative sexual behaviors will decrease. As for the fortunes of war, the terrorism and the atrocities of war, we can only hope to reduce them by working for peace.

Chapter 12

Equal Opportunity

My Country 'Tis of Thee, Please Give Me Equality
—Suffragette Song

A parallel exists between the suffragette movement and the women in combat movement. One has only to examine the lyrics of suffragette songs to see the similarity. Women's suffrage is now almost universal, but history shows long delays between women's right to vote and men's. The delay was on the average 47 years, but the range was 1 to 134 years.[1] Ruth Leger Sivard points out that although getting the vote under the law is now past history for almost all countries, the effective use of it to get political equality is still a distant goal.

In 1997, I heard Frieda Mae Hardin, 101 years old, at the dedication services for the Women in Military Service for America (WIMSA) Memorial speak to Sivard's conclusion. Hardin, a veteran Navy yeoman of World War I, told the crowd that when she was young, "women weren't even allowed to vote." The most important achievement is "the progress of women taking their rightful place in society."

According to Col. Kelly Hamilton, USAF (Ret.), "Social climate and legal attempts to limit the opportunities for women to serve in combat situations have not stopped their participation in war. Defense of the freedom they value is important. They understand and accept the risk involved. The oath women take upon entering the service is exactly the same as their male counterparts: 'to protect and defend the Constitution of the United States.'"[2]

Hamilton believes that women's desire to serve in the military may be idealistic, but since women have always been the "true volunteer force," there seldom is another explanation. "The accepted rewards offered to their male counterparts, public recognition, advancement opportunities, and hero status, were factors which until very recently were not a consideration," she adds.

MAJ Paul Christopher, USA, concludes there is "no good reason to exclude females from filling combat roles in our armed forces." He also thinks the burden of justification should be on those people who would exclude women from certain jobs, rather than on those who advocate total equality.[3] While it is true that the goal of military women is to be soldiers in service of their country, the political-civilian component has to be addressed. In fact, the commander in chief, the president of the United States, is at the apex of both the civilian and military structures, which are intricately intertwined. This intricacy becomes more apparent when we realize that combat ground is where the military exercises the rights it has gained, while continuing to defend those rights for all, civilian and military.

MIRROR OF SOCIETY

Mady Segal states that "The more egalitarian the social values about gender, the greater women's representation in the military."[4] Her past research on Canada and the European Community shows that civilian law prohibiting discrimination based on gender is driving an increase in women's representation in society.[5]

One person who testified before a House subcommittee stated, "Civil society protects individual rights, but the military, which protects civil society, must be governed by different rules."[6] Active duty military personnel must often serve around-the-clock for months on end. But having different internal rules does not free them from having many of the interpersonal problems of the larger society. The early 1990s presented us with tremendous change. As the larger society grappled with the Anita Hill–Clarence Thomas debacle, the military struggled with the Tailhook '91 event. The Gulf War saw a country calling upon its reserve units to help meet readiness needs. The reserves were filled with women who went to war and served valiantly alongside men and in wartime roles equal to men. As President George Bush's Commission on the Assignment of Women in the Armed Forces was narrowly deciding against women serving in combat, United States law was being repealed to allow women aboard ships and in combat aircraft, rendering moot the narrow victory of members of the Commission who opposed having women in combat.

THE COVETED HIGH RANKS

While career aspirations or interests are subordinate to military mission, it was not right that women served in combat roles without access to the higher ranks. What the "old way" said was that "you can help out in necessity," but you cannot use that valuable experience to go up to the higher, coveted ranks. A valuable resource was being lost.

Opponents of women in combat often argue that career aspirations or interests are subordinate to military mission. If that were truly so, recruiting methods would differ in some ways. Youth, as we saw in Desert Storm and in earlier conflict, often "join up" to take advantage of the G.I. Bill. Serving your country is one way to finance an education and improve your career options.

But, opponents of women in combat aren't talking about what happens after the enlistment period is over. What do they mean then, that they haven't cared about some of the men advancing so that we would have capable leadership for our young men and women? If I understand correctly, they mean that career aspirations of women are subordinate to the military mission. If the mission is to be ready to protect and defend at all times, then it should allow qualified women as well as men to have career aspirations. Progress has been made, but given the cyclical nature of the issue, some gains could be lost. At any rate, serving in combat is necessary to attain the coveted high ranks.

Opponents say that the military is not the place for social experiments. According to MGen. Jeanne Holm, "It was never about women's equality to the exclusion of readiness considerations. It was about the privilege of serving one's country without artificial barriers based solely on gender."[7] In the August 1997 issue of *Proceedings of the U.S. Naval Institute*, Col Paul E. Roush, USMC (Ret.), said, "But it is simply not true that women in the military are a social experiment; we have decades of experience by which to access the performance of women."

RMC Roxine C. Hart gives a slightly different perspective: "[It is] a hard fact that if the military doesn't experiment during the relative security of peacetime, it will almost surely be forced to do so in the exigency of war."[8]

In spite of women's record that they are able to serve, the intent of Congress and military policy prohibits women from serving in positions involving direct combat. According to the research of Megan Craven, Jennifer Kopper, and Stacey Rohrer, "These policies prohibit women, on the basis of gender only, from over twelve percent of the skill positions and thirty-nine percent of the total positions offered by the Department of Defense."[9] They suggest that Congress repeal these policies that exclude women from combat. The Equal Protection Clause of the Fourteenth Amendment does not apply to the federal government, they say, but the Supreme Court said the Due Process Clause in the Fifth Amendment prohibits the federal government from making unreasonable classifications. Craven, Kopper, and Rohrer argue that the set policies "that exclude women from combat ... violate the Fifth Amendment and deny women their fundamental right to engage and excel in their chosen occupation." No court case, they add, has challenged the constitutionality of the laws and regulations banning women from combat. In their opinion, three court cases have, however, involved women in combat. *Frontiero v. Richardson* rejected the idea that "man is, or should be, woman's protector or defender," an idea that the authors say in reality put women "not on a pedestal, but in a cage." *Satty v. Nashville Gas Co.* stated that gender does not determine who is able to perform capably as a soldier.[10] *Schlesinger v. Ballard* held that combat exclusion hinders women from gaining experience needed for promotion in the military.

Ground combat, explains CAPT Rosemary Mariner, USN, is the last preserve. If individual qualifications are the basis of the argument, it may take an

Amazon and requisite personality traits. Women have already served in ground combat, for example, in the World War II guerrillas and Tito's resistance forces in Yugoslavia. Mariner notes Plato held the real issue of being a warrior was not strength, but speed. Sometimes if you cannot fall back on anything, you can rely on strength as a prerequisite because it falls back on class differences.[11] Mariner's reasoning is supported by RADM Paul T. Gillcrist, who says, "The subtle but more significant element is the psychological impact. It says, 'There is an element we notice, for example, the Navy has a seesaw battle—one wins—one loses, etc. We saw it in the Civil War. It could be the general waving a sword or Molly Pitcher waving a flag.'"[12]

The 1994 ground combat hearings were filled with testimony from people holding different philosophies than those which Mariner, Gillcrist, and Pfluke believe. One example of such testimony is the following:

> The charge that barring women from combat units inhibits their career advancement is groundless. According to Department of Defense (DOD) statistics, even with the combat exclusion for women, the services are promoting females at similar or faster rates than men. Expanding combat "opportunities" places the aspirations of feminist activists ahead of the wishes of most military women, who have expressed consistently strong personal resistance to being assigned to combat.[13]

Although the U.S. military is improving, we have a history of having an exclusively male military, and at present it remains so in direct ground combat assignments.[14] Addis points out that among the disadvantages of an exclusively male military are economic inferiority and dependency (see Chapter 7).

In spite of the difficulties in direct ground combat assignments, symbolic progress is being made in other units. On March 22, 1996, SGT Heather Lynn Johnsen became the first woman in the Army's history to guard the Tomb of the Unknown Soldier in Arlington National Cemetery. True to military demeanor, SGT Johnsen said, "I realize the significance of my accomplishment, but it's not an issue with me. I think of myself as a soldier."[15] According to Kristin Patterson, *Army Times*, the unit Johnsen applied to, the military police platoon attached to E Company Honor Guard, 3d Infantry Regiment (Old Guard), is the oldest unit in the Army and one of its most elite.[16] On February 4, 1997, SGT Danyell Elaine Wilson became the first black female to guard the Tomb according to *MINERVA's Bulletin Board*'s 1997 spring issue.

The Navy established its Ceremonial Guard in 1931. Seaman Apprentice (SA) Vanessa L. Encarnacion, Ceremonial Guard, USN, was on duty at President Clinton's 1997 inauguration. I asked her how she came to be in the Ceremonial Guard. "I volunteered," she replied, with an infectious smile. "In boot … I was a recruit. I made a high score on the entrance exams; I interviewed and they liked me."[17] Encarnacion said her duties as a Ceremonial Guard included assisting in such events as the inauguration, parades, funerals, and arrivals of dignitaries. She also performed her duty at White House events. The Navy, she said, has 200 Ceremonial Guards, with 30 being female.

ARMY

Perhaps nowhere in the military is progress as difficult to identify as it is in the army. In 1989, 1LT Sonja Smith commanded a lance nuclear missile platoon and led her soldiers on war drills a few miles from the East German border. She hid with her troops under camouflage nets in the woods during the day and slept in a tent alongside them at night. After Smith had spent 19 months making the platoon combat ready, the Army reassigned her to a desk job, saying women should not be sent so close to potential front lines. Molly Moore, a *Washington Post* writer, says Smith's transfer reflects the struggles of thousands of American women as they try to overcome discrimination and contradictions to gain a place of honor and reward in the U.S. military. It also represents, she says, the conflict within the military.[18]

CPT Lee J. Whiteside, 27, who in 1989 was the commander of the 4th Lance Battalion's Headquarters Company in West Germany, notes: "The average American thinks females are filling clerical rear support-type jobs in the Army. It's not so. I've got females who would be required to lay [communication] wire across the battlefield. If people don't think they'll get shot at, they don't understand combat."[19]

In June 1993, the Army graduated 2LT Charlene Wagner, a female combat helicopter pilot, and assigned her to a Cobra attack helicopter unit in South Korea.[20]

The Army's first female brigadier general, Dorothy B. Pocklington (Ret.), received the Army's highest medal for a noncombat role, the Distinguished Service Medal. She believes that one of the reasons so few women reach high-ranking positions is the lack of support from commanding officers. "Women in the Army," she says, "should have any assignment that they can meet the standards for. They should have that option."[21]

In 1996, Secretary of the Army Togo D. West, Jr., appointed retired BG Evelyn "Pat" Foote as his adviser on the Army sex scandal. Foote was the first woman to command Ft. Belvoir and the first to teach at the Army War College; she was also a vocal advocate for assigning women to combat.

MARINES

The major increases that come from career opportunities for women in the Marine Corps are in aviation. The direct combat units, those that locate, close with, and destroy the enemy by fire, maneuver, and shock effect remain closed.[22] The Marine review proposed that the following units be opened:

Expeditionary Unit command element and service support elements, all helicopter squadrons, Harrier jet squadrons, and Marine air support squadrons. Fixed wing operations, according to Lt Gen George R. Christmas, Deputy Chief of Staff for Manpower and Reserve Affairs, USMC, were already open, and with the integration of fighter attack-squadrons aboard aircraft carriers, he expected to see female Marines embarked as those ships were converted.

Historically, the Marines have dragged their feet. According to Holm, the Marine Corps was in 1975 the last service to offer coed officer training and in 1984 was the last to allow women combat training during recruit boot operations. The Marine Corps also did not expand its use of women in the 1980s as fast as the other services. In the Gulf War, their support base, female and noncombatant, was set up well forward of most infantry units. When the ground offensive started, infantry units went in front of the support unit to attack the enemy. The Marine Corps was slow to repeal combat restrictions.[23]

In 1994 the Marine Corps voiced concerns about its ability to recruit quality women and the impact of pregnancy on deployments. According to Christmas, the concerns were the basis for the Marine Corps "go-slow approach in implementation."[24] Women will receive additional combat training at the conclusion of recruit training, the only difference being women will not receive instruction in ambush techniques.[25] It would seem that training was not totally the same for males and females. Yet according to Under Secretary of Defense Dorn, when deployment occurs: "Equal opportunity brings equal obligation. Men and women will be treated the same with regard to hardship conditions. They will be expected, with their male cohorts, to deploy whenever called upon to do so."[26]

The Marine Corps has made progress. In July 1996, Carol R. Mutter became the first woman three-star general in the Corps.[27] Capt Sarah M. Deal joined the Corps in 1991 and four years later in April 1995 became the first female pilot to pin on naval flight wings. Thus she changed the face of the Marines forever. In 1993, Deal was the only female applicant who reported with six other Marines to the naval air station in Pensacola, Florida, for flight training. Deal said that there were no "in-between" attitudes. People either thought that there was "no way" they were going to fly with her or that it was great women were finally flying. Four months after graduation from flight school she was stationed at Heavy Helicopter Squadron–466, Marine Corps Air Station, Tustin, California. Soon she deployed to Okinawa. Deal reports: "I couldn't wait to go, and I'd be doggoned if I'd pass this chance up. I finally feel like part of the fleet."[28] In 1997, Gen Charles C. Krulak, Commandant of the Marine Corps, ordered combat training in a mixed-gender setting (see Chapters 10, 11, 14). According to the Summer 1997 MINERVA'S Bulletin Board, the Marines awarded wings to their first female flight officer, 1st Lt Jeanne Buchanan, in 1997.

NAVY

In January 1992, Congresswoman Beverly B. Byron (D-Md.) said the repeal of the exclusionary rule on women in combat aircraft occurred because in the "modern battle where mobility and long-range standoff weapons have made even rear-echelon lethal, the argument that women should not be exposed to danger no longer has any meaning."[29] In July 1992, MGen. Jeanne M. Holm, USAF (Ret.), characterized the exclusionary rule as the "last vestige of the 1948 law."[30] It was time to allow women on combatant ships.

The Navy has many "firsts." CAPT Rosemary Mariner was in the first group of eight women to earn the naval aviator gold wings. In 1974, Mariner was the first woman to fly the A-4E/L Skyhawk. In 1975 she became the first military woman to fly the A-4L and A-4E, a high-performance jet. In 1976 she flew the A-7E, a front-line light attack aircraft. In 1990, Mariner became the first military woman to command an operational aviation squadron, a Navy tactical electronic warfare squadron.[31] The Navy's first female aviator, LCDR Barbara Allen Rainey, died in a plane crash in 1982.[32]

In 1996, RADM Patricia Tracey, 45, was promoted to Vice Admiral and thus became the first woman to wear three stars in the Navy as the Chief of Naval Education and Training. Tracey and Maj Gen Carol Mutter of the Marine Corps, who achieved a three-star lieutenant general rank, are the highest-ranking women ever to serve.[33] (See Table 4.6.)

LT Shannon Workman, a 1988 Naval Academy graduate, became in 1993 the first female to break into the elite world of combat jet pilots. She joined an EA-6B Prowler squadron at Whidbey Island, Washington. In December 1994 she set sail aboard the USS *Eisenhower*, the first "combat vessel" to allow women combatants, with 4 other female pilots, 400 women, and 5,000 officers and crew for a six-month deployment to the Mediterranean and Adriatic. Her job was patrolling the skies from Bosnia-Herzegovina to Iraq. The Prowlers would lead the way into hostile territory should action come and try to take out enemy radar installations. Workman, like most military females, does not want to be singled out as a woman, but as a Navy pilot, and like most fighter pilots who make carrier landings, she easily says, "Night landings are definitely the hardest by far."[34] Two other women, LT Terry Lynn Bradford, 26, a 1990 Naval Academy graduate, and LT Sally Fountain joined the combat jet pilots.

In 1995, Workman's progress slowed. She was reassigned to fly a cargo jet in a support squadron because she had trouble landing on the carrier. In the *Baltimore Sun*, Bowman said ten female aviators, including six pilots, remained on the *Eisenhower* and were performing well.[35] One male, LCDR Gerald Dileonardo, who flew in the same squadron, was ordered to return to the squadron's base for further training. The findings were approved by VADM Richard C. Allen, Commander of the Naval Air Force, Atlantic Fleet.

In 1993, women made impressive progress in leadership positions in the

Navy. Patricia Tracey became one of the youngest flag officers, male or female, as director for Manpower and Personnel. RADM Louise Wilmont became the first women to command a U.S. naval base, in Philadelphia.[36] In surface warfare, two women officers joined the USS *Fox* for full deployment.[37]

In 1994, 500 women boarded combat ships and a handful of other women became members of combat squadrons. How did some of these first females feel? Chief Petty Officer (CPO) Mindee Wolven, assigned to the USS *Eisenhower* nuclear aircraft carrier after 14 years of service, said that she felt as if she had just joined the Navy. "We've been supporting the Navy; now we're in the Navy."[38] Petty Officer Theresa Walker entered the Navy in 1987 in a desk job. Six years later she became a damage control person prepared to fight fires, clean up oil spills, and keep a damaged ship from flooding. Aboard the USS *Mt. Whitney* with 80 other women, she felt her male colleagues gave her the opportunity to prove herself. CAPT Lin Hutton, also aboard the *Whitney*, served as the Second Fleet's new air operations officer. Hutton managed all aircraft from all branches of the military that trained with the Second Fleet. She became the seventh woman to earn her wings and the first woman aviator to be named commander of a Navy Atlantic Coast aviation squadron.

Since combat assignments opened up after the Tailhook '91 event and the Navy's resulting anti–sexual harassment programs, one woman, Airman (Amn) Malissia Chester, who was temporarily stationed on the aircraft carrier USS *America* in the Mediterranean Sea and off the coast of Somalia, said, "With sexual harassment (concerns) in the Navy now, (men on ship) had to be careful. We'd walk through passageways and they'd slam their bodies to the side, like we had some horrible disease." Men on board ship may no longer feel they have to "slam their bodies to the side," with the Navy's new approach to boot camp that focuses on better treatment for all recruits and the treatment of sexual harassment as a readiness issue.[39]

More than 4,000 women are now assigned to 59 combatant ships, and the number of mixed-gender combatant ships is projected to increase to 72 by the end of the 1997 fiscal year. Women are assigned to all 12 carriers. According to the Assistant Secretary of the Navy for Manpower and Reserve Affairs, Bernard D. Rostker, "command surveys indicate that women are more fully accepted in their combat roles."[40] Rostker also said that the Marine Corps has 279 female officers and 3,849 enlisted females in combat-related units. Female Marine recruits must complete the Crucible, and female Marine privates must complete Marine combat training. Recently, female Marines shot live ammunition from heavy weapons in combat training for the first time.

Basic combat skills are very important as the world hotspots are reshaped, according to CPL William M. Lisbon.[41] Any area can become a combat zone, and front lines are a thing of the past. The Crucible training "gives Marines the knowledge to set up a defensive perimeter or operate a heavy weapon."

According to Rostker in 1997, the Navy had 135 women aviators. Fifty-three were tactical aircraft aviators. It had 36 females in aviator training pipelines, with 15 women in pipelines for combatant aviation. The Marine Corps had 29 women aviators in combat squadrons and combat aviation pipelines. In 1998, CDR Trish Beckman, USN, summarized very well the responsibilities of men and women alike:

> Every American citizen is a rugged individualist. He/she should contribute to our nation's defense based on his/her individual capabilities, not on arbitrary assumptions of what is 'average' for each gender. Women will never be given the full rights of citizenship until they accept the full responsibilities of citizenship."

AIR FORCE

In January 1992, LGen. Billy J. Boles, Deputy Chief of Staff, Personnel, said the best-qualified person should be assigned to combat and said he anticipated the repeal of the law prohibiting the assignment of women to aircraft in combat.[42] At the time of the July 1992 hearings, the Air Force's first woman aviator was flying a U-2 on station in Korea.[43]

Capt. Susan M. Cunningham, an Air Force pilot who flew a transport plane to Grenada in 1983, thought at the time, "In reality, I think that's how it's going to happen, women are going to be launched before they [the Air Force] realized the women are launched. But they certainly aren't going to advertise it."[44] [In fact, one female flew unnoticed on six missions aboard an Air Force C-141 transport plane during the height of the invasion.]

Many firsts happened in 1993 in the Air Force. Lt. Col. Susan Helms became the first woman to graduate from the USAF Test Pilot School, and Maj. Jacquelyn Parker became the first female Air Force fighter pilot.[45] In April 1993, 27-year-old 1st Lt. Jeannie Flynn was chosen as the first woman to train as a combat-qualified fighter pilot, and in February 1994, she graduated from Luke Air Force Base. She trained to fly the F-15E Strike Eagle.[46] The Strike Eagles, considered to be the most advanced aircraft in the world, led an attack on Iraqi forces on January 16, 1991.[47] Gen. Merrill McPeak, Air Force Chief of Staff, said in February 1994 that the Air Force's move to a 100-percent merit-based assignment system was smooth because it had 97 percent of its positions already open to women. At the time, 13 women were either in training or scheduled to start training for combat aircraft. McPeak went on to say that the Air Force had not raised or lowered its standards to qualify Flynn, who said she had not encountered resistance. The policy changed, and the timing was right for her to take advantage of the opportunity. "If people had their opinions, they kept them to themselves and they did their best to train me. And they did very good."[48] She adds that whether people disagree at this point is irrelevant because they will follow policy. If a person is qualified, he or she will be accepted. Like other military women, Flynn saw herself as being no different from any other student. She definitely thought it was more exciting to fly F-15s than other aircraft, however, because they demand more skill. "We started out in basic air-to-air ... with two airplanes and fight against each other. Once you get the handle on how to do that, both offensive, defensive, then they throw another airplane in and there's three airplanes and you have to deal with that. And there's just so many different things that this aircraft does, because then we got into the special tasks of dropping the bombs. And this aircraft is very well equipped for flying at night, low level."

Also in 1993, Lt. Col. Patricia Farns, Minot Air Force Base in North Dakota, became the first woman in the Air Force to take command of a missile squadron.[49] In 1996, Lt. Bobbi Doorenbos got her wings at Reese Air Force Base in Lubbock. Second in her class, she received the top flying grades among the fighter-bomber students. She was on track to become the first woman in Air National Guard history to be selected and trained as an F-16 pilot.[50] Doorenbos said her instructors and other students had an accepting attitude.

In July 1996, astronaut Shannon Lucid, 53, a NASA biochemist, broke the U.S. space flight endurance record of 115 days, 9 hours, 43 minutes and spent an additional six weeks in space because of problems with the Atlantis shuttle launch. She returned successfully.[51] Maj. Eileen Isola, USAF and president of Women Military Aviators in 1998, said compared to the past "you can go anywhere you want in the Air Force."

Dynamic and rapid changes in the international security environment that occurred five years ago changed the face of air mobility, according to Maj. Michael J. Petersen, USAF.[52] The focus is regional and fragmented. It is uncertain, he says, where the next trouble spot will occur. Being able to respond to those hotspots quickly is key to national security. Aerospace's ability "to display presence" promotes national influence as well as security. "Both reach and power are inseparable aspects of the same single entity—aerospace power," says Petersen. "Today's aerospace power doesn't mean bombing necessarily, but lending a helping hand through humanitarian efforts. In Desert Shield, aerospace power was there within 24 hours flying defensive patrols. Between 1970 and 1992, aerospace forces engaged in only 7 combat operations, while engaging in 42 presence missions and shows of force, 84 air movements of national influence, and 197 humanitarian missions."

"The post–Cold War era has made strategic mobility, especially air mobility," writes Maj. Philip A. Bossert, Jr., "a first among equals with the traditional 'combat forces.'"[53] Technological advances have made the terms *strategic* and *tactical* along with *combat* and *combat support* beside the point. Bossert says, "A C-141 or C-17 [that] flies just hundreds of feet above the ground dropping paratroopers in a blazing shower of gunfire and AAA [antiaircraft artillery] is as much a combat aircraft as a F-15 or F-22 circling at 35,000 feet ready to pound on any enemy." Bossert feels the Air Force is not unlike most large organizations "steeped in history and bureaucratic habit"; some in it resist change.

COAST GUARD

According to the Association of the New York City Bar, the Coast Guard situation is unique.[54] In peacetime, it falls under the Department of Transportation, and during war, under the Department of Defense. All Coast Guard positions have been open to women since 1978. In war, The Coast Guard would be under the command of the Navy, and women might have to be removed from the ships.

Conclusion: Déjà Vu?

Col. Kelly Hamilton writes that in her interview with the first Air Force woman pilot assigned to an operational fighter aircraft, 1st Lt. Jeannie Flynn, she listened to Flynn's dreams. "It was like déjà vu."[55] Hamilton joined the Air Force in 1973. Although women were not allowed to fly, Hamilton says that she knew without a doubt that she would be an Air Force pilot. It would only be a matter of time. When she became an Air Force pilot, she felt the same way about the combat exclusion law; it was only a matter of time until its repeal. Hamilton has some inspiring philosophy for young people, "The future can only be realized by meeting the challenges placed before you head-on. I encourage you to be an advocate for change. Create a professional environment in all that you do. Most importantly, recognize the power of committing to your dreams."[56]

Chapter 13

Family

Speak to me. Take my hand. What are you now?
—Muriel Rukeyser[1]

How can it pass that my mother is in the military?
No, It cannot be, but it is
—A Soldier

There are not any woman war heros, tv, movies, newspapers.
Nowhere.
—Richard Webb[2]

The Larger Society

DIFFERENTIATION BETWEEN WORK AND FAMILY

By working, the American woman maximizes her potential as a fully functioning member of society. She acquires and makes full use of skills, attitudes, and objectives. Women in our culture have a Puritan work ethic. Regardless of position, they often play a constructive role in the American workforce.

This benefit to society should be viewed, however, in a total context. There are issues that confront the American woman every day in the workforce. History recounts how early industrial capitalism developed. Factories hired young, unmarried women who were not expected to earn a living wage. In the nineteenth and early twentieth centuries, although more women entered the workforce, they were kept in low-paying jobs. Recent statistics indicate, however, that the workforce is changing. More women are becoming executives and professionals; nearly 40 percent of executives and slightly over 50 percent of professionals are women. More women are entering the fields considered "non-traditional." Women, however, still dominate the "administrative support, including clerical" and "service occupations" categories.[3]

The entrance of women into the labor force has not always resulted in equal status for women, particularly with regard to income in the United States. Organizations are not only structures; they are environments within which people live and work. Stratification in society, organizational theory, and practice provide an appropriate larger context for examining inequality and inequity. The American female military soldier must be understood in the organizational setting if we are to see clearly the impact and effects of inequality and inequity on her job and life satisfaction and the far-reaching positive contributions of the latter to our society as a whole. The majority of contemporary American women still view their primary role as caring for home and family, but most also spend many years contributing human capital to the nation's economy in the form of paid employment. Men and women work for the same reasons: to meet economic needs, become independent, have greater control over their environment and future, contribute meaningfully to the needs of society, interact with other adults engaged in productive work, develop and use skills and talents, and experience growth and personal fulfillment. One must realize that it is human motives for activity, exploration, and independence that are reflected in women's desire to work. These motives, which stimulate both men and women, make for a better society. Women are making a positive contribution to American society, but gender-status difference questions remain: How does the United States resolve the obstacles to status inequality? Is it a hangover from an earlier era that is currently evolving? Will it disappear with time?

In order to answer these questions adequately, it is critical that we realize the genitalia identity given at birth is perhaps the deepest concept we hold of ourselves. Gender identity determines many of the directions our lives will take.[4] Although each culture determines the content of gender roles in its own way, for the purposes of this book, we will limit our discussion to the culture of the United States.

Bryan Strong and Christine DeVault note in their book a significant shift from traditional toward more egalitarian gender roles over the past generation. Women have made more progress than men, but men are also changing. Gender roles are becoming more androgynous, that is, they are incorporating both masculine and feminine traits. This makes for more flexible and fulfilling relationships and lives. Strong and DeVault also note that gender roles are becoming more egalitarian as opposed to hierarchical.[5]

Most women will be gainfully employed at sometime in their life as workers and professionals. Entrance into work or career does not exclude a woman from more traditional roles as wife and mother, but the roles can conflict. Strong and DeVault say that men are not asked to choose, but women are still asked to deal with the conflict. Cynthia Costello and Barbara Krimgold report that in 1994 dual-earner married couples accounted for more than four in ten families, up from fewer than one in ten in 1940.[6]

THE NEED FOR NEW IMAGES DURING SOCIAL CHANGE

Some women question motherhood and some women reject motherhood because of the conflicts having children creates. Twenty to 25 percent of baby boomers chose to remain childless and maximize work opportunities and time with their husbands, compared to 10 percent of the previous generation.[7] Women began having fewer children or remaining childless because motherhood symbolizes the acceptance and limitations of traditional gender roles. The idea that men's work conflicts with family roles has been rarely explored, however, according to Strong and DeVault. They do note that some research indicates that men perceive their family roles as being much greater than merely being the family breadwinner.[8]

To threaten an individual's gender role is to threaten his or her gender identity as a male or female. These threats are an important psychological mechanism keeping people in traditional but dysfunctional gender roles, according to Strong and DeVault. The gender schema of the larger society initially carried over into the military. We treat both objects and behavior as if they were masculine or feminine or in some way related to gender. These gender divisions form a complex structure of associations that affect our perceptions of reality. As we are socialized, we learn what constitutes appropriate behavior for males and females. We also categorize jobs, toys, clothes, and mannerisms by gender.[9]

There is no one definition of the American family; there are only families in America that vary considerably according to historical period, the place in which they are located, and the class and cultural background of the individuals composing those families.

Robert V. Wells writes that we would do well not to be too rigid in our expectations about the interpretations of family life.[10] Families have been and will continue to be a vital and important part of American society, but that vitality has come more from their capacity to adapt to changes in demographic and economic patterns. Family life in the United States is evolving. Wells believes that no aspect of American life has been more profoundly influenced by the demographic structures and changes than the family. One of the most obvious links between demography and the family is that the central life events of birth, death, marriage, and migration occur within the context of family life. Although Wells was not focusing on the military family, the events that are perhaps more pertinent to the military family are death and migration. Death, according to Wells, is not always as directly linked to family life as are marriage or childbirth, but this most fundamental of all changes frequently occurs within the context of the family. Migration likewise changes within the context of the family, particularly the military family. Parts of the family move either together or sequentially, with one family member being assigned to a new duty and then other members following.

If we believe as Strong and DeVault that being born a particular gender is the most intimate definition of self, it is little wonder then that family issues are also among the most controversial no matter what we are discussing, but particularly if we are discussing women serving in combat. The strong cultural values within our country must be viewed in the light of a changing world that the military must be ready to meet.

Military Family Life

It is little wonder then that MAJ Mary Finch, USA, writes that the U.S. Presidential Commission's "recommendations regarding parental and family policies are extremely controversial." Although its recommendations were overwhelmingly approved by a vote of nine to one, with one abstention, tensions ran so high that the issue was voted on during a walkout of conservatives.[11] To ensure that children are not separated from their parent or both parents for long periods, the Commission recommended that single custodial parents and one member of a dual-career couple be assigned to nondeployable positions. There are not very many nondeployable positions (they are found primarily only in military schools). The policy would thus stall or end careers. The second alternative recommended is that one parent in a dual-career service couple be forced to leave the services or give the separation decision to the discretion of the commander. Although regulations that service members have a family-care plan were in effect at the time of the Gulf War, some were out of date and unworkable or unrealistic. Since then, says Finch, commanders have been reviewing plans with service members.

A discussion of the military family involves two very powerful institutions that do more than tug at each other. The research of MAJ Angela Manos, USA, demonstrates that from the Revolutionary War to the present, these two institutions of the family and the military hang in the balance of a power struggle. Mady Wechsler Segal portrays the military and the family as being what are called greedy institutions.[12] The study of military families, Segal explains, involves analysis of how two societal institutions intersect, both making great demands on the individual's commitments, loyalty, time, and energy. They therefore have the characteristics of what Lewis Coser, in his book, calls "greedy" institutions.[13] Writing in 1986, Segal contended that as the result of various social trends there is greater conflict now than in the past between these two greedy institutions.

Angela Manos and David Segal's 1996 study reenforces the belief that the two institutions are still in struggle. Soldiers on their fourth or more deployment within three years say separations have a substantial impact on finances, education, and future planning. Soldiers told Manos and Segal that they have "a love for soldiering, but love for their family and burn-out is becoming stronger than their love for soldiering."[14] Another statement the authors heard was, "being a soldier is just costing me and my family too much financially and in time together." The soldiers were concerned about lost time with their spouses and missing out on important events in their children's lives. When a soldier deploys, she or he sets up two households and costs in long-distance phone calls to families soar. In response, Manos and Segal say allowing separation rations, morale calls to families, e-mail, and video-teleconferences are ways the institution of the military seeks to assuage the institution of the family in today's Army.

Major Manos's research demonstrates that interest in America's Army family remains high and is a direct result of common and significant findings that "the Army family is 'here to stay' and without question Army families do have 'an effect' on military readiness."[15] She notes, however, that researchers differ in their analysis of the effects.

In the past, Army leaders expected soldiers to be ready to go to war. Now, according to Manos, the Army expects soldiers and their families to be ready. The challenge of leadership is to let soldiers and families know what is expected of them. Based on this premise, mandatory education programs were developed for the Army family "regardless of their demographic status or demographic category" to ensure their readiness at all times.

Kris Warner, Family Action Program, USMC, says that "It [the dual-career military family] is tremendously hard. There is competition, being in the same place at the same time. There are dynamics not that different from same career families except in civilian life they may relocate and spend a lot of time separate. Everything is kind of intensified."[16]

According to Manos, little research was done prior to the 1960s on the military family. Initially, there was no need for research because the traditional soldier was single, had never been married, and had no children. It wasn't until World War II and the Korean War that the mobilizations drew large numbers of married soldiers. The Army had no policies forbidding women to follow their husbands previous to these two wars, but family members were considered a hindrance. Soldiers had to take care of their families because the Army was not economically capable of doing so. The wives were known as camp followers.[17]

It wasn't until 1917, according to Manos, that Congress formally recognized the Army family by increasing pay and extending the privileges of the allotment act for both commissioned officers and enlisted men.[18] In 1925 the Army rewrote policy to allow enlisted men to marry, with a provision that held until World War II that a Specialist (SPC) E4 or lower could be discharged if he married without permission. But it marked a shift from single soldiers without dependents to enlisted soldiers and families who lived in poverty.[19] By 1939 an estimated 45,000 dependents of enlisted soldiers were suffering in deplorable living conditions. The Army Chief of Staff instituted a policy that all enlisted men who married without permission would be discharged and would not be allowed to reenlist. The policy change stopped the growth of the number of enlisted families but did nothing to help the families already in the Army.[20] World War II brought larger numbers of married men with dependents into the armed forces and Congress passed the *Servicemen's Dependents Allowance Act* to supplement the soldier's pay and provide some medical benefits to him and his family. The Army was unprepared, however, to assist families. The American Red Cross, says Manos, provided support until its resources were no longer adequate. Military leaders were convinced that by providing families with care, they would have a better force, and benefits improved.[21] The Army saw taking care of its families as protecting the soldiers from outside distractions, thus giving them a sense of security, increasing morale, and cultivating a sense of unity. The Army adopted the slogan, "The Army Takes Care of Its Own."[22] After World War II, Congress reverted, however, and took dependents' allowances away.

Congress conducted a second study in 1952 on retention and readiness that resulted in identifying a general lack of social services.[23] Very little changed, according to Manos, until 1954, when the Army instituted support programs, recognizing the family as a support system for the soldiers.[24] In 1965 the beginning of the Vietnam era saw men going to war and wives remaining at home. It was during this time that the basic fabric of family services as we know it today was formed.[25]

After the Vietnam War, the Army shifted from conscription to volunteerism. The volunteer force consisted primarily of married people. The Army as an institution began a shift from discouraging to encouraging enlisted married soldiers, and the Supreme Court ruled that spouses of female soldiers would receive the same benefits as spouses of male soldiers.[26] Manos says, "The role of the officer's wife had begun to reflect the changing gender roles in the larger society." Nancy L. Goodman and David R. Segal called it a shift from a "militarism institution" to a "familism institution."[27]

Today's soldier, says Manos, is more likely to be married because of the emphasis on retention of enlisted personnel. In May 1995, about 65 percent of the force was married. Mady Segal and Jessie J. Harris found that the average number of children a soldier has is positively related to unit readiness. The proportion of dual-military couples and the proportion of soldiers living off-post are inversely related to unit readiness.[28]

According to Manos, the Army conducted extensive research about issues relating to military families during the 1980s and 1990s. Manos found several things in her review of the dual-military couple. During the period 1989–91, approximately seven to ten percent of all soldiers were in dual-military marriages.[29] The increase in dual-military couples is related to the increase in the number of women in the Army. Dual-military families are promoted faster, perform better, and get along well on joint assignments.[30] They are less likely to have children, but if they do, it is harder to have suitable child-care arrangements. They are more likely to be late or miss alerts, and they face the risk of both parents being called for extra duty when army child-care facilities are not open.[31]

Manos notes Kathleen Coolbaugh and Alvin Rosenthal's most significant findings in 1992 regarding family separations were that they were widespread and indiscriminate.[32] Not only did they find that a soldier's sense of family well-being while he or she was deployed affected job performance and readiness, but also that separations play a part in how the family experiences and adapts to war and they influence spousal support for retention.

Army research found the higher the average number of children the soldiers in a unit have, the higher the unit readiness, but the higher the number of dual-military married couples with children in the unit, the lower the readiness. Also the higher the number of soldiers living off-post, the lower the unit readiness.[33] The Army also found that soldiers who are married before entering the service or who get married during their first term are less likely to finish their tour of duty. It is this soldier's family that has the most problems adapting to military life because he or she may have to change duty stations as many times as three times during the first year.

Manos reports that in 1993 approximately 12 percent of the Army was female, compared to 2 percent in 1973. Fifty-three percent of the females and 43 percent of the males were minorities. Women were less likely to be married and to have children, but were in general younger and better educated than men. They were, however, lower in rank than men.

"The Army has changed," according to Manos, "from a global war, forward based, large Army, to a regional war, primarily CONUS (Continental U.S. minus Alaska and Hawaii) based, power projection Army that is ready to respond to a wide spectrum of missions—ranging from major regional conflicts to operations other than war."[34] Our Army, she continues, evolved from a conscript force of single males with no children to a volunteer, gender-integrated force with 65 percent of its soldiers married. Seventy percent of the spouses work outside of the home, and 17,000 of the military are male spouses. Thirteen percent of the active soldiers are female. Women leave at a lower rate than men and get promoted at proportionally higher rates. Manos points out that in all this change, one thing remains constant. War in the future will still require well-trained and -equipped men and women who are willing to put their lives on the line and do the hard, dirty things war requires.

To better serve its soldiers and their families, the Army has designed an Army Family Team Building concept which is not new, but is about readiness, both military and family.[35] It is the challenge of leadership to know the familial status of those soldiers in the unit. The other key to its success is family members teaching family members. Some soldiers still have a mind-set that an informed spouse is a threat. The program's goal is to teach soldiers that the more informed the spouse, the better chance of having a successful career. It does not replace any other program such as Family Support Groups.

MAJ Connie L. Reeves, USA (Ret.), herself a dual-service parent for 10 years and an extensive researcher of the military family, found that although military leaders often state that the military is not the venue for social experiments, nor is it a welfare agency, military personnel do represent the American society, with all its various problems.[36] Military personnel, however, have a special mission to defend the Constitution of the larger society. The fulfillment of that mission dictates special circumstances under which family life exists. Reeves says that over time the military has developed a system to guarantee a service member's deployability. She points out that Mady Wechsler Segal's research on "Greedy Institutions" says that when the military questions the compatibility of parenthood with readiness, women are usually targeted. At any rate, dual-parent and single-parent soldiers are required to ensure that their families will be cared for if they should have to deploy, with little notice and for a long period of time.[37] The system isn't foolproof because of varying degrees of competency of able spouses left behind and because the plan does not ensure that military members with temporary dependent-care problems are deployable. The issues are not simple, according to Reeves's review of the literature, and misinformation that a serviceperson has doesn't help. The understanding most military personnel have is that even if their arrangements for family care fail, they must still report to duty. Reeves says service members whose child-care arrangements have failed will not be required to deploy. The parent will be given reasonable time to make new plans. It is also true, she writes, that even the best-laid plans may fail. For example, a wife could be run over by a truck the day after her husband deploys. Reeves believes that all military personnel should be required to maintain dependent-care plans or alternate-care plans in case the primary caregiver is no longer available. Her research concluded that the military is more likely to offer an exemption to the traditional military parent who becomes temporarily nondeployable than the single or dual-service parents.

Reeves chips away at the myths surrounding parenting and the military. The idea that keeping single parents in the military risks deployability is not valid in her opinion.[38] Not only do single parents work extra and perform the same duty as their married counterparts, they are less likely to voice deployability problems than married men. Despite their deployments to Saudi Arabia, custodial single-parents were committed to the military. A very real research implication, says Reeves, is whether single military parents are relying upon placing their children into the care of the noncustodial parent who is also a deployable military member.

A female soldier serving in Bosnia whom I interviewed told me that upon receiving a promotion she decided she would retire. Her two preschool children were in the care of the father, also a potentially deployable military member. She said she felt very fortunate that he did not have to deploy at the same time. She thought, however, that being a parent and being deployed was just too much, so, she planned to retire from military service. Her feelings are probably not uncommon. A friend of mine who is a longtime military person has two daughters serving on active duty. The daughters both have deployable husbands. "It doesn't work," he told me.

But in spite of the hardships, some people make it work, according to Reeves. The military insures income and security. Single parents will go to great lengths to retain their positions. They will often remain quiet rather than risk retribution.

CAPT Rosemary Mariner, USN, believes that Desert Storm was a watershed.[39] It demonstrated that codifying was absurd. Reeves notes that it was the first time in which large numbers of American women have gone to war. Family-care plans were critical, particularly for dual-service and single parents in the military. How does grief affect the military children when a parent dies? Her discussion is thought provoking, but she believes the issue is too "labyrinthian" for definitive conclusions. Reeves finds that our country's acceptance of women as soldiers stops somewhere short of the acceptance of mothers as soldiers.[40]

In a 1996 interview, Linda Grant De Pauw said that the Gulf War caused the American people to view the woman or mother as a victim rather than a warrior. For example, she said, "The treatment of one Prisoner of War, (POW) Rhonda Cornum was not studied until the sexual abuse came out.... The Gulf War was the strangest war ever. Women became more visible, but more questions were on the sexual abuse or the terrible mothers leaving their babies. Combat is the high probability of face-to-face combat. Currently, in Bosnia there is no way of telling where women are going."[41]

Some military males have told me in interviews that assigning women to combat will threaten the continuance of our race because the female bears the procreation role. Mady Segal says "There are times when women's military involvement may be seen as an extension of women's roles as mothers protecting their children."[42] She cites as an example the case of partisan or guerrilla activities drawing women from the ranks of the poor. Further, Segal believes women's lives are risked if society is threatened. The resistance is most likely to the idea of risking large numbers of women. Arthur would agree that the country isn't ready to see a large number of women killed on a shore.[43]

As Reeves notes, bills were introduced to protect children from becoming orphans by trying to reduce or eliminate situations in which a custodial parent or both parents would be in a war zone simultaneously. Both Congresswoman Beverly B. Byron, chair of the House Armed Services Subcommittee on Military Personnel and Compensation, and Senator Barbara Boxer submitted such bills, but the bills were defeated. Military readiness was one concern of the Pentagon and Senator John Glenn, chair of the Senate Armed

Services Subcommittee on Manpower and Personnel. Based on Glenn's recommendation, Congress adopted a resolution in 1992 that the Department of
Defense establish a standard policy "for reassignment, leave, or deferments
when family hardships arise, or to expect future legislation."[44]

Despite all of the objections in 1991, the Assistant Secretary of Defense
for Force Management and Personnel, Christopher Jehn, testified that child-
care problems were practically nonexistent during the Gulf War due to the
family-care plan policy; therefore, prohibiting dual-service parents from serving simultaneously in a war zone would be detrimental to military readiness.[45]
The war ended quickly, points out Reeves, and the policy controversy was not
solved at that time.

Counting the number of single parents is complicated and breaking out
the number of single parents with physical custody of dependents from those
who merely claim custody is currently not feasible, says Reeves. Yet the majority of single military parents are men, simply because most service members
are men. Usually fathers do not have physical custody of their children, actual
custody is the military's concern with respect to deployability. Figures indicate that in 1995 about four percent of dual-service parents deployed.[46]

The military, Reeves says, recognizes that married soldiers have fewer discipline problems. The All-Volunteer Force dictates that the military be more
tolerant of families. Military men tend to marry earlier than their civilian
counterparts and men who are married or who expect to marry within a few
years are more likely to enlist than men who expect to remain single for a long
while. If service people know their families are protected, they are more willing to risk their own lives in defense of their country. The greatest concern,
according to Reeves, is the time spent apart.[47]

Manos and Segal say the need to help families reunite continues to be a
growing issue. Domestic conflict, verbal and physical, and the use of alcohol
increase as do counseling and disciplinary problems in the unit.[48] Most family
members are concerned about the number of deployments soldiers must go on.
Some deployments are "back to back," increasing the number of what Manos
and Segal term "geographical bachelors." Family members and the soldiers are
not sure they will have a 20-year successful career and marriage. Thus the
spouse remains behind, taking care of the children and continuing with a career
as his or her "safety-net." It is no longer uncommon, the authors say, to have
over half the women in a family-member focus group say that they are going
to make their husbands leave the service because of the number of separations.

Like it or not, Reeves states, women are necessary in today's military. They
are tolerated, but in the eyes of the majority of male service members, women
do not belong. Having children also reduces the likelihood that women will
join the military in the first place, but the opposite is true for men.

Women do not cause any more lost time than males, the reasons just
differ according to Reeves. Men accrue greater amounts of lost time because

of desertion, going AWOL, and alcohol and drug abuse. The military, says Reeves, accommodates pregnant service members not to "pacify women," but because they are needed for the All-Volunteer force.

Pregnancy itself is the only viable difference in parenthood roles between a man and a woman in my opinion. Although a man shares in the act of getting a female pregnant, he cannot physically be pregnant and give birth. Other than this one isolated fact, parenthood should be the responsibility of both males and females. Yet military and civilian mothers remain primarily responsible for raising children, according to Reeves. Enlisted mothers in particular are more traditional by nature and prefer not to mix motherly roles with a military one. Reenlistment of military women decreases by 69 percent once they become mothers.[49]

An enlisted woman may have traditional values, and those values are often reinforced by men. Career women shared their thoughts with me in interviews. In answer to the following question, "You are a soldier and a mother at the same time. What has been your experience as you have performed both duties?" MAJ Mary Finch, USA, said: "Wife," then added "I have based my career decisions on what's going on in my personal life. I make my decisions that way. We (my husband and I) decided we wouldn't go back to field units where there are long separations due to deployments and exercises. Our choice has provided us freedom and flexibility for ourselves and our children."[50]

MAJ Jane McKeon, USA (Ret.), part of the 1980 class at West Point, has taught the family course at West Point. She tried to prepare cadets for a career that sells itself as a noble profession, almost a "calling." This viewpoint is necessary when you talk about the possibility of losing your life in pursuit of a successful career. The question the cadets must answer, says McKeon, is how one balances the requirements of this kind of career with a family life.

McKeon found that her role as a dual-military parent restricted her in some ways: "As soon as you start to add a traditional role like wife and mother to that of career officer, you will find it more difficult to get a mentor. Some male officers were very up-front. In fact, I was once told that a particular job I was best qualified for was going to be given to a male officer because he was the primary bread winner for his family and I had a competent husband. Men often feel a responsibility to keep mothers where they should be. Why— because we are in competition."[51]

"In the military," McKeon continued, "the male may say he is taking off for a father-son activity and it is accepted. The female may also do it, but she won't say it because it drives home the 'female agenda' that women put family first. 'Family first' is not interpreted as negatively when men are doing it." McKeon thought leaders saw her as a mother.

McKeon believes that a leader has to be nurturing and see her soldiers as valued people. "You're a soldier 24 hours a day, seven days a week—this position doesn't allow you to view people as a valued resource."

Age is a factor in acceptance according to McKeon: "Women fit in much better when we are younger. We can be viewed by senior officers as competent daughters. When we get a little older, we resemble wives and mothers too much." I asked McKeon how a mature woman gets accepted, and she replied: "We must be more competent than our male counterparts." Fortunately, most women understand human behavior and know how to get people to work together toward common goals. Real life experience adds another qualification. According to McKeon:

> The bottom line is [that] those issues [gender and age] don't stand alone for women in combat. If a person leading you is competent and whether this person will keep you alive, is what is important. The military uses those issues of gender, motherhood, and age against women. The questions that must be asked are, what are the job requirements and what is the competency level of the person available to meet these requirements. The upper levels in the military organization must support this mind set. Fortunately, most of the soldiers in the lower level jobs do—they just want their leaders to do their job, and do it well.

Reeves suggests that had the Gulf War lasted longer, there might have been orphaned children. Large numbers of orphaned children would dictate a need for serious study of the problem. Reeves believes the military recognizes the importance of family happiness and is likely to make additional efforts to support the welfare of children. If the military is designed to serve the nation, she says, then the nation should see that servicewomen have the peace of mind that their children will be no less protected than the public who is being served. Reeves concludes that since not all soldiers are needed in the combat zones, children should not have to risk losing both their parents if it can be avoided. Women are in the military because they are needed by the nation and because they wish to serve. The military should recognize the trends and changes within the larger society, such as single parenting. Reeves believes the military will not return to the way things were and it may as well meet these issues head-on.

There are many reasons that a soldier does not have to deploy: terminal illness, the death of a spouse or child within a 60-day period prior to the deployment, prolonged hospitalization of a family member, abuse of a child or spouse, pregnancy with complications lasting beyond 90 days, family members that are HIV positive, emergency dental treatment, and conscientious objector beliefs. Holm believes that pregnancy is a factor for men not deploying as well as for women. During the 1970s about 500 men a year were given a deferment because their wives were in the advanced stages of pregnancy.

In 1991 the Department of Defense released a statement that all service members must be able to deploy to any "hot spot around the world." Single and dual-service parents could not be excused from deployment or reassignments. At the same time, the DOD reiterated it would provide reassignments or discharges when family-care arrangements could not be made.

Gen C. C. Krulak, USMC Commandant, said that one indication of how well female members of the Marine Corps performed in Desert Shield/Storm was the fact that very few, when compared statistically with their male counterparts, ended up leaving for any reason. Only five females left because of pregnancies and all five were pregnant but unaware of this fact prior to deployment.[55]

DIFFERENTIATION BETWEEN WORK AND FAMILY.

In July 1996, according to Bradley Graham, *Washington Post*, the pregnancy rate in Bosnia was average in that about five percent of the troops were reassigned because of maternity.[56] In July 1996 in the *Early Bird* daily, the Pentagon said the number of pregnancies in Bosnia equaled the rate in the 1991 Persian Gulf War and was also in line with the frequency of pregnancies among all Army women during the preceding year. Women constituted only nine percent of the 17,000 soldiers in Bosnia, and they remained confined to noncombat support roles. Thus the Army appears to be inclined to accept the pregnancy rate as a fact of life. It is not against military rules to become pregnant. For those pregnant women serving in Bosnia, their pregnancy means automatic reassignment for health reasons, however, because a pregnant soldier cannot don heavy Kevlar body armor and belts that carry canteens, ammunition pouches, first-aid kits, and personal items.

EVACUATION

Commanding Gen J. A. Brabham, USMC, praised women in Desert Shield/Storm. Even though 11 were medically evacuated, 7 because of pregnancy, he believed that "In the main they proved themselves fully equal to the tasks they were assigned."[57]

Conclusions

Whatever the definition of family, as an institution it remains a strong and vital factor in military readiness. Manos's research demonstrates the military family has strong beginnings. George Washington forbade family members in the camps. The wives tended to ignore the officers' orders.[58] Today's soldiers are better equipped to perform if they know their families are being taken care of in the best possible fashion. The societally gender-constructed family role of mother will, no doubt, remain the most difficult role for the mother herself, but for society to accept. Whatever the role struggle, the concept of family as something cherished and valued remains and offers hope.

Chapter 14

Toward Strength and Equality

—Souls on Board, two.[1]

That men and women have been dying alongside each other in wars for thousands of years is nothing new. Then why does Jean Zimmerman end her book with the provocative question of whether the final frontier of equality for women and men is their flying and dying alongside one another?[2] LTC Dave Grossman, USA, introduces his 1995 book, *On Killing: The Psychological Cost of Learning to Kill in War and Society*, remarking, "War has often been a sexist environment, but death is an equal opportunity employer." Death is gender neutral. It does not discriminate. The breath of life is gender neutral. I conclude common sense prevails on the battlefield, and wounded and dying men and women will say, "Heck, yes, carry me off the battlefield." Women and men carrying one another off the battlefield is not new.

What is new is the legal right to share most military assignments and therefore be acknowledged as an equal member of the combatant team. Responding to rank is gender neutral. Equality and what equality brings, that is, more opportunity to observe women as colleagues, will improve understanding and treatment of one another. Old acculturation must give way to new ideas, leading to positive change for women and men alike and a better life for our children and grandchildren.

Meaningful change is occurring. The old argument that women do not like getting dirty is not true. Pvt Tabatha Kittleson, who participated in the "Crucible" established by Gen Krulak, the Commandant of the Marine Corps, says, "I love playing in dirt and getting dirty." Pvt Susan Miedaner and Pvt Leon Nicholas found themselves lying shoulder-to-shoulder behind one station. It is barely possible to distinguish men from women in their combat positions. Private Nicholas, 18, shrugged off the idea that a female partner might perform differently from a male one: "Men or women, that doesn't matter. We're trained as Marines, to rise above any situation of male-female. All we see is another Marine."[3] Although the women cannot serve in combat, they can be trained. These women, unlike their foremothers, will be ready should they be called to serve in direct combat. Just as important, they will be more ready to serve in noncombatant positions should they go in "harm's way."[4] According to GSgt Daniel C. Orland, "Marines receive training on heavy weapons, combat formations, land navigation, field survival, and nuclear, biological and chemical defense."[5] The change is reflected by Sgt Maj Charlene K. Wiese, USMC Headquarters, when she said, "Women get to do more than when I came in. I wish I were 25 years younger."

In spite of the gravity of war, all military personnel interviewed have a fierce loyalty to the military and to the nation. They are people with a mission; most can recall some beauty in mission even in the heat of war. In a letter home to her father in 1991, Col. Kelly Hamilton, USAF (Ret.), wrote:

> Flew a long mission yesterday and it really made me wonder how folks spend their lives earthbound. The view from above has a lot going for it. God knew a good deal when he chose the penthouse. Last night the moon gave a silver blue cast to the thousands of clouds that lay below our six-ship cell as we silently flew to meet our seven receivers in the early morning hours. At times the cumulus formations gave the impression of a series of canyons and rolling hills, a beautiful non-threatening skyscape.[6]

Hamilton adds that serene moments like observing the skyscape make it difficult to realize she is so far from the familiar sites and sounds of the United States.

MAJ Mary Finch sums up a positive reality of change:

> There are those out there who would have things change or go back to the way they were before women were integrated into the services — that isn't the way it is. Things are changing (progressing forward). The battlefield is changing, women are changing, our daughters are playing soccer, taking Tae Kwon Do, and even ice hockey. The "good old days" are not coming back. The people who said, "keep the blacks down" — haven't fared well in recent history today.[7]

Most of this book was written at an unprecedented time in the history of the military — the building and dedication of the Women in Military Service to America Memorial. According to the *St. Petersburg Times* of November 7, 1998, BGen. Wilma L. Vaught, the driving force behind the memorial, was the first woman to be named a general in the Air Force. I was fortunate to attend the dedication ceremonies and participate in the candlelight walk from the Lincoln Memorial, crossing the Memorial Bridge, to the Women's Memorial at the entrance of Arlington Cemetery. A sense of history began with the Saturday morning remarks of 101-year-old veteran of World War I, Frieda Mae Hardin, and concluded with the Saturday evening remarks of many active duty women, one of whom was Rhonda Cornum, POW during the Gulf War. The veterans, according to Cornum, made it possible for her generation to "have it all," a family and a military career. According to Defense Secretary William Cohen, "The monument is being built of stone and steel— I think an appropriate symbol of the stone courage and the steel will of all the women who have ever served to defend our country."[8] In 1996 ground was broken for the memorial's construction, and in 1997 it was dedicated. Cohen notes: "The Memorial recognizes women's contribution to our freedom, peace, and security, and it corrects a historical oversight that has long obscured [women's] contribution, because the true history shows that women have always done double duty." Women, Cohen says, have fought two battles, the first against aggression, the enemies of liberty beyond our borders, and second, the battle against sexism and prejudice, enemies of a liberty within. From the factories to just behind the front lines, American women have taken their rightful places.

Military women are now marking a significant milestone in service to their country, and with this monument, are written into history in a most magnificent way. We have begun.

Appendix A
General Chronology

This chronology is based in part on Cynthia Costello and Barbara Kivimae Krimgold, eds., The American Woman, 1996–97, Women's Research and Education Institute (New York: Norton, 1996).[1]

1993

July 27—The House and Senate Armed Services Committees approve their versions of the Department of Defense authorization bill. Both versions would repeal the last statutory barrier to women's equal participation in the military.

November 17—Shannon Faulkner may attend classes at the Citadel according to the U.S. Court of Appeals for the Fourth Circuit. The lower court is to hear her lawsuit challenging the Citadel's all-male policy.

November 30—President Clinton signs the DOD authorization bill for fiscal year 1994. The bill repeals the law barring Navy and Marine Corps women from permanent assignment on combat ships. It also authorizes gender-neutral performance standards.

December 20—A 600-page study is released by DOD indicating that there is no link between marital status and readiness. This study does away with the USMC's ban on recruiting married personnel.

Over 1,000 women participate in operations in Somalia between 1992 and 1994.

1994

January 12—Shannon Faulkner registers for classes at the Citadel, but she will not be allowed to attend because of Chief Justice William Rehnquist's order barring her for at least one week.

January 13—Secretary of Defense Les Aspin sets policy to open more positions to women in the military. This action rescinds the Risk Rule that kept women from positions exposing them to a risk of combat equal to or greater than the risk faced by the associated combat units.

March 9—The House Armed Services Committee hears four service women testify that sexual harassment is still a problem.

May 12—One of the four women testifying, LT Darlene Simmons, receives a letter of apology from Secretary of the Navy John H. Dalton for the Navy's handling of her sexual harassment complaints.

May 16—Shannon Faulkner's lawyers begin a lawsuit in federal district court over her right to attend the Citadel. She attends classes but has not been admitted to the corps of cadets.

May 18—Senator Sam Nunn, chair of the Senate Armed Services Committee, female senators, and civilian secretaries and military heads of all services meet to discuss what is being done to address equality for military women, handling of sexual harassment cases, and concern for increased military family violence.

June 1—U.S. District Court in Seattle orders Army to reinstate COL Margarethe Cammermeyer in Washington State's National Guard. In 1992, COL Cammermeyer admitted being lesbian in a security clearance interview. Current military policy would not ask her about her sexual orientation, and if an official did ask, Cammermeyer would not have to tell.

June 10—Citadel lawyers ask for a mistrial in Faulkner lawsuit.

June 13—Sgt. Zenaida Martinez, USAF, and Secretary of the Air Force Sheila Widnall meet. Widnall promises Martinez will be subject to no more reprisals because of her sexual harassment testimony and agrees that she be trained in a new career as an equal opportunity officer.

June 16—Justice Department appeals Judge Thomas Zilly's order to reinstate COL Cammermeyer in National Guard.

June 16—Judge C. Weston Houck dismisses the Citadel's motion for a mistrial. He hears final arguments in Faulkner suit.

June 28—Both Citadel and Faulkner lawyers present plans for admitting Faulkner if Judge C. Weston Houck rules she should be admitted.

July 28—Secretary of Defense William Perry announces that the military will open 80,000 additional positions to women effective October 1, 1994.

October 31—A federal jury orders the Hilton Hotel in Las Vegas to pay LT Paula Coughlin, USN, $5 million in punitive damages in addition to $1.7 million in compensatory damages for failing to provide adequate security during the 1991 Tailhook convention.

November 4—Three West Point football players are benched for sexual harassment.

November 7—The Navy investigates charges of sexual harassment at the naval training center in San Diego.

December 14—The Navy announces punishment for harassers at the naval training center in San Diego.

1995

Over 1,200 women deploy for peacekeeping duties in Haiti.

January 26—U.S. Court of Appeals for the Fourth Circuit in a 2-to-1 vote approves Virginia Military Institute's plan to establish a separate, state-subsidized program for women at Mary Baldwin College as an alternative to admitting women to VMI.

January 30—U.S. Court of Appeals for the Fourth Circuit continues to hear arguments. Faulkner continues to attend classes but cannot participate in military activities.

February 6—NBC-TV presents the movie *Serving in Silence*, true story of COL Margarethe Cammermeyer, a career Army officer discharged from Washington State's National Guard after she told a security clearance investigator that she was lesbian.

February 6—Secretary of the Navy John H. Dalton signs a Navy policy on pregnancy, the first in the military. Policy is that pregnancy is a natural event and is not a presumed medical incapacity. Pregnancy and parenthood are compatible with a naval career.

February 28—Evidence that differences between the sexes in cardiovascular capacity (men have more) and percentage of body fat (men have less) will always enable men to perform higher than women.

March 1—Hillary Rodham Clinton is the initial First Lady to speak at the Pentagon.

March 2—LCDR Wendy Lawrence, first female Navy aviator, lifts off in space shuttle *Endeavor*. Lawrence is also the first woman astronaut to have graduated from the U.S. Naval Academy.

March 6—Women account for 18 percent of new recruits to the military service for the first quarter of the year.

March 9—A federal district court judge ruled that the amount of LT Paula Coughlin's award must be reduced $1.5 from the $6.7 million because she had received a separate settlement from the Tailhook Association.

March 22—Officials on carrier USS *Eisenhower* state the announcement that 14 women crew members were sent home because of pregnancy detracted from the historic first of a carrier putting women to sea as part of the permanent crew.

Appendix B
History of Definitions
of Combat

Direct Combat at the Time of
the Persian Gulf War[1]

No statute restricted the Army from assigning women to combat positions. Title 10 U.S. Code § 3012 authorizes the Secretary of the Army to determine policy. The Secretary developed policies that, "exclude women from 'routine engagement in direct combat.'" The Army justified its policy on the basis of congressional intent manifested in the Navy and Air Force exclusionary statutes.

Direct combat at the time of the Persian Gulf War was defined as "engaging an enemy with individual or crew-served weapons while being exposed to direct enemy fire, a high probability of direct physical contact with the enemy's personnel, and a substantial risk of capture. Direct combat takes place while closing with the enemy by fire, maneuver, or shock effect in order to destroy or capture, or while repelling assault by fire, close combat or counterattack."

The 1988 Risk Rule attempted to standardize positions closed to women across the services. "Noncombat units can be closed to women on grounds of risks or exposure to direct combat, hostile fire, or capture provided the type, degree, and duration of such risks are *equal to or greater than* that experienced by combat units in the same theater of operations."

Definition of Ground Combat[2]

Army and Marine Corps directives announced on July 29, 1994, are based on the new rule and definition of combat announced by former Defense Secretary Les Aspin on January 13, 1994:

A. Rule. Service members are eligible to be assigned to all positions for which they are qualified, except that women shall be excluded from assignment to units below the brigade level whose primary mission is to engage in direct combat on the ground as defined below:

B. Definition. Direct ground combat is engaging an enemy on the ground with individual or crew served weapons, while being exposed to hostile fire and to a high probability of direct physical contact with the hostile force's personnel. Direct ground combat takes place well forward on the battlefield while locating and closing with the enemy to defeat them by fire, maneuver, or shock effect.

The new rule is slated to replace the Defense Department's long-standing Risk Rule, which was designed to limit the exposure of women in noncombat units to front-line combat on land, sea, and in the air. Both provisions represent a significant departure from previous policy.

Appendix C

THE SOLDIER'S CREED[1]

I am an American soldier, I am a soldier of the United States Army—a protector of the greatest nation on earth. Because I am proud of the uniform I wear, I will always act in ways creditable to the military service and the nation it is sworn to guard.

I am proud of my own organization. I will do all I can to make it the finest unit of the Army. I will be loyal to those under whom I serve. I will do my full part to carry out orders and instructions given me or my unit.

As a soldier, I realize that I am a member of a time-honored profession—that I am doing my share to keep alive the principles of freedom for which my country stands. No matter what situation I am in, I will never do anything, for pleasure, profit, or personal safety, which will disgrace my uniform, my unit, or my country. I will use every means I have, even beyond the line of duty, to restrain my Army comrades from actions disgraceful to themselves and the uniform.

I am proud of my country and its flag. I will try to make the people of this nation proud of the service I represent, for *I am an American soldier.*

CODE OF CONDUCT FOR MEMBERS OF THE ARMED FORCES OF THE UNITED STATES[2]

1. I am an American, fighting in the forces which guard my country and our way of life. I am prepared to give my life in their defense.

2. I will never surrender of my own free will. If in command, I will never surrender the members of my command while they still have the means to resist.

3. If I am captured, I will continue to resist by all means available. I will make every effort to escape and aid others to escape. I will accept neither parole nor special favors from the enemy.

4. If I become a prisoner of war, I will keep faith with my fellow prisoners. I will give no information or take part in any action which might be harmful to my comrades. If I am senior, I will take command. If not, I will obey the lawful order of those appointed over me and will back them up in every way.

5. When questioned, should I become a prisoner of war, I am required to give name, rank, service number, and date of birth. I will evade answering further questions to the utmost of my ability. I will make no oral or written statements disloyal to my country and its allies or harmful to their cause.

6. I will never forget that I am an American, fighting for freedom, responsible for my actions, and dedicated to the principles which made my country free. I will trust in my God and in the United States of America.

As a guardian of public trust, the soldier places loyalty to the Constitution, laws, and standards of ethical conduct above any personal gain. A military officer once told me, "A soldier will do what she or he is told even at her or his own peril."

Notes

Preface

1. Linda Grant De Pauw, Pasadena, Md., e-mail interview, March 4, 1996.
2. Lauren Cook Burgess, "'Typical' Soldier May Have Been Red-blooded American Woman; Secret Buried with Many in Blue Gray," *The Washington Times*, October 5, 1991, B3.
3. Col. Kelly Hamilton, USAF (Ret.), telephone interview, December 28, 1996.
4. *Ibid.*
5. Mady Wechsler Segal and Amanda Faith Hansen, "Value Rationales in Policy Debates on Women in the Military: A Content Analysis of Congressional Testimony, 1941–1985," *Social Science Quarterly* 73:2 (June 1992): 297.
6. Jeanne M. Lieberman, USA, "Women in Combat," *Federal Bar News and Journal* 37:1 (May 1990): 215; author interviews.
7. *Ibid.*, 220.
8. Maj. Kay Troutt, USAF, *45th Anniversary DACOWITS Defense Advisory Committee on Women in the Services*, 1996 Spring Conference, 5.
9. Holly K. Hemphill, interview, June 14, 1996.
10. *Ibid.*
11. Jean Ebbert and Marie-Beth Hall, *Cross Currents: Navy Women from World War I to Tailhook* (Washington, D.C.: Brassey's, 1993), 266.
12. Otto Kreisher, "Marines Mix Sexes in Enlisted Combat Training," *Copley News Service*, March 20, 1997.

Introduction

1. CAPT Rosemary Bryant Mariner, USN, telephone interview, February 27, 1996; Mariner, "A Soldier Is a Soldier," *Joint Force Quarterly* 3 (Winter 1993-94): 54–61.
2. MAJ Lillian A. Pfluke, USA (Ret.), testimony to the U.S. Presidential Commission on the Assignment of Women in the Armed Forces, September 12, 1992, Washington, D.C., referred to in Presidential Commission on the Assignment of Women in the Armed Forces, *Report to the President: Women in Combat* (Washington, D.C.: Brassey's, 1993), Appendix F–18.
3. *Ibid.*

4. RADM Paul T. Gillcrist, USN (Ret.), *Vulture's Row: Thirty Years in Naval Aviation* (Atglen, Penn.: Schiffer, 1996), 123.

5. RADM Paul T. Gillcrist, USN (Ret.), telephone interview, October 10, 1995.

6. Pfluke, telephone interview, March 18, 1996.

7. *Ibid.*

8. Mariner, interview, February 27, 1996.

9. Mariner, "A Soldier Is a Soldier," 61.

10. Mariner, interview, February 27, 1996.

11. Mariner, follow-up e-mail interview, April 28, 1997. She elaborates:

> Under the *Goldwater-Nichols Act*, codified under Title 10, the persons who actually are in charge of fighting wars and deployed joint operations (which all operations directed by the National Command Authorities ultimately are) are the Unified Combatant Commanders who hold "combatant command." Known as "U.S. Commanders in Chief" these are Pacific Command (CINCPAC), U.S. Atlantic Command (CINCACOM), European Command (CINCEUR), Central Command (CINCCENT), Special Operations Command (CINCSOC), Southern Command (CINCSOUTH), Space Command (CINCSPACE), Strategic Command (CINCSTRAT) and Transportation Command (CINCTRANS). For example, during the Gulf War, GEN Norman Schwarzkopf was CINCCENT. All four-star positions in rank, these CINCs are also known as Joint Force Commanders (a generic term for anyone who commands a joint force.) The Chairman of the Joint Chiefs of Staff is the senior military officer by law, the Vice Chairman of the Joint Chiefs is the second senior officer. However, the Chairman does not command anything. By law, he is the principal military advisor to the National Command Authorities (the President and the Secretary of Defense) and is usually selected from one of the serving CINCs (GEN John M. Shalikashvili was CINCEUR before selected.)

12. Mariner, "A Soldier Is a Soldier," 54–61.

13. ADM Stanley R. Arthur, former Vice Chief of Naval Operations (VCNO), former CDR of U.S. Seventh Fleet and CDR U.S. Naval Forces Central Command for Operations Desert Shield/Desert Storm, interview, June 13, 1996.

14. Gillcrist, interview, October 10, 1995.

15. CAPT James F. Amerault, USN, former Commanding Officer, USS *Samuel Gompers* (AD–37); RADM Philip M. Quast, Assistant CNO, Surface Warfare; and VADM Ronald J. Zlatoper, Deputy Chief of Naval Operations, Manpower, Personnel and Training, Chief of Naval Personnel, in U.S. Congress, House Committee on Armed Services, Military Forces and Personnel Subcommittee, *Women in Combat: Hearing Before the Military Forces and Personnel Subcommittee*, 103d Congress, 1st sess., May 12, 1993, 40–41, 51–54.

16. Ike Skelton (D-Mo.), congressman, in U.S. Congress, House Committee on Armed Services, Military Forces and Personnel Subcommittee, *Assignment of Army and Marine Corps Women Under the New Definition of Ground Combat*, 103d Cong., 2d sess., October 6, 1994, 1.

17. Jon Kyl (R-Ariz.), congressman, in U.S. Congress, House Committee, *Assignment of Army*, 2.

18. Stephen E. Buyer (R-Ind.), congressman, in U.S. Congress, House Committee, *Assignment of Army*, 4.

19. Maj Gen William M. Keys, Commanding General, 2d Marine Division, letter, March 29, 1991, two enclosures; letter, March 30, 1991, one enclosure.

20. MGen. Jeanne Holm, USAF (Ret.), *Women in the Military: An Unfinished Revolution*, rev. ed. (Novato, Calif.: Presidio, 1992), 456–60.

21. Col. Kelly Hamilton, USAF (Ret.), telephone interview, December 28, 1996.

22. Elaine Donnelly, in U.S. Congress, House Committee, *Women in Combat*, 112.

23. Susan Yoachum, "The Navy, Before and After Tailhook: An Incisive Look at the Lasting Effects of the Scandal," a review of Jean Zimmerman's *Tailspin: Women at War in the Wake of Tailhook* (New York: Doubleday, 1995), in *San Francisco Chronicle*, June 25, 1995, 3.

24. RADM Paul T. Gillcrist, USN (Ret.), *Feet Wet: Reflections of a Carrier Pilot* (New York: Pocket Books, 1990), 221–22.

Chapter 1

1. Col. Kelly Hamilton, USAF (Ret.), letter home to her father, January 15, 1991.

2. Lexis-Nexis search, March 2, 1997.

3. Jonathan Broder, Ray Mosely, and Ron Yates, "Up in Arms: 67 Years After the 'War to End Wars,' the World Remains Mired in Conflict," *Chicago Tribune*, November 10, 1985, magazine sect., 13.

4. *Ibid.*

5. *Ibid.*

6. *Ibid.*

7. "Epidemic of War Deaths; Statistics on War-Related Deaths Through History," *Science News* 134:8 (August 8, 1988): 124.

8. *Ibid.*

9. Linda Grant De Pauw, in "Gender Gulf Prospect of Women at War Faced By Some with Unease," by Charlotte Grimes, *St. Louis Post-Dispatch*, February 17, 1991, B1.

10. UN, "Women and Armed Conflict," *Report of the Fourth World Conference on Women*, Beijing, China, September 4–15, 1995. Posted online by the UN Department for Policy Coordination and Sustainable Development (DPCSD), at http://www.iisd.ca/linkages/women.html, October 17, 1995, IV E, 133.

11. RADM Paul T. Gillcrist, USN (Ret.), letter to author, November 28, 1995.

12. LTG Harold G. Moore, USA (Ret.), and Joseph L. Galloway, *We Were Soldiers Once ... and Young—Ia Drang: The Battle That Changed the War in Vietnam* (New York: Random House, 1992), viii.

13. Linda Grant De Pauw, e-mail interview, March 4, 1996.

14. Linda Grant De Pauw, e-mail interview, March 3, 1996; Linda Grant De Pauw, *Battle Cries and Lullabies: A Brief History of Women in War* (Norman: University of Oklahoma, 1998).

15. MAJ Lillian A. Pfluke, USA (Ret.), e-mail interview, April 25, 1997.

16. Ruth Seifert, "War and Rape: A Preliminary Analysis," 54, 64, 66, in Alexandra Stiglmayer, "The Rapes in Bosnia-Herzegovina," in *Mass Rape: The War Against Women in Bosnia-Herzegovina*, edited by Alexandra Stiglmayer, translated by Marion Faber (Lincoln: University of Nebraska Press, 1994), 85.

17. Roy Gutman, Foreword to *Mass Rape: The War Against Women in Bosnia-Herzegovina*, edited by Alexandra Stiglmayer, translated by Marion Faber (Lincoln: University of Nebraska Press, 1994), x; Alexandra Stiglmayer, *Mass Rape*, 88, 140, 160, 175.

18. Report of Commission of Experts to the Secretary-General of the UN, October 1992, First Interim Report (S/25274), 55, 56, 130–32, 142–43, 147–48, 251–53.

19. Beverly Allen, *Rape Warfare: The Hidden Genocide in Bosnia-Herzegovina and Croatia* (Minneapolis: University of Minneapolis Press, 1996), 43–47; 63.

20. UN, Beijing Report, 132.

21. *IoWoman* 26:1 (January-February 1996), 1; UN, Beijing Report, 131.

22. UN, Beijing Report, 134.

23. Hillary Rodham Clinton, "Women's Rights Are Human Rights," speech delivered by First Lady Rodham Clinton at the UN Fourth World Conference on Women in Beijing, China, September 5, 1995, in *Vital Speeches* 61:24 (October 1, 1995): 738ff.

24. Moore and Galloway, *We Were Soldiers Once*, 25.

25. *Ibid.*, 1.

26. MGen. Jeanne Holm, USAF (Ret.), *Women in the Military: An Unfinished Revolution*, rev. ed. (Novato, Calif: Presidio, 1992), 442–43, 464–69.

27. *Ibid.*

28. Philip Bigler, *In Honored Glory: Arlington National Cemetery, The Final Post*, 2d ed. (Arlington, Va: Vandamere, 1994), 127.

29. Hamilton, letter, January 15, 1991.

30. Gillcrist, telephone interview, October 10, 1995.

31. James Webb, *A Sense of Honor* (Englewood Cliffs, N.J.: Prentice Hall, 1981), 247.

32. Moore and Galloway, *We Were Soldiers Once*, 27.

33. John Hanchette, "Gulf War Illnesses: Questions and Answers," *Gannett News Service*, Washington, D.C., November 15, 1996, final ed.; Philip Shenon, "Oversight Suggested for Study of Gulf War Ills," *New York Times*, November 14, 1996, B12; Julie Fustanio, "Congressmen Leery of Gulf Syndrome Probe," *The Capital Times*, Madison, Wis., November 22, 1996, A2.

34. Gerald F. Linderman, *Embattled Courage: The Experience of Combat in the American Civil War* (New York: Free Press, 1987), 1.

Chapter 2

1. Philip Bigler, *In Honored Glory: Arlington National Cemetery, The Final Post*, 2d ed. (Arlington, Va.: Vandamere, 1994), 127.

2. Linda Bird Francke, *Ground Zero: The Gender Wars in the Military* (New York: Simon and Schuster, 1997), 15, 26.

3. U.S. Congress, House Committee on Armed Services, Military Forces and Personnel Subcommittee *Women in Combat: Hearing Before the Military Forces and Personnel Subcommittee*, 103d Cong., 1st sess., May 12, 1993, 106.

4. U.S. Presidential Commission on the Assignment of Women in the Armed Forces, *Report to the President: Women in Combat* (Washington, D.C.: Brassey's, 1993), 36.

5. Mary Whitley, former captain, USA, interview, June 10, 1996.

6. Whitley, follow-up e-mail interview, April 28, 1997.

7. Barbara Sweatt, former specialist, USA, telephone interview, September 15, 1996.

8. CAPT Georgia Clark Sadler, USN (Ret.), "Women in Combat: The U.S. Military and the Impact of the Persian Gulf War," in *Wives and Warriors: Women and the Military in the United States and Canada*, edited by Laurie Weinstein and Christie White (Westport, Conn.: Bergin and Garvey, 1997), 81.

9. Col. Kelly Hamilton, USAF (Ret.), letter home, January 23, 1991.

10. House Hearing, May 12, 1993, 74.

11. Title 10 U.S. Code § 3012.

12. Frank Carlucci, Secretary of Defense, memorandum, Feb. 2, 1988.

13. Presidential Commission, *Report to the President*, 36.

14. Les Aspin, Secretary of Defense (SECDEF), "Direct Ground Combat Definition and Assignment Rule," memorandum for Secretaries of the Army, Navy, and Air Force, Chairman, Joint Chiefs of Staff, Assistant SECDEF for Personnel and Readiness, and Assistant SECDEF for Reserve Affairs, January 13, 1994.

15. Edwin Dorn, Under Secretary of Defense, Personnel and Readiness, in U.S. Congress, House Committee on Armed Services, Military Forces and Personnel Subcommittee, *Assignment of Army and Marine Corps Women Under the New Definition of Ground Combat*, 103d Cong., 2d sess., October 6, 1994, 13.

16. MAJ Lillian A. Pfluke, USA (Ret.), e-mail interview, April 26, 1997.

17. Dorn, U.S. Congress, House Committee, *Assignment of Army*, 13.

18. Charles Duncan, Deputy Secretary of Defense, House Committee on Armed Services, hearings on Military Posture and Assignment of Women to Ships—Hearings on H.R. 10929 and H.R. 7431, 95th Cong., 2d sess. (Serial No. 95–96, February 15, 1978) at 1179–88, 1190–1192, in Committee on Military Affairs and Justice, Association of the Bar of the City of New York, "The Combat Exclusion Laws: An Idea Whose Time Has Gone," May 17, 1991, note 63, 16–17.

19. Bar of New York, "The Combat Exclusion Laws," 17–21.

20. *Ibid.*

21. *Ibid.*

22. *Ibid.*

23. CAPT P. W. Kelley, Department of the Navy (DON), Office of the Judge Advocate General (OJAG), memorandum to CAPT T. D. Keating, JAGC, USN, November 24, 1993; memorandum from OJAG staff, November 23, 1993, 1–2 of 7; enclosure (5), Spring 1993 bullets on "Women in Combat," DON, memorandum for the Assistant Secretary of Defense (Force Management and Personnel), "Expansion of Women's Opportunities in the Navy," Ref: memorandum of March 25, 1993, 2 of 4.

24. LGen. Robert M. Alexander, USAF, Deputy Assistant Secretary of Defense (Military Manpower and Personnel Policy), memorandum of March 25, 1993, 4 of 4.

25. House Hearing, May 12, 1993, 42.

26. U.S. Congress, House Committee on Armed Services, Military Personnel and Compensation Subcommittee, *Women in the Military: Hearing Before the Military Personnel and Compensation Subcommittee*, 101st Cong., 2d sess., March 20, 1990, 25.3.

27. House Hearing, May 12, 1993, 52–53.

28. Sadler, "Women in Combat," 82.

29. Kelley, memorandum, November 24, 1993, enclosure (5), 1 of 4.

30. Presidential Commission, *Report to the President*, 28–29.

31. MAJ Mary Finch, USA, "Women in Combat: One Commissioner Reports," paper presented at the Military Manpower Conference: A Military of Volunteers, U.S. Naval Academy, September 17, 1993, 17–20.

32. U.S. Congress, House Committee on Armed Services, Military Personnel and Compensation Subcommittee, *Implementation of the Repeal of the Combat Exclusion on Female Aviators*, 102d Cong., 2d sess., January 29, 1992, 2.

33. Les Aspin, Secretary of Defense, letter to The Honorable Ike Skelton, May 11, 1993, in U.S. Congress, House Committee, *Women in Combat*, 2–4.

34. Pat Schroeder (D-Colo.), congresswoman, in U.S. Congress, House Committee, *Women in the Military*, 8.

35. *Ibid.*, 9.

36. *Ibid.*, 9–10.

37. LTC Timothy A. Rippe, USA, professor of Military Science–ROTC, University of Northern Iowa, interview, October 28, 1995.

38. *Ibid.*

39. *Ibid.*

40. Rippe, interview, April 4, 1996.

41. Ike Skelton (D-Mo.), chair, in U.S. Congress, House Committee on Armed Services, Military Forces and Personnel Subcommittee, *Assignment of Army and Marine Corps Women Under the New Definition of Ground Combat,* 103d Cong., 2d sess., October 6, 1994, 21.

42. *Ibid.,* 20.

43. LTG Theodore G. Stroup, Jr., Deputy Chief of Staff for Personnel, USA, in U.S. Congress, House Committee on Armed Services, Military Forces and Personnel Subcommittee, *Assignment of Army and Marine Corps Women Under the New Definition of Ground Combat,* 103d Cong., 2d sess. October 6, 1994, 20.

44. Dorn, U.S. Congress, House Committee, *Assignment of Army,* 13.

45. Stroup, U.S. Congress, House Committee, *Assignment of Army,* 20–21.

46. Lt Gen George R. Christmas, Deputy Chief of Staff for Manpower and Reserve Affairs, USMC, in U.S. Congress, House Committee on Armed Services, Military Forces and Personnel Subcommittee, *Assignment of Army and Marine Corps Women Under the New Definition of Ground Combat,* 103d Cong., 2d sess., October 6, 1994, 23.

47. Christmas, U.S. Congress, House Committee, *Assignment of Army,* 27, 28, 30, 33.

48. 1st Lt Theodore "Ted" Thomey, USMC (Ret.), "No Reverse," *Retired Officer Magazine* (April 1996): 38–42.

49. Col. Kelly Hamilton, USAF (Ret.), telephone interview, December 28, 1996.

50. Maj Gen William M. Keys, Commanding General, 2d Marine Division, letter, March 29, 1991, enclosure 1.

51. *Ibid.*

52. B Gen C. C. Krulak, "Comments on the Contribution of Women," n.d., 1, in Lt Gen W. E. Boomer, Commanding General, I Marine Expeditionary Force, FPO San Francisco, Calif., letter to Gen A. M. Gray, Commandant of the Marine Corps, March 30, 1991, 1–2, enclosure 3.

53. Accident Mishap Board, *F-14A Mishap Investigation Report (MIR),* Military City Online, March 1995, 1.

54. CDR Jay B. Yakeley, USN Carrier Group THREE, memorandum to Office of the JAG (OJAG), February 19, 1995, 34–35.

55. ADM R. J. Spane, memorandum to OJAG, February 24, 1995, 37.

56. LT Michael Kilian, "A Becoming Legend; Bright and Shining, LT Hultgreen Deserved Better," *Chicago Tribune,* March 12, 1995, Tempo, 6.

57. RADM Paul T. Gillcrist, USN (Ret.), telephone interview, December 14, 1995.

58. "More Criticism of the AX and F/A-18 Upgrade Services," *Navy News & Undersea Technology* 9:9 (March 2, 1992): 1.

59. RADM Paul T. Gillcrist, USN (Ret.), *Tomcat! The Grumman F-14 Story* (Atglen, Pa.: Schiffer, 1994), 57.

60. Gillcrist, interview, December 14, 1995.

61. Gillcrist, *Tomcat!* 190–92.

62. Jean Zimmerman, *Tailspin: Women at War in the Wake of Tailhook* (New York: Doubleday, 1995), 294; Accident Mishap Board, *F-14A Mishap,* (8) Chronology, (E); Rosemarie Skaine, *Power and Gender: Issues in Sexual Dominance and Harassment* (Jefferson, N.C.: McFarland, 1996), 308–09.

63. John Corry, "The Death of Kara Hultgreen," in Rosemarie Skaine, *Power*

and Gender: Issues in Sexual Dominance and Harassment (Jefferson, N.C.: McFarland, 1996), 308–09.

64. Marina Pisano, "Military Sex Bias Blamed on Resisters," *Dayton Daily News*, November 23, 1994, A9; Jim Gogek, "Women Saw Combat Horrors, Public Snubs," *The San Diego Union Tribune*, November 21, 1994, A2, 1–3.

65. Tom Morganthau with Carroll Bogert at West Point, John Barry in Washington, and Gregory Vistica in San Diego, "The Military Fights the Gender Wars," *Newsweek*, November 14, 1994, 35.

66. Susan Barnes, posted to H-MINERVA "H-NET List for Discussion of Women and the Military and Women in War," at http://www.h-net.msu.edu./~minerva/archives/threads/pres.com.html June 26, 1996.

67. CAPT Rosemary Mariner, USN (Ret.), telephone interview, February 27, 1996.

68. CAPT Rosemary Mariner, USN (Ret.), ABC, *Nightline*, February 28, 1995; Mariner, e-mail interview, September 25, 1998.

69. ADM Stanley R. Arthur, USN (Ret.), "LT Hultgreen Wasn't A 'Quota' Pilot," *The Washington Times*, May 28, 1995, B5.

70. CDR James D. McArthur, Jr., investigation into Death of LT Hultgreen, public report, February 14, 1995, 33.

71. Corry, "Death of Kara Hultgreen," in Skaine, *Power and Gender*, 308–09.

72. RADM Paul T. Gillcrist, USN (Ret.), *Feet Wet: Reflections of a Carrier Pilot* (New York: Pocket Books, 1990), 258.

73. *Ibid.*, 258–64.

74. Accident Mishap Board, *F-14A Mishap*, (8) Chronology, (A)(P).

Chapter 3

1. Christine de Pisan's last poem in Frances Gies, *Joan of Arc: The Legend and the Reality* (New York: Harper and Row, 1981), 241.

2. Francine D'Amico, "Feminist Perspectives on Women Warriors," *Peace Review* 8:3 (September 1996): 379–84.

3. Plato, *The Republic*, with an English translation by Paul Shorey (London: W. Heinemann, 1930–35), 452a, 473d.

4. CAPT Rosemary Bryant Mariner, USN, "The Battle Over Women in Combat; Equality, Full Citizenship Back Women in Combat," *Baltimore Sun*, May 26, 1996, G6.

5. Aristotle, *The Politics of Aristotle*, translated by Ernest Barker (Oxford: The Clarendon, 1946), 1259a35–1260b25.

6. CAPT Rosemary Bryant Mariner, follow-up e-mail interview, April 28, 1997.

7. Thomas K. Lindsay, "Was Aristotle Racist, Sexist, and Anti-Democratic? A Review Essay," *Review of Politics* 56:1 (Winter 1994): 127–28.

8. Aristotle, quoted in Thomas K. Lindsay, "Was Aristotle Racist?" 151.

9. Aristotle, *Generation of Animals*, translated by A. L. Peck, rev. ed. (London: W. Heinemann, 1963), 737a28–29.

10. Darrell Dobbs, "Family Matters: Aristotle's Appreciation of Women and the Plural Structure of Society," *American Political Science Review* 90:1 (March 1996): 80.

11. The term is *parekbebēke*, see Dobbs, "Family Matters," 80.

12. The Holy Bible, Judges, 4 and 5.

13. Richard Hall, *Patriots in Disguise: Women Warriors of the Civil War*, 1st ed. (New York: Paragon House, 1993), xii.

14. *Ibid.*

15. Reina Pennington, ed., *Military Women Worldwide: A Biographical Dictionary* (Westport, Conn.: Greenwood Press, forthcoming), posted to H-MINERVA, at http://www. h-net.msu.edu/logs, log is 9701e, December 29, 1996.

16. Helen Solterer, "Figures of Female Militancy in Medieval France," *Signs* 16:3 (Spring 1991): 522–25.

17. *Ibid.*, 527.

18. *Ibid.*, 534.

19. *Ibid.*, 535–49.

20. Nancy Caciola, "Performance and Gender," Medieval Masculinities Discussion Archive, week two, Georgetown Online, at http://www.georgetown.edu/labyrinth /e-center/interscripta/archive2.html, October 28, 1995, 9–10.

21. *United States Code Annotated, Title 10, Armed Forces*, SS 5001 to 8010, "Navy and Marine Corps," Subt. C, § 6015, (St. Paul, Minn.: West; Brooklyn, N.Y.: Edward Thompson, 1959), 336. "Women members: duty; qualifications; restrictions," states in part:

> Women may not be assigned to duty in aircraft that are engaged in combat missions… nor may they be assigned to duty on vessels of the Navy other than hospital ships and transports. August 10, 1956, c. 1041, 70A Stat., 375, 336.

Update: Armed Forces

> Women may not be assigned to duty on vessels that are engaged in combat missions (other than as aviation officers as part of an air wing or other air element assigned to such a vessel) nor may they be assigned to other than temporary duty on other vessels of the Navy except hospital ships, transports, and vessels of similar classification not expected to be assigned combat missions. (As amended Oct. 20, 1978, Pub. L. 95–485, Title VIII, S 808, 92 Stat. 1623; Dec. 12, 1980, Pub. L. 96–513, Title V, S. 503(44), 94 Stat. 2914; Dec. 5, 1991, Pub. L. 102–190, Div. A. Title V, S 531(b), 105 Stat. 1365), 87.

Armed Forces, Notes of Decisions, no. 4,
Assignment of female personnel

> Alleged morale and discipline problems caused by integration of men and women aboard Navy ships furnished no basis for upholding ban on assignment of female personnel to duty on Navy vessels other than hospital ships and transports since whatever problems might arise from integrating ships and crews were matters that could be dealt with through appropriate training and planning. *Owens v. Brown*, D.C. D.C. 1978, 455F. Supp. 291, 88.

> The fact that military affairs were implicated did not mean that challenge to ban on assignment of female personnel to duty on Navy vessels other than hospital ships and transports raised a nonjustifiable political question. Id.

> Likelihood of influencing legislative efforts to revise ban on assignment of female personnel to duty on Navy vessels other than hospital ships and transports did not afford a principled basis for avoiding a determination of whether ban violated U.S.C.A. Const. Amend. 5. Id.

No. 5, Class action

Action challenging bar on assignment of female personnel to duty on Navy vessels other than hospital ships and transports was certified as class action, notwithstanding concern that some female personnel might not share representative plaintiff's desire to remove such bar, since issue was not whether Navy must assign female personnel to ship duty against their wishes but whether Navy authorities must exclude women from ship assignments whether or not they wish to go to sea. *Owens v. Brown*, D.C.D.C. 1978, 455 F. Supp. 291, 89.

22. U.S. Congress, House Committee on Armed Services, Military Forces and Personnel Subcommittee, *Women in Combat: Hearing Before the Military Forces and Personnel Subcommittee*, 103d Cong., 1st sess., May 12, 1993, 39–45, 99, 180.

23. James L. Matterer, "Jeanne La Pucelle and the Dying God," posted to http://www.contrib.andrew.cmu.edu/~sca/src/contributed/yapm97a@prodigy.com/jnofarc.html, verified March 21, 1997.

24. Eric Jennings, "'Reinventing Jeanne': The Iconology of Joan of Arc in Vichy Schoolbooks, 1940–44," *Journal of Contemporary History* 29 (1994): 713.

25. *Ibid.*, 711.

26. *Ibid.*, 713.

27. Frances Gies, *Joan of Arc: The Legend and the Reality* (New York: Harper and Row, 1981): 83–88.

28. Leonard Cohen, "Songs of Love and Hate" and "Joan of Arc," Excite, Britannica Online, sponsored by Sun Microsystems, Inc., Mt. Vicie, Calif., Architext Software, Netscape, copyright 1995.

29. Women in the Military Service for America Memorial Foundation, Inc. (WIMSA), *Change the Face of Monumental Washington: Help Build the Memorial to America's Military Women, Past, Present and Future*, brochure (Washington, D.C.: WIMSA, 1994); Kathryn Sheldon, *Did You Know...?* Women's History Month (Washington, D.C.: WIMSA, 1996), 1-2; Helen Rogan, *Mixed Company: Women in the Modern Army* (New York: G. P. Putnam's Sons, 1981), 120–23.

30. RMC Roxine C. Hart, *Women in Combat*, Research Division, Defense Equal Opportunity Management Institute, Patrick AFB, Fla., February 1991, 4–5.

31. Col. Kelly Hamilton, USAF (Ret.), letter to Amy Talkington, 1993.

32. Kathryn Sheldon, *American Military Women at War* (Washington, D.C.: WIMSA, 1996), 2.

33. Hall, *Patriots in Disguise*, 48–50.

34. Steve Clark, "Life Up North Is Much Sweeter Now," *Richmond Times-Dispatch*, November 30, 1996, B1.

35. Lauren Cook Burgess, ed., *An Uncommon Soldier: The Civil War Letters of Sarah Rosetta Wakeman, alias Private Lyons Wakeman, 153rd Regiment, N.Y. State Volunteers* (Pasadena, Md.: The MINERVA Center, 1994), 1.

36. Linda Grant De Pauw, quoted in "'Typical' Soldier May Have Been Red-Blooded American Woman; Secret Buried with Many in Blue Gray," by Lauren Cook Burgess, *The Washington Times*, October 5, 1991, B3.

37. Linda Grant De Pauw, telephone interview, March 21, 1996.

38. DeAnne Blanton, "Cathay Williams: Black Woman Soldier (1866–1868)," *MINERVA: Quarterly Report on Women and the Military*, X:3,4 (Fall-Winter 1992): 1–12; National Archives, Record Groups 15, 94, in Kathryn Sheldon, *A Brief History of Black Women in the Military* (Washington, D.C.: WIMSA, 1996), 2.

39. Sheldon, *American Military Women at War*, 1996.

40. Mary Elizabeth Massey, *Bonnet Brigades* (New York: Alfred A. Knopf, 1966), 96.

41. Hart, *Women in Combat*, 5.

42. Mattie E. Treadwell, *The Women's Army Corps*, Office of the Chief of Military History, Department of the Army (Washington, D.C.: GPO, 1954), copyright 1953, 50.

43. Hall, *Patriots in Disguise*, 3–4.

44. C. Kay Larson, *'Til I Come Marching Home: A Brief History of American Women in World War II* (Pasadena, Md.: The MINERVA Center, 1995), xiii.

45. William M. Fowler, Jr., "Relief on the River: The *Red Rover*," *Naval History* (Fall 1991): 19, in Sheldon, *A Brief History*, 1.

46. Thomas Wentworth Higginson, *Army Life in a Black Regiment* (New York: Longmans, Green, 1869), 262–63.

47. William M. Fowler, Jr., in Sheldon, *A Brief History*, 1.

48. National Archives, Record Group 94, in Sheldon, *A Brief History*, 1.

49. Patricia Romero, ed., *A Black Woman's Civil War Memoirs* (Princeton: Markus Wiener, 1988), 42, 52, in Sheldon, *A Brief History*, 2.

50. Hart, *Women in Combat*, 2.

51. CAPT Rosemary Bryant Mariner, USN, telephone interview, February 27, 1996.

52. Mady Wechsler Segal, "Women's Military Roles Cross-Nationally: Past, Present, and Future," *Gender and Society* 9:6 (December 1995): 764–65.

53. LTC Carolyn M. Feller, ANC, USAR, and MAJ Constance J. Moore, ANC, *Highlights in the History of the Army Nurse Corps*, rev. and exp. ed. (Washington, D.C.: U.S. Army Center of Military History, 1995), CMH Pub 85–1, 3.

54. John Rees, "'The Multitude of Women,' An Examination of the Numbers of Female Camp Followers with the Continental Army," *MINERVA: Quarterly Report on Women and the Military* XIV:2 (Summer 1996): 1–8, 30–32.

55. Sheldon, *A Brief History*, 1.

56. LTG Theodore G. Stroup, Jr., Deputy Chief of Staff for Personnel, USA, prepared statement, U.S. Congress, House Committee on Armed Services, Military Forces and Personnel Subcommittee, *Assignment of Army and Marine Corps Women Under the New Definition of Ground Combat*, 103d Cong., 2d sess., October 6, 1994, 18–19.

57. Sheldon, *Did You Know...?* 1–2.

58. Information paper for use by Fred Pang, prepared by LTC Jose R. Maldonado, USA, OASD(FMP)(MPP)/O&EPM. Received through FOIA requests 1996–97, date of accompanying letter to author, October 31, 1996.

59. Feller and Moore, *Army Nurse Corps*, 7, 9, 23.

60. Sheldon, *Did You Know...?* 1–2.

61. Feller and Moore, *Army Nurse Corps*, 6–7.

62. Kathryn Sheldon, *Important Dates in the History of Women in the Military*, Women's History Month (Washington, D.C.: WIMSA, 1996), 1–3.

63. Kathryn Sheldon, interview, June 11, 1996.

64. Harriet Camp Lounsbery, secretary and treasurer, "Order of Spanish-American War Nurses," *Trained Nurse and Hospital Review* 23 (1899): 81.

65. *Ibid.*, 80–81.

66. Sheldon, *American Military Women at War*, 3.

67. Sheldon, *A Brief History*, 3.

68. Feller and Moore, *Army Nurse Corps*, 7, 9, 23.

69. U.S. Army, *The Women's Army Corps: A Commemoration of World War II Service* (Washington, D.C.: U.S. Army Center of Military History, [1993?]) CMH Pub 72–15, 9.

70. *Ibid.*, 13–14.

71. *Ibid.*, 17–18.

72. *Ibid.*, 30–31.

73. MAJ Mary E. V. Frank, ANC, *Army and Navy Nurses Held As Prisoners of War During World War II*, Office of the Assistant Secretary of Defense, Manpower, Installations and Logistics, April 1985, 1–9.

74. Andrée Marechal-Workman, "Margaret (Peggy) Nash Speaks of Her Experience as a World War II POW," essay, courtesy of WIMSA, September 10, 1992, 1–11. Assistance provided by USA CMH on June 13, 1996.

75. Elizabeth M. Norman and Sharon Eifried, "How Did They All Survive? An Analysis of American Nurses' Experiences in Japanese Prisoner-of-War Camps," *Nursing History Review* 3 (1995): 108.

76. MAJ Lillian A. Pfluke, USA (Ret.), interview, April 26, 1997; "Protocol Additional to the Geneva Conventions of 12 August 1949, and Relating to the Protection of Victims of International Armed Conflicts (Protocol I)," Part I, Article 12—Protection of Medical Units, in *Documents on the Laws of War*, edited by Adam Roberts and Richard Guelff (New York: Clarendon, 1982), 397–98.

77. CPT Sharon Grant Wildwind, ANC, USA (Ret.) interview, December 15, 1996.

78. Norman and Eifried, "How Did They All Survive?" 114.

79. Marechal-Workman, "World War II POW," 1–11.

80. Sheldon, *American Military Women at War*, 3; Sheldon, *Important Dates*, 1–3.

81. Sheldon, *A Brief History*, 3.

82. National Archives, Record Group 112, in Sheldon, *A Brief History*, 3.

83. Sheldon, *American Military Women at War*, 3–4.

84. *Ibid.*

85. Sheldon, *A Brief History*, 4.

86. Sheldon, *American Military Women at War*, 3–4.

87. Information paper, Maldonado.

88. Hart, *Women in Combat*, 8.

89. Sheldon, *Important Dates*, 1–3.

90. John Martin, "How R.I. Remembers Vietnam," *Providence Journal-Bulletin*, April 26, 1995, F1.

91. Sheldon, *A Brief History*, 5.

92. Mary. L. Hanes, "Fact Sheet, U.S. Army Women in Vietnam," courtesy of WIMSA, 1–2.

93. Feller and Moore, *Army Nurse Corps*, 42, 45, 58.

94. Sheldon, *Important Dates*, 1–3.

95. *Women's Armed Services Integration Act of 1948*, ch. 449, § 102, 202, 62 Stat. 356, 357, 363, § 104(d)(3), 203, 62 Stat. 358, 363, 10 U.S. Code, Supp. I, § 559(b)(1) (1988).

96. Information paper, Maldonado.

97. Sheldon, *Did You Know...?* 1–2.

98. Hart, *Women in Combat*, 10–11.

99. *Frontiero et vir v. Richardson, Secretary of Defense, et al.*, 411 U.S. 677, U.S. Supreme Court, argued January 17, 1973, decided May 14, 1973.

100. Information paper, Maldonado.

101. Rosemarie Skaine, "Harassment Is a Leadership Issue," *Des Moines Register*, November 29, 1996, A13.

102. Joseph McCullough, interview, November 30, 1996; Feller and Moore, *Army Nurse Corps*, 27.

103. Judi Hasson, "Top Woman Vet Pushes Memorial," Gannett News Service, Washington, D.C., November 7, 1989.

104. Joseph P. Ferry, "Backers Mobilize for War Memorial: Women's Military Group Seeks Funding for Arlington Project," *Morning Call*, Allentown, Pa., June 13, 1994, B1.

Chapter 4

1. Rosemarie Skaine, *Power and Gender: Issues in Sexual Dominance and Harassment* (Jefferson, N.C.: McFarland, 1996), 307.

2. Les Aspin, Secretary of Defense, letter to The Honorable Ike Skelton, chair, Subcommittee on Military Forces and Personnel, Committee on Armed Services, May 11, 1993, in U.S. Congress, House Committee on Armed Services, *Women in Combat: Hearing Before the Military Forces and Personnel Subcommittee*, 103d Cong., 1st sess., May 12, 1993, 2–4.

3. Women's Research and Education Institute (WREI), "Women in the Military: Where They Stand," in Kathryn Sheldon, *American Military Women at War* (Washington, D.C.: WIMSA, 1996), 6; U.S. Department of Defense, Defense Manpower Data Center, September 30, 1996, in Georgia C. Sadler, Annette M. Wiechert, and Dina A. Warnken, *Women in the Military: Statistical Update 1997* (Washington, D.C.: WREI, 1997).

4. Information paper for use by Fred Pang, prepared by LTC Jose R. Maldonado, USA, OASD(FMP)(MPP)/O&EPM, received through FOIA requests 1996–97, letter to author, October 31, 1996.

5. RMC Roxine C. Hart, *Women in Combat*, Research Division, Defense Equal Opportunity Management Institute, Patrick AFB, Fla., February 1991, 13.

6. *Ibid.*, 10–11.

7. Information paper, Maldonado.

8. Kathryn Sheldon, *Important Dates in the History of Women in the Military*, Women's History Month (Washington, D.C.: WIMSA, 1996), 1–3.

9. Hart, *Women in Combat*, 13.

10. *Ibid.*, 14.

11. *Ibid.*

12. *Ibid.*, 15–16.

13. *Ibid.*, 16.

14. Sheldon, *American Military Women*, 5–6.

15. Sheldon, *Important Dates*, 1–3.

16. Sheldon, *American Military Women*, 6.

17. Hart, *Women in Combat*, 16.

18. BGen Margaret A. Brewer, USMC (Ret.), written interview, April 25, 1997.

19. MGen. Jeanne Holm, USAF (Ret.), *Women in the Military: An Unfinished Revolution*, rev. ed. (Novato, Calif.: Presidio, 1992), 445–46, in Sheldon, *American Military Women*, 6.

20. Carolyn Becraft, *Women in the U.S. Armed Services: The War in the Persian Gulf* (Washington, D.C.: WREI, 1991), 1–4.

21. Skaine, *Power and Gender*, 307.

22. *Ibid.*, 315–16, 354.

23. Les Aspin, chair, Defense Policy Panel, and Beverly B. Byron, chair, Military Personnel and Compensation Subcommittee, House Committee on Armed Ser-

vices, *Women in the Military: The Tailhook Affair and the Problem of Sexual Harassment Report* (Washington, D.C.: GPO, 1992), 1–121.

24. *Ibid.*

25. Skaine, *Power and Gender*, 54.

26. House Hearing, May 12, 1993, 1.

27. Aspin, letter to Skelton, 2–4.

28. *Ibid.*

29. Sheldon, *Important Dates*, 1–3.

30. Mark Conrad, posted to H-MINERVA, at http://www.h-net.msu.edu, August 28, 1996, from SPC Brett C. Traver, "Local Soldiers Return from Snow, Mud," in the *(Ft.) Monmouth (N.J.) Message* 53:34 (August 23, 1996).

31. Sheldon, *Important Dates*, 1–3.

32. *Ibid.*

33. Rowan Scarborough, "Female Bombers Achieve Milestone; But Pentagon Keeps Profile Low," *The Washington Times*, December 23, 1998, A1.

34. Ray Moseley, "Women Ear Their Wings; U.S. Female Fighter Pilots in Combat for 1st Time," *Chicago Tribune*, December 21, 1998, News, North Sports Final Edition, 1.

35. Scarborough, "Female Bombers," A1.

36. Richard Sisk, "Five Female Pilots Launch First Aerial Combat Missions: Women Fly Into History," *New York Daily News*, December 22, 1998, 18.

37. CAPT Georgia Clark Sadler, e-mail interview, April 27, 1997.

38. *Ibid.* ("Data includes Coast Guard and larger number includes Guard and Reserves who are not on active duty.")

39. MAJ Angela Maria Manos, USA, and David R. Segal, "What Every Leader Wants to Know," Behavioral Science Research in Support of Soldiers and their Families, Alexandria, Va., Center for Army Lessons Learned (CALL), Ft. Leavenworth, Ks., 1996, 1–21.

40. *Ibid.*

41. MAJ Angela Manos, USA, interview, May 24, 1996.

42. PL 94–106.

43. Kathryn Sheldon, *Did You Know...?* Women's History Month (Washington, D.C.: WIMSA, 1996), 1–2.

44. Hart, *Women in Combat*, 12–13.

45. MAJ Lillian A. Pfluke, USA (Ret.), telephone interview, April 25, 1997.

46. Ailene Voisin, "Women at the Military Schools; Closing Ranks," *Atlanta Journal-Constitution*, October 15, 1995, F1.

47. William L. Chaze and Sara A. Peterson, "Where 'Ma'am' Can Command," *U.S. News and World Report*, May 26, 1980, 35.

48. MAJ Lillian A. Pfluke, USA (Ret.), e-mail interview, March 9, 1996.

49. MAJ Lillian A. Pfluke, USA (Ret.), telephone interview, April 26, 1997.

50. Ed Timms, "From Antarctica to Outer Space, First Female Cadets Have Excelled; Three Who Entered Academies in '76 Reflect on Making History," *Dallas Morning News*, May 5, 1996, A30.

51. Matthew McAllester and Somini Sengupta, "The Women Who Fought Before," *Newsday*, August 20, 1995, A3.

52. Capt Kim Hunter, USMC, posted to H-MINERVA, at http://www.h-net.msu.edu, January 26, 1997.

53. Mary Whitley, former USA captain, interview, June 10, 1996.

54. Maj. Lillian A. Pfluke, USA (Ret.), interview, March 18, 1996.

55. Timms, "From Antarctica to Outer Space," A30.

56. MAJ Carol Barkalow, with Andrea Raab, *In the Men's House* (New York: Poseidon, 1990), 20, 23.

57. MAJ Mary Finch, USA, telephone interview, August 17, 1997.

58. MAJ Mary Finch, USA, e-mail interview, August 15, 1997.

59. Victoria Irwin, *Christian Science Monitor*, midwestern ed., May 27, 1980, 14.

60. Danna Maller, former USA captain, interview, June 10, 1996.

61. James F. Vesely, "The Wrong Solution at VMI," *Seattle Times*, June 28, 1996, B4.

62. Justice Ruth Bader Ginsburg, U.S. Supreme Court, 94–1941 and 94–2107, opinion, *United States of America v. Commonwealth of Virginia* (hereafter cited as *U.S. v. Virginia*), June 26, 1996, 23, n. 13.

63. *Ibid.*, 23.

64. Rosemary Yardley, "Officers and Gentlemen to Be Joined by Women Who Are 'Seeking and Fit,'" *News & Record*, Greensboro, N.C., June 28, 1996, A13.

65. Peter Hardin, "Female Officers Join VMI Legal Battle," *Richmond Times-Dispatch*, December 4, 1995, A1.

66. MAJ Lillian A. Pfluke, USA (Ret.), "VMI Should Follow West Point's Lead," *Richmond Times-Dispatch*, December 12, 1995, A11.

67. "West Point Women Compare Past Horrors with Present," *All Things Considered*, National Public Radio, transcript #2269, segment 16, July 9, 1996.

68. Pfluke, e-mail interview, March 9, 1996.

69. Hardin, "Female Officers," A1.

70. Jim Mallory, "General Foresees Space Explorers in USAF Class of 2000," *Denver Post*, June 28, 1996, B5.

71. Chaze and Peterson, "Where 'Ma'am' Can Command," 35.

72. Capt. Alison M. Weir, USAF Academy, posted to H-MINERVA, at http://www.h-net.msu.edu, February 10, 1997.

73. Jim Mallory, "Academy Grads Leave Nest; 916 Cadets Turned Out as Second Lieutenants," *Denver Post*, May 30, 1996, B5.

74. Scott Shane, JoAnna Daemmrich, and Tom Bowman, "Women at the Naval Academy: 20 Years Later," first of three parts, *Baltimore Sun*, February 9, 1997, Telegraph, A1.

75. Chaze and Peterson, "Where 'Ma'am' Can Command," 35.

76. JoAnna Daemmrich and Scott Shane, "Women at the Naval Academy: 20 Years Later," second of three parts, *Baltimore Sun*, February 10, 1997, Telegraph, A1.

77. JoAnna Daemmrich, "Women at the Naval Academy: 20 Years Later," last of three parts, *Baltimore Sun*, February 11, 1997, Telegraph, A1.

78. *Ibid.*

79. Angela Callahan, "Mids Make Career Choices Under Cloud of Scandal," *Capital*, February 3, 1994, Arundel, B1.

80. Linda Grant De Pauw, *Baptism of Fire* (Pasadena, Md.: The MINERVA Center, 1993.

81. Linda Grant De Pauw, posted to H-MINERVA, at http://www.h-net.msu.edu, February 10, 1997.

82. *Ibid.*

83. Daemmrich, "Women at the Naval Academy," A1.

84. "Women Graduate from Academies," *Facts on File World News Digest*, June 6, 1980, C1, 428.

85. Chaze and Peterson, "Where 'Ma'am' Can Command," 35.

86. "VMI, Gen. Jackson? Well, It's Coed Now," *Morning Star*, Wilmington, N.C., June 28, 1996, editorial, A8.

87. Donald P. Baker and Ann O'Hanlon, "VMI Mourns a Tradition Lost," *Washington Post*, June 27, 1996, B1.

88. ADM Stanley R. Arthur, e-mail interviews, July 17 and 18, 1996.

89. Danna Maller, former USA captain, e-mail interview, June 18, 1996.

90. MAJ Lillian A. Pfluke, USA (Ret.), e-mail interview, June 30, 1996.

91. *U.S. v. Virginia*, C.A. No. 90–0126–R, the U.S. District Court for the Western District of Virginia, Roanoke Division; Activities by the Virginia Military Institute in Preparation for the Admission of Women in August 1997, "First Quarterly Report," December 2, 1996.

92. "VMI Considers Mentor Program," Associated Press, January 20, 1997, posted to H-MINERVA, at http://www.h-net.msu.edu, January 20, 1997.

93. Citadel Board of Visitors, "The Citadel Approved Plan for Assimilation of Female Cadets," memorandum for Lt. Gen. Claudius E. Watts III, July 30, 1996.

94. Michael Janofsky, "Citadel Bowing to Court, Says It Will Admit Women," *New York Times*, June 29, 1996, 6.

95. Yardley, "Officers and Gentlemen," A13.

96. MAJ Lillian A. Pfluke, USA (Ret.), posted to H-MINERVA, at http://www.h-net.msu.edu, July 10, 1996.

97. Citadel Board of Visitors, memorandum July 30, 1996.

98. "VMI Considers, January 20, 1997; Bruce Smith, "'Hell Week' Begins For 4 Female Cadets At Citadel," *Chattanooga (Tenn.) Free Press*, August 26, 1996.

99. Tim Kulp, counsel, on CNN, *Burden of Proof*, hosted by Greta Van Susteren and Roger Cossack, transcript # 96122601V12, December 26, 1996.

100. Maj. Gen. Clifton Poole, Citadel president, on CNN, *Burden of Proof*, December 26, 1996.

101. *Webster's New Universal Unabridged Dictionary*, 2d ed., 1983, posted to H-MINERVA, at http://www.h-net.msu.edu, February 10, 1997; Reina Pennington, ed., *Military Women Worldwide: A Biographical Dictionary* (Westport, Conn.: Greenwood Press, forthcoming).

102. Dorothy H. Mackey, posted to H-MINERVA, at http://www.h-net.msu.edu, February 3, 1997.

103. Gene Moser, posted to H-MINERVA, at http://www.h-net.msu.edu, March 11, 1997.

104. Linda Wertheimer, "Citadel Punishment," *All Things Considered*, National Public Radio, transcript # 97031010–212, March 10, 1997.

105. Joan Biskupic, "Supreme Court Invalidates Exclusion of Women by VMI," *Washington Post*, June 27, 1996, A1; *U.S. v. Virginia*, U.S. Court of Appeals for the Fourth Circuit, 44 F.3d 1229, Lexis 1504, 1233–1234.

106. Linda Greenhouse, "At the Supreme Court: Discrimination; Military College Can't Bar Women, High Court Rules," *New York Times*, June 27, 1996, A1.

107. *U.S. v. Virginia*, Lexis 1504, 1233–1234.

108. *Ibid.*, 1234.

109. *Ibid.*, 1244.

110. Chief Justice William H. Rehnquist, U.S. Supreme Court, 94–1941 and 94–2107, concurring, *U.S. v. Virginia*, June 26, 1996, 1.

111. Rehnquist, *U.S. v. Virginia*, 2.

112. Dan Casey and Jennifer Miller, "Lexington Reactions Divided over Ruling," *(Norfolk) Virginian-Pilot*, June 27, 1996, A11; Allison Blake, "Court Rules Against VMI," *Virginian-Pilot*, June 27, 1996, A1.

113. Pamela Stallsmith, "VMI Crossroads; Court Scored; Most Respondents Appear Disgusted," *Richmond Times-Dispatch*, June 28, 1996, A1.

114. "Norwich University Official Comment on Virginia Military Institute Supreme Court Decision," PR Newswire Association, June 28, 1996.

115. Linda McAffrey, St. Louis, Missouri., posted to H-MINERVA, at http://www.h-net.msu.edu, September 9, 1996.

Chapter 5

1. PL 80–625, 62 Stat. 356 (1948).

2. 10 U.S. Code § 3013(g), (1), (3), in James D. Milko, "Beyond the Persian Gulf Crisis: Expanding the Role of the Servicewomen in the United States Military," *American University Law Review* 41 (Summer 1992): 1302.

3. Milko, "Beyond the Persian Gulf Crisis," 1302.

4. Information paper for use by Fred Pang, prepared by LTC Jose R. Maldonado, USA, OASD(FMP)(MPP)/O&EPM, received through FOIA requests 1996-97, letter to author, October 31, 1996.

5. *U.S. Code Annotated, Title 10 Armed Forces,* Subt. C, § 6015, (St. Paul, Minn: West; Brooklyn, N.Y.: Edward Thompson, 1959), 336. (As subsequently amended by *National Defense Authorization Act for Fiscal Years 1992 and 1993,* PL 102–190, § 531[a], 105 Stat. 1290, 1365 [1991].)

6. Committee on Military Affairs and Justice, Association of the Bar of the City of New York, "Equality for Women in Combat Aviation: Addressing Whether the Response of the Executive Branch to Public Law 102–190, the Legislative Repeal of the Combat Exclusion Laws for Women Aviators, Violates the Equal Protection Guarantees of the Fifth Amendment," October 26, 1992, 1–3.

7. VADM Ronald J. Zlatoper, Deputy Chief of Naval Operations, Manpower, Personnel and Training, Chief of Naval Personnel, Department of the Navy, in U.S. Congress, House Committee on Armed Services, Military Forces and Personnel Subcommittee, *Women in Combat: Hearing Before the Military Forces and Personnel Subcommittee,* 103d Cong., 1st sess., May 12, 1993, 11-13.

8. PL 102-90, Div. A, Title V, § 531(a)(1), 105 Stat. 1290, 1365 (1991), 1302.

9. Act of PL 90–130, 81 Stat. 374, November 8, 1967.

10. Information paper, Maldonado, enclosure.

11. Milko, "Beyond the Persian Gulf Crisis," 1306, n. 22, *Hill v. Berkman,* 635 F. Supp. 1228, 1231, 1232, 1234, 1242 (E.D.N.Y. 1986).

12. Information paper, Maldonado, enclosure.

13. *Ibid.*

14. *Goldman v. Weinberger* in 475 U.S. 503 (1986).

15. Milko, "Beyond the Persian Gulf Crisis," 1309; Bar of N.Y., "Equality for Women," 9.

16. *Schlesinger v. Ballard,* 419 U.S. 498, 510 (1975), in Milko, "Beyond the Persian Gulf Crisis," 1310, n. 43.

17. *Campbell v. Beaughler,* 519 F. 2d 1307, 1308 (9th Cir. 1975), *cert. denied,* 423 U.S. 1073 (1976), in Milko, "Beyond the Persian Gulf Crisis," 1310, n. 44.

18. *Kovach v. Middendorf,* 424 F. Supp. 72 (D. Del. 1976), in Milko, "Beyond the Persian Gulf Crisis," 1310, n. 45.

19. *Lewis v. U.S. Army,* 697 F. Supp. 1385, 1393 (E.D. Pa. 1988), in Milko, "Beyond the Persian Gulf Crisis," 1310, n. 45.

20. CDR P. W. Kelley, JAGC, USN, memorandum to chair, Women in Combat Aviation Working Group, October 18, 1991, 1.

21. *Rostker v. Goldberg,* 453 U.S. 57, 83 (1981), in Milko, "Beyond the Persian Gulf Crisis," 1310, n. 47.

22. *Hill v. Berkman,* 635 F. Supp. 1238 (E.D.N.Y. 1986), in Milko, "Beyond the Persian Gulf Crisis," 1309, n. 41.

23. *Owens v. Brown,* 455 F. Supp. 291 (1978), in B Gen G. L. Miller, "Historical Perspective of Women in Combat Legislation," information paper, 5800 JAR\9501, Headquarters Marine Corps, NAVMC HQ–335 (REV. 5–89), June 14, 1991, 1.

24. PL 95–485.

25. *Chandler v. Callaway,* No. C–741249 RHS, at 2 (N.D. Calif. November 1, 1974); *U.S. v. Cook,* 311 F. Supp. 618 (W.D. Pa. 1970); *U.S. v. St. Clair,* 291 F. Supp. 122, 124 (S.D.N.Y. 1968); and *U.S. v. Yingling,* 368 F. Supp. 379, 386 (W.D. Pa. 1973); in Milko, "Beyond the Persian Gulf Crisis," 1314, n. 65.

26. *Crawford v. Cushman,* 531 F. 2d 114 (2d Cir. 1976), in Bar of N.Y., "Equality for Women," 9, n. 3.

27. *Kovach v. Middendorf,* 424 F. Supp. 72 (D. Del. 1976), in Milko, "Beyond the Persian Gulf Crisis," 1310, n. 45.

28. *U.S. v. Dorris,* 319 F. Supp. 1306, 1308 (W.D. Pa. 1970), in Jeanne M. Lieberman, "Women in Combat," *Federal Bar News & Journal* 37:1 (May 1990): 218, n. 29, 221.

29. *U.S. v. Clinton,* 310 F. Supp. 333, 336 (E.D.La.1970), in Lieberman, "Women in Combat," 218, n. 30, 221.

30. *Barbier v. Connolly,* 113 U.S. 27 (1885), 32; *Ferguson v. Skrupa,* 372 U.S. 726 (1963), 732.

31. *Kovach v. Middendorf,* in Milko, 1310.

32. *Lindsley v. Natural Carbonic Gas Co.,* 220 U.S. 61 (1911); *R.S. Royster Guano Co. v. Virginia,* 253 U.S. 412 (1920).

33. Lt. Col. Tucker, JAG, USAF, "Memorandum of Law on the Constitutional Issues Surrounding Assignment of Women to Combat," 3.

34. Rosemarie Skaine, *Power and Gender: Issues in Sexual Dominance and Harassment* (Jefferson, N.C.: McFarland, 1996), 105.

35. CDR Thomas N. Ledvina, JAGC, USN, Telecopier Transmittal Sheet, release for transmission, June 10, 1991, memorandum on proposed legislation re Women in Combat, to Ledvina, 1 of 2, June 8, 1991, 1.

36. *Roper v. Department of the Army,* 832 F. 2d 247 (2d Cir. 1987), in Ledvina, memorandum.

37. U.S. Constitution, art. 1, sect. 8, cl. 14, in Jack S. Groat, "Assessment of the Litigation Risk Posed by the Constitutional Challenges to Limitations Upon the Assignment of Female Service Members," to CDR Thomas N. Ledvina, JAGC, June 7, 1991.

38. Richard B. Morris, *The Forging of the Union, 1781–1789* (New York: Harper and Row, 1987), 193. On p. 191, Morris includes a letter that Massachusetts patriot John Adams (later the second president), wrote to a friend on the subject of qualifications for voting in his home state:

> [I]t is dangerous to open so fruitful a source of controversy and altercation as would be opened by attempting to alter the qualifications of voters; there will be no end of it. New claims will arise; women will demand a vote; lads from twelve to twenty-one will think their rights not enough attended to; and every man who has not a farthing, will demand an equal voice with any other, in all acts of state. It tends to confound and destroy all distinctions, and prostrate all ranks to one common level.

Reprinted in Justice Ruth Bader Ginsburg, U.S. Supreme Court, 94–1941 and 94–2107, opinion, *U.S. v. Virginia,* June 26, 1996, 34, n. 21.

39. See Morris, *Forging of the Union*, 29, n. 16.

40. *Ibid.* Ginsburg, opinion, 34.

41. *Ibid.*, 1241. Ginsburg, opinion, 10.

42. *Ibid.*, 1250. Ginsburg, opinion, 30.

43. Ginsburg, opinion, 21.

44. 52 F. 3d, 93, in Ginsburg, opinion, 22.

45. Ginsburg, opinion, 13, 21, 26, 28.

46. 458 U. S. 718 (1982), in Ginsburg, opinion, 5.

47. Ginsburg, opinion, 5.

48. *Frontiero et vir v. Richardson, Secretary of Defense, et al.*, 411 U.S. 677, 684 (1973).

49. As Thomas Jefferson stated the view prevailing when the Constitution was new: "Were our State a pure democracy ... there would yet be excluded from their deliberations ... women, who, to prevent depravation of morals and ambiguity of issue, should not mix promiscuously in the public meetings of men." Letter from Thomas Jefferson to Samuel Kercheval, September 5, 1816, in *Ten Writings of Thomas Jefferson*, ed. P. Ford (New York: Putnam's 1899), 45–46, n. 1, in Ginsburg, opinion, 12, n. 5.

50. "See *Goesaert v. Cleary*, 335 U.S. 464, 467 (1948), rejecting the challenge of a female tavern owner and her daughter to a Michigan law denying bartender licenses to females—except for wives and daughters of male tavern owners, Court would not 'give ear' to the contention that 'an unchivalrous desire of male bartenders to ... monopolize the calling' prompted the legislation," in Ginsburg, opinion, 12.

51. *Reed v. Reed*, 404 U.S. 71 (1971), in Ginsburg, opinion, 12; Ginsburg, opinion, 13.

52. Justice Antonin Scalia, 94–1941 and 94–2107, dissent, *U.S. v. Virginia*.

53. Editorial, "The VMI Ruling and Beyond," *Washington Post*, June 27, 1996, A28.

54. Judith Lichtman, president of the Women's Legal Defense Fund, in Linda Greenhouse, "At the Supreme Court: Discrimination; Military College Can't Bar Women, High Court Rules," *New York Times*, June 27, 1996, A1.

55. RADM Merlin H. Staring, JAGC, USN, "Training and Assignment of Women Aviators," memorandum for the Assistant Deputy Chief of Naval Operations (Air Warfare), JAG:131.3:PLJ:cck, Ser: 8777, November 29, 1974, 1.

56. CAPT P. W. Kelley, OJAG, USN, draft point paper, 10 U.S. Code § 6015, Combat Exclusion, enclosure in memorandum to chair, Women in Combat Aviation Working Group, October 18, 1991, enclosure (2), 1–2.

57. CAPT R. E. Coyle, JAGC, USN, memorandum to CAPT Schachte, JAGC, USN, "Subj.: Women on Vessels of the Navy," August 29, 1985.

58. RADM H. B. Robertson, Jr., JAGC, USN, Deputy JAG, letter to VADM Robert B. Baldwin, USN, Commander, Naval Air Force, U.S. Pacific Fleet, May 23, 1974, 1–2.

59. House subcommittee hearings on § 1641, *Women's Armed Forces Integration Act of 1948* (Subcommittee No. 3, Organization and Mobilization, of the House Armed Services Committee, 80th Cong., 2d sess., 1948, 5711, 5712–13, in Robertson, letter to Baldwin, 1–2, enclosure memorandum for the Secretary of the Navy, "Navy Women in Aircraft," JAG:131.4:JMT:cck, Ser: 4631, June 1, 1973, 1–2.

60. Robertson, enclosure memorandum, "Navy Women in Aircraft," in Robertson, letter to Baldwin, May 23, 1974.

61. JAG memo to Chief of Naval Personnel, JAG:131.7:PLJ:cck Ser: 979, February 6, 1973, in Robertson, letter to Baldwin, May 23, 1974.

62. CAPT E. R. Fink, memorandum on Women in the Navy, JAG:14:ERF:vme, May 25, 1973, 1.

63. Miller, "Historical Perspectives," 1.

64. *Ibid.*

65. *Ibid.*, 2.

66. Bar of N.Y., "Equality for Women," 12.

67. Miller, "Historical Perspectives," 3.

68. *Ibid.*

69. *Ibid.*, 4-5.

70. Kelley, draft point paper, 1991, in memorandum to CAPT T.D. Keating, JAGC, USN, November 24, 1993, enclosure (2), 7.

71. *Ibid.*

72. LT M. Deere, JAGC, USN, point paper, 1300, 131.2/4–1781, 1991; Kelley, draft point paper, in memorandum to Keating, 8.

73. CAPT T. D. Keating, JAGC, USN, memorandum for Director, Officer and Enlisted Personnel Management, June 12, 1991; CDR Frank Prochazka, JAG 131, 614–1781, issue paper, "Exclusion of Women from Combat," n.d.

74. Stephen J. Shapiro, chair, Committee on Military Affairs and Justice, Association of the Bar of the City of New York, to Dick Cheney, Secretary of Defense, May 17, 1991.

75. U.S. Congress, House Committee on Armed Services, *National Defense Authorization Act for Fiscal Years 1992 and 1993*, report on H.R. 2100 together with dissenting views, May 13, 1991, 240.

76. *Congressional and Administrative News, 103d Congress—First Session, 1993*, vol. 2, (St. Paul, Minn.: West, 1994), 150.

77. U.S. Code § 8549 (1976).

78. Bar of New York, "The Combat Exclusion Laws: An Idea Whose Time Has Gone," May 17, 1991, 5.

79. Civil law opinion of the Judge Advocate General of the Air Force (OPJAGAF) 1973/67, April 27, 1973, 237.

80. MGen. Jeanne Holm, USAF (Ret.), *Women in the Military: An Unfinished Revolution*, rev. ed. (Novato, Calif.: Presidio, 1992), 337, n. 2, in Bar of N.Y., "Equality for Women," n. 44, 12.

81. "Task Force Report," in *Women in the Military*, House Hearings, 1987–88, 147.

82. *Ibid.*

83. Karla R. Kelly, "The Combat Exclusion; Withstanding Challenge," working manuscript for OJAG, April 28, 1983, 6.

84. Milko, "Beyond the Persian Gulf Crisis," 1302.

85. 10 U.S. Code § 3013(g) (1988).

86. MAJ Lillian A. Pfluke, USA (Ret.), "Chronology of Recent History to Open Combat Roles," July 29, 1996, 1, enclosure (1), 10 U.S. Code §3013, Subtitle D—Women in the Service, sec. 541, 543.

87. 10 U.S. Code § 3013, Subtitle D—Women in the Service, sec. 542,(a) (1) (2), (b).

88. MAJ Mary Finch, USA, "Women in Combat: One Commissioner Reports," paper presented at the Military Manpower Conference: A Military of Volunteers, U.S. Naval Academy, September 17, 1993, 17–20.

89. Presidential Commission, *Report to the President*, 93.

90. Finch, "Women in Combat," 19–20.

91. LGen. Henry Viccellio, Jr., USAF, Director, Joint Staff, Joint Staff memorandum for Army, Navy, Air Force and Marine Corps Operations Deputy, June 4, 1992, 1 of 2.

92. *Ibid.*

93. Department of Defense, Office of Assistant Secretary of Defense (Public Affairs), "Secretary of Defense Aspin Expects to Open New Opportunities for Women with New Direct Ground Combat Rule," news release, Washington, D.C., January 13, 1994, 1.

94. MAJ Lillian A. Pfluke, "Direct Ground Combat in Bosnia—Clear as Mud," *Minerva's Bulletin Board* IX:1 (Spring 1996): 10–11.

95. Linda Grant De Pauw, interview, March 21, 1996.

96. Les Aspin, Secretary of Defense, memorandum on policy, "The Assignment of Women in the Armed Forces," April 28, 1993, 2.

97. U.S. Code Service, Advance Legislative Service, 1993 Lawyers Cooperative Publishing, PL 103–160, § 541, 103d Cong., 1st sess., November 30, 1993.

98. John Lancaster, "Army, Marines Resisting Combat Role for Women; Policy Paper Severely Limits Females," *Washington Post*, June 18, 1993, A1.

99. *Ibid.*

100. Pfluke, "Chronology," 1, enclosure (3).

101. MAJ Lillian A. Pfluke, "Combat Bans Force Army Women Behind," opinion, *Army Times*, November 22, 1993, reprinted in *Women Military Aviators Newsletter* (Winter-Spring, 1993–1994).

102. MAJ Lillian A. Pfluke, interview, September 28, 1996.

103. John Lancaster, "Combat Plan for Women Put on Hold," *Washington Post*, January 6, 1994, 1, 8; "Women Soldiers, Step by Step," *Washington Post*, January 9, 1994, C6.

104. GEN Gordon R. Sullivan, Chief of Staff, USA, and Togo D. West, Jr., Secretary of the Army, memorandum for Secretary of Defense, Direct Combat Definition and Assignment Rule, January 12, 1994, 1; Togo D. West, Jr., Secretary of the Army, and GEN Gordon R. Sullivan, Chief of Staff, USA, "Statement: Direct Combat Definition and Assignment for Women," January 13, 1994, 1.

105. *Ibid.*

106. Office of Assistant Secretary of Defense (Public Affairs), "Secretary of Defense Aspin," 1. Attachments: (1) memorandum regarding this subject, (2) an April 28, 1993, memorandum on Assignment of Women in the Armed Forces, (3) a list of Areas for Examination by the Services, and (4) the Former Risk Rule.

107. Eric Schmitt, "Aspin Moves to Open Many Military Jobs to Women," *New York Times*, January 14, 1994, 1, 22; Phyllis W. Jordan, "New Military Policy Could Open Jobs to Women," *(Norfolk) Virginian-Pilot*, January 14, 1994, 1.

108. MAJ Lillian A. Pfluke in Rowan Scarborough, "Aspin Announces Rules for Women in Ground Combat," *The Washington Times*, January 14, 1994, 3–4.

109. GEN John M. Shalikashvili, Chairman of the Joint Chiefs of Staff, memorandum for the Secretary of Defense, CM–224–94, April 22, 1994, 1.

110. MAJ Lillian A. Pfluke, "Special Forces—the Last Word?" posted to H-MINERVA, "H-NET list for Discussion of Women and the Military and Women in War," November 4, 1996, at http://www.h-net.msu.edu, log is 9611.

111. MAJ Lillian A. Pfluke, Ordnance Corps Officer, Marine Corps Command and Staff College at Quantico, Virginia, "Some Ideas Are As Outmoded As the Horse Cavalry," *Army Times*, May 2, 1994, 10.

112. 1st Lt. Faith Richards, USAFR, e-mail interview, October 26, 1998; RADM Paul T. Gillcrist, USN (Ret.), *Feet Wet: Reflections of a Carrier Pilot* (New York: Pocket Books, 1990), 125.

113. Pfluke, "Some Ideas," 10.

114. Togo D. West, Jr., Secretary of the Army, working memorandum for the Secretary of Defense, "Recommendations for Opening Additional Positions for

Women Under the DOD Assignment Policy—DECISION MEMORANDUM," June 1, 1994, 1–9.

115. *Ibid.*

116. Sara E. Lister, Assistant Secretary of the Army (Manpower and Reserve Affairs), memorandum for the Secretary of the Army, "Application of DOD Policy in the Assignment of Women," June 13, 1994, 1-4.

117. GEN Gordon R. Sullivan, Chief of Staff, memorandum for the Secretary of the Army, "Women in Combat—Expanding Career Opportunities for Women in the Army," n.d., 2.

118. Holm, *Women in the Military*, 451–452.

119. *Ibid.*

120. Togo D. West, Jr., Secretary of the Army, memorandum for the Secretary of Defense, "Women in Combat, Assignment Policy Proposal—Action Memorandum" (prepared by GEN Gordon R. Sullivan, Chief of Staff), circa June 1994, 4.

121. GEN Gordon R. Sullivan, Chief of Staff, "Increasing Opportunities for Women in the Army," January 28, 1994, 1–3. (Extract CSA Weekly Summary, January 28, 1994.)

122. Pat Schroeder, Olympia Snowe, Marilyn Lloyd, Connie Morella, Elizabeth Furse, Tillie Fowler, Maxine Waters, Arma Eshoo, Karen Shepherd, Eleanor Holmes Norton, Carolyn Maloney, Karan English, Carrie Meek, Jill Long, and Leslie Byrne, Congressional Caucus for Women's Issues, U.S. Congress, Washington, D.C., letter to Secretary of Defense William J. Perry, June 14, 1994, 1–2.

123. Togo D. West, Jr., Secretary of the Army, "Increasing Opportunities for Women in the Army," memorandum for the Under Secretary of Defense (Personnel and Readiness), July 27, 1994, 1–7.

124. *Ibid.*

125. William J. Perry, Secretary of Defense, "Application of the Definition of Direct Ground Combat and Assignment Rule," memorandum for the Secretaries of the Army, Navy, Air Force, and Under Secretary of Defense (Personnel and Readiness), July 28, 1994, 1.

126. William J. Perry, Secretary of Defense, letter to The Honorable Sam Nunn (D-Ga.), chair, Senate Committee on the Armed Services, July 28, 1994, 2.

127. Office of Assistant Secretary of Defense (Public Affairs), "Secretary of Defense Perry Approves Plans to Open New Jobs for Women in the Military," news release, no. 449–94, July 29, 1994, 1.

128. MAJ Christine Hallisey and BG R. Dennis Kerr, "Women in the Army," information paper, Deputy Chief of Staff of the Army for Personnel–Human Resources (DAPE-HR-S), September 19, 1994, 1–3.

129. *Ibid.*, 3.

130. *Ibid.*

131. Pfluke, "Chronology," 2.

132. LTC Karen McManus, USA, "Women in the Army Policy Update," *Army Women's Professional Association*, March 26, 1996.

133. Holly K. Hemphill, chair, Defense Advisory Committee on Women in the Services (DACOWITS), interview, Washington, D.C., June 14, 1996.

134. Pfluke, "Chronology," 2.

135. Pfluke, interview, September 28, 1996.

136. Headquarters, Department of the Army, *Tactics, Techniques, and Procedures for the Multiple Launch Rocket System (MLRS) Operations*, FM–6–60 (original document), September 16, 1992, 1–1.

137. Headquarters, Department of the Army, *Tactics, Techniques, and Procedures*

for the MLRS Operations, FM–6–60, C1, September 30, 1993, 1–1. (C1 means change number 1; new material is indicated by a star.)

138. Headquarters, Department of the Army, *Tactics, Techniques,* September 16, 1992, 4–1.

139. Headquarters, Department of the Army, *Tactics, Techniques,* September 30, 1993, 4–3.

140. Pfluke, interview, September 28, 1996.

141. COL Barbara Lee, USA, interview, September 19, 1996.

142. Pfluke, interview, September 28, 1996.

143. Headquarters, Department of the Army, 7NR 44444, R 0223447 November 1995, 707 720 T All U.S. Army, U.S. Army REPs and ACT, August 1995 (picked up September 2, 1996), 1–6.

144. Headquarters, Department of the Army, message, "Subject: Expanded Roles for Women in the Army," 121301Z August 1994, 1–4.

145. Headquarters, Department of the Army, message, "Subject: Coding of Tables of Distribution and Allowances (TDA)," 061614Z January 1993, 1–5.

146. Rosemarie Skaine, letter to Togo D. West, Jr., Secretary of the Army, October 27, 1996.

147. LTC John S. Westwood, USA, chief, Leadership Division, letter to Rosemarie Skaine, n.d. (metered date on envelope is November 14, 1996); 1-2.

148. *Ibid.*

Chapter 6

1. Roscoe Bartlett (R-Md.), congressman, in U.S. Congress, House Committee on Armed Services, *Women in Combat: Hearing Before the Military Forces and Personnel Subcommittee,* 103d Cong., 1st sess., May 12, 1993, 39, 80.

2. ADM Stanley R. Arthur, USN (Ret.), FAX, January 30, 1996.

3. Mady Wechsler Segal and Amanda Faith Hansen, "Value Rationales in Policy Debates on Women in the Military: A Content Analysis of Congressional Testimony, 1941–1985," *Social Science Quarterly* 73:2 (June 1992): 294, 299, 301, 304, 306–07.

4. John A. Rawls, *A Theory of Justice* (Cambridge: Harvard University Press, 1971), 380, 390, quoted in CPT A. Dwight Raymond, USA, "Soldiers, Unjust Wars, and Treason," in James C. Gaston and Janis Bren Hietala, *Ethics and National Defense: The Timeless Issues* (Washington, D.C.: National Defense University Press, 1993), 66–67.

5. Peter L. Berger, *Invitation to Sociology: A Humanistic Perspective* (Garden City, N.Y.: Doubleday, 1963), 5, 12–13, 16.

6. Elaine Sciolino, "Battle Lines Are Shifting on Women in War," *New York Times,* January 25, 1990, A1.

7. United Press International, "Survey: I'd Let My Daughter Fight," April 9, 1990; PR newswire, April 9, 1990.

8. Karlyn H. Keene, Everett Carll Ladd, Jennifer Baggette, John Benson, and Karl Zinsmeister, "Women and the Use of Force," *Public Perspective* 2:3 (March-April 1991): 85.

9. "Most Callers: Allow Military Women in Combat Zones," *Orlando Sentinel Tribune,* February 5, 1991, A9.

10. U.S. Congress, House Committee, *Women in Combat,* 47; U.S. Presidential Commission on the Assignment of Women in the Armed Forces, *Report to the President: Women in Combat* (Washington: Brassey's, 1993), Appendix D–5.

11. MAJ Mary Finch, USA, "Women in Combat: One Commissioner Reports,"

paper presented at the Military Manpower Conference: A Military of Volunteers, U.S. Naval Academy, September 17, 1993, 9–10.

12. Capt. Georgia Clark Sadler, USN (Ret.), "The Polling Data," *Proceedings of the U.S. Naval Institute* 119:2 (February 1993): 51.

13. *Ibid.*, 51–52.

14. *Ibid.*, 54.

15. *Ibid.*, 53–54.

16. *Ibid.*, 52.

17. *Ibid.*, 52–53.

18. *Ibid.*, 53.

19. *Ibid.*, 54.

20. Presidential Commission, *Report to the President*, Appendix D-7.

21. Finch, "Women in Combat," 11.

22. MAJ Mary Finch, e-mail interview, April 7, 1997.

23. Some other studies on women in the military are *Women in the Military: More Military Jobs Can Be Opened Under Current Statutes* (Washington, D.C.: GAO/[National Security and International Affairs Division] NSIAD, 1988); *Women in the Military: Career Progression Not a Problem But Concerns Remain* (Washington, D.C.: GAO/NSIAD, 1989); *Women in the Military: Attrition and Retention* (Washington, D.C.: GAO/NSIAD, 1990); *Opinion on Women in Combat*, USAF Personnel Survey Branch, 1992; Gordon George, Paul Bierly, Laurie Davison, and Nancy DiTmaso, *Recommendations Related to the Culture and Climate Assessment of the U.S. Coast Guard Academy* (Princeton, N.J.: Princeton Economic Research, 1992); and M. C. Devilbliss, "Gender Integration and Unit Deployment: A Study of GI Jo," *Armed Forces and Society* 11:4 (Summer 1985): 523–52.

24. Pamela Johnston Conover and Virginia Sapiro, "Gender, Feminist Consciousness, and War," *American Journal of Political Science* 37:4 (November 1993): 1079, 1095–97.

25. *Ibid.*, 1079.

26. *Ibid.*

27. *Ibid.*

28. UN, "Women and Armed Conflict," *Report of the Fourth World Conference on Women*, Beijing, China, September 4–15, 1995. Posted online by the UN Department for Policy Coordination and Sustainable Development (DPCSD), at http://www.iisd.ca/linkages/women.html, October 17, 1995, IV E, 134.

Chapter 7

1. Louis A. Zurcher, Jr., "Navy Boot Camp: Role Assimilation in a Total Institution," in *Sociology: Windows on Society*, 3d ed., John W. Heeren and Marylee Mason (Sweet Springs, Mo.: Roxbury, 1994), 56.

2. Erving Goffman, *Asylums* (New York: Doubleday, 1961), xiii, 237–38, in Zurcher, "Navy Boot Camp," in *Sociology*, Heeren and Mason, 56.

3. Goffman, *Asylums*, 51.

4. Frederick Elkin, "The Soldier's Language," *American Journal of Sociology* (March 1946): 414, in Zurcher, "Navy Boot Camp," 59.

5. Goffman, *Asylums*, 61–63.

6. "Faulkner Quits the Citadel," *Dayton Daily News*, August 19, 1995, A1.

7. Rosemary Yardley, "Shannon Faulkner Set Up to Fail at the Citadel," *News & Record*, Greensboro, N.C., August 23, 1995, A13.

8. Anne-Marie Hilsdon, "From Civilian to Military: Bodily Transformations and

Transgressions in Philippine Militaries," MINERVA: *Quarterly Report on Women and the Military* XIV: 3, 4 (Fall-Winter 1996): 89.

9. *Ibid.*, 71.

10. *Ibid.*, 91.

11. *Ibid.*, 92–93.

12. *Ibid.*, 101–03, 120.

13. Chris Burritt, "Citadel Cadet Disciplined Cadets for Hazing," *Atlanta Journal-Constitution*, December 15, 1996, A7.

14. Dirk Johnson, "New Messages Sent at Navy Boot Camp; A Focus on Treating All Recruits Better," *New York Times*, March 17, 1997, A10.

15. Gerald F. Linderman, *Embattled Courage: The Experience of Combat in the American Civil War* (New York: Free Press; 1987), 266–75.

16. Cpl Timothy Sexton, USMC Reserve, interview, January 30, 1996.

17. Sgt Maj Charlene K. Wiese, USMC, interview, August 15, 1996.

18. ADM Stanley R. Arthur, USN (Ret.), interview, February 8, 1996.

19. Lewis A. Coser, *The Functions of Social Conflict* (New York: Free Press, 1964), 113–14.

20. RADM Paul T. Gillcrist, USN (Ret.), interview, October 10, 1995.

21. *Ibid.*

22. MGen. Jeanne Holm, USAF (Ret.), *Women in the Military: An Unfinished Revolution*, rev. ed. (Novato, Calif.: Presidio, 1992), 461.

23. Elisabetta Addis, "Women and Economic Consequences of Being a Solider," in *Women Soldiers: Images and Realities*, edited by Elisabetta Addis, Valeria E. Russo, and Lorenza Sebesta (New York: St. Martin's, 1994), 3–27.

24. Maj R. S. Lenac, Assistant Chief of Staff, G-1, comments on the contribution of women from the staff of Command Element, I Marine Expeditionary Force, 1, in Lt Gen W. E. Boomer, Commanding General, I Marine Expeditionary Force, FPO San Francisco, Calif., letter to Gen A. M. Gray, Commandant of the Marine Corps, March 30, 1991, 1–2, enclosure 4.

25. *Ibid.*

26. Linda Grant De Pauw, in Charlotte Grimes "Gender Gulf Prospect of Women at War Faced by Some with Unease," *St. Louis Post-Dispatch*, February 17, 1991, B1.

27. Linda Grant De Pauw, e-mail interview, March 3, 1996.

28. Mady Wechsler Segal, "Women's Military Roles Cross-Nationally: Past, Present, and Future," *Gender & Society* 9:6 (December 1995): 770.

29. Francine D'Amico, "Feminist Perspectives on Women Warriors," *Peace Review* 8:3 (September 1996): 379.

30. CPT Sharon Grant Wildwind, ANC, USA (Ret.), interview, December 15, 1996.

31. Linda Grant De Pauw, e-mail interview, March 4, 1996.

32. Segal, "Women's Military Roles," 757–59.

33. *Ibid.*, 758, 761, 771.

34. Pamela Johnston Conover and Virginia Sapiro, "Gender, Feminist Consciousness, and War," *American Journal of Political Science* 37:4 (November 1993): 1080–81.

35. Sara Ruddick, *Maternal Thinking: Towards a Politics of Peace* (Boston: Beacon Press, 1989), 161, in Conover and Sapiro, "Gender," 1081.

36. UN, "Women and Armed Conflict," *Report of the Fourth World Conference on Women*, Beijing, China, September 4–15, 1995. Post online by the UN Department for Policy Coordination and Sustainable Development (DPCSD), at http://www.iisd.ca/linkages/women.html, October 17, 1995, IV E, 139–40.

37. *Ibid.*, 134.

38. Conover and Sapiro, "Gender," 1081–82.

39. *Ibid.*, 1079, 1095–97.

40. Rosalyn Diprose, *The Bodies of Women: Ethics, Embodiment and Sexual Difference* (New York: Routledge, 1994), vii–viii, xi.

41. *Ibid.*, xi.

42. *Ibid.*, 18.

43. *Ibid.*, 1–3.

44. *Ibid.*, 2.

45. *Ibid.*, x, 1, 20.

46. B Gen Thomas V. Draude, USMC (Ret.), in U.S. Congress, House Committee on Armed Services, Military Forces and Personnel Subcommittee *Women in Combat: Hearing Before the Military Forces and Personnel Subcommittee*, 103d Cong., 1st sess. May 12, 1993, 102.

47. *Ibid.*, 75.

48. Diprose, *Bodies of Women*, vi, 11.

49. *Ibid.*, 10–12.

50. *Ibid.*, vii, viii, 36–37.

51. *Ibid.*, vii, 19.

52. *Ibid.*, viii, ix, 1–17.

53. Michel Foucault, *Discipline and Punish: The Birth of the Prison*, trans. by Alan Sheridan, (Harmondsworth, Middlesex: Penguin, 1979), in Diprose, *Bodies of Women*, ix, 18–37.

54. Hilsdon, "Civilian to Military," 72, 77, 80, 102.

55. Diprose, *Bodies of Women*, 38.

56. *Ibid.*, 38–81.

57. Daniel Callahan, "How Shall We Incorporate Ethics Instruction at All Levels?" in *Ethics and National Defense: The Timeless Issues*, by James C. Gaston and Janis Bren Hietala (Washington, D.C.: National Defense University Press, 1993), 136–43.

58. Diprose, *Bodies of Women*, 18–19.

59. Col. Michael O. Wheeler, USAF, "Thinking Ethically About the Strategic Defense Initiative: Some Preliminaries," and MAJ H. F. Kuenning, USA, "Small Wars and Morally Sound Strategy," in *Ethics and National Defense: The Timeless Issues*, by James C. Gaston and Janis Bren Hietala (Washington, D.C.: National Defense University Press, 1993), 172, 189–93.

60. CPT A. Dwight Raymond, USA, "Soldiers, Unjust Wars, and Treason," in *Ethics and National Defense: The Timeless Issues*, by James C. Gaston and Janis Bren Hietala (Washington, D.C.: National Defense University Press, 1993), 63–69.

61. James H. McGrath, "The Officer's Oath: Words That Bind," in *Ethics and National Defense: The Timeless Issues*, by James C. Gaston and Janis Bren Hietala (Washington, D.C.: National Defense University Press, 1993), 17–33.

62. Sexton, interview, January 30, 1996.

63. Headquarters Department of the Army, "The Soldier's Creed" and "Code of Conduct," *Soldier's Handbook*, January 1, 1993, ii, 66.

64. CPT Thomas J. Begines, USA, "Special Trust and Confidence," in *Ethics and National Defense: The Timeless Issues*, by James C. Gaston and Janis Bren Hietala (Washington, D.C.: National Defense University Press, 1993), 3–15.

65. Diprose, *Bodies of Women*, x, 38–64.

66. *Ibid.*, x, 65–81.

67. *Ibid.*, xi, 82–101.

68. Conover and Sapiro, "Gender," 1080–81.

69. Diprose, *Bodies of Women*, 131.

Chapter 8

1. MAJ Jane McKeon, USA (Ret.), telephone interview, August 12, 1996.

2. Gen. Charles Krulak, Commandant of the USMC, testimony before the Senate Armed Services Committee, Readiness Subcommittee, March 14, 1996, *Federal News Service*, March 15, 1996.

3. ADM Stanley R. Arthur, statement before House Appropriations Committee, National Security Subcommittee, April 6, 1995, Federal Document Clearing House (FDCH) Congressional Testimony, April 6, 1995.

4. *Ibid.*

5. MAJ Lillian A. Pfluke, USA (Ret.), e-mail interview, March 18, 1996, referring to Office of Assistant Secretary of Defense (Public Affairs), "Secretary of Defense Perry Approves Plans to Open New Jobs for Women in the Military" news release, no. 449–94, July 29, 1993, 1.

6. Mady Wechsler Segal, "Women's Military Roles Cross-Nationally: Past, Present, and Future," *Gender and Society* 9:6 (December 1995): 760–62.

7. ADM Stanley R. Arthur, interview, January 5, 1996.

8. Segal, "Women's Military Roles," 762–68.

9. Bernard D. Rostker, statement before the Senate Armed Services Committee, Subcommittee on Personnel, *Federal News Service*, April 8, 1997.

10. Dorothy Schneider and Carl J. Schneider, *Sound Off! American Military Women Speak Out* (New York: Dutton, 1988), 149.

11. Elaine Donnelly in U.S. Congress, House Committee on Armed Services, Military Forces and Personnel Subcommittee, *Women in Combat: Hearing Before the Military Forces and Personnel Subcommittee*, 103d Cong., 1st sess., May 12, 1993, 61.

12. *Ibid.*, 112.

13. Elaine Donnelly in U.S. Congress, House Committee on Armed Services, Military Forces and Personnel Subcommittee, *Assignment of Army and Marine Corps Women Under the New Definition of Ground Combat*, 103d Cong., 2d sess., October 6, 1994, 62–64; Dirk Johnson, "New Messages Sent at Navy Boot Camp; A Focus on Treating All Recruits Better," *New York Times*, March 17, 1997, A10.

14. Brian Mitchell, *Weak Link: The Feminization of the American Military* (Washington, D.C.: Regnery Gateway, 1989), 5–7.

15. *Ibid.*, 218–22.

16. CDR John Calande, Jr., e-mail interview, April 18, 1997.

17. Joe Helmick, e-mail interview, February 22, 1996.

18. Pfluke, e-mail interview, March 22, 1996.

19. MAJ Mary Finch, USA, "Women in Combat: One Commissioner Reports," paper presented at the Military Manpower Conference: A Military of Volunteers, U.S. Naval Academy, September 17, 1993, 2–3.

20. U.S. Presidential Commission on the Assignment of Women in the Armed Forces, *Report to the President: Women in Combat*, (Washington, D.C.: Brassey's, 1993), 40.

21. Dick Kirschten, "The Flap Over Draft Registration—Only the Public Seems to Like It," *National Journal* 12:16 (April 19, 1980): 645.

22. Richard L. Lyons, "Draft Registration Plan Passed by House, 218–188," *Washington Post*, April 23, 1980, A35.

23. John K. Cooley, "Draft Sign-Up Opponents Enlist Strong Aid in Senate," *Christian Science Monitor*, April 24, 1980, 4.

24. Arthur, interview, January 5, 1996.

25. *Ibid.*

26. BGen. Wilma Vaught, USAF (Ret.), interview, June 11, 1996.

27. House Hearing, *Women in Combat*, May 12, 1993, 43–45.

28. *Ibid.*, 45.

29. Capt. Patricia A. Gavin, USAF, posted to H-MINERVA, at http://www.h-net.msu.edu, February 11, 1997.

30. ADM Stanley R. Arthur, interview, February 8, 1996.

31. Segal, "Women's Military Roles," 761–62, 765.

32. James D. Milko, "Beyond the Persian Gulf Crisis: Expanding the Role of the Servicewomen in the United States Military," *American University Law Review* 41 (Summer 1992): 1302–03.

33. LTG Harold G. Moore, USA (Ret.), and Joseph L. Galloway, *We Were Soldiers Once ... and Young—Ia Drang: The Battle That Changed the War in Vietnam* (New York: Random House, Inc.: 1992), 39, 341.

34. David R. Segal, Joseph C. Jones, Angela M. Manos, and David E. Rohall, "Meeting the Missions of the 1990s with a Down-Sized Force: Human Resource Management Lessons From the Deployment of PATRIOT Missile Units to Korea," forthcoming; David R. Segal, Joseph C. Jones, and Angela Maria Manos, "Citizen Soldiers in the Sinai: The Evolution of a Composite Active/Reserve Component American Battalion for a Peacekeeping Mission," forthcoming.

35. Segal, "Women's Military Roles," 760–61.

36. CAPT P. W. Kelley, Department of the Navy (DON), Office of the Judge Advocate General (OJAG), memorandum to CAPT T. D. Keating, JAGC, USN, November 24, 1993, memorandum from OJAG Staff, November 23, 1993, 1–2 of 7, 5 enclosures.

37. *Ibid.*, 2 of 7.

38. Kelley, memorandum, enclosure (1), papers from file entitled "DOD Response to Draft Registration Questions by Senator Sam Nunn," COL Kenneth A. Deutsch, Director, Officer and Enlisted Personnel Management, Military Manpower and Personnel Policy, Office of the Assistant Secretary of Defense for Force Management and Personnel, memorandum to CAPT T. D. Keating, July 2, 1991, 3 of 7.

39. Kelley, memorandum, enclosure (1), transcript from Hearing on Women in the Military, June 18, 1991, 4 of 7 – 7 of 7.

40. Kelley, memorandum, enclosure (2), draft point paper, "10 U.S. Code § 6015, Combat Exclusion," 6.

41. *Ibid.*, 7.

42. Kelley, memorandum, enclosure (3), lists of tabs within Code 13 subj. file: "Women in Combat—Historical Work Product," Tab B; Kelley, "The Combat Exclusion: Withstanding the Challenge," *JAG Journal*, working manuscript, 1983.

43. Kelley, memorandum, enclosure (2), 7.

44. *Ibid.*; see 50 U.S. Code App. § 467(c).

45. Francine D'Amico, posted to H-MINERVA, at http://www.h-net.msu.edu, April 29, 1996.

46. Marian Neudel, posted to H-MINERVA, at http://www.h-net.msu.edu, April 30, 1996.

47. Col. Kelly Hamilton, USAF (Ret.), interview, December 28, 1996.

48. Arthur, telephone interview, February 8, 1996; RADM Paul T. Gillcrist, USN (Ret.), telephone interview, December 14, 1995.

49. Gillcrist, telephone interview, October 10, 1995.

50. RMC Roxine C. Hart, *Women in Combat*, Research Division, Defense Equal Opportunity Management Institute, Patrick AFB, Fla., February 1991, 19–20.

51. Presidential Commission, *Report to the President*, 2.5.4B, Appendix C-85, in House Hearing, *Women in Combat*, May 12, 1993, 76.

52. Hamilton, interview, December 28, 1996.

53. Presidential Commission, *Report to the President*, Appendix C-93, 86–87, 93.

54. CAPT Georgia Clark Sadler, USN (Ret.), and Patricia J. Thomas, "Rock the Cradle, Rock the Boat?" *Proceedings of the U.S. Naval Institute* 121:4 (February 1993): 53–54.

55. *Ibid.*, 55.

56. "Department of the Navy (DON) Policy on Pregnancy," SECNAVINST 1000, February 6, 1995, in Sadler, "Rock the Cradle," 56.

57. *Ibid.*, 51.

58. *Ibid.*, 53–54.

59. *Ibid.*, 54.

60. *Ibid.*, 55.

61. BGen. Mike Hall, testimony before the Presidential Commission, *Report to the President*, 1992, 257.

62. Hart, *Women in Combat*, 20.

63. Gillcrist, interview, December 14, 1995.

64. Elaine Sciolino, "Female P.O.W. Is Abused, Kindling Debate," *New York Times*, June 19, 1992, A1.

65. Col. Kelly Hamilton, letter to Amy Talkington, 1993.

66. MAJ Mary Finch, USA, "Women in Combat," 4–5.

67. MAJ Mary Finch, USA, e-mail interview, April 7, 1997; Beverly B. Byron (D-Md.), chair, U.S. Congress, House Committee on Armed Services, Military Forces and Personnel Subcommittee, *Gender Discrimination in the Military*, 102d Cong., 2d sess., July 29 and 30, 1992, 2.

68. Col. Kelly Hamilton, USAF (Ret.), letter home January 23, 1991.

69. *Ibid.*

70. Hamilton, letter to Amy Talkington, 1993.

71. Hart, *Women in Combat*, 20.

72. Finch, "Women in Combat," 5.

73. *Ibid.*, 7–8.

74. Pfluke, interview, March 18, 1996.

Chapter 9

1. A. J. Langguth, *Patriots: The Men Who Started the American Revolution* (New York: Simon and Schuster, 1988), 535.

2. MAJ Mary Finch, USA, "Women in Combat: One Commissioner Reports," paper presented at the Military Manpower Conference: A Military of Volunteers, U.S. Naval Academy, September 17, 1993, 11–13.

3. Col Paul E. Roush, USMC (Ret.), "A Tangled Webb," *Proceedings of the U.S. Naval Institute* 123:8 (August 1997), 42–45.

4. James Webb, Jr., "Women Can't Fight," *The Washingtonian*, November 1979, 144.

5. RADM Paul T. Gillcrist, USN (Ret.), interview, October 10, 1995.

6. M. C. Devilbliss, "Gender Integration and Unit Deployment: A Study of GI Jo," *Armed Forces and Society* 11:4 (Summer 1985): 523–52.

7. Tom Bowman, "Webb's Views Opposing Women in Combat Called 'Propaganda': Professor Accuses Writer of Fostering Resentment," *Baltimore Sun*, April 6, 1997, 7, A3.

8. Michael Rustad, *Women in Khaki: The American Enlisted Woman* (New York: Praeger, 1982), 90–91, 147–52, 193–94, 231.

9. MAJ Paul Christopher, USA, "Women in Combat Roles?" in James C. Gaston and Janis Bren Hietala, *Ethics and National Defense: The Timeless Issues* (Washington, D.C.: National Defense University Press, 1993), 227–30.

10. BGen. Wilma Vaught, USAF (Ret.), interview, June 11, 1996.

11. BGen. Mike Hall, testimony before the U.S. Presidential Commission on the Assignment of Women in the Armed Services, September 11, 1992, *Report to the President: Women in Combat* (Washington, D.C., Brassey's, 1993), 247–48.

12. *Ibid.*, Hall, 248.

13. *Ibid.*, 248, 255.

14. MAJ Mary Finch, USA, interviews, 1996.

15. MGen. Jeanne Holm, USAF (Ret.), *Women in the Military: An Unfinished Revolution*, rev. ed. (Novato, Calif.: Presidio, 1992), 444, 459–61; Jean Zimmerman, *Tailspin: Women at War in the Wake of Tailhook* (New York: Doubleday, 1995), xvi.

16. Holm, *Women in the Military*, 459–61.

17. *Ibid.*, 438, 448, 460–61.

18. Dorothy Schneider and Carl J. Schneider, *Sound Off! American Military Women Speak Out* (New York: Dutton, 1988), 154.

19. *Ibid.*, 144–147.

20. Lt Col Greg Morin, USMC, interview, June 12, 1996.

21. Danna Maller, former USA captain, interview, June 10, 1996.

Chapter 10

1. Mady Wechsler Segal, "Women's Military Roles Cross-Nationally: Past, Present, and Future," *Gender and Society* 9:6 (December 1995): 768.

2. U.S. Congress, House Committee on Armed Services, Military Forces and Personnel Subcommittee *Women in Combat: Hearing Before the Military Forces and Personnel Subcommittee*, 103d Cong., 1st sess., May 12, 1993, 67–68, 79, 115; U.S. Congress, House Committee on Armed Services, Military Forces and Personnel Subcommittee, *Assignment of Army and Marine Corps Women Under the New Definition of Ground Combat*, 103d Cong., 2d sess., October 6, 1994, 2–3; U.S. Presidential Commission on the Assignment of Women in the Armed Forces, *Report to the President: Women in Combat* (Washington, D.C.: Brassey's, 1993), 4–14.

3. Segal, "Women's Military Roles," 768.

4. LT Michael J. Frevola, USNR, "Damn the Torpedoes, Full Speed Ahead: The Argument for Total Sex Integration in the Armed Services," *Connecticut Law Review* 28 (Spring 1996): 637–41.

5. B Gen Margaret A. Brewer, USMC (Ret.), written interview, April 25, 1997.

6. RMC Roxine C. Hart, *Women in Combat*, Research Division, Defense Equal Opportunity Management Institute, Patrick AFB, Fla., February 1991, 14–15.

7. *Ibid.*, 15.

8. MAJ Paul Christopher, USA, "Women in Combat Roles?" in James C. Gaston and Janis Bren Hietala, *Ethics and National Defense: The Timeless Issues* (Washington, D.C.: National Defense University Press, 1993), 226.

9. MAJ Lillian A. Pfluke, USA (Ret.), e-mail, "PT Tests Don't Determine Qualification," March 12, 1996; see also *The Washington Times*, Part Symposium, May 8, 1985, 21.

10. House Hearings, May 12, 1993, 45.

11. Helen Rogan, *Mixed Company: Women in the Modern Army* (New York: G. P. Putnam's Sons, 1981), 291.

12. U.S. Army Research Institute of Environmental Medicine report, January 26, 1996, in J. Michael Brower, "New Army Study Undermines Old Taboo," posted to H-MINERVA at http://www.h-minerva, log is 9607b, July 11, 1996. Versions also appeared in *Armed Forces Journal International* (May 1996): 13; *Stars and Stripes*, domestic ed., March 25–31, 7; and *Pentagram*, Ft. McNair, Washington, D.C., March 22, 1996, 14.

13. Hugh McManners, *Sunday Times*, London, December 3, 1995, Home News, in Brower, "New Army Study," July 11, 1996.

14. Brower, "New Army Study," July 11, 1996.

15. J. Michael Brower, "The Mother of All Future Debates: Women in Combat," *MINERVA: Quarterly Report on Women in the Military* XIV:3, 4 (Fall-Winter 1996): 1.

16. *Ibid.*, 4.

17. *Ibid.*, 8.

18. Hart, *Women in Combat*, 17.

19. *Ibid.*, 17–18.

20. *Ibid.*

21. *Ibid.*; ADM Stanley R. Arthur, USN (Ret.), interview, February 8, 1996.

22. Pam Proctor, "The Stormy Life of Navy Pilot Judy Neuffer," *Parade*, October 13, 1974, 12, 17.

23. CAPT Larry G. Parks, Assistant JAG, prepared April 11, 1975, memorandum for the Chief of Information (OI 210), "Physical Qualifications of Women Naval Aviators," JAG:131.3:PLJ:sba, Ser: 3828, April 14, 1975, enclosure 1, 1.

24. R. E. Smith, Ph.D., letter to CNO, enclosure in Parks, April 11, 1975, memorandum, enclosure 1, 1.

25. *Griggs v. Duke Power Company*, 401 U.S. 424 (1971) applies to Title VII of the *Civil Rights Act of 1964*, PL No. 88–352, 78 Stat. 241, in letter referenced as proposed reply to R. E. Smith, JAG:131.3:PLJ:sba, 1–2, enclosure in Parks, memorandum for the Chief of Information (OI 210), "Physical Qualifications," enclosure 1, 1.

26. *Schlesinger v. Ballard*, 43 U.S.L.W. 4158 (January 15, 1975) in letter referenced as proposed reply to Smith, JAG:131.3:PLJ:sba, 1–2, enclosure in Parks, memorandum for the Chief of Information (OI 210), "Physical Qualifications," enclosure 1, 1.

27. MAJ Lillian A. Pfluke, USA (Ret.), e-mail interview, August 15, 1996; Pfluke, "Question: Will Combat Roles for Women Downgrade Military Readiness? No: Women Have Proved They Can Do the Job," *The Washington Times*, May 8, 1995, Part Symposium, 21.

28. Letter referenced as proposed reply to Smith, JAG:131.3:PLJ:sba, 1–2, enclosure in Parks, memorandum for the Chief of Information (OI 210), "Physical Qualifications," enclosure 1, 2.

29. CAPT Rosemary Mariner, USN, ABC News, *Nightline*, transcript # 3592, February 28, 1995.

30. James W. Crawley, "Navy Grounds Female F-14 Pilot for Evaluation of Flying Skills," *San Diego Union-Tribune*, June 30, 1995, B1.

31. "*Chapter II* CMR Fights Back," Center for Military Readiness (CMR), *V.I.P. Notes, CMR Insider News and Views*, no. 20, Livonia, Mich., July 20, 1996, 1, 3.

32. Elaine Donnelly, "Dear CMR Friend," letter, CMR, Livonia, Mich., February 1997, 2.

33. *Ibid.*, 2, 3.

34. RADM Paul T. Gillcrist, USN (Ret.), interview, March 19, 1996.

35. ADM Stanley R. Arthur, "LT Hultgreen Wasn't a 'Quota' Pilot," *The Washington Times*, May 28, 1995, Op.Ed., B5.

36. Susan Barnes, posted to H-MINERVA at http://www.h-net.msu.edu, February 2, 1997.

37. Evan Thomas and Gregory L. Vistica, "Falling Out of the Sky," *Newsweek,* March 17, 1997, 26.

38. "Rash of Jet Accidents in Pacific Baffles Navy," (*Phoenix*) *Arizona Republic,* March 3, 1996, A19.

39. Gillcrist, interview, March 19, 1996.

40. House Hearings, May 12, 1993, 45.

41. *Ibid.,* 101.

42. *Ibid.,* 40–41.

43. BGen. Wilma L. Vaught, USAF (Ret.), interview, June 11, 1996.

44. MAJ Mary Finch, e-mail interview, August 15, 1996.

45. Vaught, interview, June 11, 1996.

46. Presidential Commission, *Report to the President,* Appendix C–72.

47. MAJ Mary Finch, USA, "Women in Combat: One Commissioner Reports," paper presented at the Military Manpower Conference: A Military of Volunteers, U.S. Naval Academy, September 17, 1993, 8–9.

48. BGen. Mike Hall, testimony before the Presidential Commission, September 11, 1992, *Report to the President,* 234–44.

49. *Ibid.,* 247.

50. *Ibid.,* 234–44.

51. Pfluke, interview, March 18, 1996.

52. Lt Col Greg Morin, interview, June 12, 1996.

53. Michael Janofsky, "Women in the Marines Join the Firing Line," *New York Times,* April 1, 1997, A10.

54. Otto Kreisher, "Marines Mix Sexes in Enlisted Combat Training," Copley News Service, March 20, 1997.

55. Arthur, USN (Ret.), interview, June 13, 1996.

Chapter 11

1. RADM D. M. Williams, Jr., USN (Ret.), letter to author, April 24, 1997.

2. Richard Cohen, "Duty, Gender, Country," *Washington Post,* April 24, 1997, Op. Ed., A25.

3. Williams, letter, April 24, 1997.

4. B Gen Margaret A. Brewer, USMC (Ret.), letter to author, April 25, 1997.

5. Cpl William M. Lisbon, "First Females Graduate Marine Combat Training," *Marines* (March 1997): 5.

6. LT Michael J. Frevola, USN Reserve, "Damn the Torpedoes, Full Speed Ahead: The Argument for Total Sex Integration in the Armed Services," *Connecticut Law Review* 28 (Spring 1996): 667.

7. Tamara Jones, "The Pilot's Cloudy Future; She Was the First Woman to Fly a B-52, Then She Fell in Love and the Sky Fell In," *Washington Post,* April 29, 1997, D1.

8. "Female Pilot, Air Force Achieve a Compromise," Associated Press, *Waterloo* (*Iowa*) *Courier,* May 23, 1997, 1.

9. National Organization for Women Action Center, "NOW Action Alert: Speak Out on Lt. Flinn's Case," May 22, 1997, posted to H-MINERVA, at http://www. h-net.msu.edu, May 22, 1997.

10. U.S. Presidential Commission on the Assignment of Women in the Armed

Forces. *Report to the President: Women in Combat* (Washington, D.C.: Brassey's, 1993), Appendix C–88.

11. Presidential Commission, *Report to the President*, C-89, in MAJ Mary Finch, USA, "Women in Combat: One Commissioner Reports," paper presented at the Military Manpower Conference: A Military of Volunteers, U.S. Naval Academy, September 17, 1993, 12.

12. Rosemarie Skaine, *Power and Gender: Issues in Sexual Dominance and Harassment* (Jefferson, N.C.: McFarland, 1996), 16, 185.

13. Rosemarie Skaine, "Harassment Is a Leadership Issue," *Des Moines Register*, November 29, 1996, A13.

14. MAJ Mary Finch, USA, e-mail interview, August 15, 1996.

15. Linda Grant De Pauw, interview, March 21, 1996.

16. LTC Timothy A. Rippe, USA, interview, October 28, 1995.

17. ADM Stanley R. Arthur, USN (Ret.), telephone interview, February 8, 1996.

18. CAPT Rosemary Mariner, USN, interview, February 27, 1996.

19. *Ibid.*

20. Arthur, telephone interview, February 8, 1996.

21. *Ibid.*

22. BGen. Mike Hall, testimony before the Presidential Commission, September 11, 1992, *Report to the President*, 258–60.

23. MAJ Mary Finch, USA, interview, August 17, 1996.

24. MAJ Paul Christopher, "Women in Combat Roles?" in *Ethics and National Defense: The Timeless Issues*, edited by James C. Gaston and Janis Bren Hietala (Washington, D.C.: National Defense University Press, 1993), 232–34.

25. Skaine, *Power and Gender*, 44–46, 307–21.

26. "Army Trainers Charged with Rape of Female Soldiers," Associated Press, on CNN Interactive, U.S. News, at http://www.cnn.com., November 7, 1996.

27. MAJ Lillian A. Pfluke, USA (Ret.), "Every Day Is a Fight," *Newsweek*, November 25, 1996, 32.

28. "West Point Women Compare Past Horrors with Present," *All Things Considered*, National Public Radio, transcript #2269, segment 16, July 9, 1996.

29. *Ibid.*

30. Ruth Seifert, "War and Rape: A Preliminary Analysis," in *Mass Rape: The War Against Women in Bosnia-Herzegovina*, edited by Alexandra Stiglmayer and translated by Marion Faber (Lincoln: University of Nebraska Press, 1994), 66–67.

31. Rhonda Copelon, "Surfacing Gender: Reconceptualizing Crimes Against Women in Time of War," in *Mass Rape*, 205–06.

32. Capt. Patricia A. Gavin, USAF, posted to H-MINERVA, "H-NET List for Discussion of Women and the Military and Women in War," at http://www.h-net.msu.edu., February 11, 1997.

33. Sgt. Sharon F. Daugherty II, USA, posted to H-MINERVA, at http://www.h-net.msu.edu, March 29, 1997.

34. RADM Paul T. Gillcrist, USN (Ret.), interview, December 14, 1995.

Chapter 12

1. Ruth Leger Sivard, *Women ... a World Survey* (Washington, D.C.: World Priorities, 1995), 32, 37.

2. Col. Kelly Hamilton, USAF (Ret.), letter to Amy Talkington, 1993.

3. MAJ Paul Christopher, USA, "Women in Combat Roles?" in *Ethics and*

National Defense: The Timeless Issues, by James C. Gaston and Janis Bren Hietala (Washington, D.C.: National Defense University Press, February 1993), 223–24.

4. Mady Wechsler Segal, "Women's Military Roles Cross-Nationally: Past, Present, and Future," *Gender and Society* 9:6 (December 1995): 769.

5. Christopher Dandeker and Mady Wechsler Segal, "The Social Construction of Gender Integration in Armed Forces: Recent Policy Developments in the United Kingdom," paper presented at the World Congress of Sociology, July 22, 1994, Bielefeld, Germany; David R. Segal and Mady Wechsler Segal, "Female Combatants in Canada: An Update, *Defense Analysis* 5 (1989): 372–73; Sandra Carson Stanley and Mady Wechsler Segal, "Military Women in NATO: An Update," *Armed Forces and Society* 14, (1988): 559–85 in Mady Wechsler Segal, "Women's Military Roles Cross-Nationally: Past, Present, and Future," *Gender and Society* 9:6 (December 1995): 769.

6. U.S. Congress, House Committee on Armed Services, Military Forces and Personnel Subcommittee, *Women in Combat: Hearing Before the Military Forces and Personnel Subcommittee*, 103d Cong., 1st sess., May 12, 1993, 68.

7. MGen. Jeanne Holm, USAF (Ret.), *Women in the Military: An Unfinished Revolution*, rev. ed. (Novato, Calif.: Presidio, 1992), 508.

8. RMC Roxine C. Hart, *Women in Combat*, Research Division, Defense Equal Opportunity Management Institute, Patrick AFB, Fla., February 1991, 20.

9. Megan Craven, Jennifer Kopper, Stacey Rohrer, Category: Laws, at http://www.SchoolSucks.com/scripts/$itePass.exe?sucks/New-ShowPaper.sql/2228, December 15, 1996, 1.

10. *Ibid.*, 1–2.

11. CAPT Rosemary Bryant Mariner, USN, telephone interview, February 27, 1996.

12. RADM Paul T. Gillcrist, USN (Ret.), telephone interview, October 10, 1995.

13. U.S. Congress, House Committee on Armed Services, Military Forces and Personnel Subcommittee, *Assignment of Army and Marine Corps Women Under the New Definition of Ground Combat*, 103d Cong., 2d sess., October 6, 1994, 60–61.

14. Elisabetta Addis, "Women and Economic Consequences of Being a Soldier," and Cynthia Enloe, "The Politics of Constructing the American Women Soldier," in *Women Soldiers: Images and Realities*, edited by Elisabetta Addis, Valeria E. Russo, and Lorenza Sebesta (New York: St. Martin's, 1994), 3–27, 94, 95–104.

15. SGT Heather Lynn Johnsen in "The New Old Guard," by Kristin Patterson, *Army Times* 16:37 (April 8, 1996): 16.

16. Kristin Patterson, "The New Old Guard," *Army Times* 37 (April 8, 1996): 16.

17. SA Vanessa L. Encarnacion, USN, interview, January 20, 1997, and phone interview, April 19, 1997.

18. Molly Moore, "Open Doors Don't Yield Equality; 'Combat' Ban Symbolizes Limits to Female Advancement in Services," *Washington Post*, September 24, 1989, A1.

19. *Ibid.*

20. "Air Force Woman Set to Pilot Combat Jet (February 16/WT)," *The Washington Times*, Periscope Daily Defense News Capsules, February 16, 1994, A3.

21. Joe Sherry, "1st Female Brigadier General Retires from Reserve," *Baltimore Sun*, April 25, 1994, B3.

22. Lt Gen George R. Christmas, in U.S. Congress, House Committee on Armed Services, Military Forces and Personnel Subcommittee, *Assignment of Army and Marine Corps Women Under the New Definition of Ground Combat*, 103d Cong., 2d sess., October 6, 1994, 27–28.

23. Holm, *Women in the Military*, 270, 416, 418, 448–49.

24. Christmas, *Assignment of Army*, 23–24.

25. *Ibid.*, 33.

26. Edwin Dorn, Under Secretary of Defense, Personnel and Readiness, testimony in U.S. Congress, House Committee on Armed Services, Military Forces and Personnel Subcommittee, *Assignment of Army and Marine Corps Women Under the New Definition of Ground Combat*, 103d Cong., 2d sess., October 6, 1994, 37.

27. Francine D'Amico, posted to H-MINERVA, at http://www.h-net.msu.edu, August 2, 1996.

28. Frankie Lorence Rasmussen, posted to H-MINERVA, at http://www.h-net.msu.edu, October 28, 1996, from LCpl Teresa A. Brown, "Corps' First Female Pilot Heads to Okinawa on Unit Deployment Program," Division of Public Affairs, Headquarters, USMC, Washington, D.C., October 25, 1996.

29. Beverly B. Byron (D-Md.), congresswoman, subcommittee chair, in U.S. Congress, House Committee on Armed Services, Military Personnel and Compensation Subcommittee, *Implementation of the Repeal of the Combat Exclusion on Female Aviators*, 102d Cong., 2d sess., January 29, 1992, 2.

30. MGen. Jeanne M. Holm, USAF (Reg.), in U.S. Congress, House Committee on Armed Services, Military Personnel and Compensation Subcommittee, *Gender Discrimination in the Military*, 102d Cong., 2d sess., July 29 and 30, 1992, 15.

31. Holm, *Women in the Military*, 429–30, 489.

32. Carl M. Cannon, "President Uses Holiday to Praise U.S. Diversity, *Baltimore Sun*, May 30, 1995, Telegraph, A1.

33. "Black Woman Nominated for High U.S. Navy Posts," *Reuters North American Wire*, May 13, 1996.

34. Tom Bowman, "Flying Into the History Books," *Baltimore Sun*, October 2, 1994, B1.

35. Tom Bowman, "Navy's First Female Combat Pilot Reassigned to Cargo Jet Squadron," *Baltimore Sun*, March 1, 1995, B2.

36. "Remarks by Les Aspin, Secretary of Defense, to the Women Officers Professional Association Annual Symposium," Fort McNair Officers Club, Washington, D.C., *Federal News Service*, July 14, 1993 Defense Department Briefing.

37. *Ibid.*

38. A. Scharnhorst, "Females Ahoy!; First on Combat Ships or in Squadrons Welcome Chance to Prove Themselves," *Chicago Tribune*, August 7, 1994, Womanews, 5.

39. Bernard D. Rostker, Assistant Secretary of the Navy for Manpower and Reserve Affairs, in U.S. Congress, Senate Armed Services Committee, Subcommittee on Personnel, "Concerning Manpower and Personnel Issues," *Federal News Service*, April 8, 1997, News.

40. *Ibid.*

41. Cpl William M. Lisbon, "First Females Graduate Marine Combat Training," *Marines* (March 1997): 5.

42. LGen. Billy J. Boles, USAF, in U.S. Congress, House Committee on Armed Services, Military Personnel and Compensation Subcommittee, *Implementation of the Repeal of the Combat Exclusion on Female Aviators*, 102d Cong., 2d sess., January 29, 1992, 13.

43. Byron, U.S. Congress, House Committee, *Implementation of the Repeal*, 2.

44. Molly Moore, "Open Doors Don't Yield Equality; 'Combat' Ban Symbolizes Limits to Female Advancement in Services," *Washington Post*, September 24, 1989, A1.

45. Daniel M. Sheehan, "An Enriching Tradition," *Air Force Magazine* (June 1995): 83.

46. "Chicken Pox Targets 1st Woman Fighter Pilot," Associated Press, in *(Phoenix) Arizona Republic*, B2.

47. Ray Delgado, "First U.S. Woman Fighter Pilot Ready to Take Wing; Lt. Jeannie Flynn Bided Her Time in Flight Instructor's Course Until the Air Force's Combat Ban Was Lifted. Now She Will Fly the F-15E," *Los Angeles Times*, February 16, 1994, 5.

48. Gen. Merrill McPeak and 1st Lt. Jeannie Flynn, "Special Pentagon Briefing," Washington, D.C., Federal Information Systems Corporation, *Federal News Service*, February 15, 1994, Defense Department Briefing.

49. "Remarks by Les Aspin," *Federal News Service*, July 14, 1993.

50. Bill Bell, Jr., "On Track to Become a Fighter Pilot," *Des Moines Register*, July 21, 1996, Metro Iowa, 2.

51. Francine D'Amico, posted to H-MINERVA, at http://www.h-net.msu.edu, August 2, 1996.

52. Maj. Michael J. Petersen, USAF, "Indivisible Global Reach—Global Power," *Airlift Tanker Quarterly* 4:4 (Fall 1996): 29.

53. Maj. Philip A. Bossert, Jr., "Strategic Mobility and the Moral Imperative," *Airlift Tanker Quarterly* 4:4 (Fall 1996): 29.

54. Committee on Military Affairs and Justice, Association of the Bar of the City of New York, "The Combat Exclusion Laws: An Idea Whose Time Has Gone," May 17, 1991, 18.

55. Hamilton, letter to Amy Talkington, 1993.

56. *Ibid.*

Chapter 13

1. Muriel Rukeyser, "Effort at Speech Between Two People," in *Patterns for Living*, 3d ed., edited by Oscar J. Campbell, Justin Van Gundy, and Caroline Shrodes (New York: Macmillan, 1952), 145.

2. Richard Webb, "I Am a Soldier's Son," unpublished poem, 1997.

3. Rosemarie Skaine, *Power and Gender: Issues in Sexual Dominance and Harassment* (Jefferson, N.C.: McFarland, 1996), 83–91.

4. Bryan Strong and Christine DeVault, *The Marriage and Family Experience*, 6th ed. (St. Paul, Minn.: West, 1995), 79.

5. *Ibid.*, 96.

6. Strong and DeVault, *The Marriage and Family Experience*, 95–103; Cynthia Costello and Barbara Kivimae Krimgold, eds., *The American Woman, 1996–97*, Women's Research and Education Institute (New York: Norton, 1996), 52.

7. Strong and DeVault, *Marriage and Family Experience*, 96–103.

8. *Ibid.*, 97–98.

9. *Ibid.*, 81–82.

10. Robert V. Wells, "Demographic Change and Family Life in American History: Some Reflections," in *The Family Experience: A Reader in Cultural Diversity*, edited by Mark Hutter (New York: Macmillan, 1991), 41–62.

11. MAJ Mary Finch, USA, "Women in Combat: One Commissioner Reports," paper presented at the Military Manpower Conference: A Military of Volunteers, U.S. Naval Academy, September 17, 1993, 14–16.

12. Mady Wechsler Segal, "The Military and the Family As Greedy Institutions," *Armed Forces and Society* 13:1 (Fall 1986): 9–38.

13. Lewis A. Coser, *Greedy Institutions: Patterns of Undivided Commitment* (New York: Free Press, 1974), in Segal, "The Military and the Family," 9–38.

14. MAJ Angela Maria Manos, USA, and David R. Segal, "What Every Leader Wants to Know," Behavioral Science Research in Support of Soldiers and Their Families, Alexandria, Va., Center for Army Lessons Learned (CALL), Ft. Leavenworth, Ks., 1996, 6-7.

15. MAJ Angela M. Manos, USA, "America's Army Family: Yesterday, Today, and Tomorrow," unpublished material used at the Command and General Staff College, 1993.

16. Kris Warner, USMC, interview, August 25, 1996.

17. MAJ Angela M. Manos, "Remarks U.S. Army America's Army Family: Yesterday, Today, and Tomorrow and Army Family Team Building," unpublished slide presentation script, May 1995, 3.

18. Manos, "America's Army Family," 7.

19. *Ibid.*

20. *Ibid.*

21. *Ibid.*

22. Manos, "Remarks," 15.

23. *Ibid.*, 13.

24. Manos, "America's Army Family," 11.

25. *Ibid.*

26. *Frontiero et vir v. Richardson, Secretary of Defense, et al.*, 411 U.S. 677, U.S. Supreme Court, argued January 17, 1973, decided May 14, 1973.

27. Nancy L. Goodman, "Revolution and Peacekeeping, Trends In Family Patterns of U.S. Military Personnel During the 20th Century," in *The Social Psychology of Military Service*, edited by Nancy L. Goodman and David R. Segal, Sage Research Progress Series on War (Beverly Hills, Calif.: Sage, 1976), 8, 119, in Manos, "Remarks," 26, 34-35.

28. Mady Wechsler Segal and Jessie J. Harris, *What Leaders Need to Know About Army Families* (Alexandria, Va.: U.S. Army Research Institute for the Behavioral and Social Sciences, 1993), 4, in Manos, "America's Army Family," 16-17.

29. Zita M. Simutis, D. Bruce Bell, and Paul A. Gade, "The U.S. Army Family Research Program: How Family Programs Impact Soldier Retention and Readiness," paper presented at Defense Analysis Seminar VII, 1993, 5, in Manos, "America's Army Family," 18.

30. Walter R. Schumm, D. Bruce Bell, and Giao Q. Tran, *The Demography of Army Families: A Review of Findings*, Research Report 1642, (Alexandria, Va.: U.S. Army Research Institute for the Behavioral and Social Sciences, n.d.), 41-42, in Manos, "America's Army Family," 18.

31. Segal and Harris, *What Leaders Need*, 10, in Manos, "America's Army Family," 18.

32. K. W. Coolbaugh and A. Rosenthal, "Family Separations in the Army," Technical Report 964 (Alexandria, Va.: U.S. Army Research Institute for the Behavioral and Social Sciences, 1992), AD A258-274.

33. Manos, "Remarks," 34-35.

34. Manos, "America's Army Family," 22-23; MAJ Angela Maria Manos, USA, "The Army and Women Today," remarks to the American Red Cross Service to Military Families annual meeting, Syracuse, New York, September 28, 1995, 2.

35. Manos, "Army and Women Today," 39-59.

36. Barry Robinson, ed., *Fifty Years of Military Life: 1940–1990* (Springfield, Va.: Times Journal Co., 1990), 150, in Connie L. Reeves, "Dual-Service and Single Parents: What About the Kids?" *MINERVA: Quarterly Report on Women and the Military* XIII:3, 4 (Fall-Winter 1995): 52.

37. Reeves, "Dual-Service," 52.

38. *Ibid.*, 50–51.

39. CAPT Rosemary Mariner, USN, telephone interview, February 27, 1996.

40. Martin Binkin, "The New Force of the American Military: The Volunteer Force and the Persian Gulf War," *The Brookings Review* 9 (Summer 1991): 6–13, in Reeves, "Dual-Service," 26.

41. Linda Grant De Pauw, telephone interview, March 21, 1996.

42. Mady Wechsler Segal, "Women's Military Roles Cross-Nationally: Past, Present, and Future," *Gender and Society* 9:6 (December 1995): 761–62.

43. ADM Stanley R. Arthur, USN (Ret.), e-mail interview, August 25, 1996.

44. William Matthews, "Senate Votes Down Wider Combat Exemptions," *Air Force Times*, March 4, 1991, 16, "The Combat Exclusion Laws: An Idea Whose Time Has Gone," May 17, 1991, in Committee on Military Affairs and Justice, Association of the Bar of the City of New York, 48, in Connie L. Reeves, "Dual-Service" *MINERVA*, 26–29.

45. Rick Maze, "McPeak, Navy Chief Backs Exempting Infants' Mothers," *Air Force Times*, April 1, 1991, 6, in Reeves, "Dual-Service" *MINERVA*, 28.

46. Reeves, "Dual-Service" 44–51.

47. *Ibid.*, 31–34.

48. Manos and Segal, "What Every Leader," 18–20.

49. Patricia M. Shields, "Sex Roles in the Military," in *The Military: More Than Just a Job?* edited by Charles C. Moskos and Frank R. Wood (Mclean, Va.: Pergamon-Brassey's, 1988), in Reeves, "Dual-Service" *MINERVA*, 43.

50. MAJ Mary Finch, USA, interview, August 17, 1997.

51. MAJ Jane McKeon, USA (Ret.), telephone interview, August 12, 1996.

52. U.S. Army, *All Ranks Update, AR 614–30, Overseas Assignment*, 1990, 10, 27, in Reeves, "Dual-Service," *MINERVA*, 56–57.

53. MGen. Jeanne Holm, USAF (Ret.), *Women in the Military: An Unfinished Revolution*, rev. ed. (Novato, Calif.: Presidio, 1992), 101.

54. Matthews, "Senate Votes Down," in Reeves, "Dual Service," *MINERVA*, 55.

55. Gen C. C. Krulak, Commandant of the U.S. Marine Corps, "Comments on the Contribution of Women," n.d., 1, in Lt Gen W. E. Boomer, Commanding General, I Marine Expeditionary Force, letter to Gen A. M. Gray, Commandant of the Marine Corps, March 30, 1991, 1–2, enclosure 3.

56. "Pregnancy Rate of Unit in Bosnia Hits Army Average; About 5% of U.S. Female Troops Reassigned Because of Maternity," Bradley Graham, *Washington Post*, July 23, 1996, A15.

57. B Gen J. A. Brabham, letter, March 28, 1991, 1, in Lt Boomer, letter to Gen A. M. Gray, 1–2, enclosure 2.

58. Manos, "Remarks," 4.

Chapter 14

1. Accident Mishap Board, *F-14A Mishap Investigation Report* (MIR), Military City Online, March 1995, (6), Personnel.

2. Jean Zimmerman, *Tailspin: Women at War in the Wake of Tailhook* (New York: Doubleday, 1995), xvi.

3. Michael Janofsky, "Women in the Marines Join the Firing Line, *New York Times*, April 1, 1997, A10.

4. *Ibid.*

5. Cpl William M. Lisbon, "First Females Graduate Marine Combat Training," *Marines* (March 1997): 5.

6. Col. Kelly Hamilton, USAF (Ret.), letter home, January 7, 1991.

7. MAJ Mary Finch, USA, interviews during 1996.

8. "Remarks by Defense Secretary William Cohen at Department of Defense Ceremony Held in Observance of Women's History Month, the Pentagon," *Federal News Service*, March 24, 1997.

Appendix A

1. Based in part on Cynthia Costello and Barbara Kivimae Krimgold, eds., *The American Woman, 1996–97*, Women's Research and Education Institute (New York: Norton, 1996), 177–245.

Appendix B

1. Based on Carolyn Becraft, "Women in the U.S. Armed Services: The War in the Persian Gulf," Women's Research and Education Institute, Washington, D.C., March 1991. All quotes in this section are from Becraft.

2. Elaine Donnelly, in U.S. Congress, House Committee on Armed Services, Military Forces and Personnel Subcommittee, *Assignment of Army and Marine Corps Women Under the New Definition of Ground Combat*, 103d Congress, 2d sess., October 6, 1994, attachment to testimony, 67–68.

Appendix C

1. Headquarters, Department of the Army, "The Soldier's Creed," *Soldier's Handbook*, January 1, 1993, ii.

2. Headquarters, Department of the Army, "Code of Conduct," *Soldier's Handbook*, January 1, 1993, 66.

Bibliography

Accident Mishap Board. *F-14A Mishap Investigation Report (MIR)*, March 1995. Military City Online.

Addis, Elisabetta. "Women and Economic Consequences of Being a Soldier." In *Women Soldiers: Images and Realities*, edited by Elisabetta Addis, Valeria E. Russo, and Lorenza Sebesta. New York: St. Martin's, 1994.

"The Airlift/Tanker Hall of Fame." Special convention edition, *Airlift/Tanker Quarterly* 4:4 (Fall 1996): 8–9.

Allen, Beverly. *Rape Warfare: The Hidden Genocide in Bosnia-Herzegovina and Croatia.* Minneapolis: University of Minnesota Press, 1996.

American Forces Information Service (AFIS/OATSD-PA). *Current News Early Bird*, January 14, 1994.

Aristotle. *Generation of Animals*. Rev. ed. Translated by A. L. Peck. London: W. Heinemann, 1963.

_____. *The Politics of Aristotle*. Translated by Ernest Barker. Oxford: Clarendon Press, 1946.

Arthur, ADM Stanley R., USN, former Vice Chief of Naval Operations. Statement before National Security Subcommittee of the House Appropriations Committee, April 6, 1995. Federal Document Clearing House. Congressional Testimony, April 5 and 6, 1995.

_____. Interview, 1996; Telephone interviews, 1996.

Aspin, Les, Secretary of Defense. Memorandum on policy, "The Assignment of Women in the Armed Forces." Directed to all of the Services. April 28, 1993.

_____. Memorandum for Secretaries of the Army, Navy and Air Force; Chairman, Joint Chiefs of Staff; Assistant Secretary of Defense (SECDEF) (Personnel and Readiness), and Assistant SECDEF (Reserve Affairs). "Direct Ground Combat Definition and Assignment Rule," January 13, 1994.

_____. Letter to The Honorable Ike Skelton, chair, Military Forces and Personnel Subcommittee. House Committee on Armed Services, May 11, 1993. In U.S. Congress. House Committee on Armed Services. *Women in Combat: Hearing Before the Military Forces and Personnel Subcommittee.* 103d Cong., 1st sess., May 12, 1993.

Aspin, Les, chair, Defense Policy Panel, and Beverly B. Byron, chair, Military Personnel and Compensation Subcommittee. House Committee on Armed Services. *Women in the Military: The Tailhook Affair and the Problem of Sexual Harassment Report.* Washington, D.C.: GPO, 1992, 1–121.

Barbier v. Connolly. Supreme Court of the United States, 113 U.S. 27; 5 Sup. Ct. 357;

1885. U.S. Lexis 1647; 28 L. Ed. 923. Submitted November 25, 1884. Decided January 5, 1885.

Barkalow, CAPT Carol, with Andrea Raab. *In the Men's House*. New York: Poseidon, 1990.

Barnes, Susan. H-MINERVA. "H-NET List for Discussion of Women and the Military and Women in War." Posted June 26, 1996. http://www.h-net.msu.edu.

Becraft, Carolyn. *Women in the U.S. Armed Services: The War in the Persian Gulf.* Women's Research and Education Institute, Washington, D.C., March 1991.

Berger, Peter L. *Invitation to Sociology: A Humanistic Perspective*. Garden City, N.Y.: Doubleday, 1963.

Bigler, Philip. *In Honored Glory: Arlington National Cemetery, The Final Post*. 2d ed., Arlington, Va.: Vandamere, 1994.

Blanton, DeAnne. "Cathay Williams: Black Woman Soldier (1866–1868)," *MINERVA: Quarterly Report on Women and the Military* X:3, 4. (Fall-Winter 1992): 1–12.

Boomer, Lt Gen W. E. Letter to Gen A. M. Gray, Commandant of the Marine Corps, March 30, 1991, 1–2. Enclosures 4: (1) Memorandum from Maj Gen Wiliam M. Keys, Commanding General, 2d Marine Division, May 29, 1991, with 2 enclosures: (a) The Women Marines of Headquarters Battalion, March 29, 1991, 1–2, (b) The Women Marines of 10 Marines, March 27, 1991, 1–2; (2) Letter from B Gen J. A. Brabham, Commanding General, 1st Force Service Support Group, March 28, 1991, 1; (3) Comments on the Contribution of Women from B Gen C. C. Krulak, Commanding General, 2d Force Service Support Group, n.d., 1; (4) Comments on the Contribution of Women from the Staff of Command Element, I Marine Expeditionary Force, n.d., 1–3.

Borkholder, Philip L. Prepared testimony before the House Appropriations Committee, VA, HUD, and Independent Agencies Subcommittee. *Federal News Service*, May 10, 1996. Sect. In the News Section.

Bossert, Maj. Philip A., Jr. "Strategic Mobility and the Moral Imperative." Special convention edition, *Airlift/Tanker Quarterly* 4:4 (Fall 1996): 29.

Bradwell v. Illinois. Supreme Court of the United States, 83 U.S. 130 (1872). U.S. Lexis 1140; 21 L. Ed. 442, December 1872, Term.

Brewer, B Gen Margaret A., USMC (Ret.). Written interview, April 25, 1997.

Brower, J. Michael. "The Mother of All Future Debates: Women in Combat." *MINERVA: Quarterly Report on Woman and the Military* XIV:3, 4 (Fall-Winter, 1996): 1–10.

_____. "New Army Study Undermines Old Taboo." Posted to H-MINERVA, July 11, 1996. http://www.h-net.msu.edu.

_____. "Undermining Old Taboos." *Armed Forces Journal International*, May 1996. http://www.afji.com/Mags/1996/undermining.html.

Brown, LCpl Teresa A. "Corps' First Female Pilot Heads to Okinawa on Unit Deployment Program." Division of Public Affairs, Headquarters, U.S. Marine Corps, Washington, D.C., October 25, 1996. Posted by Frankie Lorence Rasmussen on H-MINERVA, October 28, 1996. http://www.h-net.msu.edu.

Brownmiller, Susan. *Against Our Will: Men, Women and Rape*. New York: Simon and Schuster, 1975.

Burgess, Lauren Cook. "'Typical' Soldier May Have Been Red-Blooded American Woman; Secret Buried With Many in Blue Gray." *The Washington Times*, October 5, 1991, B3.

Burgess, Lauren Cook, ed. *An Uncommon Soldier: The Civil War Letters of Sarah Rosetta Wakeman, alias Private Lyons Wakeman, 153rd Regiment, N.Y. State Volunteers*. Pasadena, Md.: The MINERVA Center, 1994.

Burns, Ken, and John Colby. *The Civil War: Original Soundtrack Recording*. Elektra Entertainment, Columbia House, 1990. Side Two.

Caciola, Nancy. "Performance and Gender." Medieval Masculinities Discussion Archive. Week Two. Georgetown Online, October 28, 1995, 9–10. http://www.georgetown.edu/labyrinth/e-center/interscripta/archive 2.html.

Callahan, Daniel. "How Shall We Incorporate Ethics Instruction at All Levels?" In *Ethics and National Defense: The Timeless Issues*, by James C. Gaston and Janis Bren Hietala, 135–44. Washington, D.C.: National Defense University Press, 1993.

Campbell v. Beaughler. 519 F.2d 1307, 1308 (9th Cir. 1975), *cert. denied*, 423 U.S. 1073 (1976).

Center for Military Readiness (CMR). *V.I.P. Notes*, CMR *Insider News and Views*. Livonia, Mich., July 20, 1996, 1, 3.

Chandler v. Callaway. No. C-741249 RHS, at 2 (N.D. Calif. November 1, 1974).

Christopher, MAJ Paul, USA. "Women in Combat Roles?" In *Ethics and National Defense: The Timeless Issues*, by James C. Gaston and Janis Bren Hietala, 223–36. Washington, D.C.: National Defense University Press, 1993.

Citadel Board of Visitors. "The Citadel Approved Plan for Assimilation of Female Cadets." Memorandum for Lt. Gen. Claudius E. Watts III, July 30, 1996.

Clinton, Hillary Rodham. "Women's Rights Are Human Rights." Speech delivered by First Lady Rodham Clinton at the UN Fourth World Conference on Women in Beijing, China, September 5, 1995. *Vital Speeches* 61:24 (October 1, 1995): 738ff.

Cohen, Leonard. "Songs of Love and Hate" and "Joan of Arc." Excite, Britannica Online. Sponsored by Sun Microsystems, Inc., Mt. Vicie, Calif. Architext Software, Netscape, copyright 1995.

Committee on Military Affairs and Justice. Association of the Bar of the City of New York. "The Combat Exclusion Laws: An Idea Whose Time Has Gone," May 17, 1991.

_____. "Equality for Women in Combat Aviation: Addressing Whether the Response of the Executive Branch to Public Law 102–190, The Legislative Repeal of the Combat Exclusion Laws for Women Aviators, Violates the Equal Protection Guarantees of the Fifth Amendment, October 26, 1992.

Conover, Pamela Johnston, and Virginia Sapiro. "Gender, Feminist Consciousness, and War." *American Journal of Political Science* 37:4 (November 1993): 1079–99.

Coolbaugh, K. W., and A. Rosenthal. "Family Separations in the Army." Technical Report 964. Alexandria, Va., U.S. Army Research Institute for the Behavioral and Social Sciences (AD A258–274). In "America's Army Family: Yesterday, Today, and Tomorrow," by MAJ Angela M. Manos, USA. Unpublished material used at the Command and General Staff College, 1993.

Copelon, Rhonda. "Surfacing Gender: Reconceptualizing Crimes Against Women in Time of War." In *Mass Rape: The War Against Women in Bosnia-Herzegovina*, edited by Alexandra Stiglmayer and translated by Marion Faber, 197–218. Lincoln: University of Nebraska Press, 1994.

Coser, Lewis A. *The Functions of Social Conflict*. New York: Free Press, 1964.

Costello, Cynthia, and Barbara Kivimae Krimgold, eds. *The American Woman, 1996–97*. Women's Research and Education Institute. New York: Norton, 1996.

Coughlin, LT Paula A., USN. Letter to The Honorable John H. Dalton, Secretary of the Navy, Washington, D.C., February 7, 1994.

Craven, Megan, Jennifer Kopper, and Stacey Rohrer. Category: Laws. December 15, 1996, 1–2. http://www.SchoolSucks.com/scripts/$itePass.exe?sucks\New=Show-Paper. sql/2228.

Crawford v. Cushman. 531 F. 2d 114 (2d Cir. 1976).

D'Amico, Francine. "Feminist Perspectives on Women Warriors." *Peace Review* 8:3 (September 1996): 379–84.

De Pauw, Linda Grant. *Baptism of Fire*. Pasadena, Md.: The MINERVA Center, 1993.

_____. *Battle Cries and Lullabies: A Brief History of Women in War*. Norman: University of Oklahoma, 1998.

_____. Interview, 1996; E-mail interviews, 1996, 1997; Telephone interviews, 1996.

Deere, Lt M. JAG, USN. Point paper, 1300, 131.2/4–1781, 1991. Department of Defense (DOD). Office of Assistant Secretary of Defense (Public Affairs). "Secretary of Defense Aspin Expects to Open New Opportunities for Women with New Direct Ground Combat Rule." News release, Washington, D.C., January 13, 1994.

Devilbliss, M. C. "Gender Integration and Unit Deployment: A Study of GI Jo." *Armed Forces and Society* 11:4 (Summer 1985): 523–52.

Diprose, Rosalyn. *The Bodies of Women: Ethics, Embodiment and Sexual Difference*. New York: Routledge, 1994.

Dobbs, Darrell. "Family Matters: Aristotle's Appreciation of Women and the Plural Structure of Society." *American Political Science Review* 90:1 (March 1996): 74–88.

Dvir, Taly, Dov Eden, and Michael Lang Banjo. "Self-Fulfilling Prophecy and Gender: Can Women Be Pygmalion and Galatea?" *Journal of Applied Psychology* 80:2 (1995): 253–70.

Earley, Charity Adams. *One Woman's Army: A Black Officer Remembers the WAC*. College Station: Texas A and M University Press, 1989.

Ebbert, Jean, and Marie-Beth Hall. *Cross Currents: Navy Women from World War I to Tailhook*. Washington, D.C.: Brassey's, 1993.

Encarnacion, SA Vanessa L., USN. Interview, 1997; Telephone interviews, 1997.

Feller, LTC Carolyn M., ANC, USA, and MAJ Constance J. Moore, ANC. *Highlights in the History of the Army Nurse Corps*. Rev. and exp. ed. Washington, D.C.: U.S. Army Center of Military History, 1995. CMH Pub 85–1.

Ferguson v. Skrupa. 372 U.S. 726 (1963).

Finch, MAJ Mary, USA. "Women in Combat: One Commissioner Reports." Paper presented at the Military Manpower Conference: A Military of Volunteers. U.S. Naval Academy, September 17, 1993.

_____. Telephone interviews, 1996; E-mail interviews, 1996.

Fowler, William M., Jr. "Relief on the River: The *Red Rover*." *Naval History* (Fall 1991).

Frank, MAJ Mary E. V., ANC. *Army and Navy Nurses Held As Prisoners of War During World War II*. Office of the Assistant Secretary of Defense, Manpower, Installations and Logistics, April 1985.

Freivogel, William H. "An Empty Room with a View." *St. Louis Post-Dispatch*, September 25, 1995, B15.

Frevola, LT Michael J., USN Reserve. "Damn the Torpedoes, Full Speed Ahead: The Argument for Total Sex Integration in the Armed Services." *Connecticut Law Review* 28 (Spring 1996): 621–67.

Frontiero et vir v. Richardson, Secretary of Defense, et al. No. 71–1694. 411 U.S. 677 (1973). Supreme Court of the United States. Argued January 17, 1973. Decided May 14, 1973.

Gaston, James C., and Janis Bren Hietala. *Ethics and National Defense: The Timeless Issues*. Washington, D.C.: National Defense University Press, 1993.

Gies, Frances. *Joan of Arc: The Legend and the Reality*. New York: Harper and Row, 1981.

Gillcrist, RADM Paul T., USN (Ret.). *Feet Wet: Reflections of a Carrier Pilot*. New York: Pocket Books, 1990.

_____. *Tomcat! The Grumman F-14 Story*. Atglen, Pa.: Schiffer, 1994.

_____. *Vulture's Row: Thirty Years in Naval Aviation*. Atglen, Pa.: Schiffer, 1996.

_____. Telephone interviews, 1995–98; Letters and e-mail to author 1995–98.

Ginsburg, Justice Ruth Bader. Delivering the opinion of the Supreme Court of the United States. Nos. 94–1941 and 94–2107. *United States of America*, Petitioner, 94–1941, *v. Commonwealth of Virginia, et al. Commonwealth of Virginia, et al.*, Petitioners, 94–2107, *v. United States of America.* On writs of certiorari to the U.S. Court of Appeals for the Fourth Circuit, June 26, 1996.

Goffman, Erving. *Asylums.* New York: Doubleday, 1961.

Goodman, Nancy L. "Revolution and Peacekeeping, Trends in Family Patterns of U.S. Military Personnel During the 20th Century." In *The Social Psychology of Military Service*, edited by Nancy L. Goodman and David R. Segal, 6. Beverly Hills, Calif.: Sage, 1976.

Goldman v. Weinberger. 475 U.S. 503 (1986).

Gutman, Roy. Foreword to *Mass Rape: The War Against Women in Bosnia-Herzegovina*, edited by Alexandra Stiglmayer and translated by Marion Faber. Lincoln: University of Nebraska Press, 1994.

Hall, BGen. Mike. Testimony before the U.S. Presidential Commission on the Assignment of Women in the Armed Forces, September 11, 1992. *Report to the President: Women in Combat*, 234–61.

Hall, Richard. *Patriots in Disguise: Women Warriors of the Civil War.* 1st ed. New York: Paragon House, 1993.

Hallisey, MAJ Christine, and BG R. Dennis Kerr. "Women in the Army." Information paper, Deputy Chief of Staff of the Army for Personnel–Human Resources (DAPE-HR-S), September 19, 1994, 1–3.

Hamilton, Col. Kelly, USAF (Ret.). Telephone interview, 1996; Letters and e-mail to author 1996–98.

_____. Letter to Amy Talkington, 1993.

_____. Letters home, October 20, 1990; December 5, 1990; January 7, 1991; January 15, 1991; and January 23, 1991.

Hanes, Mary L. "Fact Sheet, U.S. Army Women in Vietnam." Courtesy of Women in Military Service for America Memorial Foundation, Inc. (WIMSA), Washington, D.C., 1–2.

Hart, RMC Roxine C. *Women in Combat.* Research Division, Defense Equal Opportunity Management Institute, Patrick AFB, Fla., February 1991.

Hemphill, Holly K., chair, 1996 Defense Advisory Committee on Women in the Services (DACOWITS). Interview, 1996.

Higginson, Thomas Wentworth. *Army Life in a Black Regiment.* New York: Longmans, Green, 1869.

Hill v. Berkman. 635 F. Supp. 1228, 1238 (E.D.N.Y. 1986).

Hilsdon, Anne-Marie. "From Civilian to Military: Bodily Transformations and Transgressions in Philippine Militaries." *MINERVA: Quarterly Report on Women and the Military* XIV:3, 4 (Fall-Winter 1996): 69–126.

H-MINERVA. "H-NET List for Discussion of Women and the Military and Women in War," 1996, 1997. http://www.h-net.msu.edu.

Holm, MGen. Jeanne, USAF (Ret.). *Women in the Military: An Unfinished Revolution.* Rev. ed. Novato, Calif.: Presidio, 1992.

Iowa Democratic Activist Women's Network. November 11, 1995, Newton, Iowa.

IoWoman 26:1 (January-February 1996): 1.

Jennings, Eric. "'Reinventing Jeanne': The Iconology of Joan of Arc in Vichy Schoolbooks, 1940–44." *Journal of Contemporary History* 29 (1994): 711–34.

Jennings, Marianne Moody. "Women Ask, 'Is This All There Is?'" *(Phoenix) Arizona Republic*, September 17, 1995, F3.

Johnsen, SGT Heather Lynn. In "The New Old Guard," by Kristin Patterson. *Army Times*, no. 37 (April 8, 1996), 16.

Jones, James E., Jr. Memorandum for Lt. Gen. Claudius E. Watts III, July 30, 1996. "Plan for Assimilation of Female Cadets into the South Carolina Corps of Cadets."

Judge Advocate General (JAG) Investigation Report, USN. "F-14A Aircraft Accident on 25 October 1994 That Resulted in the Death of LT Kara S. Hultgreen, USN, and Injury of LT Matthew P. Klemish, USN, 14 February 1995."

Keating, CAPT T. D., JAGC, USN. Memorandum for Director, Officer and Enlisted Personnel Management, June 12, 1991.

Kelley, CAPT. P. W., OJAG, USN. Memorandum to CAPT T. D. Keating, JAGC, USN, November 24, 1993, memorandum from OJAG staff, November 23, 1993, 1–2 of 7. 5 Enclosures: Enclosure (1)—Papers from file entitled "DOD Response to Draft Registration Questions by Senator Sam Nunn." Col. Kenneth A. Deutsch. Memorandum to CAPT T. D. Keating, July 2, 1991, 3 of 7; Transcript from Hearing on Women in the Military, June 18, 1991, 4 of 7 – 7 of 7. Enclosure (2)—draft point paper, "10 U.S. Code 6015—Combat Exclusion," 6–7. Enclosure (3)—Lists of Tabs within Code 13 Subj. File: "Women in Combat—Historical Workproduct," 1–8. Enclosure (4)—Les Aspin, Secretary of Defense, memorandum, "Policy on the Assignment of Women in the Armed Forces," April 28, 1993, 1–2. Enclosure (5)—Spring 1993 bullets on "Women in Combat" and copies of memoranda for ASD (FMP) and ASN (M&RA), 1–4.

_____. Memorandum to Chair, Women in Combat Aviation Working Group. October 18, 1991, 1–4, enclosures.

Kelly, Karla R. "The Combat Exclusion: Withstanding Challenge." Working manuscript, April 28, 1983, 1–50, plus enclosure.

Kilian, Michael. "A Becoming Legend; Bright and Shining, LT Hultgreen Deserved Better." *Chicago Tribune*, March 12, 1995, Tempo Section, 6.

Kovach v. Middendorf. 424 F. Supp. 72 (D. Del. 1976).

Krulak, Gen Charles, Commandant of the Marine Corps. Testimony before the Senate Armed Service Committee, Readiness Subcommittee, March 14, 1996. *Federal News Service*, March 15, 1996.

Kuenning, MAJ H. F., USA. "Small Wars and Morally Sound Strategy." In *Ethics and National Defense: The Timeless Issues*, by James C. Gaston and Janis Bren Hietala, 187–222. Washington, D.C.: National Defense University Press, 1993.

Kulp, Tim. On CNN, *Burden of Proof.* Hosted by Greta Van Susteren and Roger Cossack. Transcript # 96122601V12, December 26, 1996.

Langguth, A. J. *Patriots: The Men Who Started the American Revolution.* New York: Simon and Schuster, 1988.

Larson, C. Kay. *'Til I Come Marching Home: A Brief History of American Women in World War II.* Pasadena, Md.: The MINERVA Center, 1995.

Lawrence, VADM William P., USN (Ret.). "The Commission." *Proceedings of the U.S. Naval Institute* 119:2 (February 1993): 48–51.

Ledvina, CDR Thomas N., JAGC, USN. Telecopier Transmittal Sheet, June 10, 1991. Memorandum on Proposed Legislation re Women in Combat, to Ledvina, June 8, 1991.

Lee, COL Barbara. Telephone interview, 1996.

Lewis v. U.S. Army. 697 F. Supp. 1385, 1393 (E.D. Pa. 1988).

Lieberman, Jeanne M. "Women in Combat." *Federal Bar News and Journal* 37:1 (May 1990): 215–22.

Linderman, Gerald F. *Embattled Courage: The Experience of Combat in the American Civil War.* New York: Free Press, 1987.

Lindsay, Thomas K. "Was Aristotle Racist, Sexist, and Anti-Democratic? A Review Essay." *Review of Politics* 56:1 (Winter 1994): 127–51.

Lindsley v. Natural Carbonic Gas Co. No. 260, Supreme Court of the United States, 220 U.S. 61; 31 Sup. Ct. 337; 1911. U.S. Lexis 1661; 55 L.Ed. 369. Argued January 3 and 4, 1911. Decided March 13, 1911.

Lisbon, Cpl William M. "First Females Graduate Marine Combat Training." *Marines* (March 1997): 5.

Lister, Sara E. Memorandum for the Secretary of the Army. "Application of DOD Policy in the Assignment of Women," June 13, 1994, 1–4.

Lounsbery, Harriet Camp. "Order of Spanish-American War Nurses." *Trained Nurse and Hospital Review* 23 (1899): 80–81.

McCullough, Joseph. Telephone interview, 1996.

McGrath, James H. "The Officer's Oath: Words That Bind." In *Ethics and National Defense: The Timeless Issues*, by James C. Gaston and Janis Bren Hietala, 17–33. Washington, D.C.: National Defense University Press, 1993.

McKeon, MAJ Jane, USA (Ret.). Telephone interview, 1996.

MacKinnon, Catharine A. "Turning Rape into Pornography: Postmodern Genocide." In *Mass Rape: The War Against Women in Bosnia-Herzegovina*, edited by Alexandra Stiglmayer and translated by Marion Faber, 73–81. Lincoln: University of Nebraska Press, 1994.

McManus, LTC Karen. "Women in the Army Policy Update." *Army Women's Professional Association*, March 26, 1996.

McPeak, Gen. Merrill, and 1st Lt. Jeannie Flynn. "Special Pentagon Briefing." *Federal News Service*, February 15, 1994, Defense Department Briefing Section.

Maller, Danna. Interview, 1996.

Manos, MAJ Angela M., USA. "America's Army Family: Yesterday, Today, and Tomorrow." Unpublished material used at the Command and General Staff College, 1993.

_____. "The Army and Women Today." Remarks to the American Red Cross Service to Military Families Annual Meeting. Syracuse, N.Y., September 28, 1995.

_____. "Remarks U.S. Army America's Army Family: Yesterday, Today, and Tomorrow and Army Family Team Building." Unpublished slide presentation script, May 1995.

_____. Interview, 1996.

Manos, MAJ Angela Maria, USA, and David R. Segal. "What Every Leader Wants to Know." Behavioral Science Research in Support of Soldiers and Their Families, Alexandria, Va.; Center for Army Lessons Learned (CALL), Ft. Leavenworth, Ks.; 1996.

Marechal-Workman, Andrée. "Margaret (Peggy) Nash Speaks of her Experience as a World War II POW." Essay. Courtesy of Women in the Military Service for America Memorial Foundation, Inc. (WIMSA), September 10, 1992.

Mariner, CAPT Rosemary Bryant, USN. "A Soldier Is a Soldier." *Joint Force Quarterly* 3 (Winter 1993–94): 54–61.

_____. Interview, 1996.

Massey, Mary Elizabeth. *Bonnet Brigades*. New York: Alfred A. Knopf, 1966.

Matterer, James L. "Jeanne La Pucelle and the Dying God." Posted to http://www.contrib.andrew.cmu.edu/~sca/src/contributed/yapm97a@prodigy.com/jnofarc.html. Verified March 21, 1997.

Matthews, William. "Senate Votes Down Wider Combat Exemptions." *Air Force Times*, March 4, 1991, 16.

Milko, James D. "Beyond the Persian Gulf Crisis: Expanding the Role of the Servicewomen in the United States Military." *American University Law Review* 41 (Summer 1992): 1302–37.

Miller, B Gen G. L. "Historical Perspective of Women in Combat Legislation." Information Paper, 5800 JAR\9501. Headquarters. U.S. Marine Corps. NAVMC HQ–335 (REV. 5–89), June 14, 1991, 1–5.

———. "Point Paper, Subj. Women in Combat." 1300 Ser JAR/9454. Judge Advocate Division. Headquarters. U.S. Marine Corps, May 29, 1991, 1–2.

MINERVA: Quarterly Report on Women and the Military IX:4 (Winter 1991): 1–55.

Mississippi University for Women v. Hogan. 458 U.S. 718 (1981).

Mitchell, Brian. *Weak Link: The Feminization of the American Military.* Washington, D.C.: Regnery Gateway, 1989.

Moore, LTG Harold G., USA (Ret.), and Joseph L. Galloway. *We Were Soldiers Once … and Young—Ia Drang: The Battle That Changed the War in Vietnam.* New York: Random House, 1992.

"More Criticism of the AX and F/A-18 Upgrade Services," *Navy News & Undersea Technology* 9:9 (March 2, 1992): 1.

Morin, Lt Col Greg. Interview, 1996.

Myles, Bruce. *Night Witches, The Untold Story of Soviet Women in Combat.* Novato, Calif.: Presidio, 1981.

Navy News & Undersea Technology 9:9 (March 2, 1992): 1.

Norman, Elizabeth M., and Sharon Eifried. "How Did They All Survive? An Analysis of American Nurses' Experiences in Japanese Prisoner-of-War Camps." *Nursing History Review* 3 (1995): 105–27.

Office of Assistant Secretary of Defense (Public Affairs). "Secretary of Defense Perry Approves Plans to Open New Jobs for Women in the Military." News release, no. 449–94, July 29, 1994, 1.

Owens v. Brown, 455 F. Supp. 291 (D.C. D.C. 1978).

Parks, CAPT Larry G., Assistant JAG. Memorandum prepared April 11, 1975, for the Chief of Information (OI 210). "Physical Qualifications of Women Naval Aviators." JAG:131.3:PLJ:sba, Ser: 3828, April 14, 1975, enclosure 1, 1–5. Proposed reply letter to R. E. Smith, Ph.D. JAG:131.3:PLJ:sba, February 25, 1975, 1–2. CNO Routing Slip Control No. 5u23287 to NOP–007, 1. R. E. Smith, Ph.D., letter to CNO, February 25, 1975, and attachment, "The Stormy Life of Navy Pilot Judy Neuffer," *Parade,* October 13, 1974, 12, 17.

Patterson, Kristin. "The New Old Guard." *Army Times,* no. 37 (April 8, 1996): 16.

Pennington, Reina, ed. *Military Women Worldwide: A Biographical Dictionary.* Forthcoming, Greenwood Press. Posted to H-MINERVA, December 29, 1996. http://www.h-net.msu.edu.

Perry, William J., Secretary of Defense. "Application of the Definition of Direct Ground Combat and Assignment Rule." Memorandum for the Secretaries of the Army, Navy, Air Force, and Under Secretary of Defense (Personnel and Readiness), July 28, 1994.

———. Letter to The Honorable Sam Nunn (D-Ga.), chair, Senate Committee on the Armed Services, July 28, 1994.

Petersen, Maj. Michael J., USAF. "Indivisible Global Reach—Global Power." *Airlift/Tanker Quarterly* 4:4 (Fall 1996): 29.

Pfluke, MAJ Lillian A., USA (Ret.). "Chronology of Recent History to Open Combat Roles." Correspondence with author, July 29, 1996.

———. "Combat Bans Force Army Women Behind." *Army Times,* November 22, 1993.

———. "Direct Ground Combat in Bosnia—Clear as Mud." *MINERVA's Bulletin Board* IX:1 (Spring 1996): 10–11.

_____. "Every Day Is a Fight." *Newsweek*, November 25, 1996, 32.

_____. "Question: Will Combat Roles for Women Downgrade Military Readiness? No: Women Have Proved They Can Do the Job." *The Washington Times*, May 8, 1985, Part Symposium, 21.

_____. "Some Ideas Are As Outmoded As the Horse Cavalry." *Army Times*, May 2, 1994, 10.

_____. Testimony to the U.S. Presidential Commission on the Assignment of Women in the Armed Forces. September 12, 1992, Washington, D.C. Referred to in *Report to the President: Women in Combat*. Washington: Brassey's, 1993, Appendix F–18.

_____. Telephone interviews, 1996–98; Letters and e-mail to author 1996–98.

Pine, Art. "U.S. Missiles to Be Re-Aimed at Distant Seas." *Los Angeles Times*, Washington edition, January 13, 1994, 1, 14. In American Forces Information Service (AFIS/OATSD-PA), *Current News Early Bird*, Arlington, Va. January 14, 1994, 1, 5.

Plato, *The Republic*. Translated by Paul Shorey. London: W. Heinemann, 1930–35.

"Protocol Additional to the Geneva Conventions of 12 August 1949, and Relating to the Protection of Victims of International Armed Conflicts (Protocol I)." Part I, Article 12—Protection of Medical Units. In *Documents on the Laws of War*, edited by Adam Roberts and Richard Guelff, 397–98. New York: Clarendon Press, 1982.

R. S. Royster Guano Co. v. Virginia. 253 U.S. 412 (1920).

Raby, Lt. Col. Kenneth A. "Flight Training for Women." December 1, 1972, DAJA-AL 1972/5294, CMT2, LTC Raby/kd/74088.

Raymond, CPT A. Dwight, USA. "Soldiers, Unjust Wars, and Treason." In *Ethics and National Defense: The Timeless Issues*, by James C. Gaston, and Janis Bren Hietala, 57–71. Washington, D.C.: National Defense University Press, 1993.

Rees, John. "'The Multitude of Women,' An Examination of the Numbers of Female Camp Followers with the Continental Army." *MINERVA: Quarterly Report on Women and the Military* XIV:2 (Summer 1996): 1–47.

Reeves, Connie L. "Dual-Service and Single Parents: What About the Kids?" *MINERVA: Quarterly Report on Women and the Military* XIII:3, 4 (Fall-Winter 1995): 52.

Rehnquist, Chief Justice William H. Supreme Court of the United States. Concurring opinion. 94–1941 and 94–2107. *United States v. Commonwealth of Virginia*, June 26, 1996.

Rejali, Darius M. "After Feminist Analyses of Bosnia Violence." *Peace Review* 8:3 (September 1996): 365–71.

Report of Commission of Experts to the Secretary-General of the UN. October 1992, First Interim Report (S/25274), 55, 56, 130–32, 142–43, 147–48, 251–53. In *Rape Warfare: The Hidden Genocide in Bosnia-Herzegovina and Croatia*, by Beverly Allen. Minneapolis: University of Minnesota Press, 1996.

Rippe, LTC Timothy A., USA. Interviews, 1995–96.

Robertson, Adam, and Richard Guelff, eds. *Documents on the Law of War*. New York: Clarendon, 1982.

Robertson, RADM H. B. Jr., JAGC, USN. Letter to VADM Robert B. Baldwin, USN, Commander, Naval Air Force, U.S. Pacific Fleet, May 23, 1974, 1–2. Enclosure memorandum for the Secretary of the Navy, "Navy Women in Aircraft." Prepared by Captain J. M. Tompkins, USMC Reserve, May 31, 1973, JAG:131.4:JMT:cck, Ser: 4631, June 1, 1973, 1–3. CAPT E.R. Fink, Memorandum on Women in the Navy, JAG:14:ERF:vme, May 25, 1973, 1. CDR William C. Lynch, JAGC, USN, Memorandum for the JAG, Navy Women in Aircraft, May 17, 1973, 1.

Rogan, Helen. *Mixed Company: Women in the Modern Army*. New York: G. P. Putnam's Sons, 1981.

Rogers, Robin. "Comment: A Proposal for Combating Sexual Discrimination in the Military: Amendment of Title VII." *California Law Review* (1990): 165–94.

Romero, Patricia, ed. *A Black Woman's Civil War Memoirs*. Princeton: Markus Wiener, 1988.

Rostker, Bernard D. Statement before the Senate Armed Services Committee. Subcommittee on Personnel Concerning Manpower and Personnel Issues. *Federal News Service*, April 8, 1997.

Rostker v. Goldberg. 453 U.S. 57, 83 (1981).

Roper v. Department of the Army. 832 F. 2d 247 (2d Cir. 1987).

Ruddick, Sara. *Maternal Thinking: Towards a Politics of Peace*. Boston: Beacon, 1989.

Rustad, Michael. *Women in Khaki: The American Enlisted Woman*. New York: Praeger, 1982.

Sadler, CAPT Georgia Clark, USN (Ret.). "The Polling Data." *Proceedings of the U.S. Naval Institute* 119:2 (February 1993): 51–54.

_____. "Women in Combat: The U.S. Military and the Impact of the Persian Gulf War." In *Wives and Warriors: Women and the Military in the United States and Canada*, edited by Laurie Weinstein and Christie White. Westport, Conn.: Bergin and Garvey, 1997.

Sadler, CAPT Georgia Clark, USN (Ret.), and Patricia J. Thomas. "Rock the Cradle, Rock the Boat?" *Proceedings of the U.S. Naval Institute* 121:4 (February 1993): 51–56.

Sander, Helke. "Prologue." In *Mass Rape: The War Against Women in Bosnia-Herzegovina*, edited by Alexandra Stiglmayer and translated by Marion Faber, xvii–xxiii. Lincoln: University of Nebraska Press, 1994.

Scalia, Justice Antonin. Supreme Court of the United States. Dissenting opinion. 94–1941 and 94–2107. *United States v. Commonwealth of Virginia*.

Schlesinger v. Ballard. 419 U.S. 498, 510 (1975).

Schneider, Dorothy, and Carl J. *Sound Off! American Military Women Speak Out*. New York: Dutton, 1988.

Schroeder, Pat, Olympia Snowe, Marilyn Lloyd, Connie Morella, Elizabeth Furse, Tillie Fowler, Maxine Waters, Arma Eshoo, Karen Shepherd, Eleanor Holmes Norton, Carolyn Maloney, Karan English, Carrie Meek, Jill Long, and Leslie Bryne. Congressional Caucus for Women's Issues. Letter to Secretary of Defense William Perry, June 14, 1994.

Schumm, Walter R. D., Bruce Bell, and Giao Q. Tran. *The Demography of Army Families: A Review of Findings*. Alexandria, Va.: U.S. Army Research Institute for the Behavioral and Social Sciences. In "America's Army Family: Yesterday, Today, and Tomorrow," by Maj. Angela M. Manos, USA. Unpublished material used at the Command and General Staff College, 1993.

Segal, David R., Joseph C. Jones, and Angela Maria Manos. "Citizen Soldiers in the Sinai: The Evolution of a Composite Active/Reserve Component American Battalion for a Peacekeeping Mission." Forthcoming.

Segal, David R., Joseph C. Jones, Angela M. Manos, and David E. Rohall. "Meeting the Missions of the 1990s with a Down-sized Force: Human Resource Management Lessons from the Deployment of PATRIOT Missile Units to Korea." Forthcoming.

Segal, Mady Wechsler. "The Military and the Family As Greedy Institutions." *Armed Forces and Society* 13:1 (Fall 1986): 9–38.

_____. "Women's Military Roles Cross-Nationally: Past, Present, and Future." *Gender and Society* 9:6 (December 1995): 757–75.

Segal, Mady Wechsler, and Amanda Faith Hansen. "Value Rationales in Policy Debates on Women in the Military: A Content Analysis of Congressional Testimony, 1941–1985." *Social Science Quarterly* 73: 2 (June 1992): 294–309.

Segal, Mady Wechsler, and Jessie J. Harris. "What Leaders Need to Know About Army Families." Alexandria, Va.: U.S. Army Research Institute for the Behavioral and Social Sciences, 1993. In "America's Army Family: Yesterday, Today, and Tomorrow," by Maj. Angela M. Manos, USA. Unpublished material used at the Command and General Staff College, 1993.

Seifert, Ruth. "War and Rape: A Preliminary Analysis." In *Mass Rape: The War Against Women in Bosnia-Herzegovina*, edited by Alexandra Stiglmayer and translated by Marion Faber, 54–72. Lincoln: University of Nebraska Press, 1994.

Sexton, Cpl Timothy, USMC Reserve. Interview, 1996.

Shalikashvili, GEN John M., Chairman of the Joint Chiefs of Staff. Memorandum for the Secretary of Defense, CM–224–94, April 22, 1994, 1.

Shapiro, Stephen J. Chair, Association of the Bar of the City of New York. Letter to Secretary of Defense Dick Cheney, May 17, 1991.

Sheehan, Daniel M. "An Enriching Tradition." *Air Force Magazine* (June 1995): 83.

Sheldon, Kathryn. *American Military Women at War*. Washington, D.C.: Women in the Military Service for America Foundation, Inc. (WIMSA), 1996.

_____. *A Brief History of Black Women in the Military*. Washington, D.C.: WIMSA, 1996.

_____. *Did You Know...?* Women's History Month. Washington, D.C.: WIMSA, 1996.

_____. *Important Dates in the History of Women in the Military*. Women's History Month. Washington, D.C.: WIMSA, 1996.

_____. Interview, June 11, 1996.

Simutis, Zita, M.D., Bruce Bell, and Paul A. Gade. "The U.S. Army Family Research Program: How Family Programs Impact Soldier Retention and Readiness." Paper presented at Defense Analysis Seminar VII, 1993, 5. In "America's Army Family: Yesterday, Today, and Tomorrow," by MAJ Angela M. Manos, USA. Unpublished material used at the Command and General Staff College, 1993.

Sivard, Ruth Leger. *Women ... a World Survey*. Washington, D.C.: World Priorities, 1995.

Skaine, Rosemarie. "Harassment Is a Leadership Issue." *Des Moines Register*, November 29, 1996, A13.

_____. *Power and Gender: Issues in Sexual Dominance and Harassment*. Jefferson, N.C.: McFarland, 1996.

Solterer, Helen. "Figures of Female Militancy in Medieval France." *Signs* 16:3 (Spring 1991): 522–49.

Spane, CDR R. J., Naval Air Force. Office of the Judge Advocate General. Investigation into the VF–213 F-14A Aircraft Accident on 25 October 1944 that resulted in the Death of LT Kara S. Hultgreen, USN, 450–59–6806/1310 and Injury of LT Matthew P. Klemish, USN (USN Public Report).

Staring, RADM Merlin H., JAGC, USN. "Training on Assignment of Women Aviators." Memorandum for the Assistant Deputy Chief of Naval Operations (Air Warfare). Prepared by LT P. L. Joffe, JAGC, USN. JAG:131.3:PLJ:cck, Ser: 8777, November 29, 1974, 1.

Stiglmayer, Alexandra. "The Rapes in Bosnia-Herzegovina." In *Mass Rape: The War Against Women in Bosnia-Herzegovina*, edited by Alexandra Stiglmayer and translated by Marion Faber, 82-169. Lincoln: University of Nebraska Press, 1994.

_____. "The War in the Former Yugoslavia." In *Mass Rape: The War Against Women in Bosnia-Herzegovina*, edited by Alexandra Stiglmayer and translated by Marion Faber, 1–34. Lincoln: University of Nebraska Press, 1994.

Strong, Bryan, and Christine DeVault. *The Marriage and Family Experience.* 6th ed. St. Paul, Minn.: West, 1995.

Sullivan, GEN Gordon R., USA. "Increasing Opportunities for Women in the Army." Extract Chief of Staff of the Army (CSA) Weekly Summary, January 28, 1994, 1–3.

_____. Memorandum for the Secretary of the Army. "Women in Combat—Expanding Career Opportunities for Women in the Army," n. d., 2.

Sullivan, GEN Gordon R., USA, and Togo D. West, Jr., Secretary of the Army. Memorandum for the Secretary of Defense. "Direct Combat Definition and Assignment Rule," January 12, 1994, 1.

Sweatt, Barbara, former specialist, USA, Telephone interview, 1996.

Thomas, Dorothy Q., and Regan E. Ralph. "Rape in War: Challenging the Tradition of Impunity." *SAIS Review* 14 (Winter-Spring 1994), 81–99.

Thomey, 1st Lt Theodore, USMC Reserve (Ret.). "No Reverse." *Retired Officer Magazine* (April 1996): 38–42.

"Those Daring Young Women in Military Flying Machines." *Airlift/Tanker Quarterly* 4:4 (Fall 1996): 11, 54–55.

Traver, SPC Brett C. "Local Soldiers Return from Snow, Mud." *(Ft.) Monmouth (N.J.) Message* 43:34 (August 23, 1996). Posted to H-MINERVA "H-NET List for Discussion of Women and the Military," August 28, 1996. http://www.h-net.msu.edu.

Treadwell, Mattie E. *The Women's Army Corps.* Office of the Chief of Military History. Department of the Army. Washington, D.C.: GPO, 1954.

Troutt, MAJ Kay, USAF. Producer of the 1996 Spring Conference of the Defense Advisory Committee on Women in the Services (DACOWITS). *45th Anniversary DACOWITS Defense Advisory Committee on Women in the Services.*

Tucker, Lt. Col., JAG, USAF. "Memorandum of Law on the Constitutional Issues Surrounding Assignment of Women to Combat."

United Nations. "Women and Armed Conflict." *Report of the Fourth World Conference on Women,* Beijing, China, September 4–15, 1995. Posted online by the United Nations Department for Policy Coordination and Sustainable Development (DPCSD). http://www.iisd.ca/linkages/woman.html. October 17, 1995, IV E, 131–49.

U.S. Air Force. Civil Law Opinion of the Judge Advocate General, (OpJAGAF) 1973/67, 27, April 1973, 237 of USAF FOIA.

U.S. Army. *All Ranks Update, AR 614–30, Overseas Assignment,* 1990.

_____. *The Women's Army Corps: A Commemoration of World War II Service.* Washington, D.C.: U.S. Army Center of Military History, [1993?]. CMH Pub 72–15, 1–32.

U.S. Army. Headquarters. Message. "Subject: Coding of Tables of Distribution and Allowances (TDA)," 061614Z January 1993, 1–5.

_____. Message. "Subject: Expanded Roles for Women in the Army," 121301Z August 1994, 1–4.

_____. *Tactics, Techniques, and Procedures for the Multiple Launch Rocket System (MLRS) Operations.* FM-6-60. Original document, September 16, 1992, 1–1, 4–3.

_____. *Tactics, Techniques, and Procedures for the Multiple Launch Rocket System (MLRS) Operations.* FM-6-60. C1, (change 1), September 30, 1993, 1–1, 4–3.

_____. Washington, D.C. 7NR 44444, R 0223447 November 1995, 707 720 T All U.S. Army, U.S. Army REPs and ACT, August 1995 (picked up September 2, 1996), 1–6.

U.S. Army. Research Institute of Environmental Medicine Report, January 26, 1996. In "New Army Study Undermines Old Taboo," by J. Michael Brower. Posted to H-MINERVA, July 11, 1996; http://www.h-net.msu.edu. Versions also appeared in *Armed Forces Journal International* (May 1996): 13; *Stars and Stripes,* Domestic edition, March 25–31, 7; and Pentagram, *Ft. McNair,* March 22, 1996, 14.

_____. "The Soldier's Creed" and "Code of Conduct." In *Soldier's Handbook*, January 1, 1993, ii, 66.

U.S. Code Annotated, Title 10 Armed Forces, Subt. C, § 6015. St. Paul, Minn.: West; Brooklyn, N.Y.: Edward Thompson, 1959.

U. S. Code Congressional and Administrative News, 103d Congress—First Session, 1993. Vol. 2. Public Laws 103–140 to 103–210 (107 Stat. Pages 1485 to 2498), Legislative History: Public Laws 103–1 to 103–66. St. Paul, Minn.: West, 1994.

U.S. Code. Subtitle D—Women in the Service, Sect. 541, 543.

U.S. Congress. House. Committee on Armed Services. Hearings on Military Posture and Assignment of Women to Ships: Hearings on H.R. 10929 and H.R. 7431. 95th Congress, 2d sess., 1978.

U.S. Congress. House. Committee on Armed Services. Military Forces and Personnel Subcommittee. *Gender Discrimination in the Military.* 102d Cong., 2d sess., July 29 and 30, 1992.

U.S. Congress. House. Committee on Armed Services. Military Forces and Personnel Subcommittee. *Hearings on Women in Combat.* 103d Cong., 1st sess., May 12, 1993.

U.S. Congress. House. Committee on Armed Services. Military Forces and Personnel Subcommittee. Hearings on Women in the Military, 100th Cong., 1st and 2d sess., 1987 and 1988.

U.S. Congress. House. Committee on Armed Services, Military Personnel and Compensation Subcommittee. *Assignment of Army and Marine Corps Women under the New Definition of Ground Combat*, 103d Cong., 2d sess., October 6, 1994.

U.S. Congress. House. Committee on Armed Services. Military Personnel and Compensation Subcommittee. *Implementation of the Repeal of the Combat Exclusion on Female Aviators.* 102d Cong., 2d sess., January 29, 1992.

U.S. Congress. House. Committee on Armed Services. Military Personnel and Compensation Subcommittee. *Women in the Military.* 101st Cong., 2d sess., March 20, 1990.

U.S. Congress. House. Committee on Armed Services. *National Defense Authorization Act for Fiscal Years 1992 and 1993.* Report on H.R. 2100 together with dissenting views, May 13, 1991.

U.S. Constitution, art. 1, sect. 8, clause 14. In "Assessment of the Litigation Risk Posed by the Constitutional Challenges to Limitations Upon the Assignment of Female Service Members." Communication from Jack S. Groat to CDR Thomas N. Levins, JAGC, June 7, 1991.

U.S. Presidential Commission on the Assignment of Women in the Armed Forces. *Report to the President: Women in Combat.* Washington, D.C.: Brassey's, 1993.

U.S. v. Clinton. 310 F. Supp. 333, 336 (E.D.La.1970).

U.S. v. Cook. 311 F. Supp. 618 (W.D. Pa. 1970).

U.S. v. Dorris. 319 F. Supp. 1306, 1308 (W.D. Pa. 1970).

U.S. v. St. Clair. 291 F. Supp. 122, 124 (S.D.N.Y. 1968).

U.S. v. Virginia. Fourth Circuit Court of Appeals, 44 F. 3d 1229, *1244; 1995 U.S. App. Lexis 1504, **, Curiae. No. 94–1667–94–1712.

U.S. v. Yingling. 368 F. Supp. 379, 386 (W.D. Pa. 1973).

United States of America v. Commonwealth of Virginia, et al. C.A. No. 90–0126–R. The U.S. District Court for the Western District of Virginia. Roanoke Division. Activities by the Virginia Military Institute in Preparation for the Admission of Women in August 1997. "First Quarterly Report," December 2, 1996.

Vaught, BGen. Wilma, USAF (Ret.). Interview, June 11, 1996.

Vesely, James F. "At the Wrong Solution at VMI." *Seattle Times*, June 28, 1996, B4.

Viccellio, Lt. Gen. Henry, Jr., USAF. Joint Staff memorandum for Army, Navy, Air Force and Marine Corps Operations Deputy, June 4, 1992.

Warner, Kris, USMC. Interview, 1996.
Webb, James. *A Sense of Honor.* Englewood Cliffs, N.Y.: Prentice Hall, 1981.
_____. "Women Can't Fight." *The Washingtonian,* November 1979.
Webb, Richard. Unpublished poem, 1997.
Weinstein, Laurie, and Christie White, eds. *Wives and Warriors: Women and the Military in the United States and Canada.* Westport, Conn.: Bergin and Garvey, 1997.
Wells, Robert V. "Demographic Change and Family Life in American History: Some Reflections." In *The Family Experience: A Reader in Cultural Diversity,* edited by Mark Hutter. New York: Macmillan, 1991.
West, Togo D., Jr., Secretary of the Army. Working memorandum for the Secretary of Defense. "Recommendations for Opening Additional Positions for Women Under the DOD Assignment Policy—Decision Memorandum," June 1, 1994, 1–9.
_____. Memorandum for the Secretary of Defense. "Women in Combat, Assignment Policy Proposal—Action Memorandum." Prepared by GEN Gordon R. Sullivan, Chief of Staff, USA, circa June 1994.
_____. Memorandum for the Under Secretary of Defense (Personnel and Readiness). "Increasing Opportunities for Women in the Army," July 27, 1994.
West, Togo D., Jr., Secretary of the Army, and Gen Gordon R. Sullivan, Chief of Staff of the Army. "Statement: Direct Combat Definition and Assignment for Women," January 13, 1994.
Westwood, LTC John S., USA. Letter to author, no date (metered date on envelope November 14, 1996).
Wheeler, Col. Michael O., USAF. "Thinking Ethically about the Strategic Defense Initiative: Some Preliminaries." In *Ethics and National Defense: The Timeless Issues,* by James C. Gaston and Janis Bren Hietala, 169–236. Washington, D.C.: National Defense University Press, 1993.
Whitley, Mary, former captain, USA. Interview, 1996.
Wildwind, CPT Sharon Grant, USA (Ret.), ANC 1969–1972. Telephone interview, 1996.
Williams, RADM D. M., Jr., USN (Ret.). Telephone interview, 1997.
Women in Military Service for America Memorial Foundation, Inc. "Change the Face of Monumental Washington: Help Build the Memorial to America's Military Women, Past, Present and Future." Washington, D.C.: WIMSA, 1994.
Women's Armed Services Integration Act of 1948, Ch. 449, Stat. 356, 357, 363. PL 80–625, codified 10 U.S. Code.
Zimmerman, Jean. *Tailspin: Women at War in the Wake of Tailhook.* New York: Doubleday, 1995.
Zurcher, Louis A. Jr. "Navy Boot Camp: Role Assimilation in a Total Institution." In *Sociology: Windows on Society.* 3d ed., by John W. Heeren and Marylee Mason, 56–61. Sweet Springs, Mo.: Roxbury, 1994.

Index